Capital Punishment
in America

Capital Punishment in America

Raymond Paternoster

LEXINGTON BOOKS
An Imprint of Macmillan, Inc.
NEW YORK

Maxwell Macmillan Canada
TORONTO

Maxwell Macmillan International
NEW YORK OXFORD SINGAPORE SYDNEY

This book is published as part of the Lexington Books Series on Social Issues, George Ritzer, general editor.

Library of Congress Cataloging-in-Publication Data

Paternoster, Raymond.
    Capital punishment in America / by Raymond Paternoster.
    p. cm.—(Lexington Books social issues series)
    Includes bibliographical references and index.
    ISBN 0-669-21409-4 (alk. paper).—ISBN 0-669-21993-2 (pbk.: alk. paper)
    1. Capital punishment—United States.   I. Title.   II. Series.
HV8699.U5P37   1991   91-11300
364.6'6'0973—dc20   CIP

Lexington Books
An Imprint of Macmillan, Inc.
866 Third Avenue, New York, N. Y. 10022

Maxwell Macmillan Canada, Inc.
1200 Eglinton Avenue East
Suite 200
Don Mills, Ontario M3C 3N1

Macmillan, Inc. is part of the Maxwell Communication Group of Companies.

Printed in the United States of America

printing number
1   2   3   4   5   6   7   8   9   10

This book is dedicated to my parents, Florence and Anthony. Everything that is good in me has come from them.

Contents

List of Figures and Tables

Figures

Tables

Preface

T here are few topics as controversial as capital punishment. It seems to stir great passion and debate among those who support its infliction on serious criminal offenders and those who oppose it. It is also a very curious phenomenon, in that it seems that the United States has a somewhat schizophrenic attitude toward the imposition of death on one of its citizens, even one who has killed another. It would appear at first that public support for the death penalty is quite strong, reflecting some sort of national consensus on the issue. In a 1988 Gallup poll, for example, approximately 80 percent of those sampled expressed approval of the death penalty, at least for those who commit murder. What might underlie this sentiment, however, may be not a moral endorsement of the death penalty, but a simple desire to punish harshly those who commit serious crimes and to be protected from dangerous criminal offenders. When given an alternative penal sanction that promises severe punishment and offers almost the same kind of protection as capital punishment —such as life imprisonment without the possibility of parole, with restitution for the surviving family of the victim—support for the death penalty declines substantially.

Further evidence of the "softness" of public approval for capital punishment can be seen from the fact that when confronted with the reality of the death penalty, the public begins to lose its stomach for it. For example, during an eight-week period from June to August of 1987 the state of Louisiana executed eight persons. It put another offender to death in March of 1988, a second one in April of that year, and a third in June. The citizens of Louisiana, then, witnessed eleven executions from June of 1987 until June of 1988. This is the highest number of executions in any one state over a twelve-month period since executions resumed in the United States in 1977 after a ten-year moratorium. It may be that Louisianans have had (at least temporarily) their fill of executions, since from June of 1988 until September of 1990 only one other execution was performed in that state.

It is not clear, therefore, how much the public actually favors the imposition of capital punishment—beyond their inclination to express approval when asked, "Do you favor or oppose the death penalty for convicted murderers?"

What is more clear is that the public labors under many misconceptions about the death penalty. Some of these misconceptions are that capital punishment is inflicted in an evenhanded and fair manner and that it is inflicted only for the most serious and heinous murders; that it protects the public better than life imprisonment by incapacitating murderers who are likely to repeat their crime if ever released and by deterring would-be murderers; that persons are sentenced to death only after legal proceedings that are procedurally sound and that give accused murderers who are on trial for their life the best opportunity to prove their innocence; that the execution of convicted murderers is a far less costly system of punishment than one based on life imprisonment; and that trial judges and juries are able to select only the most deserving capital defendants for the ultimate penalty of death.

This book is an attempt to understand these many issues about the death penalty and to bring some understanding to a volatile topic where debate has unfortunately brought more heat than light. The book is divided into five parts. The first part (Chapter 1) presents an overview of capital punishment in the United States. It provides a brief history and describes both the bulging population on death rows across the United States today and the frequency (more properly, infrequency) of executions relative to the far larger number of capital offenses. This chapter will also discuss the imposition of the death penalty primarily in the southern United States (both in the past and in recent history) and on black defendants, and the public's ongoing love–hate relationship with the death penalty. The issues raised in this introductory chapter give rise to a set of questions and topics that will be addressed in the remainder of the book.

One of the more curious features about the death penalty in the United States is the ten-year moratorium on executions that occurred from 1967 until 1977, even though public approval of the death penalty for murder was increasing. In addition, despite the fact that in 1989 public approval of capital punishment was at an all-time high and over 2,300 persons were on death row, fewer than 150 condemned offenders were executed in the thirteen years after 1977. This raises two important questions. Why was there a ten-year hiatus in the use of capital punishment from 1967 to 1977? And why have there been so few executions relative to the large number of death sentences imposed, causing such an accumulation of inmates on death row? These questions provide the background for Part II, Constitutional and Legal Issues in Capital Punishment, composed of Chapters 2 and 3.

Chapter 2 presents a chronology of the strategy and efforts of a group of abolitionist lawyers working for the NAACP Legal Defense Fund in the 1960s and 1970s to have the United States Supreme Court review the constitutionality of capital punishment. This work succeeded in delaying a return of the death penalty to the United States for ten years, and culminated in two important death penalty cases, *McGautha v. California* (1971) and *Furman v. Georgia* (1972). This chapter reviews the thorny issues in these two critical cases and attempts to provide a rationale to an anomaly which has perplexed both observers of the Court and legal scholars—how the Supreme Court could hold in 1971 that standardless and single-verdict capital juries were constitutional under the Fourteenth Amendment's "due process" clause *(McGautha)*, and then declare just one year later that such practices were unconstitutional under the Eighth Amendment's "cruel and unusual punishments" clause *(Furman)*. This is particularly perplexing given the previous decisions of the Court that suggested that the death penalty did not contravene the Eighth Amendment's prohibition against cruel and unusual punishment. Chapter 2 will discuss the apparent requirements of a constitutionally acceptable versus unacceptable system of capital punishment, and what the *Furman* Court specifically found to be objectionable to existing state death penalty statutes.

Chapter 3 surveys the Supreme Court's death penalty decisions after *Furman,* and provides a brief overview of death penalty law. It details the attempt by state legislatures to fashion death penalty statutes that would pass constitutional muster. Two different types of capital statutes are described in this chapter, those that promised to guide the discretion of the jury and those that would eliminate it. This chapter analyzes the Supreme Court's review of these two types of death sentencing schemes in *Gregg v. Georgia* (1976) and its companion cases, and why the Court found those statutes that guided sentencing discretion to be acceptable and those that eliminated it to be constitutionally infirm.

The Supreme Court's interest in state death penalty practices did not cease with the *Gregg* decision, however, as it has continued to take an active role in examining the constitutionality of state death penalty practices, both substantively (as to what crimes may be punished by death) and procedurally (what protections and legal procedures must be in place for a death penalty scheme to meet constitutional requirements). This has led the Court to probe such issues as the constitutionality of capital punishment for rape, "nontriggerman" killings, juveniles, and the mentally retarded and insane, as well as what kinds of information the jury is permitted (and forbidden) to hear, what defines competent counsel in capital cases, and the requirements of appellate review of death sentences. This chapter provides a review of the long and arduous attempt by the Court to reform state death penalty practices, and of how the legal complexity of the death penalty today has inevitably resulted in long stays on death row and relatively few and long-delayed executions.

Having discussed the death penalty as it exists in law, Chapters 4 and 5 examine its actual operation both historically and under current statutes. In the execution data presented in Chapter 1, two curiosities will be noted: the death penalty appears to have been imposed disproportionately on black offenders (and those who slay whites), particularly in the South; and the death penalty is imposed for only a small proportion of the capital offenses committed. This raises two questions: Is the death penalty imposed in a racially discriminatory manner? And, given its infrequency, is the death penalty inflicted on only the most egregious offenders or is it instead the result of a random or chance process?

Both of these questions go to the heart of the issue of what constitutes evenhanded imposition of capital punishment. A punishment, such as the death penalty, can fail to be inflicted in an evenhanded manner for one of two reasons: if it is systematically inflicted on the basis of criteria that are clearly irrelevant to the goals of punishment, or if it is inflicted on no apparent rational basis. An example of the first type of "nonevenhandedness" is the imposition of the death penalty in part because of one's race, gender, or hair color. This systematic departure from evenhandedness results in capital sentences that are the product of discrimination. An example of the second type of nonevenhandedness would be if death sentences were imposed by a chance process or if they were influenced by irrelevant sentencing considerations such as the geographical location of the crime. Ideally, if not all convicted capital offenders are sentenced to death, then those who are should be distinguished from those given life sentences on some meaningful, rational basis. Those condemned to die, for example, should be the most remorseless and brutal offenders. If there is no rational way to distinguish those sentenced to death from those whose lives are spared, then the imposition of capital punishment becomes a macabre game of chance—the lucky live while the hapless await their death.

Chapter 4 takes up the first of these departures from evenhanded capital sentencing—discrimination. It reviews historical evidence that suggests that traditionally black Americans have been afforded unequal treatment in the hands of the law. This history reveals that as victims of the crimes committed by whites, blacks have not received the full protection of the law, and that blacks who commit offenses against white victims have often received more severe penalties than white offenders. The role of race in the imposition of capital punishment is examined under both pre- and post-*Furman* capital statutes. This chapter will end with a somewhat detailed discussion of the presentation of social scientific information about racial discrimination to the courts, in particular the United States Supreme Court, and how these courts have come to interpret what this evidence does and does not say about how color-blind the executioner has been and is currently in the United States.

Chapter 5 concerns the second type of departure from evenhanded capital sentencing, that is, whether the death penalty is imposed in an arbitrary and capricious fashion. This issue was before the U.S. Supreme Court in *Furman v. Georgia*. *Furman* struck down existing state capital punishment statutes because the infrequent imposition of the death penalty suggested that it was being imposed in a "freakish" and "wanton" manner. The infliction of the death penalty appeared to work much like a lottery system; there was no meaningful distinction between those receiving life and those receiving death sentences. In *Furman* the Court essentially thought that the penalty of death was being imposed without consistency or rationality—that its infrequency did not mean that it was reserved only for those who committed the most deplorable offenses.

One of the promises of post-*Furman* procedurally reformed statutes was that capital sentences would no longer be as random or irrational as under pre-*Furman* laws. Chapter 5 examines the imposition of death sentences under several post-*Furman* statutes to determine whether or not they are still being imposed in an arbitrary manner. It begins with a working definition of what an arbitrary death sentence is, and distinguishes between two forms of arbitrariness —arbitrariness by infrequency and arbitrariness by irrelevance. In this chapter we will examine the social scientific research that has investigated the imposition of death sentences under procedurally reformed post-*Furman* statutes. The review of this empirical evidence will suggest that although there may be some rationality to current capital sentencing systems, a substantial number of death sentences continue to be imposed in a fashion that can only be described as "freakish."

The fourth section of the book attempts to shed some light on what has been referred to in this preface as misconceptions about the death penalty. The chapters in Part IV, entitled Arguments For and Against the Death Penalty, examine whether or not capital punishment is economically more cost effective than life imprisonment, whether the death penalty protects public safety better than life imprisonment, and whether death is the only deserved punishment for those who deliberately take the life of another.

Chapter 6, The Cost of Life and Death, compares the cost of maintaining a system of justice that includes capital punishment with the cost of one based on life imprisonment. It will be argued that the cost of executing a condemned prisoner today may actually greatly exceed that required for a life prison term. Several reasons are explored in this chapter that help account for the high cost of a system of capital punishment. These include the length of the pretrial process (particularly jury selection and investigation), the complexity of the capital trial itself, which is actually two separate trials (a trial over guilt and a trial over penalty), and the lengthy appeals process in capital cases.

Chapter 7, Public Protection and the Death Penalty, reviews the argument that suggests that capital punishment is a more effective way to protect the public from murderers than life imprisonment. This argument takes two different forms. One is that capital punishment is necessary to threaten and deter would-be offenders from committing a murder. This is the notion of general deterrence. The second states that capital punishment is the only way to prevent those who have already murdered from killing again. This is the idea of incapacitation.

At first, these appear to be difficult arguments for those who would like to see the death penalty abolished. Executed offenders are quite unlikely to repeat their crimes, but those sentenced to life may commit other murders either while confined in prison or if released out into the community. In addition, since death certainly must be a more frightful and feared punishment than life imprisonment, it must be more effective in dissuading would-be murderers from committing their crimes. The notions of incapacitation and general deterrence become a little more complex, however, when it is recognized that there are two real issues: first, whether or not those sentenced to life imprisonment constitute such a risk of offending again that the only way to keep them from committing more offenses is to put them to death; and second, whether or not death is so much more feared than life imprisonment that it deters crimes that the threat of a life prison term would not. An extensive review of both the general deterrence and incapacitation literature in Chapter 7 will indicate that there is virtually no solid empirical evidence to support the public protection argument.

The final chapter of this section deals with the issue of deserved punishment. A frequent and passionate argument of death penalty proponents is that under the guiding principle of "an eye for an eye," those who intentionally murder another person deserve themselves to be punished with an identical amount of harm and injury—the penalty of death. Chapter 8, Death as Deserved Punishment, will first examine the philosophy of retribution, or "just deserts." A retributive philosophy presents the idea that murderers deserve the death penalty (and nothing less than the death penalty) in a moral sense—"they have it coming to them." The notion that those persons who intentionally kill another thereby forfeit their right to life and must be executed is a persuasive one. Chapter 8 will, however, present counterarguments to this literal "eye-for-an-eye" philosophy. It will be asserted that the idea that the murderer must be harmed to exactly the same extent as the victim is both impractical and barbaric in modern civilized society. In this chapter we will entertain the thought that perhaps we can do justice to both murderers and their victims with a punishment less severe than death.

The final section and chapter of the book will be devoted to an understanding of where capital punishment may be going in the future. We will examine the prospect of reducing the logjam of condemned inmates on death rows today by massive executions—a virtual "blood bath." We will conclude by suggesting an alternative course of action for states to take. This would include the eventual abolition of the death penalty and its substitution with the penalty of life imprisonment without parole. This alternative will be looked at in terms of a worldwide trend toward the abolition of capital punishment and how life without parole will offer the kind of protection and community safety citizens demand without the brutality of a death penalty.

Acknowledgments

There are many people I would like to thank for helping me complete this book. Many of the chapters began as course lectures for a seminar on the death penalty which I have been teaching at the University of Maryland. I would like to thank the many (and unnamed) students who took this course and helped me to slowly develop the arguments that appear in this book. The Director of the Institute of Criminology, Dr. Charles F. Wellford, has been kind enough to let me teach this seminar even though there were always other classes that I should have been teaching. I owe him a great deal of debt, not only for that, but for creating the most conducive working environment that a scholar could ever hope for. He has always provided me with both encouragement and opportunity. I owe a special thanks to a colleague of mine, Douglas Smith, who has always been a good friend and who helped keep me sane over the past year and a half. I have also been very lucky in having four tireless students assist me with a great deal of the research, Dayna Kate Better, James M. Cronin, Alex R. Piquero, and Lisa van Kesteren. I could not have finished this book without their efforts. I am grateful for the efforts of two other former students, now professors, LeeAnn Iovanni and Ruth Triplett, who read the first draft of the book and commented on it extensively. I also had the good fortune of having three excellent reviewers of the first draft of the manuscript. I owe a great deal to Professors William Bowers, Michael Radelet, and Gennaro Vito. What lies within is far better because of their keen eyes. Finally, I am deeply grateful to Ronet Bachman for providing the critical observation, supportive touch, humorous story, and a peaceful site to both write a few of the more difficult chapters of this book and polish all of them during the last few months. Thank you all.

College Park, Maryland
February 1991

I
Introduction

1
Executions in the United States

This is a book about the death penalty in the United States. The problem of capital punishment is both old and new. It is old in that the death penalty has been on the U.S. criminal justice scene since the country's very beginnings. The first known execution occurred in 1608 when Captain George Kendall, one of the original councilors of Jamestown Colony, was put to death (Espy and Smykla 1987, i). Criminal defendants in the American colonies were executed for numerous crimes, and most of the Framers of the Constitution were both knowledgeable and tolerant of the death penalty. Since the Fifth Amendment ensured that no person could be deprived of *life,* liberty, or property without due process of law, the implication was that *with* such due process of law such deprivations were acceptable.

But the problem of capital punishment is also a new and very foreboding one. There are currently over 2,300 convicted capital offenders on death row across the United States today,[1] more than at any time in the history of our country. In fact, if the states' death rows were one long row of cells, each 5 × 7 feet, there would be a line of convicted capital defendants awaiting death over two miles long. Even if we were to begin to execute one person each day (and we show no inclination to put to death anywhere near that number), it would take over six years to eliminate the current backlog of condemned persons.

In this chapter we will briefly examine the earliest history of capital punishment in the United States. We will learn that capital punishment existed in England, was adopted early in the colonies, and continued well into the 1900s, and that the performance of executions during these years was under local rather than state control. We will then examine what we call the "pre-modern period" of capital punishment, the period between the years 1930 and 1972. The early part of this period was an active one for the executioner, but after the 1940s the number of executions declined substantially until they stopped altogether, temporarily, in 1967. One of the most interesting features about capital punishment during this period was the infrequency of executions relative to the number of capital offenses, despite general (though intermittent) public approval for the death penalty.

In the final section of the chapter we will examine what we call the "modern period" of capital punishment, the period after 1972. Two important events mark this modern period, the constitutional approval given to procedurally reformed state death penalty statutes (the subject of Chapters 2 and 3), and the resumption of sporadic executions in 1977 after a ten-year interruption.

The Early History of Capital Punishment in the United States

The Continuation of an English Tradition

As the execution of Captain George Kendall in 1608 suggests, capital punishment in the United States has an early history. The very best historical accounting is the data collected by Watt Espy, an Alabama historian (Espy 1980; Espy and Smykla 1987; Schneider and Smykla 1991; Radelet 1989). Espy collected information on some 16,000 executions. Using the Espy data set, Schneider and Smykla (1991, 6) reported the number of executions on U.S. soil from the 1600s to the 1920s (see Table 1–1).[2] They found that Espy was able to document some 162 executions during the 1600s, 1,391 during the 1700s, 2,451 in the decades before and during the Civil War (1800–1865), and 820 in the years immediately after that (1866–1879). After the 1870s there were approximately 1,000 executions each decade up to 1930.

It should not be surprising that capital punishment has an early history in the United States. Colonial society, and this would certainly include its legal and penal institutions, was strongly influenced by English traditions, and capital

Table 1–1
Number and Percent of Executions Performed under State and Local Authority in the United States: 1600s–1920s

Years	Local Authority (%)	State Authority (%)	Total
1600s	162 (100%)	0	162
1700s	1391 (100%)	0	1391
1800–1865	2441 (99%)	10 (1%)	2451
1866–1879	805 (97%)	15 (3%)	820
1880s	989 (98%)	16 (2%)	1005
1890s	949 (86%)	149 (14%)	1098
1900s	997 (78%)	283 (22%)	1280
1910s	397 (36%)	694 (64%)	1091
1920s	274 (21%)	1015 (79%)	1289

Adapted from V. Schneider and J. O. Smykla, "A Summary Analysis of Executions in the United States, 1608–1987: The Espy File," in R. Bohm, *The Death Penalty in America: Current Research* (Cincinnati, Ohio: Anderson Publishing, 1991), Table 1-2, 7. Reprinted with permission.

punishment was no stranger to English law. Historical evidence from England paralleling the U.S. data presented in Table 1-1 documents the fact that capital punishment is an Anglo-American custom. Radzinowicz (1948, 140–42) has reported that in the years of Henry VIII's reign (1509–1547) there were approximately 3,780 executions in England, an average of 140 per year. Immediately after that, in the years of King Edward VI's rule (1547–1553), there were 3,360 executions in England, an average of 560 per year. The frequency of capital punishment declined in subsequent years, although there was never a time during this period when it was abolished either *de jure* (by law) or *de facto* (in practice). During the reign of Charles I (1625–1649), 2,160 persons were executed (90 per year), and 990 more during the ten years of the Commonwealth under Oliver Cromwell (1649–1658). As in the United States, English use of capital punishment extended well into the 1800s. Radzinowicz (1948, 147–48) reported that from 1749 to 1799 there were 1,696 executions in London and Middlesex County alone, and 354 executions for all of England and Wales during the years 1805–1810. Although the frequency of executions declined and the number of capital offenses was reduced over time, the death penalty was a well-established English practice. Rather than being unique to the New World, then, the institution of capital punishment in the colonies was merely an extension of an English legal tradition.

Although English influence on the practice of capital punishment in the colonies was pervasive, the kinds of offenses for which offenders were put to death during this early period reflect a more distinctly American tenor. Serious crimes such as murder and rape were capital offenses in all of the colonies that had the death penalty, but since there was no uniform American "criminal law," and the adoption of English law was not consistent, each colony developed somewhat unique capital statutes. Given the fact that some colonies were heavily influenced by the church, it is not surprising that a large proportion of the executions in these jurisdictions were for religious transgressions. The capital crimes of the colony at Massachusetts Bay, for example, included idolatry, witchcraft, blasphemy, bestiality, adultery, man stealing, and related sexual transgressions (Bowers 1984, 133–34; Bedau 1982, 7). After the American Revolution, the theocratic Massachusetts Bay Colony became Massachusetts the Commonwealth; and capital crimes were both reduced in number and reflected a more secular society (murder, sodomy, burglary, buggery, arson, rape, and treason; see Powers 1966). The colony of North Carolina had a more extensive and different list of capital crimes reflecting local conditions. North Carolina had no established penitentiary system for the long-term incarceration of offenders, and it had a plantation economy which relied on forced (slave) labor. Bedau (1982, 8) and Bowers (1984, 139–40) note that as late as 1837, North Carolina had over twenty capital offenses, including concealing a slave with intent to free him, slave stealing, and inciting slaves to insurrection or circulating seditious literature among slaves.

Restricting the Use of the Death Penalty

It was mentioned above that after the American Revolution Massachusetts began to restrict its number of capital offenses. This was generally true of all the states at the time, and represents a profound difference with English trends. The capital punishment laws of Massachusetts around the mid-1600s listed over twelve capital crimes (Powers 1966; Bedau 1982, 7). In the post–revolutionary war period, the capital statutes of Massachusetts and Pennsylvania included only eight capital offenses, and the 1830 capital statue in Virginia included only five capital crimes for whites (but seventy for blacks; see Bowers 1984, 139–40). At the same time, under English law in 1819, some 223 potentially capital offenses existed (Bowers 1984, 136).

In addition to a restriction in the number of capital offenses, American states in the post–revolutionary war period also began to narrow the application of capital punishment through the development of degrees of murder and the extension of sentencing discretion. Under English law, and as it was first adopted in the colonies, there was only one degree of murder, and the mandatory punishment was death. The idea of a mandatory death sentence upon the conviction of any murderer did not set well with many juries, which refused to convict persons (or convicted them of a lesser offense) who may have been guilty of murder but who were not seen as deserving of a death sentence. The problem in these cases of juries disregarding their oaths ("jury nullification") provided the impetus for a reform of capital statutes which had the effect of restricting the use of the death penalty.

After the Revolution state legislatures began to devise degrees of murder, restricting capital punishment to only the most serious, or first-degree murder. In 1794 Pennsylvania became the first state to enact into law the notion of degrees of murder (Keedy 1949). Under the Pennsylvania reform, only murder in the first degree was punishable by death; for all other crimes the death penalty was abolished. The purpose of devising degrees of murder was to give the jury the kind of discretion they were in fact exercising; they now had the legal authority to reserve the death penalty for only the most serious murders. By the 1900s most states followed the example of Pennsylvania and adopted two or three degrees of murder, with death penalty jurisdictions restricting capital punishment only for murder in the first degree.

The adoption of different degrees of murder was one way in which the use of the death penalty was contained. It was not a complete solution to the problem of jury nullification, however. Under the Pennsylvania law, first-degree murder included a deliberate and premeditated killing as well as any murder committed in the commission of arson, rape, robbery, or burglary (Keedy 1949, 727). Any defendant committing a deliberate armed robbery whose victim was unintentionally killed would face a mandatory death sentence if convicted of first-degree murder. Juries would often circumvent the rigor of these laws by acquitting defendants or convicting them of a lesser degree of murder. To extend to the capital jury the option to impose a sentence other than death in even first-degree murder cases, state legislatures began to revise their capital statutes to include sentencing discretion. Under the Maryland statute of 1809, which included degrees of murder, the jury was given the discretion to impose a noncapital sentence for treason, rape, and arson (but not homicide; see Bedau 1982, 10). Tennessee in 1838 and Alabama in 1841 were the first states to extend sentencing discretion to juries in capital murder cases, and Louisiana did so for all its potentially capital crimes in 1846 (Bedau 1982, 10). By 1930, most death penalty states had abandoned mandatory death penalty statutes for discretionary ones.

Making Capital Punishment Centralized and Private

In addition to a restriction in the use of capital punishment by reducing the number of capital crimes, devising degrees of murder, and extending sentencing discretion, there was another important development in the institution of capital punishment during this period. Early executions in the United States were both public and conducted under the authority of local officials (Table 1–1 reports the percent of executions that were conducted under state and local authority during the time period 1600–1929). Immediately after the Revolution, almost all executions were performed under local authority. Local authorities maintained control over the executions of condemned offenders until the early part of the twentieth century. The first execution to take place under state authority occurred in Vermont, and not until January 20, 1864 (Bowers 1984, 43). Although the centralization of capital punishment under state control came slowly, it had (except in the South) replaced local authority by the 1920s. In the 1890s, 86 percent of all executions were performed under local authority, but by the 1920s almost eight out of every ten executions were conducted under state authority.

Consistent with English custom, most executions in the United States not only were local events, but were performed as public spectacles, in front of great throngs. Despite substantial and early opposition to public executions, reform was slow in coming. It was not until 1834 in Pennsylvania that the first law prohibiting public executions was passed. New York, New Jersey, and Massachusetts followed in 1835 and several other states thereafter (Bowers 1984, 8; Zimring and Hawkins 1986). By the end of the 1800s the practice of public executions had been generally discontinued; a few were performed as late as 1936 and 1937.

Capital Punishment as Discipline

The passing reference earlier to the use of capital punishment against slaves and those who would try to free them points to a disturbing feature about capital punishment in this period of U.S. history. The death penalty was imposed not only on criminal populations (those who murdered or raped), but on what could be described as "problem populations" (Spitzer 1975)—persons who pose a danger or threat to constituted authority. In the theocratic Massachusetts Bay Colony, the problem population included those who questioned religious authority, such as witches and blasphemers. Under the slave economies of the South, the problem population included runaway or rebellious slaves and those who assisted them in their effort. The specific use of capital punishment against slaves and opponents of slavery was only part of a more general use of the criminal law to control the slave population in southern states. The odious Slave Codes of the pre–Civil War South included a long list of behaviors punishable if committed by blacks, and the list of capital offenses was far more numerous for slaves than for free persons. The attempt to maintain racial discipline continued after the Civil War with the Black Codes, which called for harsher sanctions for offenses committed by blacks. This included the disproportionate infliction of the death penalty on black offenders. We will deal with the issue of racial discrimination and the imposition of the death penalty more specifically in Chapter 4.

No discussion of capital punishment during this early period would be complete without some mention of the existence of an extralegal form of capital punishment—lynching. Lynching, primarily by vigilante groups, was frequently used by majority groups to keep minorities oppressed. Bowers (1984, 54) has reported that in the 1890s some 1,540 lynchings were conducted. During that decade there were more instances of illegal lynchings than there were of state or local legally authorized executions (1,098; see Table 1–1). The number of lynchings declined in subsequent years; there were 885 reported by Bowers in the 1900s, 621 in the 1910s, and 315 in the 1920s. This trend coincides with the centralization of the death penalty first under local then state control.

Tentative Movement toward Abolition

As we have learned, since the American Revolution there has been growing sentiment toward restricting the use of capital punishment. Several reforms of the death penalty, such as a reduction in the number of capital crimes, the adoption of degrees of murder, and the granting of sentencing discretion, have all tended to narrow the opportunity for imposing a sentence of death. In addition to attempts at reform, post–revolutionary war Americans witnessed attempts to have the death penalty abolished. Prior to the Civil War, abolitionist societies emerged along with antislavery and temperance organizations and pressed their claims on state legislatures. Not only were these abolitionist groups locally organized to fight capital punishment in death penalty states, in 1845 a national organization was created, the American Society for the Abolition of Capital Punishment (Bedau 1982, 21).

These early abolitionist movements met with some success. The territory of

Michigan abolished the death penalty for all crimes except treason in 1846, and became the first political jurisdiction in the English-speaking world to do so. Other states soon followed. Rhode Island abolished capital punishment for all crimes (including treason) in 1852, Wisconsin did the same in 1853, Iowa in 1872, and Maine in 1876. After this initial success the abolitionist movement met with resistance. Other state legislatures were ready to reform, but not get rid of, their provisions for capital punishment. It was not until the early 1900s that the abolitionists were to secure more victories, when several states either abolished the death penalty completely or severely restricted its use; Kansas in 1907, Minnesota in 1911, Washington in 1913, Oregon in 1914, North Dakota, South Dakota, and Tennessee in 1915, Arizona in 1916, and Missouri in 1917. These were, however, only partial victories for the abolitionists, because with only a few exceptions (Michigan, Wisconsin, Rhode Island, Minnesota, and North Dakota) those states that experimented with the abolition of capital punishment soon reinstated it. Iowa, for example, abolished the death penalty in 1872 but restored it in 1878, Maine's period of abolition lasted from 1876 to 1883, Colorado's only from 1897 to 1901. Whatever the reasons, few states became long-term abolitionist states, and most that experimented with it had reinstated death penalty statutes by 1930.

Capital Punishment during the Pre-Modern Period: 1930–1972

The Declining Use of the Death Penalty

One of the features of capital punishment during the pre-modern period was its centralization under state authority. Beginning in 1930, the National Bureau of the Census included for all states the category "death by execution" as a cause of death in its *Mortality Statistics,* and with this publication we begin to get a precise accounting of the frequency with which executions were performed.

Table 1–2 reports the annual number of executions in the United States from 1930 until the end of 1969, as well as the average for each five-year period. Figure 1–1 illustrates in graphic form the trend of executions performed annually over the same period, during which time a total of 3,859 executions took place under state and federal authority. Both Table 1–2 and Figure 1–1 show that executions were far more common during the 1930s and 1940s than over the next two decades. The frequency of executions was greatest during the 1930s; there was an execution in the United States almost every other day. The annual average number of executions declined from about 166 during the 1930s to approximately 130 during the 1940s—a decrease in executions of about 36 per year (see Table 1–2). There was also a sharp decline in the number of executions from the 1940s to the 1950s, from about 130 a year to approximately

75. Capital punishment declined steadily during the 1960s and stopped temporarily, after 1967.

Another way to look at the infrequency of capital punishment is to examine the number of executions relative to the number of homicides committed.[3] For the years 1930 to 1967, Table 1-3 reports the number of executions (column 1), the estimated number of homicides (column 2), the number of homicides in death penalty states (column 3), and the estimated number of executions per 100 homicides in death penalty states (column 4). A few things are clear from this table. One of them is that in spite of the large number of homicides committed in any given year, very few resulted in an execution. There have been no more than 2 executions per 100 homicides (column 4: 1938) during this period. The rate of execution was highest during the 1930s and 1940s, although even then fewer than 2 out of 100 homicides resulted in an execution.

Because of the high number of homicides committed during the 1930s, the frequency of executions was higher during that decade than during the 1940s, but the rate of execution was somewhat higher during the 1940s. The second thing to observe from Table 1-3 is that the execution rate had declined almost steadily since the 1940s. While the execution rate was almost 2 out of 100 homicides from the mid-1930s to the late 1940s, it drops to less than 1 in 100 after the mid-1950s, and declines to less than 1 in 1,000 by the mid-1960s.

One reason for this generally low execution rate, of course, is that most of

Table 1-2
Yearly Number of Executions in the United States and Five-Year Averages: 1930-1970

	1930s				*1940s*	
1930	155	1935	199	1940	124	1945	117
1931	153	1936	195	1941	123	1946	131
1932	140	1937	147	1942	147	1947	153
1933	160	1938	190	1943	131	1948	119
1934	168	1939	160	1944	120	1949	119
Five-year average	155		178	Five-year average	129		128

	1950s				*1960s*	
1950	82	1955	76	1960	56	1965	7
1951	105	1956	65	1961	42	1966	1
1952	83	1957	65	1962	47	1967	2
1953	62	1958	49	1963	21	1968	0
1954	81	1959	49	1964	15	1969	0
Five-year average	83		61	Five-year average	36		2

Source: *Capital Punishment—1982* (Washington, D.C.: U.S. Department of Justice, Bureau of Justice Statistics, 1984), Table 1, 14.

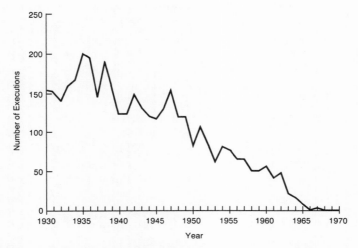

Source: T. J. Flanagan and K. Maguire, *Sourcebook of Criminal Justice Statistics 1989.* (Washington, D.C.: U.S. Department of Justice, Bureau of Justice Statistics, 1990), Table 6.95, 632.

Figure 1–1. Annual Number of Executions: 1930–1970

the homicides that occur in any year are not capital offenses and so are not eligible for the death penalty. Unfortunately, there are no separate records kept on capital murders by the FBI in its *Uniform Crime Reports,* and definitions of what a "potentially capital crime" is have varied across legal jurisdictions, so we have no clear way of knowing how many murders committed in any given year were "death-eligible," or capital, homicides. It has been estimated, however, that capital murders make up about 15 to 20 percent of all homicides during this period (Wolfgang 1958). On the assumption that the execution rates for death-eligible murders is about five times that shown in column 4 of Table 1–3 throughout the time period, we can see that the rate of execution for even capital murders was quite low, with no more than 10 executions for every 100 capital homicides.

The Geographical Distribution and Methods of Capital Punishment

The frequency of executions was not evenly distributed throughout the United States during this period. Table 1–4 reports for each state the number of executions that occurred in the United States from 1930 to 1967. From 1930 to the end of 1970 there were 3,859 executions under state or federal authority (and another few hundred under military authority). During these years, forty-two of fifty U.S. states had a death penalty statute at some time and

Number of Executions, Number of Homicides, and the Rate of Execution in Death Penalty States: 1930–1967

Years	Number of Executions (1)	Number of Homicides That Year [a] (2)	Number of Homicides in Death Penalty States in the Prior Year (3)	Executions per 100 Homicides in Death Penalty States[b] (4)
1930	155	10,617	9,509	1.63
1931	153	11,160	10,625	1.44
1932	140	11,035	11,290	1.24
1933	160	12,124	11,034	1.45
1934	168	12,055	11,586	1.45
1935	199	10,587	11,503	1.73
1936	195	10,232	10,156	1.92
1937	147	9,811	9,866	1.49
1938	190	8,799	9,453	2.01
1939	160	8,394	8,511	1.88
1940	124	8,208	8,104	1.53
1941	123	7,929	7,935	1.55
1942	147	7,743	7,656	1.92
1943	131	6,690	7,443	1.76
1944	120	6,553	6,417	1.87
1945	117	7,412	6,290	1.86
1946	131	8,784	7,081	1.85
1947	153	8,555	8,407	1.82
1948	119	8,536	8,207	1.45
1949	119	8,033	8,207	1.45
1950	82	7,942	7,736	1.06
1951	105	7,495	7,609	1.38
1952	83	8,054	7,155	1.16
1953	62	7,640	7,750	.80
1954	81	7,735	7,297	1.11
1955	76	7,418	7,397	1.03
1956	65	7,629	7,065	.92
1957	65	7,641	7,303	.89
1958	49	7,815	7,206	.68
1959	49	8,159	7,424	.66
1960	56	8,421	7,778	.72
1961	42	8,543	7,924	.53
1962	47	8,987	8,103	.58
1963	21	9,192	8,750	.24
1964	15	9,771	8,824	.17
1965	7	10,663	8,750	.08
1966	1	11,560	10,000	.01
1967	2	13,381	10,000	.02

Source: From W.J. Bowers, G.L. Pierce, and J.F. McDevitt, *Legal Homicide: Death as Punishment in America, 1864–1982* (Table 1–4, 25–26). Copyright © 1974, 1984 by W.J. Bowers. Reprinted by permission of Northeastern University Press.

[a]These figures pertain only to the continguous United States, excluding Alaska, Hawaii, and other territories and possessions. The annual number of homicides for Texas was not included in the Vital Statistics until 1933 when Texas reported 965 homicides. Thus, the national totals from 1930 through 1932 underestimate the actual number of homicides in the country by as much as 1,000 per year.

[b]The execution rate for a given year is based on the previous year's homicides in death penalty jurisdictions only. Specifically, for all abolitionist jurisdictions in the designated year, homicides committed the year before were subtracted from the national total in the preceding year. Since the number of homicides is unavailable for Texas prior to 1933, executions performed by Texas from 1930 through 1933 were excluded in the calculations of the execution rates for these years.

Table 1–4
Number of Executions in the United States by Jurisdiction: 1930–1967

Georgia	366
New York	329
Texas	297
California	292
N. Carolina	263
Ohio	172
Florida	170
S. Carolina	162
Mississippi	154
Pennsylvania	152
Alabama	135
Louisiana	133
Arkansas	118
Kentucky	103
Tennessee	93
Virginia	92
Illinois	90
New Jersey	74
Maryland	68
Missouri	62
Oklahoma	60
Washington	47
Colorado	47
Indiana	41
W. Virginia	40
Dist. of Columbia	40
Arizona	38
Federal System	33
Nevada	29
Massachusetts	27
Connecticut	21
Oregon	19
Iowa	18
Kansas	15
Utah	13
Delaware	12
N. Mexico	8
Wyoming	7
Montana	6
Vermont	4
Nebraska	4
Idaho	3
S. Dakota	1
N. Hampshire	1
Wisconsin	0
Rhode Island	0
N. Dakota	0
Minnesota	0
Michigan	0
Maine	0
Hawaii	0
Alaska	0

Source: *Capital Punishment—1982* (Washington, D.C.: U.S. Department of Justice, Bureau of Justice Statistics, 1984), Table 2, 15.

executed at least one offender (there were also executions in the District of Columbia under federal jurisdiction, as well as other federal executions, such as the Rosenbergs, executed for espionage in 1951).

Although a majority of states have had death penalty statutes, most of the executions occurred in only a few of them. From 1930 to 1967 over 60 percent (2,257) took place in just ten states: Georgia, New York, Texas, California, North Carolina, Ohio, Florida, South Carolina, Mississippi, and Pennsylvania (see Table 1–4). The imposition of capital punishment also seems to be distributed by region of the country. Almost one half of the 1930–1967 executions occurred in nine southern states: Georgia, Texas, North Carolina, Florida, South Carolina, Mississippi, Alabama, Louisiana, and Arkansas (see Table 1–4). Figure 1–2 further illustrates the regional nature of the imposition of capital punishment in the United States during the pre-modern period. It reports the number of executions over the period 1930–1970 for four geographical areas of the country, the Northeast (Massachusetts, Connecticut, New Hampshire, New Jersey, Pennsylvania, Vermont, New York, Maine, and Rhode Island), the North Central (Illinois, Indiana, Missouri, Nebraska, Ohio, South Dakota, Michigan, Wisconsin, Minnesota, Iowa, North Dakota, and Kansas), the South (Alabama, Arkansas, Delaware, Florida, Georgia, Maryland, District of Columbia, Virginia, West Virginia, North Carolina, South Carolina, Kentucky, Tennessee, Mississippi, Louisiana, Oklahoma, and Texas), and the West (Montana, Idaho, Wyoming, Colorado, New Mexico, Arizona, Utah, Nevada, Washington, Oregon, California, Alaska, and Hawaii). This figure shows quite vividly that throughout this period the frequency of executions was higher in the South than in any other region. Of the 3,859 executions that were performed in the fifty United States and the District of Columbia over the years 1930–1970, 2,306 (60%) occurred in seventeen southern states, an average of 135 executions per death penalty state. The number of executions that were performed in the South over this period was more than that in all other regions combined.

Most of the persons executed during the years 1930–1967 were put to death by electrocution. During this period twenty-five states and the District of Columbia used the electric chair at one time or another, eleven employed a gas chamber, thirteen used hanging, and in two others the method was death by firing squad. Prior to the 1900s the most frequent form of execution was hanging. In 1888, however, the New York legislature abolished its practice of death by hanging and substituted the new, more humane method of death by electrocution. The motivation of the New York legislature was ostensibly to develop "the most humane and practical method known to modern science of carrying into effect the sentence of death in capital cases."[4]

There was some doubt at the time, however, how humane death by electrocution was, and the first condemned offender scheduled to be electrocuted contested this method on the grounds that it constituted "cruel and unusual" punishment in violation of the 8th Amendment (see Miller and

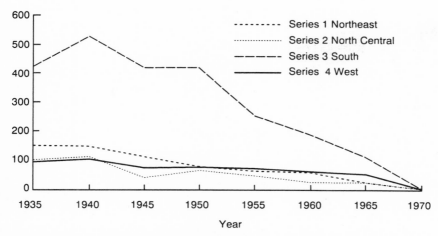

Source: *Capital Punishment–1982*. U.S. Department of Justice Bureau of Justice Statistics. Washington, D.C.: U.S. Government Printing Office, Table 2, 15.

Figure 1–2. Executions by Region: 1930–1970

Bowman 1988). The United States Supreme Court decided in *In re Kemmler,* 136 U.S. 436 (1890), however, that death by electrocution did not violate the 8th Amendment because it was an "instantaneous, and, therefore, painless death."[5] Ohio followed the New York example in 1897, and by 1930 more than half the states with capital punishment statutes adopted the electric chair as its method of carrying out executions. An additional "reform" of the method of execution, the adoption of lethal gas, occurred during the 1930s in some states, three of which had previously used the electric chair (Bowers 1984, 12).

Capital Offenses and Capital Statutes during the
Pre-Modern Era

Most executions during the pre-modern period were for the offense of murder. Of the 3,859 executions under state and federal jurisdiction that occurred from 1930 to 1967, 3,334 (86%) were for murder, 455 (12%) were for rape, 25 (.65%) for armed robbery, 20 (.52%) for kidnapping, and 25 (.65%) for other offenses such as burglary, aggravated assault, and federal espionage offenses.

One interesting feature about the imposition of capital punishment for different offenses is that the region of the country and race of the offender has been, at least in the past, an important correlate. Although blacks comprised about 10 to 12 percent of the total U.S. population during this period, of the 3,334 executions for murder about 50 percent involved black defendants (see Figure 1–3). Black offenders are even more conspicuously prominent in the rape execution figures. Of the 455 executions for rape, 405 (89%) involved non-whites (see Figure 1–3). Furthermore, 97 percent of all executions for rape occurred within southern states, and in 400 (90%) of these 443 southern executions for rape the condemned offender was nonwhite. These data would suggest that for the offenses of murder and particularly rape, the imposition of the death penalty, at least in the South, may have been affected by racial discrimination. As was true during its early years, capital punishment during the pre-modern period may also have been disproportionately inflicted upon unpopular groups and those perceived by powerful groups to be in need of discipline and control. We will examine the issue of racial discrimination in the imposition of capital punishment, both historically and under current death penalty statutes, in greater detail in Chapter 4.

Earlier in this chapter we learned that when death penalty laws were first adopted, they took the English common law form of mandatory statutes. Since it became clear that juries were attempting to mitigate the harshness of the law by refusing to convict those defendants not believed to be deserving of a death sentence, most states began to extend sentencing discretion to juries. Tennessee was the first state to abandon mandatory death sentences for murder in 1838, followed by Alabama in 1841 and Louisiana in 1876. By the 1920s, all but eight states had adopted a discretionary capital statute, and by 1963 all states with capital statutes had done so.[6] Although the precise nature of these discretionary statutes varied from state to state, all of them gave the capital sentencer the opportunity to return a sentence less than death for the conviction of a capital crime. Juries were typically instructed that when making their penalty determination they were to consider all factors that would argue for a death sentence

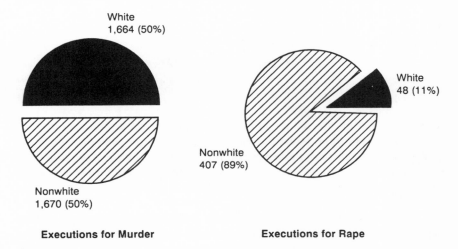

Executions for Murder   **Executions for Rape**

Source: T. J. Flanagan and K. Maguire, *Sourcebook of Criminal Justice Statistics 1989* (Washington, D.C.: U.S. Department of Justice, Bureau of Justice Statistics, 1990), Table 6.95, 632.

Figure 1–3. Murder and Rape Executions by Race

and all extenuating circumstances that would support a noncapital sentence. There did not have to be any established findings of fact, and the jury was left free to act according to its own unfettered judgment. The instructions given to the jury in the case of *McGautha v. California,* 402 U.S. 183 (1971) at pp. 189–190 (a case we will discuss in more detail in the next chapter) are instructive of the kind of discretionary capital statute we are talking about.

> . . . in arriving at this [penalty] determination you should consider all of the evidence received in court here presented by the People and defendants throughout the trial before this jury. You may also consider all of the evidence of the circumstances surrounding the crime, of each defendant's background and history, and of the facts in aggravation or mitigation of the penalty which have been received here in court. . . . Notwithstanding facts, if any, proved in mitigation or aggravation, in determining which punishment shall be inflicted, you are entirely free to act according to your own judgment, conscience, and absolute discretion.

These instructions make clear that capital juries during this pre-modern period were given virtually unrestricted freedom to return life or death sentences. Ironically, it was just this sentencing freedom, and the irrational pattern of death sentences this freedom produced, that led to the temporary suspension of the death penalty in the United States.

Furman v. Georgia *and the Suspension of Executions*

One by-product of the existence of sentencing discretion in capital cases was that juries began to return death sentences in only a minority of death eligible cases. The sporadic use of the death penalty could have meant that juries were being selective in their penalty decision. That is, juries could have been reserving the penalty of death for only the most egregious murderers, and sparing the lives of those murderers whose crimes were less brutal. It is also possible, of course, that the infrequency of death sentences could have been the product of a more random and irrational process. Juries could have been using their sentencing discretion to sentence some offenders to death and others to life for no clear or meaningful reason.

This latter scenario poses a problem, for it suggests that those sentenced to die are not the most serious offenders but those who happen to be unlucky— unlucky in the sense that their life might have been spared had they only been sentenced by a different jury. It is also possible that extending sentencing discretion to the capital jury gives it the opportunity to act on extralegal considerations in its penalty determination. Juries given the option of returning a life sentence may be more inclined to do so for white offenders and to be far less merciful on black offenders, particularly when they cross racial lines and slay a white. Another dark side of capital sentencing discretion, therefore, could be racial discrimination.

One of the facts about capital punishment which is very clear is that executions became more and more infrequent toward the end of the pre-modern period. By the mid-1960s the number of executions had dwindled to a mere handful. There were only 56 executions in 1960, fewer than 50 in both 1961 and 1962, 21 in 1963, only 15 in 1964, and from 1965 until 1969 there were only 10 executions (see Table 1–2 and Figure 1–1). The last execution for nearly ten years took place on June 2, 1967 when Louis Jose Monge was hung by the state of Colorado (Bowers 1984, 419). The use of capital punishment in the United States did not resume until the execution of Gary Gilmore in Utah by firing squad on January 17, 1977. This ten-year period when there were no executions was probably due to two related factors: (1) a *de jure* moratorium on capital punishment while the United States Supreme Court examined the constitutionality of state death penalty statutes, and (2) declining public approval for the death penalty.

By the late 1960s the Supreme Court had received numerous appeals from condemned offenders questioning the constitutionality of capital punishment. Legal claims had been raised that suggested that the administration of some state death penalty laws was discriminatory, while others raised the more general objection that discretionary capital statutes were in violation of the U.S. Constitution. The death penalty was then in legal limbo, and few state executives were willing to allow persons to be put to death until those issues were definitively resolved by the courts. This legal examination did ultimately occur, and the consequence was not favorable for those who wished to retain the death penalty in its current form.

Existing discretionary capital statutes were reviewed and declared unconstitutional in their application in 1972 when the Supreme Court decided *Furman v. Georgia,* 408 U.S. 238 (1972). This decision invalidated capital punishment laws in some forty states, and resulted in the vacating of death rows throughout the United States. As a result of the *Furman* decision over 600 condemned persons were resentenced to life terms, and some observers were prophesying dire consequences. Meltsner (1973, 290–91) has reported that Lester Maddox, Georgia's lieutenant governor, called the Court's decision "a license for anarchy, rape, and murder"; Bill Price, the chief of police in Memphis, suggested that "people who hesitated to pull the trigger before just might go ahead and do it now"; while Jack Greenberg, an abolitionist lawyer who worked on the *Furman* case for the NAACP's Legal Defense Fund, predicted that "there will no longer be any more capital punishment in the United States." The legal battle that was waged over the constitutionality of capital punishment and the aftermath of *Furman* will be the topic of Chapters 2 and 3. It is sufficient to note at this point that neither those who predicted a crime spree nor those foretelling the end of capital punishment were correct. The practical effect of the 1972 *Furman* decision was that the moratorium on executions that had existed since 1967 would continue, and lead to a reform of state death penalty law.

In addition to the important legal questions being raised, by the mid-1960s public support for the death penalty was at an all-time low. It was one of the few times in our history when a majority of the populace did not approve of capital punishment. Figure 1–4 reports the percent of the public expressing approval of the death penalty for persons convicted of murder during the period 1936– 1969. It can be seen that public support for capital punishment was high during the late 1930s and in the mid-1950s but began to decline thereafter for a few years. A Gallup opinion poll indicated that in 1953 68 percent of the American public expressed approval of the death penalty for those convicted of murder (Gallup 1988). This approval declined to 53 percent in 1960. By the mid-1960s this decline continued, and fewer than half expressed approval of the death penalty for murder. The year 1966 marked the low point for public sentiment: only 42 percent of the public expressed approval of capital punishment for murderers. Perhaps not surprisingly, and reflecting this public antipathy against capital punishment, executions had trickled to only a handful of cases in the mid-1960s, and by 1967 they stopped altogether for ten years (see Figure 1–1). With the *Furman* decision and the suspension of executions which began in 1967, it may have appeared by the 1970s that the death penalty would be abolished. Such, however, was most definitely not to be the case.

Capital Punishment in the Modern Era: The Executioner Returns

Enactment of New Death Penalty Statutes

The Supreme Court's *Furman* decision in 1972 did strike down existing capital punishment statutes and vacated death rows throughout the United States. *Furman* did *not,* however, declare that capital punishment was *per se* unconstitutional, that is, that the death penalty was under any circumstances cruel and unusual punishment. What *Furman* declared was simply that existing state capital punishment statutes, which granted juries unguided and virtually unregulated discretion, were unconstitutional. In sum, *Furman* held only that existing *procedures* for imposing death sentences were unconstitutional, not the practice of capital punishment itself. Although *Furman* did empty death rows across the country, it had none of the dire consequences that were being predicted by its critics, nor was Greenberg's statement true that "there will no longer be any more capital punishment in the United States" (Meltsner 1973, 291).

One of the consequences of *Furman* was the swift drafting of new death penalty statutes by state legislatures. These new capital punishment laws were fashioned in such a way as to remedy the major constitutional defect of previous

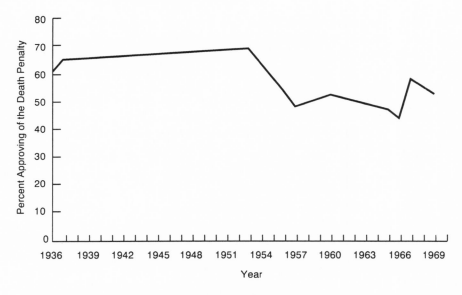

Sources: G. Gallup, *Public Opinion, 1985* (Wilmington, Delaware: Scholarly Resources Press, 1986), 36, 269; T. J. Flanagan and K. Maguire, *Sourcebook of Criminal Justice Statistics 1989* (Washington, D.C.: U.S. Department of Justice, Bureau of Justice Statistics, 1990), Figure 2.1, 169.

Figure 1–4. Death Penalty Approval for Murder

statutes identified by the *Furman* Court—unregulated and unrestricted sentencing discretion. These statutes, the subject of more detailed discussion in Chapters 2 and 3, took one of two general forms. One type attempted to remedy the problem of capital sentencing discretion by completely taking such discretion away. These statutes, referred to as mandatory statutes, required the imposition of a death sentence upon the conviction of a narrowly defined class of capital crimes. They were comparable to the very early mandatory death penalty statutes of post–revolutionary war America. The second type of new capital statute sought to remedy the problem of unregulated sentencing discretion, not by eliminating discretion altogether as mandatory statutes did, but by providing capital sentencers with some guidance and direction in their sentencing decision. These statutes, called guided discretion statutes, provided the jury with an implicit or explicit set of factors they should consider when making their penalty determination.

By the mid-1970s, some thirty-five states attempted to reinstate the death penalty by drafting new death penalty statutes which were hoped to pass constitutional muster. Guided discretion and mandatory capital statutes were reviewed by the United States Supreme Court; their decision, handed down in 1976 in *Gregg v. Georgia*, 428 U.S. 153 (1976) and its companion cases,[7] was that capital punishment for the offense of murder was acceptable under guided discretion statutes but unconstitutional under mandatory ones.[8] The ultimate effect of the Court's *Gregg* decision was the reappearance of the death penalty in the United States. With the enactment of new state death penalty statutes death rows once again began to fill up. Once these statutes were given constitutional approval by the U.S. Supreme Court it was only a matter of time before the moratorium on executions in existence since 1967 would come to a halt. The moratorium ended on January 17, 1977 with the voluntary execution of Gary Gilmore in Utah.

Executions and Death Sentences in the Modern Period

Table 1–5 reports the total number of executions performed in each state from January of 1977 until September of 1990, the number of condemned offenders on death row as of that date, and the current method of executions. During the approximate thirteen-year period there have been only 140 executions conducted in the United States. The "peak" execution year was 1987 when only twenty-five executions occurred. These data suggest that although the death penalty is back, the frequency of executions during the modern era is nowhere near its previous levels. Since the reinstatement of capital punishment only a handful of offenders have been executed each year.

If executions are infrequent, death sentences certainly are not. Table 1–5 reports that as of September 1990 there were 2,393 persons on state death rows, ranging from a high of 324 in Texas to two in Connecticut, New Mexico, and Wyoming. In looking at Table 1–5 we see that consistent with the pre-modern period, most of the executions and most of the condemned offenders awaiting death are in southern states. Of the 140 executions from 1977 to 1990, 123 (88%) were performed in the South,[9] and of the 2,393 offenders awaiting their deaths as of September 1990, over one half are in southern states. Current trends in the imposition of the death penalty, then, closely follow historical patterns in the carrying out of death sentences. Although not exclusively a southern phenomenon, southern states have and continue to rely on the penalty of death more than other states.

As we have seen in previous sections, historically, offenders in the United States have been executed for numerous offenses, including murder, rape, kidnapping, armed robbery, burglary, and arson. The post-*Furman* statutes of several states included offenses besides murder (armed robbery, rape, kidnapping) as capital crimes. In 1977, in the case of *Coker v. Georgia*, 433 U.S. 584 (1977), the United States Supreme Court reviewed the constitutionality of the death penalty for the rape of an adult woman. In ruling that the death penalty for rape under these circumstances was unconstitutional, under the "cruel and unusual punishments" clause of the 8th Amendment, the Court in *Coker* held that capital punishment was an excessive penalty for an offense that involved no loss of life.[10] The *Coker* Court's conclusion that capital punishment is

Table 1–5

Number of Executions in the United States by Jurisdiction, Number of Inmates on Death Row, and Method of Execution: 1977–1990

	Executions 1977–Sept. 1990	Inmates on Death Row—Sept. 1990	Method of Execution
Alabama	8	108	Electrocution
Arizona		89	Gas chamber
Arkansas	2	35	Lethal injection[a]
California		284	Gas chamber
Colorado		3	Lethal injection
Connecticut		2	Electrocution
Delaware		7	Lethal injection[b]
Florida	24	313	Electrocution
Georgia	14	106	Electrocution
Idaho		20	Lethal injection or firing squad
Illinois	1	132	Lethal injection
Indiana	2	52	Electrocution
Kentucky		26	Electrocution
Louisiana	19	32	Electrocution
Maryland		18	Gas chamber
Mississippi	4	46	Gas chamber
Missouri	5	71	Lethal injection
Montana		6	Lethal injection or hanging
Nebraska		12	Electrocution
Nevada	5	55	Lethal injection
New Hampshire[c]			Lethal injection
New Jersey		12	Lethal injection
New Mexico		2	Lethal injection
North Carolina	3	95	Lethal injection or gas chamber
Ohio		101	Electrocution
Oklahoma	1	115	Lethal injection
Oregon		23	Lethal injection
Pennsylvania		123	Lethal injection
South Carolina	3	44	Electrocution
South Dakota[c]			Lethal injection
Tennessee		80	Electrocution
Texas	37	324	Lethal injection
Utah	3	10	Lethal injection or firing squad
Virginia	9	44	Electrocution
Washington		9	Lethal injection
Wyoming		2	Lethal injection
Federal System		5	Lethal injection

Sources: NAACP Legal Defense and Education Fund, Death Row, U.S.A. (New York: NAACP Legal Defense and Education Fund, September 1990); D. Colburn, "Lethal Injection," Washington Post, Health: A Weekly Journal of Medicine, Science and Society 6(1990):12–14.

[a]Choice of lethal injection or electrocution for those sentenced before March 4, 1983.

[b]Choice of lethal injection or hanging for those sentenced before June 13, 1986.

[c]Existing death penalty statue but no death sentences have been imposed.

excessively severe when there is no loss of life prohibited its imposition for other nonlethal offenses such as armed robbery, kidnapping, and burglary. All persons executed since 1977 were convicted of murder.

There is one thing that has changed very little over the years, the disproportionate imposition of capital punishment on unpopular groups and those that may constitute a threat to those in powerful, established positions. We noted earlier in the chapter that the penalty of death has been frequently imposed on minority groups, whether religious or racial. This trend appears to be characteristic of the modern period of capital punishment, though in slightly altered form. During the days of the plantation economy and in the decades after, capital punishment was disproportionately imposed on black offenders. In the years after 1972, the penalty of death is often reserved for those minority offenders who victimize majority group members. Studies of the post-*Furman* capital sentencing schemes of several states have convincingly shown that black offenders who slay white victims are more likely to be charged with capital murder, more likely to be convicted of capital murder, and more likely to be sentenced to death than blacks who kill other blacks (Baldus et al. 1990; Bowers and Pierce 1980; Paternoster 1984; Nakell and Hardy 1987; Gross and Mauro 1989). Even under procedurally reformed capital statutes, then, there is some evidence to suggest that the death penalty is still a means of forging racial and political discipline.

A final point to be noted here concerns method of execution. During the pre-modern period, most states executed offenders by electrocution (25 states), with hanging (13 states) and lethal gas (11 states) as the next most popular methods. We noted earlier that during the pre-modern period many states changed their method of capital punishment to electrocution because it was thought to be more humane and painless. In recent years there has been a movement away from the use of the electric chair, hanging, and poison gas. Many states have abandoned these methods and adopted lethal injection as the means of carrying out death sentences. In 1990, twenty-one jurisdictions used lethal injection as their method of execution; only thirteen states still used the electric chair, five the gas chamber, two the firing squad, and only one has retained hanging (see Table 1–5).

Like the movement toward electrocution before it, the trend in recent years toward the adoption of lethal injection is based in large measure on the belief that an injection of lethal drugs is a far more civilized, humane, and painless way to put persons to death. There is some irony in these reform movements toward a "civilized and humane" method of execution, since first-person accounts of both electrocution and lethal gas suggest that neither may be as painless as believed.

In 1983 in Alabama, for example, John Louis Evans was struck initially with 1,900 volts of electricity for approximately thirty seconds. This jolt was not sufficient to kill Evans, but it did ignite the electrode attached to his leg. Smoke billowed around the leg and under the mask that covered his face. A second thirty-second burst of electricity was administered which caused further sparking of Evans's leg and head. John Evans survived this second jolt of electricity and a third was finally administered. The third thirty-second charge was sufficient to kill Evans, although the execution took nearly fifteen minutes.[11] A similar fate awaited Alpha Otis Stephens. The first two-minute jolt of electricity failed to kill him and he gasped for breath in Georgia's electric chair for eight minutes before a second, fatal current of two additional minutes duration was administered. In October of 1990 the state of Virginia put to death Wilbert Lee Evans. During the course of the electrocution, which sent 2,400 volts of electricity through Evans's body, blood poured from under the mask that concealed his head. A second jolt of electricity was required before killing him.

In recognition of the horrors of death by electrocution and other more archaic means (and perhaps of the expense of repairing existing methods of execution that had been dormant since before 1967), state legislatures began to adopt a new mode of administering capital punishment. In 1977 Oklahoma became the first state to adopt lethal injection as the method of execution, and in 1982 the first such execution occurred in Texas. In death by lethal injection, the condemned inmate is strapped to a hospital gurney with an intravenous line (IV) inserted in his arm. Typically, three different drugs are injected, a non-lethal dose of sodium thiopental (a barbiturate to induce sleep), and lethal doses of pancuronium bromide and potassium chloride. The former drug is a muscle relaxer; potassium chloride brings on cardiac arrest (Colburn 1990; Amnesty International 1989). The procedure is similar to a hospital patient being anesthetized, except in death by lethal injection the drugs are given in fatal doses, and the condemned offender is literally put to sleep for good.

The popularity of lethal injection is not difficult to understand. It is claimed to be a far more humane and civilized way to execute persons than the more painful means of electrocution, hanging, or poison gas. It also holds great political appeal since juries may be far less reluctant to simply put offenders to sleep than to sentence them to death in the electric chair or gas chamber.

Death by lethal injection comes with its share of controversy, however. One area of concern is the role of the medical profession in this method of execution, since the offender is injected with medical drugs. It may appear that doctors are directly involved in the state's taking of a life. The American Medical Association declared in 1982, however, that a physician could not be a participant in a legal execution, except to pronounce the person dead (Amnesty International 1989). Executions by lethal injection are performed by "technicians," although several states have used a "death machine" which mixes and administers the lethal doses of drugs.

In addition to the medical controversy, death by lethal injection may not be as painless and humane as touted. Condemned offenders with a history of intravenous drug use (as many convicted murderers have) may not have good veins within which to fix the IV. In 1985 it took medical technicians almost forty-five minutes before they could find a suitable vein to execute Stephen Morin (Colburn 1990, 15). Witnesses at the execution of James Autry in 1984 noted that it took ten minutes for him to die and that he appeared to be in great pain. A prison doctor later explained that the intravenous needle may have become clogged, slowing down the execution (Amnesty International 1989, 60). Although it may make capital punishment more palatable to juries, death by lethal injection may not be as civilized as believed.

Popular Approval of the Death Penalty

It was noted earlier that public approval for the death penalty was at an all-time low in the mid-1960s. In 1966, only 42 percent expressed support for the death penalty for those convicted of murder. After these years, however, public support for the death penalty began to increase. Figure 1–5 shows the percent of public approval for the death penalty for murderers during the years from 1971 to 1988. In 1972, the year that *Furman* was decided, a majority of the public (57%) did approve of the death penalty, and this approval rating increased somewhat (to 60%) by the mid-1970s. Just before the *Gregg* decision, which gave constitutional approval to state death penalty statutes, Americans expressed a 2–1 approval for capital punishment.[12] This approval for the death penalty for murderers continued to increase throughout the 1970s and 1980s. In a 1988 Gallup poll (Gallup 1988) nearly 80 percent of the public expressed approval of the death penalty for murder, the highest level of support since the question was first asked in the 1930s.

Public Opinion Polls and the Death Penalty: What Does "Approval" Mean?

In examining the empirical data with respect to public opinion polls and capital punishment during the modern period, one cannot help noticing an apparent contradiction. For several years now opinion polls have indicated that public opinion is strongly in favor of the death penalty for those offenders who commit murder, yet there are only a handful of executions each year. For example, in 1988 when nearly 80 percent of the public expressed approval of the death penalty only eleven persons were executed. Only sixteen were executed the year after that. If the public endorses the death penalty so fervently, why are there so few executions? There are two possible interpretations of this paradox.

The Public Wants More Executions. One of these interpretations is frequently expressed by death penalty opponents, as well as by some conservative members of the Supreme Court.[13] This argument holds that public opinion polls

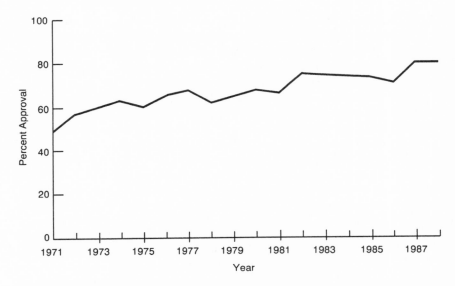

Source: G. Gallup, *Public Opinion, 1985* (Wilmington, Delaware: Scholary Resources Press, 1986), pp. 36, 269; T. J. Flanagan and K. Maguire, *Sourcebook of Criminal Justice Statistics 1989* (Washington, D.C.: U.S. Department of Justice, Bureau of Justice Statistics, 1990), Figure 2.1, 169

Figure 1–5. Public Approval for the Death Penalty

accurately gauge the depth and strength of support for the death penalty in the United States, and that the only reason so few executions are actually performed is because of the interminable delays caused by appeals courts. There is some evidence to support this interpretation.

One piece of evidence comes from additional research on U.S. public opinion about the death penalty. Ellsworth and Ross (1983) conducted an opinion survey of 500 adult residents in the San Francisco Bay area in 1974. It revealed that almost 60 percent of the respondents expressed approval of the death penalty for murder (the same percent in the 1974 Gallup poll, see Figure 1–5). If we were to hypothesize that these persons were in any way reluctant to see death sentences carried out, they would voice more support for death penalty statutes that gave juries the discretion to impose life or death sentences than mandatory ones that required the imposition of the death penalty for any person convicted of a capital crime. But in fact, Ellsworth and Ross (1983; 129) found that almost 50 percent of all respondents and 76 percent of those who expressed approval for capital punishment favored mandatory death sentences. They also asked their respondents what proportion of convicted capital defendants should be executed, and again there was little evidence of a reluctance to see death sentences carried out. Forty-two percent of respondents said that all convicted capital offenders should be executed, and two thirds said that half or more should be. These percentages were higher for death penalty proponents. Of those who favored the death penalty 66 percent thought that all convicted capital offenders should be executed and 95 percent said that half or more of them should be.

There is a second piece of evidence that might suggest that high public approval for the death penalty is an accurate indicator of the depth and strength of support that Americans have for capital punishment. This evidence comes from capital sentencing data. Figure 1–6 reports the number of death sentences imposed in the United States beginning in 1973 (the year after *Furman*). It shows, rather clearly, that the public, through the voice of the capital jury, may in fact strongly support the death penalty, because it continues to sentence large numbers of persons to death. The number of death sentences rose sharply from 1973 to 1975. Although death sentences declined in 1976 and 1977, this was primarily because mandatory death statutes were struck down by the Supreme Court in 1976, and death penalty states had to revise their laws. After 1977, there is an almost steady increase in the number of new commitments to death row, and since 1982 almost 300 new death sentences a year are imposed.

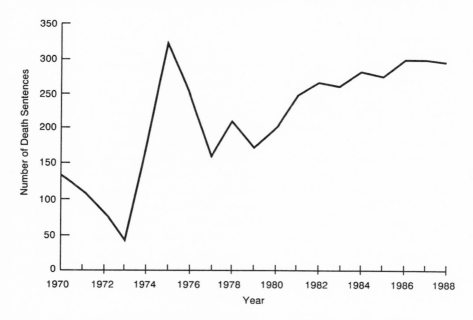

Source: T. J. Flanagan and K. Maguire, *Sourcebook of Criminal Justice Statistics 1989* (Washington, D.C.: U.S. Department of Justice, Bureau of Justice Statistics, 1990), Table 6.89, 625.

Figure 1–6. Number of Death Sentences: 1970–1988

These two pieces of evidence do not completely solve the paradox, however, for a relevant question at this juncture may be, if the public is so supportive of capital punishment, as evidenced by the fact that they express approval for it both in the abstract through public opinion polls and concretely by sentencing large numbers of persons to death, why are so few death sentences actually carried out? The answer to this critical question, from those who believe that public opinion polls are accurate reflections of public sentiment, would be that the "will of the public," which is that the frequency of executions be increased, is being thwarted by federal and state appeals courts which reverse a large proportion of death penalty cases.

There is evidence that the extra scrutiny of death penalty cases by appeals courts may have a great deal to do with the infrequency of executions during the modern period. One of the most distinctive features about the post-*Furman* system of capital punishment is that capital offenders have numerous avenues through which to appeal their case, for example, dual collateral review of capital convictions; automatic state review of death sentences and *habeas corpus* proceedings in federal courts.

The effect of this dual system of review is twofold. First, it provides opportunity for the reversal of a large proportion of death sentences. Second, it produces great delay in executions since offenders cannot have their death sentences carried out while they are pursuing their appeals. A report by the U.S. Department of Justice in 1987 revealed that the average length of time between the imposition of a death sentence and the execution of an offender is almost six and one half years.[14] Furthermore, delay has increased from an average of five years during the period 1977–1983 to over seven years during 1986 and 1987 (Bureau of Justice Statistics 1988). This report also indicated that from 1974 until the end of 1987, 3,404 persons had been sentenced to death. Of these 3,404 condemned men and women, only 93 (3%) had been executed while 1,984 (58%) were still on death row awaiting the final legal resolution of their case. In another 1,164 cases (34%) an appeals court had already overturned the state's death penalty statute, the defendant's conviction, or sentence. Many of those defendants whose conviction or death sentence had been overturned may be reconvicted and sentenced to death, and many of the 1,984 offenders awaiting their appeals may also have their convictions or sentences reversed by the courts. The small number of executions since 1977, then, may have far less to do with the lack of public support or a reluctance to see condemned offenders die, and more to do with the long and generally successful appeals process in capital cases.

The Public Wants Protection—Not the Death Penalty. A second and very different interpretation of public opinion poll data suggests that the public may support the death penalty but may not want many offenders put to death nor necessarily prefer capital punishment to other severe punishments. According to this argument, the public's expressed "approval" for capital punishment in the polling data is a reply to an abstract question and does not really support capital punishment.

The belief that Americans are in favor of capital punishment only in the abstract has been expressed by Hugo Bedau (1982, 68), a prominent critic of capital punishment. Bedau describes his position in the following way:

> One might hazard the hypothesis that the average person seems convinced that the death penalty is an important legal threat, abstractly desirable as part of society's permanent bulwark against crime, but that he or she is relatively indifferent to whether a given convict is executed on a given date as scheduled, or is indeed ever executed. To put it another way, there is no evidence that the two-to-one majority in favor of the death penalty for murder is also a two-to-one majority in favor of executing right now the hundreds of persons currently under death sentence.

Margaret Radin (1978, 1040–1042) has expressed this same idea. She suggests that what is important is not an "approval" answer to a public opinion question, but whether or not persons are able to adopt a "coherent moral position" with respect to the death penalty. This coherent moral position would require that the expression of a general support for the death penalty be consistent with other beliefs and actions—could those who approve of the death penalty also vote in favor of a death penalty referendum, could they vote for the death penalty if on a capital jury, and could they "pull the switch"? The essence of this position regarding the infrequency of executions is that in spite of an apparent high level of support, the public is in favor of capital punishment only "on the books" and only imposed on a few, isolated, and especially deplorable offenders, but is basically morally squeamish about its more widespread infliction.

One piece of information in support of this conjecture is the general disinclination of capital juries to sentence most convicted capital offenders to death. For example, in their study of the Georgia capital sentencing system, Baldus and his colleagues (1990, 111) found that of approximately 206 defendants who had been convicted of murder in a jury trial, only 112 (54%) received a death sentence. Even when defendants were convicted of a capital crime, then, almost one half of the juries in Georgia declined to impose a death sentence.

There is even more compelling information to indicate that Americans are not really expressing strong approval for the death penalty when asked about it in public opinion polls. This evidence suggests that what they are expressing is a desire to be protected, and that they would support other ways of incapacitating and punishing dangerous and serious offenders, ones that did not necessarily involve their execution. For example, a 1986 Gallup poll (Gallup 1986) revealed that while 70 percent of those surveyed approved of the death penalty for murder, this support declined to 55 percent if an alternative punishment, live imprisonment without the possibility of parole, was available. William Bowers (1990) reported that a recent California poll showed that 82 percent were in favor of the death penalty, but only 25 percent favored the death penalty over a sentence of life imprisonment without parole that also involved restitution to the victim's family. He also reported that public opinion polls in Florida showed that while 84 percent said they approved of the death penalty for murder, this declined to 24 percent when the alternative was life without the possibility of parole with restitution. In a New York survey, support for the death penalty declined from 72 to 32 percent.

These more refined public opinion polls are extremely important. They suggest that public opinion questions that simply ask whether the person approves of capital punishment for convicted murderers are a very misleading indicator of the strength of public support for the death penalty. These questions, which have been asked since the 1930s, have formed the basis of a folklore that Americans mandate capital punishment. This folklore has informed the attitudes of both state legislatures and Supreme Court justices who are led by these opinion polls into believing that this represents "the will of the people." What Americans may be expressing, however, is a desire for protection against dangerous criminals, not a desire for capital punishment. More sophisticated polling questions indicate that the public does not necessarily want to repay one life with another, but wants the murderer to be unable to offend again, and to ease the hardship and loss for those left behind.

In sum, there is evidence to suggest that there may be truth to both interpretations of the high public approval/low execution frequency paradox. On the one hand, juries seem reluctant to impose a death sentence on a large proportion of convicted capital defendants, and a significant proportion of those who express approval of capital punishment would be disinclined to impose a death sentence if there were a comparably severe noncapital sentence available (life without the possibility of parole). On the other hand, consistent with the level of public approval of capital punishment, juries continue to sentence large numbers of persons to death while appeals courts frustrate the carrying out of these sentences by carefully scrutinizing death cases for errors of law and reversing a substantial proportion of them. If there were greater use of severe but non-lethal penalties for murder, such as life imprisonment without parole with restitution, it is entirely possible that the public demand for harsh punishment and protection from dangerous criminals would be met, and such punishment would be carried out with greater dispatch than death sentences. The other unanswered question is whether Americans would continue to voice support for capital punishment if there were a substantial increase in the number of executions. Perhaps only then will we know if the United States, like most

Western nations, has evolved to the point where capital punishment is considered a morally intolerable practice.[15]

Summary and Conclusions

In this chapter we have learned that capital punishment has been with us since colonial days. Historical data show that, consistent with our English heritage, the death penalty has been with us since the 1600s. In this early period, executions (and "extralegal" executions in the form of lynchings) were frequently performed on unpopular groups such as religious dissenters and those who would question or disrupt the slave regimes of the South. Most executions performed during these years were under local rather than state control, and most were conducted in public. In spite of the established existence of capital punishment in colonial and post–revolutionary war society, there were several early attempts to restrict the use of the death penalty. These reforms included creating a distinction between different degrees of murder, a reduction in the number of capital crimes, and a movement away from mandatory to discretionary death sentences. Other reforms included the centralization of capital punishment under state control, making executions private rather than public events, and an early, though generally unsuccessful, effort in some states to have the death penalty abolished.

The years 1930–1972 were identified as the pre-modern period of capital punishment. During this time over 3,800 executions were performed. Most of these executions were for murder, and most took place in southern states. Consistent with the fact that historically capital punishment was imposed on problem populations, almost one half of the executions for murder and 90 percent of those for rape involved black offenders. The number of executions was not consistent throughout this period, however. The high point was during the 1930s and 1940s, and executions declined precipitously thereafter. By the mid-1960s fewer than twenty executions a year were performed. In 1967 the last execution for almost ten years took place.

This moratorium occurred while the Supreme Court reviewed important constitutional questions about the death penalty. In 1972, in the case of *Furman v. Georgia,* the Court decided that capital punishment under the most prevalent kind of statute, a statute that vested virtually complete sentencing discretion in the hands of the capital jury, was unconstitutional. *Furman* resulted in the reversal of over 600 death sentences, but it did not spell the end to capital punishment in the United States. Less than one year after the *Furman* decision was announced, states enacted new death penalty statutes that promised to remedy the constitutional defects of older, discretionary ones. With the passage of these new laws, state death rows began to fill up once again.

One type of death penalty statute, a so-called "guided discretion" statute, did pass constitutional muster and ushered in a new era of capital punishment, the modern period. In addition to a procedural and substantive reform of state death penalty statutes, the modern era saw one other "reform." Many states changed the manner in which they would execute their condemned offenders, away from electrocution, the gas chamber, and hanging, toward the lethal injection of drugs. By 1990 more states had death by lethal injection than had any other form of execution, primarily because it was perceived to be more humane and civilized. Although the death penalty was reinstated by these new state death penalty statutes, executions in the modern period are nowhere near as frequent as they once were. The first execution in this period was in 1977. From 1977 until September of 1990 there were only 140 executions, an average of about ten per year. Although executions have not been frequent, death sentences have. As of September 1990, there were nearly 2,400 persons on death rows throughout the United States, the highest number in our history, with more condemned persons added each year.

The infrequency of executions has occurred at a time when public support for capital punishment appears to be at an all-time high. Since the *Furman* decision in 1972, public approval for capital punishment, as expressed in public opinion polls, has increased steadily. In 1988, nearly 80 percent of Americans stated that they approved of the death penalty for those convicted of murder. If capital punishment is so popular, a question arises as to why executions have been so infrequent.

We explored two possible answers to this question. One answer argues that public opinion polls are correct, that Americans are strongly in favor of capital punishment but that the number of executions is kept low because of the long and successful appeals process in capital cases. A second answer argues instead that public opinion polls give an inaccurate estimate of the depth and strength of support Americans have for capital punishment. Those who make this argument point to more detailed public opinion information which indicates that the public is more supportive of alternatives to the death penalty that offer equal protection, such as life imprisonment without the possibility of parole. They also point to the fact that juries do not sentence most convicted capital offenders to death. If asked to, then, the average citizen may be reluctant to actually impose a death sentence, even if he or she approves of capital punishment in the abstract.

In the chapters that follow we will try to answer the many questions that were only suggested by the discussion in this introductory chapter. For example, precisely why did executions stop in 1967, what were the legal objections raised by death penalty opponents, and how were these objections handled by the various courts? What legal reforms were introduced in the administration of capital punishment in the aftermath of this legal struggle to have the death penalty declared unconstitutional, and did these reforms effectively remedy defects in the various state systems of capital punishment? If capital punishment was utilized most heavily by the South, and if most rape executions were of black offenders, given the historical legacy of racial inequality in the South, is there a connection between capital punishment and racial discrimination? Since many if not most offenders convicted of capital crimes are sentenced to life rather than death, is the death penalty reserved exclusively for the most brutal and egregious offenders? What are the reasons behind persons' approval for capital punishment, and are these reasons tenable? The answers to these and other questions will occupy our attention in the remaining chapters of this book.

Notes

1. At the end of September 1990 there were 2,393 persons on death row in 34 states (NAACP Legal Defense and Education Fund, *Death Row, U.S.A.,* 1990).

2. Schneider and Smykla, using an early computer tape of the Espy data (see Espy and Smykla 1987), reported 14,570 executions. Radelet (1989, 531) noted that the Espy data set now contains information on 15,978 executions performed in the United States since 1608.

3. Although defendants have been sentenced to death for offenses other than homicide (rape, armed robbery, kidnapping, burglary, and aggravated assault), murder has been the offense for which most offenders have been executed. Of over 3,800 executions during the period 1930–1967, approximately 85 percent were for the offense of murder.

4. Quoted in *Glass v. Louisiana,* 105 S.Ct. 2159 (1985) (J. Brennan dissent mg).

5. *In re Kemmler,* 136 U.S. 436 (1890) at p. 443.

6. See *Woodson v. North Carolina,* 428 U.S. 280 (1976) at pp. 289–292.

7. Also decided that day were *Proffitt v. Florida,* 428 U.S. 242 (1976); *Jurek v. Texas,* 428 U.S. 262 (1976); *Woodson v. North Carolina,* 428 U.S. 280 (1976); and *S. Roberts v. Louisiana,* 428 U.S. 325 (1976).

8. The rationale of the Court in accepting guided discretion but rejecting mandatory capital statutes will be discussed in Chapter 2.

9. The nonsouthern states with executions were Nevada (5), Missouri (5), Utah (3), Indiana (2), Oklahoma (1), and Illinois (1).

10. The *Coker* Court made no conclusion as to the appropriateness of the death penalty in cases of rape involving a child or for other nonlethal offenses. The Mississippi capital statute makes the forcible rape of a child under the age of ten a capital offense; South Dakota includes as a capital offense kidnapping that involves the gross and permanent injury of the victim; and California's capital statute includes aggravated assault by a prisoner serving a life term, treason, and train wrecking.

11. See *Glass v. Louisiana,* 105 S.Ct. 2159 (1985).

12. This high public approval for capital punishment in the mid-1970s is important in understanding the reinstatement of the death penalty after *Furman.* The brisk legislative activity in drafting new death penalty statutes subsequent to *Furman* may in part have been in response to favorable public sentiment for capital punishment at the time. Further, in deciding whether or not the death penalty is an unconstitutional punishment for murderers, the *Gregg* Court noted that such a penalty did not seem at variance with prevailing standards of morality, as evidenced in the expressed support for capital punishment. Since the public generally seemed to favor the death penalty for

murderers, the *Gregg* Court concluded that it is not a punishment which contemporary society finds morally objectionable [*Gregg v. Georgia*, 428 U.S. 153 (1976) at p. 179].

13. Several Supreme Court justices have expressed their dismay at the delay in carrying out death sentences brought about by appellate review. In his majority opinion in the case of *Barefoot v. Estelle*, 103 S.Ct. 3383 (1983), Justice White complained about the use of federal *habeas corpus* proceedings merely to delay an execution: "Even less is federal habeas corpus a means by which a defendant is entitled to delay an execution indefinitely" (at pp. 3391–3392). Justice Powell (1989) has been no less critical of the capital appeals process: ". . . our present system of multi-layered appeals has led to excessively repetitious litigation and years of delay between sentencing and execution."

14. See *Capital Punishment—1987*.

15. Australia, Austria, Denmark, France, Germany, the Netherlands, and Sweden have abolished the death penalty for all offenses; Canada, Israel, Italy, the United Kingdom, and Switzerland have abolished it for all crimes except specific wartime offenses (Amnesty International 1989, 259–260). We will examine the worldwide trend toward abolition of the death penalty in the final chapter of this book.

II
Constitutional and Legal Issues in Capital Punishment

2
Legal Challenges to and Reform of the Death Penalty: I. The Road to *Gregg v. Georgia*

W e have seen that executions in the United States began to decline dramatically during the 1950s and reached a mere trickle in the mid-1960s. In fact, from June 2, 1967 until January 17, 1977, a few months less than ten years, there were no executions at all. This moratorium was broken with the execution by firing squad of Gary Gilmore in Utah on January 17, 1977. What accounted for this long hiatus in state executions was a *de facto* abolition of capital punishment brought on by a concerted legal effort, primarily on the part of committed lawyers working both independently and for the NAACP's Legal Defense Fund, to secure the judicial review of existing death penalty statutes.[1]

By the mid-1960s, lawyers working on behalf of this organization, armed with scholarly reviews of existing death penalty practices, had been successful in raising considerable doubt about the constitutionality of capital punishment, or at least certain features of the way it was then being administered. This work culminated in the 1972 Supreme Court decision of *Furman v. Georgia*, 408 U.S. 238 (1972), which declared existing state capital punishment schemes unconstitutional under the Eighth Amendment's prohibition against cruel and unusual punishment.[2] The practical effect of *Furman* was to empty death rows across the United States. Over six hundred condemned men and women had their death sentences vacated to a term of imprisonment as a result of this decision. The success of this legal effort was short lived, however, as states quickly responded to *Furman* by drafting revised capital punishment statutes which promised to remedy the infirmities identified by the *Furman* Court.

The purpose of this chapter and the next is to review both the important features of the legal challenges mounted against the death penalty and the nature of the legal reforms initiated by the United States Supreme Court in the 1970s and 1980s. First we will review briefly the early Supreme Court opinions that antedated the concerted legal challenges against the death penalty of the 1960s and 1970s. These decisions presumed the constitutionality of capital punishment, but did place some restrictions on the means by which death sentences could be carried out. We will then trace the chronology of the abolitionist lawyers' death penalty litigation strategy leading up to the first important death penalty case in the 1970s, *McGautha v. California.* In *McGautha* (and its companion case, *Crampton v. Ohio),* decided in 1971, the petitioners claimed that existing capital statutes that permitted standardless juries and single-jury verdicts were unconstitutional under the "due process" clause of the Fourteenth Amendment. The Court rejected the petitioners' claims in *McGautha* and capital punishment remained on the books, although no executions occurred. The very next year after *McGautha* was decided, however, the Court again ruled on the constitutionality of the death penalty. The complaint in this case, *Furman v. Georgia,* was that capital punishment was cruel and unusual and in violation of the Eighth Amendment. Before engaging in a detailed analysis of the *Furman* decision, we will first examine the meaning that the phrase "cruel and unusual punishment" has taken in death penalty jurisprudence. Although in *Furman* the Supreme Court was to hold then-existing death penalty statutes unconstitutional, this decision did not spell the end of capital punishment in the United States. Immediately after the *Furman* decision state legislatures drafted new death penalty statutes which were believed to remedy the constitutional defects identified by the *Furman* Court. In the final sections of the chapter we will review the procedural reforms these new capital punishment statutes introduced into death penalty law.

Early Challenges to the Method of Imposing Death

The legal questioning of the death penalty in the late 1960s and early 1970s was nothing new, as the United States Supreme Court had reviewed state death penalty practices in the past. For the most part, however, these earlier cases focused on the *method or manner* in which the capital defendant was put to death, not whether it was constitutional for the state to do so in the first place.[3]

In *Wilkerson v. Utah,* 99 U.S. 130 (1878), for example, the Court examined whether or not death by shooting was a violation of the Eighth Amendment's prohibition against "cruel and unusual" punishment. Noting both that death was a usual punishment for murder and that for many years it had been inflicted in the territory of Utah by shooting, the Court held that it was not, therefore, forbidden by the Constitution as cruel and unusual. The *Wilkerson* Court noted the difficulty of defining with any degree of precision the meaning of "cruel and unusual," but did suggest some limiting principles for the state's right to inflict punishment:

> Difficulty would attend the effort to define with exactness the extent of the constitutional provision which provides that cruel and unusual punishments shall not be inflicted; but it is safe to affirm that punishments of torture . . . and all others in the same line of unnecessary cruelty, are forbidden by that amendment to the Constitution. (pp. 135–136)

The "punishments of torture" alluded to by the *Wilkerson* Court above included those acts which the Framers of the Eighth Amendment found most objectionable, punishments where the criminal "was embowelled alive, beheaded, and quartered" (p. 135). The test for "cruel and unusual" suggested by *Wilkerson,* then, was that a punishment was forbidden by the Eighth Amendment if it involved "torture" or "unnecessary cruelty."

The Supreme Court had another opportunity to rule on the constitutionality of a different form of state-inflicted capital punishment, death by electrocution, in *In re Kemmler,* 136 U.S. 436 (1890). In *Kemmler* a unanimous Court acknowledged that the death penalty was not in itself cruel and unusual: "The punishment of death is not cruel, within the meaning of that word as used in the Constitution" (p. 447). In ruling that the intended New York practice of putting capital defendants to death by electrocution was constitutional, though unusual since it was the first time electrocution was employed,"[4] the *Kemmler* Court did suggest that some forms of inflicting death might violate the Eighth Amendment. In approving of the "unnecessary cruelty" test of *Wilkerson,* and supplying its own test of "manifestly cruel and unusual," the Court observed that "[p]unishments are cruel when they involve torture or a lingering death. . . . [i]t implies there something inhuman and barbarous, something more than the mere extinguishment of life" (p. 447). The Court also supplied some specific examples of "manifestly cruel and unusual" punishments that would be forbidden: "If the punishment prescribed for an offence against the laws of the State were manifestly cruel and unusual, as burning at the stake, crucifixion, breaking on the wheel, or the like, it would be the duty of the courts to adjudge such penalties to be within the constitutional prohibition" (p. 446).

A third occasion where the Court had the opportunity to pass on the constitutionality of imposing capital punishment was the unusual case of *Louisiana ex rel. Francis v. Resweber,* 329 U.S. 459, 464 (1947). In this instance, the fifteen-year-old defendant, Willie Francis, was sentenced to die in Louisiana's electric chair. During the administration of the electric current the state's portable electric chair mechanically malfunctioned and would not operate. Francis was then removed from the chair, it was subsequently repaired, and he was rescheduled for execution. Francis fought his second electrocution on the grounds that another attempt to put him to death, what Justice Burton characterized in dissent as "death by installments" (p. 474), was both tantamount to torture and degrading to a human being. In again upholding the constitutionality of the death penalty itself, the *Kemmler* Court held that the first unsuccessful electrocution was both "an unforeseeable accident" and "an innocent misadventure," rather than a conscious intention of the state (which would have made it unacceptable torture):

The cruelty against which the Constitution protects a convicted man is cruelty inherent in the method of punishment, not the necessary suffering involved in any method employed to extinguish life humanely. . . . There is no purpose to inflict unnecessary pain nor any unnecessary pain involved in the proposed execution. (p. 464)

The Court also seemed to agree with the *Wilkerson* and *Kemmler* tests of "cruel and unusual" in observing that "[t]he traditional humanity of modern Anglo-American law forbids the infliction of unnecessary pain in the execution of the death sentence" (p. 462). Nonetheless, one year after the first execution attempt Francis again sat in Louisiana's electric chair, and this time it worked (see Miller and Bowman 1988).

It is clear, then, that early Supreme Court decisions established that, at least for certain offenses such as murder, the death penalty was not inherently cruel and unusual. The Court did suggest, however, that the method of inflicting death could become unconstitutional if it involved torture or unnecessary cruelty (*Wilkerson*), was inhuman and barbarous (*In re Kemmler*), or involved the infliction of unnecessary pain (*Francis v. Resweber*). It would appear to be certain, therefore, that any legal strategy that suggested that capital punishment for the offense of murder was in violation of the Eighth Amendment's prohibition against cruel and unusual punishment was doomed to failure, unless it could be demonstrated that the method of its infliction met one of the above tests. Under this "historical" interpretation of the Eighth Amendment, what was cruel and unusual, and therefore expressly forbidden by the Eighth Amendment, was only those barbarous or unnecessarily cruel forms of punishment the Framers were knowledgeable of—those characteristic of the Stuart monarchy in England. Such specific excesses of government (disembowelment, ear cropping), it is argued by proponents of this interpretation, were those acts, and only those acts, which the Framers of the Eighth Amendment expressly intended American citizens to be protected from.[5] Within those parameters, states were free to choose whatever punishments legislatures, as expressions of "the will of the people," authorized.[6]

Given such a fixed, "historical" understanding of the "cruel and unusual punishments" clause, it would be difficult if not legally impossible for defendants to claim that nonbarbarous forms of capital punishment, such as electrocution or the lethal injection practiced today, were in violation of the Eighth Amendment. After all, capital punishment was commonly imposed in the colonies, and the Framers of the Constitution explicitly recognized the existence of the death penalty, as evidenced by the Fifth Amendment which provides that "[n]o person shall be held to answer for a *capital*, or otherwise infamous crime, unless on a resentment or indictment of a Grand Jury . . . nor shall any person be subject for the same offence to be twice put in jeopardy of *life* or limb . . . nor be deprived of *life*, liberty, or property, without due process of law. . . ." (emphasis added). In order for the death penalty to be seen as a violation of the Eighth Amendment, the "cruel and unusual punishments" clause had to be given a different interpretation, one that does not fix its meaning to those punishments thought cruel and barbarous by its Framers. This new interpretation was in fact slowly to emerge as a result of a series of U.S. Supreme Court decisions, and was instrumental in the legal challenge marshalled against death penalties in the 1970s. Before we study this attempt to interpret the "cruel and unusual punishments" clause along this more flexible line, and how it was employed in a legal attack against the death penalty, we will first examine the course of events that led to another avenue of legal challenge which preceded the Eighth Amendment challenge. This line of attack against the death penalty employed the "due process" clause of the Fourteenth Amendment.[7]

The Road to *McGautha v. California:* Legal and Academic Challenges to the Death Penalty

By the mid-1960s the death penalty in the United States seemed to be in retreat. Reflecting disenchantment with capital punishment, public support for the death penalty for murder fell from 62 percent in 1936 to 42 percent in 1966. Perhaps indicative of this decline, as we have noted in the previous chapter, the number of executions also steadily declined over time. Along with this public questioning of the death penalty, legal scholars and practitioners became more vocal about abolishing capital punishment.[8]

Although in legal journals there were frequently philosophical discourses about the death penalty, few were concerned with its essential legality. In 1961, however, The *University of Southern California Law Review* published a prescient paper by Gerald Gottlieb. Gottlieb (1961) argued that the death penalty was unconstitutional under the Eighth Amendment because it violated contemporary moral standards, what the U.S. Supreme Court in *Trop v. Dulles,* 356 U.S. 86 (1958) referred to as "the evolving standards of decency that mark the progress of a maturing society" (p. 101). That same year, a Professor Walter Oberer wrote an article published in the *University of Texas Law Review* that was critical of the common practice of "death qualifying," a process by which capital jurors who indicated a general opposition to the death penalty were removed from service. Professor Oberer (1961) claimed that such a practice purged the jury of its more compassionate members and produced a homogenous jury more likely to convict.

In addition to legal scholars, practicing lawyers and judges grew more skeptical of the wisdom and constitutionality of the death penalty. In the early 1960s, for example, the American Law Institute (ALI) drafted a Model Penal Code which included two legal reforms of the death penalty: (1) a bifurcated trial process, in which defendants are afforded a preliminary hearing in which the factual issue is one of guilt/innocence and then a second, penalty phase hearing where the issue is the imposition of a life or death sentence; and (2) enumerated aggravating and mitigating circumstances to guide and restrict the discretion of the sentencing authority. These procedural reforms of capital punishment were accepted by a formal approval of the membership of the ALI, although an unsuccessful attempt was made to include a plea for their abolition (Meltsner 1973, 21–23).

In the early 1960s, then, there was some vocal support among the public and within both the academic community and practicing bar for legal reforms of the death penalty, if not its complete abolition. These nascent efforts received some critical encouragement from an unusual source. In October of 1963, in a rare written and published dissent from a denial of *certiorari* in an Alabama rape case, *Rudolph v. Alabama,* 375 U.S. 889 (1963), Justice Arthur Goldberg (concurred in by Justices Brennan and Douglas) suggested that the entire Court ought to determine whether or not the death penalty for a rapist who has not taken a life was unconstitutional under the Eighth Amendment. This was an unusual move not only because written dissents from *certiorari* denials are rare, but also because in their brief Rudolph's lawyers did not question the constitutionality of capital punishment for rape. In his dissenting note, Justice Goldberg provided three arguments he thought the Court should consider in this matter: (1) Prevailing standards of morality both in the United States and other "peer" countries may have progressed to the point where punishing rape by death is no longer acceptable, (2) punishing by death the crime of rape where no life was taken may be constitutionally impermissible because it is excessively severe, and (3) if the legitimate purposes for punishing rape (deterrence, rehabilitation, and retribution) can be effectively secured by a punishment less than death, the infliction of the death penalty may be unconstitutional because it is unnecessarily cruel.

Although Goldberg's *Rudolph* dissent had very little practical impact, it galvanized the small band of abolitionist lawyers working at the time. That at least three of its members were sensitive to abolitionist sentiments did in fact encourage legal efforts to get the constitutionality of the death penalty before the full Supreme Court for review. This effort occurred in the case of one William L. Maxwell.

William Maxwell was a twenty-two-year-old black male who in 1962 had been convicted and sentenced to death in Arkansas for the 1961 rape of a white woman. His appeal included a claim that the death-sentencing patterns of Arkansas rape juries showed evidence of racial discrimination, but both his conviction and death sentence were affirmed by the Arkansas Supreme Court. Legal Defense Fund (LDF) lawyers assisted Maxwell's counsel in drafting a *habeas corpus* petition for review by the federal courts. This petition was rejected by both the U.S. District Court and the Court of Appeals for the Eighth Circuit in 1964. In late 1965 the U.S. Supreme Court refused to review the case. At a second *habeas* hearing before the U.S. District Court in August of 1966 LDF lawyers were able to present social scientific testimony by Professor Marvin Wolfgang that strongly suggested racial discrimination in the imposition of death sentences for rape in selected Arkansas counties (see Wolfgang 1974). The result of this second hearing was again unsuccessful for Maxwell. The district court denied all of Maxwell's claims and refused both to stay his execution and to issue a certificate of probable cause, indicating that the court saw little merit in further appeal. The Court of Appeals for the Eighth Circuit affirmed the district court's ruling.

This execution did not take place, however; Maxwell won a stay of execution by the U.S. Supreme Court in 1967. One year after the Supreme Court sent the case back to the Eighth Circuit Court of Appeals, the latter issued its opinion written by Judge (later Supreme Court Justice) Harry Blackmun, which again upheld Maxwell's death sentence. Judge Blackmun's opinion in *Maxwell v. Bishop,* 398 F. 2d 138 was delivered in July of 1968. One consequence of Maxwell's and others' legal trips up and down the courts' ladder was an unofficial moratorium on executions until some of the more thorny legal issues could be resolved. At the time of Blackmun's *Maxwell* opinion in July of 1968, there had been no executions in the United States since June of 1967. The United States Supreme Court assisted in the further delay of executions when it agreed to review Maxwell's appeal of the 1968 Eighth Circuit's denial of relief.

The year before the Supreme Court held oral arguments on Maxwell's last appeal it issued its ruling in another death penalty case, *Witherspoon v. Illinois,* 88 S.Ct. 1770 (1968). William Witherspoon was convicted of the murder of a Chicago police officer in 1960 and sentenced to death. Under existing Illinois law, and most other state death penalty statutes at the time, a juror could be challenged for cause and removed from jury service if he or she had "conscientious scruples against capital punishment, or that he is opposed to same."[9] During the questioning of Witherspoon's prospective jurors, the *voir dire,* almost one half were eliminated for cause under this rule even though only five of forty-seven expressed the belief that under no circumstances could they return a death sentence. The brief by the petitioner argued that the "death qualification" of jurors in this manner produced a jury that was biased with respect to the decision both to convict and to impose a sentence of death.

Given the prevalent practice of "death qualifying" jurors, the *Witherspoon* decision was an important one for those advancing the abolitionist cause. In its opinion the Court rejected the argument that removing scrupled jurors produced a jury more likely to convict a defendant. In upholding Witherspoon's conviction, it rejected the social scientific evidence on this issue as too "tentative and fragmentary" (p. 1774). Writing for the majority, Justice Stewart ruled that Witherspoon's death sentence was invalid because the jury had not been impartial with respect to sentence. Specifically, those jurors who simply *had doubts* about the propriety of the death penalty in Witherspoon's case had been systematically culled. In suggesting a rule for the proper exclusion of jurors, Stewart suggested that only those who would "automatically vote against the imposition of capital punishment no matter what the trial might reveal," or those who made it "unmistakably clear" that their opposition to the death penalty would prevent them from being impartial about factual issues, could appropriately be removed for cause.[10]

The practical effect of *Witherspoon* was not significant. Those defendants on death row at the time of the decision who had been sentenced to death by juries similar to Witherspoon's had to be resentenced. In many instances this meant sentences of imprisonment; in others, defendants were simply resentenced to death after new hearings or because the spirit of *Witherspoon* was eviscerated.[11] Both the *Witherspoon* decision and another capital punishment case decided that same year, *United States v. Jackson*, 390 U.S. 570 (1968) (which struck down a federal kidnapping statute providing for the death penalty for defendants who requested a trial but not if a guilty plea was entered), were important in that they served notice that the Supreme Court was aware of deficiencies in the legal treatment of capital defendants. *Witherspoon* contributed to the moratorium on state executions, and in the following year the Supreme Court heard oral arguments in two other cases concerning the death penalty, a continuation of Maxwell's case [*Maxwell v. Bishop*, 398 U.S. 262 (1970)] and *Boykin v. Alabama*, 395 U.S. 238 (1969).

Edward Boykin, Jr. was a twenty-seven-year-old black male who was convicted of a series of armed robberies in Mobile, Alabama, and sentenced to death. He was one of only a few persons on death row in the United States for an offense other than first-degree murder or rape. With the apparent consent of his court-appointed attorney, and also apparently without advisement that he could be given the death penalty, Boykin pled guilty to five counts of armed robbery. After the jury heard testimony from seven eyewitnesses, it retired to deliberate. Less than one hour after beginning their deliberations, the jury returned with five death sentences, one for each armed robbery conviction. In his appeal from these death sentences, Boykin claimed that the imposition of the death penalty was disproportionate to the offense of armed robbery and therefore a "cruel and unusual" punishment in violation of the Eighth Amendment. The Alabama Supreme Court, however, affirmed the death sentences. In reviewing Boykin's claim of "excessive" punishment, three dissenting judges of the Alabama Supreme Court, based on conversations during oral argument, noted that the trial judge had erred because he had failed to ensure that Boykin understood the consequences of his guilty plea and waived his right to a trial knowingly and voluntarily (Meltsner 1973, 183–184).

The United States Supreme Court agreed to hear Boykin's appeal on both the excessiveness of the sentence and the voluntariness of the guilty plea. The former issue is particularly important since Boykin's case was the first time that the Court was to review the constitutionality of the death penalty itself, as a *per se* "cruel and unusual" punishment. The Court was not, however, to decide the Boykin case on such sweeping grounds. True to its usual practice of deciding cases on the narrowest possible constitutional issue, it vacated Boykin's death sentences on the grounds that the trial court failed to determine whether his guilty plea was "voluntarily and understandingly entered." Meltsner (1973, 184–185) commented that the failure of the Court to rule on larger Eighth Amendment grounds may have indicated that it was not yet receptive to the abolition of the death penalty. Decisions in *Jackson, Witherspoon,* and now *Boykin,* however, provided evidence that the Court may be more receptive to a procedural reform of state death penalty practices. Meanwhile, the moratorium on executions continued and the Court had yet to rule on the *Maxwell* case.

Maxwell's case was eventually decided on June 1, 1970. Owing to the resignation of Justice Abe Fortas (a death penalty opponent), this last appeal was argued before the Supreme Court on two occasions, March 4, 1969 and May 4, 1970. The Court's opinion did not address the two issues raised by LDF lawyers in their appeal, (1) the single-verdict jury which heard both guilt and penalty issues simultaneously, and (2) the standardless jury that sentenced Maxwell to death had been given no directions or guidance in making its decision. Instead, the Court steered clear of these more difficult issues and vacated Maxwell's death sentence on the more narrow *Witherspoon* grounds that several prospective jurors were impermissibly removed because they voiced general scruples against the death penalty. With regard to the two weightier issues of single-verdict and standardless juries, the Court made comment that "[i]n the action we take today, we express no view whatever with respect to the two questions originally specified in our grant of certiorari." [*Maxwell v. Bishop,* 398 U.S. 262 (1970) at p. 267]. It is important to note, however, that in footnote 4 of the *Maxwell* decision the Court served notice that it would delay no further on these two controversial points of law, announcing that it had that day agreed to grant *certiorari* in two cases where these issues were central, which would be considered "at an early date in the 1970 term." These two cases were *Crampton v. Ohio* and *McGautha v. California,* consolidated under 402 U.S. 183 (1971).

McGautha v. California and a Fourteenth Amendment "Due Process" Challenge to Standardless and Single-Verdict Juries

The unofficial moratorium on state executions continued into 1970, as men and women on death row waited for the Supreme Court to resolve some of the complex legal issues that were in a very real sense keeping them alive. As Meltsner (1973, 214) noted, the backlog of appeals continued; forty-six petitions in death penalty cases were filled with the Supreme Court in 1969 and thirty-eight more were added in 1970. Many of these appeals involved the two issues raised in *McGautha* and *Crampton:* standardless and single-verdict juries. Oral arguments were heard on the cases before the full Supreme Court in November of 1970.[12]

The facts of McGautha's and Crampton's crimes made them far more egregious than Maxwell's, which involved a rape without murder. As the Court's opinion narrates, during the course of an armed robbery of a store McGautha and his codefendant, Wilkinson, killed the store owner's husband. Although there was some dispute as to who the "triggerman" was, both were convicted of first-degree murder at the guilt phase of California's bifurcated capital trial procedure.[13] As a result of testimony during the penalty phase, which suggested that McGautha was the one who actually fired the fatal shot, the jury sentenced Wilkinson to life imprisonment and McGautha to death.

In *Crampton v. Ohio* the defendant was convicted by an Ohio jury for the first-degree murder of his wife and sentenced to death. Under Ohio law, the jury's verdict was unitary, or single-verdict, meaning that it decided both guilt and penalty with the same evidence and with a single deliberation. Crampton, who at the time of the murder was on leave from a state mental hospital where he was receiving treatment for alcoholism and drug addiction, threatened his wife for several days before fatally shooting her in the face.

Both McGautha and Crampton were sentenced to die by juries that had virtually complete and unfettered discretion to return a life or death sentence. At the time, capital juries were usually not instructed as to which kinds of murders or murderers were deemed most deserving of death or mercy. The selection of which factors should be most determinative and the amount of weight given to them was left entirely in the hands of the jury.[14] The law informed the jury as to the elements it could and could not employ in making their sentencing decision in only the most general terms. For example, in McGautha's case the jury was provided by the trial court with the following standard set of instructions:

> In this part of the trial the law does not forbid you from being influenced by pity for the defendants and you may be governed by mere sentiment and sympathy for the defendants in arriving at a proper penalty in this case; however, the law does forbid you from being governed by mere conjecture, prejudice, public opinion or public feeling. . . .
> . . . in determining which punishment shall be inflicted, you are entirely free to act according to your own judgment, conscience, and *absolute discretion* . . .
> . . . the law itself provides no standard for the guidance of the jury in the selection of the penalty, but, rather, commits the whole matter of determining which of the two penalties shall be fixed to the judgement, conscience, and *absolute discretion* of the jury.
> [*McGautha v. California*, 402 U.S. 183 (1971) at p. 189, emphasis added][15]

The instructions given to Crampton's jury were no more instructive or guiding. The jurors were simply informed that if they found the defendant guilty of first-degree murder they were to sentence him to death, unless they recommend mercy. They were provided with no direction as to which features of the offense or offender they should consider in recommending or not recommending mercy. They were simply told in the most general terms:

> You must not be influenced by any consideration of sympathy or prejudice. It is your duty to carefully weigh all the evidence, to decide all disputed questions of

fact, to apply the instructions of the court to your findings and to render your verdict accordingly. In fulfilling your duty, your efforts must be to arrive at a just verdict.

To summarize these two cases, Crampton had been tried and sentenced to death under the most common capital punishment scheme at the time, a unitary hearing, in which the jury determined, from the same evidence, both guilt and penalty. Again consistent with prevailing state practices, both Crampton and McGautha were sentenced to death by juries that were provided with no explicit guidance or direction for deciding the appropriate penalty. Counsel for the defendants complained that both of these death penalty sentencing procedures were in violation of the "due process" clause of the Fourteenth Amendment. To understand these cases we must first ascertain the specific nature of the complaint, why do unitary hearings and standardless juries fail to afford capital defendants the full "due process" of law due them?

To begin with, in order to comprehend Crampton's objection to the unitary capital trial, it is helpful to contrast his hearing with that granted McGautha. Under existing California law, McGautha was provided with two hearings. During the guilt phase the jury heard only evidence relevant to two specific questions, was McGautha guilty of murder and was it murder in the first degree? During this phase of the bifurcated capital trial it was not necessary (nor advisable, since it could easily prejudice a jury) for him to present any reasons to the jurors why they should spare his life if they should find him guilty.

Once convicted of first-degree murder McGautha was afforded a second hearing, the penalty phase, where the jury would hear only that evidence relevant to which sentence he should receive, death or life imprisonment. It was at this hearing that McGautha could present to the jury mitigating evidence which he hoped would convince them to spare his life. For example, McGautha, testifying in his own behalf, stated that he came from a broken home, that he had been wounded in the service of his country during World War II, and that his codefendant was the one who actually did the killing. At his penalty phase hearing his codefendant, Wilkinson, testified in his own behalf that he was generally a good provider for his mother and siblings until an accidental shooting led to his being unemployed and subsequently falling into the wrong crowd. Wilkinson also called several witnesses in his behalf, absent from the guilt phase, who testified to his good character and remorse for the crime. Reflecting the advantages of a bifurcated procedure, the generally followed trial strategy is to give only that information during the guilt phase necessary to convince the jury of the defendant's innocence, and failing that, to provide them with as much information as necessary during the subsequent penalty phase to convince them that the defendant is deserving of a life sentence.[16]

Under Ohio's single-verdict capital sentencing procedure, however, Crampton did not have the advantage that McGautha and Wilkinson did under California law. Since his jury rendered both a guilt/innocence and life/death verdict after one deliberation, Crampton had to make the difficult choice of possibly biasing the jury's guilt/innocence verdict by presenting them with mitigating evidence relevant only to appropriate penalty. Specifically, Crampton argued that the unitary proceeding forces capital defendants to make a choice between two competing constitutional rights: in order to personally address the jury with respect to issues relevant solely to punishment, capital defendants must surrender their privilege to remain silent on the issue of guilt. By testifying on their own behalf about the appropriate penalty that should be imposed if found guilty, defendants may "open the door to otherwise inadmissible evidence which is damaging to his case" (*McGautha v. California*, p. 213).[17] For example, defendants may want to plea in mitigation that they committed the crime under the duress of another or under the influence of drugs. If they were to make such a plea at a unitary hearing, however, they would be admitting that they in fact had committed the offense. Under single-verdict hearings defendants are compelled to make a choice between keeping silent on the mitigating factor and incriminating themselves. Forcing such a choice, defendant Crampton argued, creates an intolerable tension between two constitutional rights in violation of the Fourteenth Amendment's "due process" clause.[18]

The common complaint of McGautha and Crampton concerned standardless capital juries. As we have seen, both McGautha's and Crampton's juries were provided with no guidance as to those factors they should be attuned to in deciding the appropriate penalty. California juries were generally instructed that they could be swayed by pity, sentiment, and sympathy for the defendants but not by "mere conjecture, prejudice, public opinion or public feeling," and Ohio juries were merely informed that they could not be influenced by sympathy or prejudice. Other than this, jurors had "absolute discretion" in determining that the appropriate penalty. The two petitioners contended that the absence of standards was constitutionally intolerable under the "due process" clause of the Fourteenth Amendment, because without guiding standards juries would act out of whim and caprice and there would be no rational basis to differentiate those condemned to die from those given life sentences.[19] Under a system of capital sentencing that allows juries such unguided discretion, variation in jury sentencing will be at a maximum. One defendant could be sentenced to life imprisonment; another, who had committed a somewhat comparable crime, could be sentenced to death by a different jury. As a result, rather than being rationally imposed, such death sentences could be "merely reflecting random or arbitrary choice."[20]

To reiterate, the two issues before the Court in *McGautha* were whether the single-verdict capital trial and standardless capital juries were unconstitutional under the "due process" clause of the Fourteenth Amendment. The Court's decisions in *McGautha v. California* and *Crampton v. Ohio* were handed down on May 3, 1971, and the news was not good for those awaiting the announcement on death rows across the United States. In a 6–3 vote, the Court held that neither standardless nor single-verdict juries were in violation of the

Fourteenth Amendment. It is essential now to understand the rationale for the Court's decision in this important case.

In writing for the majority (joined by Justices Burger, Stewart, White, and Blackmun; Justice Black concurred in the result, but for different reasons than the majority position), Justice Harlan first argued that the function of the Supreme Court is not to devise for the states what might be a better legal system for the imposition of capital punishment, but to determine whether the two practices under review are in contradiction with the Constitution. In rejecting the claim that standardless juries are unconstitutional, Justice Harlan came to two conclusions. First of all, because of the limitations of human knowledge, it was impossible to *a priori* identify those factors or circumstances of an offense (or offender) that make it more or less deserving of the death penalty.[21] In *McGautha v. California* Justice Harlan states:

> To identify before the fact those characteristics of criminal homicides and their perpetrators which call for the death penalty, and to express these characteristics in language which can be fairly understood and applied by the sentencing authority, appear to be tasks which are beyond present human ability. (p. 204)

We simply do not have the knowledge, Justice Harlan concluded, to inform the jury, before its deliberation, as to which factors it should consider in deciding which murder defendants should live and which should die.

The American Law Institute's Model Penal Code includes as sentencing criteria an enumeration of both aggravating circumstances (those factors which would argue for a sentence of death) and mitigating factors (those factors which would support a sentence other than death) for a capital jury to consider. Harlan dismissed these sentencing "guides" as too restrictive and far too general to provide any practical direction for juries, and noted that the product of any further experimentation with such guidelines would most likely produce a list of factors that juries already employ:

> It is apparent that such criteria do not purport to provide more than the most minimal control over the sentencing authority's exercise of discretion. . . . For a court to attempt to catalog the appropriate factors in this elusive area could inhibit rather than expand the scope of consideration, for no list of circumstances would ever be really complete. The infinite variety of cases and facets to each case would make general standards either meaningless "boiler-plate" or a statement of the obvious that no jury would need. (pp. 207–208)

It should be clear here that Justice Harlan is not saying that juries with unregulated discretion (like McGautha's) act irrationally or without consideration of relevant sentencing information. Quite the contrary, he emphatically points out that capital juries "confronted with the truly awesome responsibility of decreeing death for a fellow human" will and do act with all due moral solemnity and "due regard for the consquences of their decision" (p. 208).[22] What is also quite clear is that Harlan *is* skeptical of the use of rules and standards (lists of sentencing criteria) to bring any legal precision to what he believes is essentially a difficult moral decision—the decision to take the life of another human. To Harlan, this "truly awesome responsibility" cannot be made easier with standards, guidelines, or other legal formulae.[23]

In Justice Harlan's review, Crampton's claim that the single-verdict jury burdened his privilege against self-incrimination by linking it with his desire to make a personal plea of mercy to the jury was also dismissed. In a series of rather interesting remarks, Harlan admits that a single-verdict capital jury may indeed be "cruel" (p. 214) and that "bifurcated trials . . . are superior means of dealing with capital cases" (p. 221). He rejects these arguments as constitutionally compelling, however, because the Constitution "does not guarantee trial procedures that are the best of all worlds" (p. 221). While he agreed that capital defendants should be allowed to present information to the jury regarding the issue of deserved punishment, information only they may be privy to or speak eloquently of,[24] he was also adamant that this does not give them the right to be free of adverse consequences. Harlan's essential position was that criminal defendants must make tough choices throughout their ordeal, ones that sometimes come with risks and costs not unique to those on trial for their lives.[25]

The Court's decision in *McGautha* and *Crampton* in 1971 suggested that the most common capital sentencing schemes in the country at the time, those with single-verdict proceedings and standardless juries, did not deny capital defendants due process. Although it dealt a crushing blow to the abolitionist movement, which had been successful in barring executions from 1967 until 1971 when *McGautha* was announced, it was not to be their final hour. The reason was that single-verdict and standardless juries were two *procedural* claims against current capital punishment laws. Perhaps the central question remained unanswered, "was capital punishment inherently "cruel and unusual" in violation of the Eighth Amendment? Reflecting this ambiguity, executions did not immediately resume after *McGautha* was decided. Meltsner (1973, 245) noted that on the day of the decision, Governors Gilligan of Ohio and Mandel of Maryland announced that no executions would take place in their states until the resolution of the constitutionality of the death penalty.

There was an indication that neither governors nor the population of defendants on death rows throughout the United States would have to wait long for an answer. Less than two months after the *McGautha* decision, the Supreme Court on June 28, 1971 announced orders that it had granted *certiorari* to review four death penalty cases with regard to the following question: "Does the imposition and carrying out of the death penalty in [these cases] constitute 'cruel and unusual' punishment in violation of the Eighth and Fourteenth Amendments?" [403 U.S. 952 (1971)]. These cases were *Aikens v. California, Branch v. Texas, Furman v. Georgia,* and *Jackson v. Georgia.* The latter three cases were consolidated for the Supreme Court's review in *Furman v. Georgia,* 408 U.S. 238 (1972).[26]

Making an Eighth Amendment Claim: Does the "Cruel and Unusual" Punishment Clause of the Constitution Prohibit Executions?

In order to make a successful Eighth Amendment claim against capital punishment, it would have to be demonstrated that putting defendants to death constitutes the kind of "cruel and unusual" punishment forbidden by the Constitution. We referred earlier to several previous opinions by the Supreme Court (*Wilkerson, Kemmler,* and *Resweber*) which held that death is not a *per se* "cruel and unusual" punishment, although suggesting that the manner in which it is imposed may be.

In rendering these decisions, earlier Courts adopted a fixed or historical meaning of the "cruel and unusual punishments" clause of the Eighth Amendment. That is, they understood its meaning as fixed in time with the intent of the Framers of the Eighth Amendment, who sought to prohibit only the most barbarous punishments and torture of their time. That the Framers did not intend to bar the death penalty outright is clearly seen by the explicit reference to its use in the Fifth Amendment. If a claim is to be made that the death penalty is a "cruel and unusual" punishment, then, a new meaning would have to be constructed for this all-important clause of the Eighth Amendment. This new interpretation was developed in two important noncapital cases, and was to provide the legal grounds for subsequently attacking the death penalty as unconstitutional in *Furman v. Georgia.*[27]

One of these cases was decided in 1910, *Weems v. United States,* 217 U.S. 349 (1910). In *Weems,* the defendant, a U.S. Government official in the Philippines, was convicted of making two false accounting entries amounting to 616 pesos. For this crime his punishment consisted of a prison sentence of fifteen years at hard labor, being forced to carry a chain at the ankle hanging from the wrist, surveillance for life, and loss of voting rights. Weems complained that such punishment was excessive in proportion to the crime and therefore cruel and unusual.

In agreeing with the defendant's assertion, the *Weems* Court broke with a fixed interpretation of the Eighth Amendment. The position of the Court was that the "cruel and unusual" punishment clause would offer only paper, illusory protection if it was restricted solely to the intent of the Framers. It further concluded that although the clause may have arisen from an expressed intent to forbid particular forms of punishment known and experienced at the time, this and other constitutional protections must be afforded a broad interpretation so that they may be able to protect citizens from evils not envisioned at the time of their construction:

> Legislation, both statutory and constitutional, is enacted, it is true, from an experience of evils, but its general language should not, therefore, be necessarily confined to the form that evil had heretofore taken. Time works changes, brings into existence new conditions and purposes. Therefore a principle to be vital must be capable of wider application than the mischief which gave it birth. . . . In the application of a constitution, therefore, our contemplation cannot be only of what has been but of what may be. Under any other rule a constitution would indeed be as easy of application as it would be deficient in efficacy and power. Its general principles would have little value and be converted by precedent into impotent and lifeless formulas. Rights declared in words might be lost in reality. (p. 373)

The Court in *Weems,* then, made three critical pronouncements: (1) that the meaning of the Eighth Amendment is not restricted to the intent of the Framers, (2) that the Eighth Amendment bars punishments that are excessive, and (3) that what is excessive is not fixed in time but changes with evolving social conditions.

The second important Eighth Amendment case in this tradition was *Trop v. Dulles,* 356 U.S. 86 (1958). The defendant in *Trop* was stripped of his U.S. citizenship as punishment for desertion in World War II. In declaring that the penalty violated the Eighth Amendment's prohibition against "cruel and unusual" punishment, the *Trop* Court declared that "[t]he basic concept underlying the Eighth Amendment is nothing less than the dignity of man" (p. 100). The Court in *Trop* adopted the position that if a punishment is an affront to basic human dignity, if it exceeds "the limits of civilized standards" (p. 100), it is constitutionally suspect. But concepts like "human dignity" and "civilized standards" are deceptively vague. Is a punishment only constitutionally suspect when it appears to traverse the standards of civilization at the time the Eighth Amendment was constructed?

In answering this question, the *Trop* Court, following in the footsteps of *Weems* decided fifty years earlier, held that what constitutes a breach of civilized standards changes and evolves with time: "[t]he [Eighth] Amendment must draw its meaning from the evolving standards of decency that mark the progress of a maturing society" (p. 101). This quite simply means that affronts to human dignity must be judged by standards of morality prevailing at the time. More specifically, it implies that a punishment found tolerable years ago may be deemed uncivilized today by contemporary standards of decency.

The essential principle of the *Weems* and *Trop* decisions is that the Eighth Amendment's prohibition against "cruel and unusual" punishment is not restricted to those specific forms of punishment condemned by its Framers. Instead, the Eighth Amendment protects against a more general evil—inhumane and uncivilized punishment—whose specific form changes as a society progresses and becomes more civilized. In determining whether a particular punishment is forbidden by the Eighth Amendment, the Supreme Court must not simply ask whether it was banned by the Framers, but whether it comports with contemporary standards of decency. The question now becomes, does society find such a punishment intolerable, uncivilized, and therefore cruel and unusual? To make this different kind of determination, the Court must look to objective indicators of prevailing moral standards, such as the enactments of legislatures as expressions of "the will of the people," the decisions of juries, and the subjective moral judgments of members of the Supreme Court itself.

The importance of the *Weems* and *Trop* decisions cannot be overemphasized. Those who seek to have the death penalty abolished could now claim that though once an accepted form of punishment, standards of civilized treatment have evolved over the years to the point that society no longer finds it tolerable. That was the essential argument raised in *Furman v. Georgia*.

Furman v. Georgia: The Lawlessness of Standardless Juries in Capital Sentencing

At issue in *Furman* was whether or not capital punishment as it was then being administered was in violation of the Eighth Amendment. Under the capital sentencing scheme of Georgia, and all other states at the time, juries were given virtually unrestricted and unguided discretion in determining whether a defendant received a life or death sentence. In a landmark 5–4 decision that spans over 200 pages (at that time, the longest decision in its history), the Court's conclusion was that in its then current form, capital punishment was indeed a "cruel and unusual" punishment. What was extraordinary about the *Furman* decision was not only its length but the fact that there was so little agreement as to exactly what was wrong with existing capital punishment statutes—all five justices in the majority and all four dissenters filed individual opinions.

What is also remarkable about *Furman* was the Court's position on the central legal issue, standardless juries. In *Furman* three justices (Justices Douglas, Stewart, and White) held that capital juries provided with unguided discretion produce a pattern of aberrant sentences that is in violation of the Eighth Amendment's prohibition against "cruel and unusual" punishment. What made death sentences so aberrant was that with little or nothing to guide their attention or structure their decision making, capital jurors were imposing death sentences in some cases but not in others that were equally or more egregious. As a result, the death penalty cases could not be distinguished from other noncapital cases on any rational or legal basis (making imposed death sentences arbitrary and capricious), or they could be distinguished only on improper grounds, such as race or social class (making them discriminatory). What makes this analysis so remarkable is that one year before *Furman,* in *McGautha,* the Court had decided that such sentencing schemes, which were virtually indistinguishable from those in *Furman, were not* in violation of the Fourteenth Amendment's requirement of due process in capital proceedings.

It would appear that because *McGautha* was already decided, its precedent would stand, thus making moot petitioner Furman's complaint about standardless capital juries. The position that the plurality in *Furman* appeared to be taking, however, was that while *the process* of having defendants sentenced to death by juries lacking formal guidance is consistent with the Fourteenth Amendment's requirement of due process, *the product*, an arbitrary and freakish pattern of death sentencing, is condemned by the Eighth Amendment. This seeming inconsistency must have been particularly troubling for Justices Stewart and White, who voted to uphold standardless juries in *McGautha*, but struck down their "product" in *Furman*. Weisberg (1984; 315) perhaps stated this paradox best when he commented that, in *Furman*, "the Justices could take advantage of the wonderful fiction that the Due Process Clauses [of the Fourteenth Amendment] and the Eighth Amendment might have very different things to say about standardless sentencing."

What is clear today about the *Furman* decision is that it contained no real doctrinal holding.[28] In order to uncover the common ground uniting the five members of the majority,[29] it is, therefore, necessary to review briefly each of its separate opinions. Only two of the justices, Brennan and Marshall, held that the penalty of death was unconstitutional in any form. Three other justices (Justices Douglas, Stewart, and White), who together with Brennan and Marshall comprised the majority, held, for slightly different reasons, that discretionary statutes were unconstitutional *in their operation*. We will review each of their opinions first.

Justice Douglas: Justice Douglas's opinion is aptly described by Weisberg (1984, 316) as "not so much a legal opinion as a cultural document, an emotive internal monologue of American political liberalism engaged publicly in moral self-criticism during the middle of the Vietnam era." Across the pages of his often caustic though always evocative opinion, Douglas harshly rebukes those who would characterize the imposition of death sentences as in any way fairly applied, and chastises the country that he feels has strayed too far from its fundamental principles of egalitarianism and equality under law. To him, discretionary statutes are constitutionally defective because they produce a pattern of death sentences that reflects the more general persecution of those at the bottom of the American social heap—political, economic, social, and cultural outcasts:

> In a Nation committed to equal protection of the laws there is no permissible "caste aspect" of law enforcement. Yet we know that the discretion of judges and juries in imposing the death penalty enables the penalty to be selectively applied, feeding prejudices against the accused if he is poor and despised, and lacking political clout, or if he is a member of a suspect or unpopular minority,

and saving those who by social position may be in a more protected position. (p. 255)

The crucial constitutional infirmity of standardless juries for Douglas, then, is that without direction and guidance as to those legally relevant factors that should inform their decisions, jurors all too often rely on their own prejudices, what he described in his *McGautha* dissent as "man's deep seated sadistic instincts" (p. 242). In his *Furman* opinion, Douglas concludes that there is an equal protection element in the Eighth Amendment that makes a punishment "cruel and unusual" if it is not inflicted in an evenhanded manner.[30] While selectively referring to statistical evidence of discrimination in the imposition of death sentences, Douglas concluded that even if racial, political, or economic bias cannot be definitively proved, the statutes under review which provide for standardless juries are nonetheless unconstitutional because they provide the *opportunity* for such disparity:

> Thus, these discretionary statutes are unconstitutional in their operation. They are pregnant with discrimination and discrimination is an ingredient not compatible with the idea of equal protection of the laws that is implicit in the ban on "cruel and unusual" punishments. (pp. 256–257)

Justice Stewart: The principal flaw of standardless juries, according to Justice Stewart, is that they produce a pattern of capital sentencing that cannot be explained by any rational process. Stewart does not accept the evidence that unguided capital sentencing produces discrimination; for him it lacks even that predictability.[31] The process that determines which capital defendants should live and which should die is no more meaningful or rational than the random striking of lightning: "These death sentences are 'cruel and unusual' in the same way that being struck by lightning is cruel and unusual. . . . these petitioners are among a capriciously selected random handful upon whom the sentence of death has in fact been imposed" (pp. 309–310). Unable to rationally distinguish between those who receive a death sentence and those whose lives are spared, and recognizing that the penalty of death is final and irrevocable, Justice Stewart concludes that capital sentences are "wantonly and freakishly" imposed, and therefore "cruel and unusual."

Justice White: Justice White adopts a pragmatic, utilitarian position. For him, there are legitimate state objectives that may be furthered by capital punishment (retribution, deterrence), but when death sentences are so infrequently imposed, as they appear to have been under discretionary statutes, these legitimate objectives cannot be met, and the infliction of capital punishment becomes "the pointless and needless extinction of life," and therefore cruel and unusual.

Justice Brennan: Justice Brennan is one of only two justices to adopt a *per se* position regarding the constitutionality of the death penalty. For him the central infirmity of capital punishment is not that there are procedural defects in the way it is administered under standardless juries, but that it is instead "cruel and unusual" no matter what procedures or protections are in place. To Justice Brennan a punishment is "cruel and unusual" if it is an affront to basic human dignity. In order to judge whether or not a punishment comports with human dignity, Brennan supplies four principles: (1) a punishment must not be so severe that it degrades the dignity of human beings, (2) a severe punishment must not be arbitrarily inflicted, (3) a severe punishment must not be in conflict with contemporary standards of decency, and (4) a severe punishment must not be excessive, that is, there should be no other available punishment that is less severe and that will achieve the same purposes as the more severe punishment. Examined within the context of American society in 1972, Justice Brennan concluded that capital punishment violates all four principles: death is degrading to human dignity because it involves incomparable physical and mental suffering, by its very nature it forecloses the exercise of all other rights, and because it involves the calculated killing of another individual by the state it denies that person's humanity; the penalty of death is so infrequently imposed given the large number of homicides committed that it compels the conclusion that it is being inflicted arbitrarily; the penalty of death is intolerable to prevailing standards of morality as evidence by the fact that juries so infrequently impose it, and that over time we as a society have sought to restrict the crimes punishable by death; and finally, death is an excessive punishment because it is no more of an effective deterrent nor is it of more symbolic retributive value than imprisonment. For these reasons, Brennan concludes the penalty of death is inherently cruel and unusual.[32]

Justice Marshall: Justice Marshall was the one other justice who adopted the *per se* position that the penalty of death is "cruel and unusual" punishment no matter how it is administered. In his *Furman* opinion, after an extended review of Eighth Amendment case law, Marshall offers four principles of his own in guiding the Court's inquiry into what constitutes "cruel and unusual." First, he notes that there are some punishments, among them the use of the rack and thumbscrew, which by their very nature involve so much pain and suffering as to be objectionable to a civilized society. Second, punishments that are previously unknown, and are no more humane than those they displace, are unusual and therefore unconstitutional. Third, if a penalty does not serve the legitimate state interests of deterrence, rehabilitation, incapacitation, or economy, its infliction is excessive and unnecessary. Finally, a punishment may be deemed "cruel and unusual" if it is offensive to contemporary standards of decency, even if it does further a legitimate state interest.

Justice Marshall observes that the death penalty in contemporary American society does not fail the test of the first two principles: it is not barbaric along the lines of the rack or other forms of torture, nor is it a recent and therefore unusual punishment. If capital punishment is cruel and unusual, he then notes, it is because it is excessive or because contemporary society finds it offensive. Marshall's conclusion is that the penalty of death is prohibited by the Eighth Amendment for the latter two reasons. It is excessive and unnecessary because the legitimate state purposes for retaining it that he identifies may just as effectively be achieved with a penalty of long imprisonment.

In addition, Marshall notes that even if the death penalty were not excessive, it would still violate the Eighth Amendment because U.S. citizens find it morally abhorrent. In determining whether or not a given punishment is morally intolerable, Justice Marshall suggests that public opinion polls (which at the time of *Furman* indicated that a majority of the public supported the death penalty for murder) are only of limited value since people are not fully informed about the death penalty. He concludes that if the public were aware that the death penalty is applied in a discriminatory fashion, is not immune to error and miscarriages of justice, and is a no better deterrent to murder than life imprisonment, they would reject it as cruel and unusual.[33]

It can be seen from this brief review of the justices' different positions that the majority in *Furman* was indeed a fragile alliance. Two justices found the death penalty always constitutionally objectionable (Justices Brennan and Marshall). The three justices who did not find the death penalty always intolerable (Stewart, White, and Douglas) did not find anything inherently unconstitutional about it, just the sentencing outcomes produced by standardless juries vested with almost total discretion. In addition, four justices (Justices Burger, Powell, Blackmun, and Rehnquist) found nothing at all offensive about standardless juries. The message delivered to the states along with the *Furman* decision was, therefore, quite an ambiguous one. What was clear was that two justices would object to the death penalty in any form, four would find it acceptable in its current form, and three might not find it objectionable if there were sufficient procedural reforms restricting the discretion at the disposal of the jury.

In what turned out to be a rather prescient commentary about the fractured *Furman* decision, Chief Justice Burger noted, in dissent:

> While I would not undertake to make a definitive statement as to the parameters of the Court's ruling, it is clear that if state legislatures and the Congress wish to maintain the availability of capital punishment, significant statutory changes will have to be made. Since the two pivotal concurring opinions [those of Justices Stewart and White] turn on the assumption that the punishment of death is now meted out in a random and unpredictable manner, legislative bodies may seek to bring their laws into compliance with the Court's ruling by providing standards for juries and judges to follow in determining the sentence in capital cases or by more narrowly defining the crimes for which the penalty is to be imposed. If such standards can be devised or the crimes more meticulously defined, the result cannot be detrimental. (pp. 400–401)

Chief Justice Burger correctly informed the states that there is nothing to be read in the *Furman* decision that would preclude them from retaining the death penalty if they wished. He did, however, also correctly note that in order to pass constitutional muster such revised statutes would have to satisfy at least one of the two members of the plurality (Justices Stewart and White) who appeared not to oppose the death penalty if sufficient procedural protections were in place.

One way to ensure that death sentences are not wantonly and freakishly imposed, Burger suggested, was through a substantive revision of the law of criminal homicide. If a narrow definition of murder could be constructed and the imposition of capital punishment made mandatory upon conviction of that newly defined capital offense, the requirements of *Furman* would seem to be met. Under such a mandatory scheme juries would have *no* sentencing discretion to abuse. A second way to satisfy *Furman*, Burger suggested, is for state legislatures to devise standards for the guidance of juries and judges which would focus their attention on those factors most important in determining which capital defendants should live and which deserve to die.

What is most extraordinary about this latter recommendation of Chief Justice Burger is that the attempt to guide the discretion of the capital jury through the construction of statutory standards was precisely what a majority of the Court rejected but one year earlier in *McGautha v. California* as a task "beyond present human ability," an opinion in which Burger himself concurred.[34] The irony comes full circle when it is recalled that Burger's suggestion in *Furman* — that states should experiment with attempts to guide the discretion of capital juries — is precisely what Justice Brennan in his *McGautha* dissent chastised the majority for ignoring (see note 25). As we will now see, faced with the prospect of not having a death penalty, states after *Furman* began to experiment with various formulae of capital sentencing standards and statutory guides.

Whatever the legal ambiguity of the *Furman* decision, three things were clear. First, *Furman* said nothing about the constitutionality of the death penalty itself, holding only that capital punishment, as then administered, was unconstitutional. Second, the approximately 600 occupants of death rows across the United States in 1972 would not be executed. The moratorium on executions begun in 1967 would continue into the early 1970s. Third, it was also clear that, although provided with little guidance from the decision itself, if states hoped to retain capital punishment, they would have to modify their capital statutes to bring them in compliance with what they might understand to be *Furman's* ambiguous requirements.

Not surprisingly, modifications were almost immediately made in state death penalty statutes, following the two general forms suggested by Chief Justice Burger in his *Furman* dissent: Either state legislatures attempted to eliminate the problem of jury discretion altogether by drafting mandatory death penalty statutes, or they attempted to provide sentencing direction through so-called guided discretion statutes. These new legal forms would, of course, have to pass constitutional muster, and it is to this question that we now turn our attention.

The States' Response to *Furman:* Mandatory and Guided Discretion Statutes

As a backdrop to our understanding of the post-*Furman* legal reforms, it should be noted that at the time of *Furman* there was a reversal in the direction of public opinion about the death penalty. Gallup public opinion polls indicated that in 1966 only 42 percent expressed approval of capital punishment for murder; by 1973 this had increased to 59 percent (Gallup 1986).[35] At least as expressed in the abstract form of a public opinion question, by 1973 Americans were becoming more inclined toward capital punishment. Perhaps it was in part as a response to this public sentiment that many states reacted to *Furman* not by abolition but by drafting new death penalty statutes.

Florida was the first state to pass a revised death penalty law. Just five months after *Furman* a special session of the Florida legislature was convened to enact a new death penalty statute to be signed into law by the governor. Florida was not alone; in just four years after the Court's decision in *Furman,* thirty-five states had enacted new statutes that allowed for the death penalty for at least some offenses (generally murder and rape), and in 1974 the United States Congress enacted a law permitting the death penalty for aircraft piracy that resulted in a death. By 1976 defendants once again began to amass on death rows throughout the United States, pending Supreme Court approval of these newly revised statutes. Before reviewing the Court's examination of these new laws, however, it will be helpful to first have a clear understanding of the two general legal forms they took.

In response to the complaint in *Furman* that discretionary capital sentencing produced a constitutionally intolerable patterning of death sentences, some states sought to remedy the defect by relieving the jury of all sentencing discretion. Under these mandatory statutes, once defendants were convicted of narrowly defined types of murder, a death sentence was automatic. The jury simply had no life or death determination to make—only a guilt/innocence decision. An example of this was the statute of North Carolina. In 1974 the North Carolina General Assembly enacted a new death penalty statute which defined murder in the first degree and made a penalty of death the mandatory punishment. The statute read:

> *Murder in the first and second degree defined; punishment.*—A murder which shall be perpetrated by means of poison, lying in wait, imprisonment, starving, torture, or by any other kind of willful, deliberate and premeditated killing, or which shall be committed in the perpetration or attempt to perpetrate any arson, rape, robbery, kidnapping, burglary or other felony, shall

be deemed to be murder in the first degree and shall be punished with death. All other kinds of murder shall be deemed murder in the second degree, and shall be punished by imprisonment for a term of not less than two years nor more than life imprisonment in the State's prison. [N.C. Gen. Statute Sec. 14–17 (Cum. Supp. 1975)]

Under the new North Carolina statute, once a jury convicted a defendant of first-degree murder its task was completed. The automatic penalty was death. Most of the post-*Furman* mandatory death penalty statutes were generally similar to this.

Guided discretion death penalty statutes are fundamentally different from mandatory ones. Rather than solving the problem of jury discretion by removing it entirely, guided discretion statutes attempt to retain some sentencing discretion but restrict its exercise by providing a list of relevant factors which the jury must use to guide its sentencing decision. Under guided discretion statutes these factors are considered by a jury (or judge) during the penalty phase of a bifurcated capital trial. At the first or guilt phase, the jury hears factual and legally probative evidence pertaining solely to the guilt or innocence of the defendant. If convicted, and if the prosecutor so decides, the case then proceeds to the second, penalty phase where the determination of penalty is made.

Most of these guided discretion statutes are similar to Georgia's, which includes a list of aggravating factors, at least one of which the jury must find beyond a reasonable doubt before it *may* (but does not have to) impose a sentence of death. A listing of these aggravating circumstances is provided in Table 2–1. Georgia's is an example of an "aggravation only" guided discretion statute. It explicitly includes only factors in aggravation; there are no factors in mitigation of penalty enumerated in the statute. It can be seen from the list in Table 2–1 that statutory aggravating factors are those egregious features of the offense or offender the prosecution introduces to the jury (if applicable) in its attempt to argue for the defendant's execution.

Georgia juries also hear about factors in mitigation of penalty. These factors are, however, not explicitly listed in the statute. The Georgia law specifies only that the judge or jury shall also hear during the penalty phase of the capital trial "additional evidence in extenuation [and] mitigation" [Sec. 27–2503 (Supp. 1975)]. Factors in mitigation are those extenuating circumstances of the offense or offender that the defense introduces in order to convince the jury that the defendant's life should be spared. During its penalty phase deliberation, the jury then considers both relevant aggravating and mitigating circumstances, implicitly weighs the two, and comes to a sentencing decision which the trial judge is bound to. Under Georgia's guided discretion statute, the finding of one or more aggravating circumstances does not require a death sentence, it merely makes it legally permissible. Georgia juries may be swayed by mitigating circumstances and impose a life sentence no matter how many statutory aggravating factors they find, nor are they required to find any mitigating factors in order to impose a life sentence.

Other guided discretion statutes are more similar to Florida's, which enumerates both aggravating and mitigating factors (see Table 2–2). As in Georgia, Florida's post-*Furman* capital trials are bifurcated. There is first a guilt phase where if convicted of a capital crime the defendant may move on to the second or penalty phase. At the penalty phase, the jury determines if the sentence should be death or imprisonment. Evidence about both aggravating and mitigating factors in the case at hand are presented. At this penalty phase the prosecution attempts to bring out the most disreputable and dangerous features of both the defendant and the crime by proving the existence of aggravating circumstances (and dissuading the jury of mitigating ones). The intention of the defense is to "humanize" the defendant, and to offer some sort of rationale for the offense through the introduction of mitigating and extenuating information.[36] After hearing testimony with regard to both aggravating and mitigating circumstances, the Florida jury is instructed to weigh the two and determine if

Table 2–1
Georgia's Statutory Aggravating Circumstances in Capital Trials

(1) The offense of murder, rape, armed robbery, or kidnapping was committed by a person with a prior record of conviction for a capital felony, or the offense of murder was committed by a person who has a substantial history of serious assaultive criminal convictions.

(2) The offense of murder, rape, armed robbery, or kidnapping was committed while the offender was engaged in the commission of another capital felony, or aggravated battery, or the offense of murder was committed while the offender was engaged in the commission of burglary or arson in the first degree.

(3) The offender by his act of murder, armed robbery, or kidnapping knowingly created a great risk of death to more than one person in a public place by means of a weapon or device which would normally be hazardous to the lives of more than one person.

(4) The offender committed the offense of murder for himself or another, for the purpose of receiving money or any other thing of monetary value.

(5) The murder of a judicial officer, former judicial officer, district attorney or solicitor or former district attorney or solicitor during or because of the exercise of his official duty.

(6) The offender caused or directed another to commit murder or committed murder as an agent or employee of another person.

(7) The offense of murder, rape, armed robbery, or kidnapping was outrageously or wantonly vile, horrible or inhuman in that it involved torture, depravity of mind or an aggravated battery to the victim.

(8) The offense of murder was committed against any peace officer, corrections employee or fireman while engaged in the performance of his official duties.

(9) The offense of murder was committed by a person in, or who has escaped from, the lawful custody of a peace officer or place of lawful confinement.

(10) The murder was committed for the purpose of avoiding, interfering with, or preventing a lawful arrest or custody in a place of lawful confinement, of himself or another.

Georgia Code Ann. Sec. 27–2534.1 (b) (Supp. 1975).

the mitigating factors outweigh the aggravating factors. Based on these considerations the jury determines if the sentence is life imprisonment or death.[37] Florida's guided discretion statute is somewhat unique in that Florida is one of only three states (Indiana and Alabama being the other two) where the jury's sentence is only an advisory one; the actual sentence is determined by the trial judge, who may override the jury's recommendation.

There is another feature common to those states that have adopted the guided discretion approach to capital sentencing. All provide for automatic appellate review of all death sentences. In response to *Furman's* concern about the arbitrary and capricious pattern of imposed death sentences, many revised guided discretion statutes provided for a procedure to monitor the death sentences actually meted out by capital juries. In this procedure, a court with statewide jurisdiction would review each death sentence on appeal in order to determine if it is warranted by the facts and is not inconsistent with the penalty imposed in other cases. State statutes vary with regard to how specific the task of

Table 2–2
Florida's Post-*Furman* Guided Discretion Capital Statute

Aggravating Circumstances	*Mitigating Circumstances*
1. The capital felony was committed by a person under sentence of imprisonment.	1. The defendant has no significant history of prior criminal activity.
2. The defendant was previously convicted of another capital felony or of a felony involving the use or threat of violence to the person.	2. The capital felony was committed while the defendant was under the influence of extreme mental or emotional disturbance.
3. The defendant created a great risk of death to many persons.	3. The victim was a participant in the defendant's conduct or consented to the act.
4. The capital felony was committed while the defendant was engaged, or was an accomplice, in the commission of, or an attempt to commit, or flight after committing or attempting to commit, any robbery, rape, arson, burglary, kidnapping, or aircraft piracy or an unlawful throwing, placing, or discharging of a destructive device or bomb.	4. The defendant was an accomplice in the capital felony committed by another person and his participation was relatively minor.
	5. The defendant acted under extreme duress or under the substantial domination of another person.
5. The capital felony was committed for the purpose of avoiding or preventing a lawful arrest or effecting an escape from custody.	6. The capacity of the defendant to appreciate the criminality of his conduct or to conform his conduct to the requirements of law was substantially impaired.
6. The capital felony was committed for pecuniary gain.	7. The age of the defendant at the time of the crime.
7. The capital felony was committed to disrupt or hinder the lawful exercise of any governmental function or the enforcement of laws.	
8. The capital felony was especially heinous, atrocious, or cruel.	

Fla. Stat. Ann. Sec. 921.141.

the reviewing court should be. For example, the Georgia statute is very specific in defining the review function of the Georgia Supreme Court in death penalty appeals. It states that the court shall determine

(1) Whether the sentence of death was imposed under the influence of passion, prejudice, or any other arbitrary factor, and

(2) Whether, in cases other than treason or aircraft hijacking, the evidence supports the jury's or judge's finding of a statutory aggravating circumstance . . . , and

(3) Whether the sentence of death is excessive or disproportionate to the penalty imposed in similar cases, considering both the crime and the defendant. [*Ga. Code Ann. Sec. 27–2537 (Supp. 1975)*]

The Florida statute also provides for automatic appellate review of all death sentences by the state supreme court, although unlike Georgia's it does not describe the specific form that the review should take. The supreme court of Florida has, however, defined its task as similar to the Georgia court's—that of ensuring consistency and proportionality in imposed death sentences throughout the state.[38]

In sum, there were two legislative responses to *Furman,* guided discretion capital statutes and mandatory ones.[39] Guided discretion capital statutes attempted to remedy the defects of standardless juries condemned in *Furman* by providing for three remedies: a bifurcated capital hearing, sentencing directions for the jury in the form of aggravating and mitigating circumstances, and automatic appellate review for the monitoring of proportionality and consistency in death sentences actually imposed. Mandatory capital statutes sought to remedy the defect identified by *Furman* by eliminating jury discretion altogether.

It will be recalled that these two types of statutes were immediate responses by state legislatures to the *Furman* decision. Death rows across these states soon began to swell. Once again, however, executions were delayed while the constitutionality of these procedural reforms awaited review by the United States Supreme Court. That wait ended on July 2, 1976.

Gregg v. Georgia and the Future of Capital Punishment in the United States

On July 2, 1976, two days before the nation was to celebrate its bicentennial, the Supreme Court of the United States handed down death penalty decisions in five important cases, *Gregg v. Georgia, Proffitt v. Florida, Jurek v. Texas, Woodson v. North Carolina,* and *Roberts v. Louisiana.*[40] The dilemma confronting the

Court in these cases was obvious; the overwhelming legislative response to the *Furman* decision was to reinstate the death penalty with procedurally revised statutes. The popular support for the death penalty, as indicated by this legislative activity, made it difficult for the Court to conclude that capital punishment was "cruel and unusual" because it was inconsistent with contemporary standards of decency. Yet it was also clear that the Court, in attempting to remain faithful to *Furman*, might still contain a majority that would be expected to be concerned with any arbitrary and capricious infliction of that penalty. The U.S. Supreme Court would not simply "rubber-stamp" any legislative attempt to reinstate the death penalty. As will be seen below, the Court's initial resolution of this dilemma would be to preserve the death penalty while attempting to procedurally regulate the manner in which states were to inflict it.

In these 1976 cases the Court had before it for review both guided discretion (Georgia, Florida, Texas) and mandatory (North Carolina, Louisiana) death penalty statutes.[41] In three 7–2 decisions the Court determined that the guided discretion statutes of Georgia, Florida, and Texas were constitutionally acceptable. In two 5–4 decisions the Court decided that the mandatory death penalty statutes of North Carolina and Louisiana were unconstitutional and voted to strike them down. The crucial votes in these cases were passed by Justices Stewart, Powell, and Stevens. They were joined by Justice White, Rehnquist, and Blackmun and Chief Justice Burger in upholding guided discretion statutes, and by Justices Brennan and Marshall in invalidating mandatory ones. Chief Justice Burger and Justices White, Rehnquist, and Blackmun voted to uphold both kinds of statutes.

The first issue that the Court put to rest was the constitutionality under the Eighth Amendment of capital punishment for the offense of murder, an issue not resolved by its *Furman* decision. After reviewing the history of the "cruel and unusual punishments" clause and noting that "[t]he most marked indication of society's endorsement of the death penalty for murder is the legislative response to *Furman*" (p. 179), Justice Stewart, writing for a plurality of himself and Justices Powell and Stevens, concluded in *Gregg* that capital punishment for murder does not in all circumstances violate the Eighth Amendment. It was clear, then, that the Court in 1976 was convinced that the penalty of death for the offense of murder did not offend prevailing community sensibilities. Quite the contrary, it appeared as if Americans were more enamored than ever with the death penalty. A public opinion poll taken in 1976 indicated that 66 percent of the public was in favor of the death penalty for persons convicted of murder.[42]

Having affirmed the constitutionality of the death penalty for murder, at least under some sentencing schemes, the next question Justice Stewart addressed was whether the procedural reforms under the new Georgia statute were sufficient to save it from the same fate as the statute reviewed by the *Furman* Court. This was not an easy issue to resolve. Contrary to the situation confronting the Court in *Furman*, which had some statistical evidence to support its belief that capital juries with uncontrolled discretion produced arbitrary death sentences, the *Gregg* Court, because of the recency of the statutes under review, could not really evaluate how the new procedural reforms would perform in practice. What the Court did do, however, was to determine if these reforms *would appear* to remedy the defect of arbitrary and capricious death sentences if they worked as they were supposed to. A majority agreed that they would.

In commenting on the Georgia statute, Justice Stewart's plurality opinion pointed to several procedural reforms in the new post-*Furman* statute which he thought important: (1) a bifurcated proceeding where the sentencing authority can hear testimony relevant to deserved penalty, (2) statutory factors to guide the jury in its decision making, and (3) appellate review of all death sentences to ensure consistency and proportionality.[43] As suggested above, the statutes under review were so recent that there was no real experience with the pattern of sentences produced by guided discretion schemes. Justice Stewart, therefore, had no real empirical evidence upon which to base his optimism; he simply concluded that "[o]n their face these procedures seem to satisfy the concerns of *Furman*" (p. 198).

Justice White, writing for himself, Chief Justice Burger, and Justice Rehnquist also supported the facial validity of the new Georgia statute. After first approving of Georgia's attempt to restrict the sentencing discretion of capital juries by providing them with a list of aggravating circumstances, White concludes that there "is reason to expect that Georgia's current system would escape the infirmities which invalidated its previous system under *Furman*" (p. 222). The guided discretion statutes of Florida and Texas also passed the constitutional scrutiny of the Court in *Proffitt* and *Jurek,* respectively. At least, in these 1976 cases, then, the Supreme Court decided to allow states to retain the death penalty under guided discretion systems so long as it appeared that the procedural reforms which were introduced would cure some of the worst defects of the previous system.

Mandatory death penalty schemes did not enjoy a similar fate, however, as the Court struck down the statutes of both North Carolina and Louisiana. In invalidating mandatory death penalty schemes, Justice Stewart, writing in *Woodson v. North Carolina,* noted three specific defects: (1) truly mandatory statutes do not comport with contemporary standards of decency,[44] (2) the North Carolina mandatory statute merely "papers over" the problem of discretion since juries can refuse to convict those defendants deemed not deserving of a death sentence ("jury nullification"), and (3) a mandatory statute does not allow the sentencing jury to consider "the diverse frailties of humankind" (p. 304) which may argue for a sentence less than death. The central problem with mandatory statutes was that it fails to accord capital defendants any individual consideration of their unique culpability and instead treats them "as members of a faceless, undifferentiated mass to be subjected to the blind infliction of the penalty of death" (p. 305). For similar reasons, the mandatory statute of Louisiana was also invalidated. It is important to note that what *Woodson* and *Roberts* seemed to be suggesting was that in order to comport with the human dignity requirement of the Eighth Amendment, capital punishment statutes had to allow some discretion for the consideration of individualized mitigating factors.[45]

The primary effects of the 1976 Supreme Court death penalty cases were threefold. First of all, they reestablished the death penalty for murder at least under some guided discretion formulae.[46] Second, they unambiguously rejected mandatory death penalties for broadly conceived categories of capital offenses. Third, they put the Supreme Court into the business of attempting to regulate the states' death penalty cases, at least for the time being. What *Gregg* and its companion cases decidedly did not do, however, is to settle all of the constitutional questions that troubled the imposition of the death penalty in those states that sought to retain it. On the contrary, as Weisberg (1984) notes, these cases simply became the starting point for years of additional litigation over exactly what is constitutionally required in state death penalty proceedings.[47] In the next chapter we will examine the Supreme Court's long and arduous attempt to fashion constitutionally tolerable state death penalty schemes.

Summary and Conclusions

In this chapter we have examined the attempts of a small group of abolitionist lawyers to have the death penalty declared unconstitutional in the United States. These activist lawyers were successful in getting the issue of the constitutionality of capital punishment before the United States Supreme Court in the early 1970s. This was not, however, the first time that the Court has examined death penalty issues. In several cases, dating as far back as 1878, the Supreme Court has reviewed a claim that the administration of the death penalty was not constitutional.

In these early cases, which included *Wilkerson v. Utah* and *In re Kemmler,* the Court determined that particular methods of capital punishment (death by firing squad and electrocution) were constitutionally permissible. In another case, *Louisiana ex. rel. Francis v. Resweber,* the Court ruled that an unsuccessful first attempt to put an offender to death that was not intentionally botched did not bar the state from a second effort to carry out a death sentence. These cases presumed that the death penalty was not an unconstitutionally "cruel and unusual" punishment under the Eighth Amendment. They did, however, establish some limitations on the state's right to carry out the death penalty (the imposed punishment could not entail "unnecessary cruelty" or "unnecessary pain").

The first real challenge to the constitutionality of the death penalty itself came in 1971 with *McGautha v. California. McGautha* involved a Fourteenth

Amendment challenge to existing death penalty practices. Under most capital punishment statutes at the time juries determined both the guilt/innocence of the accused and the penalty in a single deliberation (so-called single-verdict juries), and were given complete discretion in making the determination of appropriate penalty (standardless juries). The defendants in *McGautha* complained that such practices denied them due process of law. These complaints were before the Court in an earlier case, *Maxwell v. Bishop,* which also included a claim that in the South death sentences for rape were imposed in a racially discriminatory manner. *Maxwell* was decided without addressing the single-verdict, standardless jury, and racial discrimination issues. The Supreme Court disagreed with the defendants' claims in *McGautha,* and the death penalty in the United States was given constitutional approval, at least for the time being.

One year after *McGautha* was decided the Supreme Court again examined the constitutionality of standardless and single-verdict capital juries in *Furman v. Georgia.* In *Furman,* however, the complaint was raised that the discretion provided to capital juries under existing statutes produced a pattern of death sentences that lacked logic or rationality. Death sentences inflicted under such statutes, it was argued, were arbitrary and capricious and therefore "cruel and unusual" under the Eighth Amendment. Since it was clear that the death penalty was not "cruel and unusual" when the Constitution was written, this Eighth Amendment challenge could only be mounted if the meaning given to the phrase "cruel and unusual punishment" was not anchored to its original denotation. In two important cases, *Weems v. United States* (1910) and *Trop v. Dulles* (1958), the U.S. Supreme Court determined that what constitutes a cruel and unusual punishment is not fixed in time but evolves as society becomes more humane and civilized. This suggests that punishments approved in the past (such as the death penalty) may be rejected by later generations as cruel and unusual.

Abolitionist lawyers used this flexible interpretation of the Eighth Amendment to challenge the acceptability of the death penalty in *Furman. Furman* was a highly divisive opinion. Only two justices declared that capital punishment was always a cruel and unusual punishment, while three others believed that death sentences imposed under discretionary statutes were unconstitutional. The "holding" in *Furman* was, therefore, a loose one, but it did suggest that arbitrary and capricious death sentences, and the statutes which produced them, were cruel and unusual. As a result of the *Furman* decision, over 600 death sentences were vacated and death rows across the United States were emptied.

In response to *Furman,* states did not abandon capital punishment but quickly attempted to draft new death penalty laws that would meet the requirements that seemed to have been established by the Court's decision. These new laws took one of two forms, mandatory statutes and guided discretion statutes. Mandatory statutes solved the problem of unfettered jury discretion by removing it entirely. Under such statutes, defendants convicted of capital crimes were automatically sentenced to death. Under guided discretion statutes capital juries would be provided some sentencing direction in the form of aggravating circumstances (which would argue in favor of a death sentence) and mitigating circumstances (which would argue in favor of a sentence less than death).

The Court rejected mandatory statutes in *Woodson v. North Carolina* and *Roberts v. Louisiana* because it was believed that they merely "papered over" the problem of jury discretion and because mandatory statutes did not allow juries to consider the unique characteristics of each defendant. Different forms of guided discretion statutes did, however, pass constitutional scrutiny in *Gregg v. Georgia, Proffitt v. Florida, and Jurek v. Texas.* Although it was not clear at the time if these were constitutional requirements, the statutes of these states provided for bifurcated capital trials, a consideration during the penalty phase of both aggravating and mitigating factors, and an independent review of the appropriateness of the death sentence. As a result of these decisions, capital punishment for murder was given constitutional sanction, and the death penalty was reinstated in a majority of U.S. states.

Notes

1. Even staunch critics of these efforts to declare the death penalty unconstitutional note the importance of a handful of abolitionist lawyers. Raoul Berger (1982, 3–4), for example, in his somewhat acerbic account of these events, notes that "[t]his constitutional earthquake resulted from the labors of a small band of dedicated abolitionists, led by a few top-flight lawyers in the service of the NAACP. . . ."

2. The Eighth Amendment to the Constitution states: "Excessive bail shall not be required, nor excessive fines imposed, nor cruel and unusual punishments inflicted."

3. There were also early attempts at procedural reform of state death penalty practices prior to the Burger Court's work beginning in the 1970s. One of these was *Powell v. Alabama,* 287 U.S. 45, 53 S.Ct. 55, 77 L.Ed. 158 (1932), involving the famous "Scottsboro boys." In this case, several black youths were charged with raping two white women. Within a week's time the defendants were arrested, tried, convicted, and sentenced to death, all without the effective assistance of counsel. In reversing its convictions, the Supreme Court held that due to the "special circumstances" of the case (the illiteracy of the defendants, their youth, public hostility, and the fact that they were detained with military escort far from their own homes and families), the due process clause of the 14th Amendment required effective representation by counsel at trial in state capital proceedings. The *Powell* case is an important one because it was the first occasion that the Court employed the due process clause of the 14th Amendment to regulate state criminal proceedings in capital cases.

4. In its decision, the *Kemmler* Court determined that a punishment, such as electrocution, is not *prima facie* unconstitutional because it is unusual so long as the authorizing legislature had a humane purpose in employing it.

5. The "historical" interpretation of the 8th Amendment, which suggests that its

meaning must be fixed with the intention of the Framers, is described in detail in Raoul Berger's *Death Penalties: The Supreme Court's Obstacle Course* (1982).

6. The position that the general Bill of Rights was not meant to extend to the restriction of state power was expressed early in the Supreme Court's history by Chief Justice John Marshall in *Barron v. Baltimore*, 32 U.S. (7 Pet.) 243 (1833): "Had Congress engaged in the extraordinary occupation of improving the constitutions of the several States by affording the people additional protection from the exercise of power by their own governments in matters which concerned themselves alone, they would have declared this purpose in plain and intelligible language."

7. The Fourteenth Amendment to the United States Constitution states that ". . . nor shall any State deprive any person of life, liberty, or property, without due process of law; nor deny to any person within its jurisdiction the equal protection of the laws."

8. The early history of the legal fight against capital punishment in the United States is traced by Michael Meltsner, one of its participants, in his book *Cruel and Unusual: The Supreme Court and Capital Punishment* (1973). A good deal of the history presented in the early part of this chapter is found in greater detail in Meltsner's thorough book.

9. Illinois Rev. Statues c. 38, Sec. 743 (1959). Jurors are challenged for cause if there are specific objections or grounds for dismissal, such as being related to one of the parties at the trial. Dismissals for cause require the approval of the trial judge. A juror may also be dismissed with a peremptory challenge. A peremptory challenge is made without justification or approval by the trial judge. Both prosecution and defense have a statutorily limited number of peremptory challenges to exercise.

10. In the famous "footnote 21" of *Witherspoon,* Justice Stewart, writing for a majority of the Court, noted that

> . . . nothing we say today bears upon the power of a state to execute a defendant sentenced to death by jury from which the only veniremen who were in fact excluded for cause were those who made unmistakably clear (1) that they would *automatically* vote against the imposition of capital punishment without regard to any evidence that might be developed at the trial of the case before them, or (2) that their attitude toward the death penalty would prevent them from making an impartial decision as to the defendant's *guilt.* [*Witherspoon v. Illinois* 88 S.Ct. 1770 (1968) at p. 1777]

11. In Michael Meltsner's book *Cruel and Unusual* (1973, 125) he documents several efforts by state courts to blunt the implication of the *Witherspoon* ruling. For example, one federal court took *Witherspoon* to mean that only the *systematic* exclusion of scrupled jurors was unconstitutional; removing a small proportion of them was not taken to be important enough to invalidate a death sentence.

12. Justice Blackmun joined the Court as its ninth member, taking the place of resigned justice Abe Fortas.

13. At the time McGautha was sentenced to death forty-one states had death penalty statutes. Thirty-four of these were single-verdict procedures where juries decided both guilt and penalty in a single deliberation, and two states had a mandatory death penalty upon conviction of specified crimes. Only four other states besides California (Connecticut, New York, Pennsylvania, and Texas) had bifurcated death penalty trials, a guilt phase and a separate penalty phase.

14. As the Court in *McGautha* noted (p. 200, note 11), of those states that decided to retain capital punishment "none of these [capital punishment] statutes have provided standards for the choice between death and life imprisonment."

15. During its penalty phase deliberations, McGautha's jury asked the trial judge whether life imprisonment meant imprisonment for life or if there was a possibility of parole. In response, the trial judge informed the jury that under California law a sentence of life imprisonment does carry the possibility of parole, but that "the matter of parole is not to be considered by you in determining the punishment for either defendant" (*McGautha v. California* at p. 190, note 4).

16. In actual trial, defense counsel must walk a very fine line between the arguments made during the guilt and penalty phases of a capital trial. If they overly protest the innocence of their client where the evidence clearly indicates guilt, counsel runs the risk of damaging their credibility before the eyes of the same jury when they plea for their client's life during the penalty phase (see Goodpaster 1983).

17. Under then Ohio law, once the defendant takes the stand, for example in order to plead his case in mitigation of penalty, he may be cross-examined with respect to not only the offense at hand but previous offenses as well. He may also be recalled for cross-examination in the state's case in rebuttal.

18. Defendants could, of course, decide not to take the stand, thus preserving their 5th Amendment right against compelled self-incrimination, and have others testify on their behalf as to their good character and other issues related to penalty. To do so, however, Justice Douglas argued in dissent, is an unacceptable compromise because there may be some relevant information privy only to the defendant, and the right to be heard entails the right to speak for one's self since others "may not be able to speak for a defendant as the defendant might, with halting eloquence, speak for himself" (quoting Justice Frankfurter in *Green v. U.S.*, 1960, 365 U.S. 301 at p. 304). Ohio did maintain the common law right of allocution, where the defendant is entitled to address the court before sentence is pronounced. Justice Douglas, however, critically denounces this right as "ritual only" in cases, such as in Ohio, where the right of allocution occurs *after* the jury's sentencing decision has been made, and cannot be overturned unless there is prejudicial error invalidating the conviction or insufficient evidence to support a conviction.

The intolerable tension is clear in Crampton's case. The record indicated that he wanted to take the stand to plea for mercy to the jury and to proffer mitigating testimony for them to do so. That mitigating testimony could easily do him great damage, however, on the question of guilt, because the state would have the opportunity to impeach him by introducing his previous criminal record.

19. The specific claim was that without guiding standards the decision of juries to sentence defendants is essentially "lawless," and therefore in violation of the 14th Amendment's requirement that no state shall deny any citizen of his life without due process of law.

20. A description provided by Justice Brennan in his dissent from *McGautha v. California*, p. 248.

21. Justice Harlan came to this conclusion after a historical review of unsuccessful attempts to identify beforehand which murder defendants should die. He noted the early rejection in this country of mandatory death penalties, and the abortive attempt by Pennsylvania to replace a mandatory death penalty for all crimes, restricting it to defined first-degree murderers. One of the problems with mandatory death sentences was the tendency of juries to thwart the law and acquit those defendants who were thought to be guilty but not deserving of the penalty of death, "jury nullification." In order to respond

to this practical imperative, states began to formally extend to juries the discretion to sentence they were already exercising.

22. As evidence of this, Justice Harlan points to McGautha's own jury. It had for its consideration evidence suggesting that McGautha and not Wilkinson was the one who fired the fatal shot, and sentenced McGautha to death and Wilkinson to life imprisonment. Harlan's approving reference to this apparently suggested to him that with unguided discretion juries are nonetheless able to successfully distinguish deserving from less culpable candidates for a death sentence:

> The ability of juries, unassisted by standards, to distinguish between those defendants for whom the death penalty is appropriate punishment and those for whom imprisonment is sufficient is indeed illustrated by the discriminating verdict of the jury in McGautha's case, finding Wilkinson the less culpable of the two defendants and sparing his life. (p. 221)

23. An excellent review of Justice Harlan's position in *McGautha* and his conflicting view on standardless juries with Justice Brennan can be found in Robert Weisberg's essay, "Deregulating Death" (1984).

24. With regard to the fact that under the Ohio single-verdict process capital defendants who exercise their 5th Amendment protection by not testifying on their own behalf may be sentenced to death "by a jury which never heard the sound of his voice" (p. 220 *McGautha v. California,* Harlan, J. opinion), Justice Harlan almost scornfully refers to the right to speak to the jury as of only "symbolic value." Ironically, his solution is the largely symbolic common law right of allocution where, under Ohio law, the defendant is entitled to speak to the court after the jury has rendered its sentence and the trial judge is virtually powerless to alter it (see Weisberg 1984).

25. Justice Douglas wrote the dissenting opinion in *Crampton,* joined by Justices Brennan and Marshall. In it, he noted that Ohio defendants who wish to speak to the jury regarding the issue of mercy can only do so by surrendering their right to be free from self-incrimination. If they choose to exercise their 5th Amendment protection, however, Douglas notes that the jury may not hear relevant mitigating evidence told most poignantly by the defendants themselves. Juries following such procedures, Douglas concluded, "are stacked in favor of death" (p. 247).

Justice Brennan wrote the dissenting opinion in *McGautha,* joined by Justices Douglas and Marshall. He notes that the Court misunderstood the essential question in McGautha's case; that the Court was not called upon to review a state's actual attempt to provide rational guidance to so important a decision as which capital defendants should live and which should die. Brennan correctly observed that neither California nor Ohio ever attempted to provide standards and criteria for its juries:

> It is of critical importance in the present cases to emphasize that we are not called upon to determine the adequacy or inadequacy of any particular legislative procedure designed to give rationality to the capital sentencing process. For the plain fact is that the legislatures of California and Ohio, whence come these cases, have sought no solution at all. We are not presented with a State's attempt to provide standards, attacked as impermissible or inadequate. We are not presented with a legislative attempt to draw wisdom from experience through a process looking toward growth in understanding through the accumulation of a variety of experiences. We are not presented with the slightest attempt to bring the power of reason to bear on the considerations relevant to capital sentencing. We are faced with nothing more than stark legislative abdication. (pp. 249–250)

Furthermore, Brennan argued that due process does not require, as Justice Harlan seemed to think, that capital sentencing decisions be made with the rigor and exactitude of mathematical formula, but that *some* direction should be provided those making such a "truly awesome" choice: "[t]he point is even if a State's notion of wise capital sentencing policy is such that the policy cannot be implemented through a formula capable of mechanical application . . . there is no reason that it should not give some guidance to those called upon to render decision" (pp. 285–286).

26. The appeal in *Aikens v. California* was dismissed since the California Supreme Court declared that capital punishment for murder was unconstitutional under the state constitution in *People v. Anderson*, 6 Cal. 3d 628, 493 P. 2d 880, 100 Cal. Rptr. 152 (1972). Nine months after *Anderson*, however, a public referendum was passed which stated that nothing in the state constitution was inconsistent with capital punishment, thus restoring it in California.

27. Raoul Berger, a leading critic of this nonhistorical interpretation of the 8th Amendment, describes it as "the abolitionist magic fountain, the primal source from which all blessings flow" (1982, 113).

28. Weisberg (1984, 315) characterized *Furman* as "not so much a case as a badly orchestrated opera, with nine characters taking turns to offer their own arias."

29. *Furman v. Georgia* was decided by a 5–4 vote. The five justices who voted to strike down existing statutes comprised the majority.

30. Justice Douglas noted that

[i]t would seem to be incontestable that the death penalty inflicted on one defendant is "unusual" if it discriminates against him by reason of his race, religion, wealth, social position, or class . . . [t]here is increasing recognition of the fact that the basic theme of equal protection is implicit in "cruel and unusual" punishments. . . . Those who wrote the Eighth Amendment knew what price their forebears had paid for a system based, not on equal justice, but on discrimination. . . . One cannot read this history without realizing that the desire for equality was reflected in the ban against "cruel and unusual punishments" contained in the Eighth Amendment." (pp. 242, 249, 255)

31. Stewart notes (p. 308) in *Furman* that

"[m]y concurring Brothers have demonstrated that, if any basis can be discerned for the selection of these few to be sentenced to die, it is the constitutionally impermissible basis of race. . . . But racial discrimination has not been proved, and I put it to one side."

32. Justice Brennan concluded his analysis as follows:

In sum, the punishment of death is inconsistent with all four principles: Death is an unusually severe and degrading punishment; there is a strong probability that it is inflicted arbitrarily; its rejection by contemporary society is virtually total; and there is no reason to believe that it serves any penal purpose more effectively than the less severe punishment of imprisonment. The function of these principles is to enable a court to determine whether a punishment comports with human dignity. Death, quite simply, does not. (p. 305)

33. What has become known in the research literature as the "Marshall Hypothesis" can be stated in his own words as follows: "Assuming knowledge of all the facts presently available regarding capital punishment, the average citizen would, in my opinion, find it shocking to his conscience and sense of justice." (p. 369)

34. It is true, however, that in *Furman* Chief Justice Burger is skeptical that sentencing standards will be remediating:

Thus, unless the Court in *McGautha* misjudged the experience of history, there is little reason to believe that sentencing standards in any form will substantially alter the discretionary character of the prevailing system of sentencing in capital cases. That system may fall short of perfection, but it is yet to be shown that a different system would produce more satisfactory results. (p. 401)

35. See Vidmar and Ellsworth, "Public Opinion and the Death Penalty" (1974).

36. For excellent and riveting accounts of the role of the defense and prosecution in the penalty phase of a capital trial, see Weisberg (1984; 360–383) and Goodpaster (1983).

37. The Florida statute stipulated that the jury is to consider "[w]hether sufficient mitigating circumstances exist . . . which outweigh the aggravating circumstances found to exist; and . . . [b]ased on these considerations, whether the defendant should be sentenced to life or death" [Fla. Stat. Ann. Sec. 921.141 (2) (b) and (c) (Supp. 1976–1977)].

38. In *State v. Dixon*, 283 So. 2d 1, 10 (1973), the Supreme Court of Florida defined its role to be to "[ensure] that the reasons present in one case will reach a similar result to that reached under similar circumstances in another case. . . . If a defendant is sentenced to die, this Court can review that case in light of the other [sentencing] decisions and determine whether or not the punishment is too great."

39. There were nine states that did not have the death penalty at the time of the *Furman* decision: Alaska, Hawaii, Iowa, Maine, Michigan, Minnesota, Oregon, West Virginia, and Wisconsin. Of these only Oregon reinstated capital punishment after *Furman*. There were two jurisdictions that had the death penalty before *Furman* but did not attempt to reinstate it: Kansas and the District of Columbia. (Massachusetts was a pre-*Furman* death penalty state that enacted a new death penalty statute in 1979. It was determined to be unconstitutional by the State supreme court in 1980). (see Zimring and Hawkins 1986, 41–45).

40. *Gregg v. Georgia*, 428 U.S. 153 (1976); *Proffitt v. Florida*, 428 U.S. 242 (1976); *Jurek v. Texas*, 428 U.S. 262 (1976); *Woodson v. North Carolina*, 428 U.S. 280 (1976); *S. Roberts v. Louisiana*, 428 U.S. 325 (1976).

41. Texas's death penalty statute is probably more appropriately described as a "quasi-mandatory" statute. Under Texas' bifurcated procedure, if a defendant is convicted of a capital offense the trial court conducts a second, penalty phase hearing. At this hearing both the prosecution and defense may present any relevant information in their argument for or against a sentence of death. In its penalty deliberation the jury is required to answer three questions:

> (1) [W]hether the conduct of the defendant that caused the death of the deceased was committed deliberately and with the reasonable expectation that the death of the deceased or another would result; (2) whether there is a probability that the defendant would commit criminal acts of violence that would constitute a continuing threat to society; and (3) if raised by the evidence, whether the conduct of the defendant in killing the deceased was unreasonable in response to the provocation, if any, by the deceased. [Tex. Code Crim. Proc., Art. 37.071 (Supp. 1975–1976)]

If the answer to each of these questions is yes beyond a reasonable doubt, a penalty of death is required. If the answer to any question is no, a sentence of life imprisonment is commanded. Although the Texas statute has an obvious mandatory quality to it, it escaped the same fate as the other mandatory statutes reviewed by the Court because the majority thought that the second question (about future dangerousness) will be interpreted broadly to allow substantial evidence of mitigating circumstances, thus allowing the sentence to be "individualized."

42. See Flanagan and Maguire, *Sourcebook of Criminal Justice Statistics 1989* (1990, p. 170, Table 2.48).

43. Justice Stewart concluded that

> . . . the concerns expressed in *Furman* that the penalty of death not be imposed in an arbitrary or capricious manner can be met by a carefully drafted statute that ensures that the sentencing authority is given adequate information and guidance. As a general

proposition these concerns are best met by a system that provides for a bifurcated proceeding at which the sentencing authority is apprised of the information relevant to the imposition of sentence and provided with standards to guide its use of the information. . . . As an important additional safeguard against arbitrariness and caprice, the Georgia statutory scheme provides for automatic appeal of all death sentences to the State's Supreme Court. (pp. 195, 198)

In fact, in his *Gregg* opinion Justice Stewart offered a ringing endorsement of capital sentencing standards, noting that "[i]t is quite simply a hallmark of our legal system that juries be carefully and adequately guided in their deliberations" (p. 193). He writes this without commenting on the fact that he concurred with Justice Harlan's assessment in *McGautha* just five years earlier that the drafting of such standards were "beyond present human ability" (p. 204).

44. Justice Stewart reviewed the history of mandatory death penalties and concluded that over time most states have either severely restricted or abandoned them in favor of giving the sentencing authority some discretion. That some state legislatures, such as North Carolina and Louisiana, have recently returned to mandatory statutes does not convince him that society now finds them morally acceptable. Instead they represent "attempts by the States to retain the death penalty in a form consistent with the Constitution" (p. 298).

45. In its 1989–1990 term the Court has stated that a capital punishment scheme can have a mandatory feature and yet still pass constitutional muster. Under the capital statute of Pennsylvania, a sentence of death "must" be imposed if the jury finds at least one aggravating circumstance and no mitigating circumstances. In *Blystone v. Pennsylvania*, 110 S.Ct. 1078 (1990) the Court held that such a scheme was constitutional. It distinguished the Pennsylvania statute from the mandatory ones it struck down in *Woodson* and *Roberts*. The North Carolina and Louisiana statutes mandated a death sentence for all those convicted of certain classes of first-degree murder. The Pennsylvania statute, however, requires the jury to consider and weigh all aggravating and a nonexclusive list of mitigating factors. One subsection of this statute stipulates that the jury may hear "[a]ny other evidence" in mitigation. The majority in *Blystone* determined that, unlike the North Carolina and Louisiana statutes which automatically require a death sentence without regard for any consideration of the unique features of the case, the Pennsylvania statute compels the jury to sentence the defendant to death only after it has appraised all aggravating and mitigating factors that are germane to the defendants' culpability and desert. This satisfies the requirement of individualized sentencing in death penalty cases.

46. These decisions said nothing, for example, about the constitutionality of the death penalty for rape or for an accomplice in a murder, nor did it rule out the possibility that a mandatory statute could exist for very narrowly constructed capital crimes, such as murder by one serving a life sentence or the killing of a police officer. These issues were taken up and decided later, and are discussed in the next chapter.

47. Weisberg (1984, 322) probably stated best the ambiguity remaining in the wake of the *Gregg* decision: "One can say little with certainty about *Gregg v. Georgia* except that it makes a great many things constitutionally significant, but it makes nothing either constitutionally necessary or clearly constitutionally sufficient."

3

Legal Challenges to and Reform of the Death Penalty: II. Beyond *Gregg v. Georgia*

B y 1976 state legislatures had gotten approval from the United States Supreme Court that at least one kind of death penalty statute for murder was constitutional, one that included a bifurcated hearing, statutory circumstances that focused the attention of the sentencing authority on relevant features of the offense and offender, and some form of direct appeal of the appropriateness of the imposed sentence. It was not at all clear, however, if a constitutionally valid statute had to include all or any of these procedural reforms,[1] nor was it clear what additional procedural or substantive reforms of state law the Constitution would compel states to provide for capital defendants.

Since 1976 both lower federal courts and the U.S. Supreme Court have been active in reviewing state death penalty practices, with the result being one of the most complex bodies of law in American jurisprudence. In the present chapter we will review some of the most important of these post-*Gregg* reforms in the procedure and substance of state death penalty law. Two things should be kept clearly in mind throughout this review. First, because of the enormous quantity of state and federal death penalty law, not all of it can be reviewed within the confines of this chapter. Second, courts are continuing their review of state death penalty practices with the result that new cases and reforms are announced each year.

Post-*Gregg* Procedural Reforms of State Death Penalty Practices

The two lead cases in the Supreme Court's 1976 quintet of death penalty decisions, *Gregg* and *Woodson*, seemed to require two different and irreconcilable things of any death penalty statute. The procedural reforms approved in *Gregg*, bifurcated hearings, guidelines for juries, and appellate review, clearly expressed the Court's demand for greater *consistency* in capital sentencing. The theme of *Woodson*, however, is that the determination of a life or death sentence must be *individualized* to the specific and unique culpability of particular defendants, possibly making for less consistency across cases. Procedural reform of state death penalty schemes was to continue, and the theme of individualized death sentences was to sound again, soon after these 1976 cases, in *Lockett v. Ohio*, 438 U.S. 586 (1978).

Sandra Lockett was a twenty-one-year-old Ohio woman who drove the getaway car for an armed robbery that resulted in the shooting death of a pawnshop owner by one of her codefendants. Although not firing the fatal shot herself, Lockett was convicted under Ohio's aiding-and-abetting murder statute and sentenced to death, after rejecting several offers by the prosecutor to plea-bargain to a lesser offense. Under the then existing Ohio death penalty statute, once a defendant was convicted of capital murder the death penalty was the required punishment unless the sentencing authority determines that at least one of three statutory mitigating circumstances exists. None of these three mitigating circumstances included the defendant's minor participation in the crime,[2] so Lockett was unable to plea as a mitigating circumstance the fact that she was only an accomplice who had not fired the fatal shot, nor intended any harm since she was not at the scene when the fatal shot was fired.

A majority of the Supreme Court voted to strike down Lockett's death sentence and Ohio's capital statute, finding that it unconstitutionally restricted the range of mitigating evidence that the sentencing authority can hear and base its life or death decision on. Relying on the theme of its *Woodson* opinion regarding the constitutional necessity to individualize death sentences, the *Lockett* Court held that the penalty phase of a bifurcated capital hearing must be thrown open to include all kinds of relevant mitigating testimony proffered by the defense in its argument for a life sentence. The sentencing authority must be given the opportunity not only to hear this evidence but also to give it independent weight in determining the defendant's deserved sentence:

> . . . we conclude that the Eighth and Fourteenth Amendments require that the sentencer, in all but the rarest kind of capital case, not be precluded from considering, *as a mitigating factor,* any aspect of a defendant's character or record and any of the circumstances of the offense that the defendant proffers as a basis for a sentence less than death. (p. 604)

The *Lockett* decision was a major defense victory since it required juries to hear and consider all mitigating evidence that pertains to the defendant's character, prior record, or offense, and appears to prohibit very little in the way of mitigating information. Its effect may also be to return to the jury ample amounts of discretion *not to impose* a death sentence. If capital juries may now hear and give independent weight to virtually any mitigating evidence, the Court, in its *Lockett* decision, may have come perilously close to returning the penalty phase of a capital trial to its *Furman* structure. Now juries may mete out mercy for very individualized reasons, which may be true to *Woodson*'s demand that capital juries consider "the diverse frailties of humankind" but may produce sentencing patterns as arbitrary and capricious as those condemned in *Furman*.[3]

With *Lockett,* the Court was far from finished with its review of state death penalty systems, though by 1983 it appeared to be retreating somewhat from its attempt to *strictly* regulate capital sentencing procedures.[4] In that year the Court advanced an interpretation of its earlier *Gregg* decision in terms of the function of aggravating circumstances in two cases, *Barclay v. Florida,* 103 S.Ct. 3418 (1983) and *Zant v. Stephens,* 103 S.Ct. 2733 (1983).

In *Zant v. Stephens* the defendant was sentenced to death by a Georgia jury that found three aggravating circumstances: (1) that the defendant had a prior conviction of a capital felony, (2) that he had an extensive history of serious and violent criminal convictions, and (3) that the murder was committed by an escapee. While Stephens's appeal was pending the Georgia Supreme Court declared in another case that the second aggravating circumstance was unconstitutionally vague. Stephens's death sentence was thus based on two legitimate and one illegitimate aggravating circumstances.[5] Although the jury could have heard testimony about Stephens's prior criminal record, it here bore the invalid appellation of a *statutory* aggravating circumstance during his penalty phase hearing. An important question, then, was whether or not the mistaken rubric of a statutory aggravating circumstance led Stephens's jury to impose a death sentence when it might not have in its absence. In its review of his case the Georgia Supreme Court concluded that the invalid aggravating circumstance did not invalidate Stephens's death sentence since it could stand on the other two legitimate aggravating circumstances.

In reviewing Stephens's claim for the U.S. Supreme Court, Justice Stevens, writing for the Court, observed that the function of Georgia's enumerated aggravating circumstances is not to restrict the attention of the jury solely to statutory aggravating factors. The function of an aggravating circumstance is simply to "narrow the class of persons eligible for the death penalty" (p. 2742). In characterizing the function of aggravating circumstances in this manner, the U.S. Supreme Court adopted the analogy of a pyramid employed by the Georgia Supreme Court. This pyramid, which consists of all cases of homicide, is separated by three planes. The first plane separates all homicide cases below it from first-degree murder cases above. The second plane separates those murder cases in which at least one valid aggravating circumstance is found from those where none exist. The former group of capital murderers constitutes all cases where the death penalty might be imposed. The third plane separates all capital murders into two groups, those in which a sentence of death is imposed and those that result in a life sentence. In passing cases beyond the third plane into the death sentenced group, the U.S. Supreme Court agreed with the characterization by the Georgia Supreme Court that the jury has "absolute discretion" (p. 2740). Once at least one valid aggravating circumstance is found, then, the capital jury has complete discretion to sentence a defendant to life imprisonment or death.

In accepting this pyramid analogy, the *Zant* Court determined that the purpose of an aggravating circumstance is simply to narrow the category of defendants eligible for a death sentence, and that the actual selection of who is given death and who mercy is "an *individualized* determination on the basis of the character of the individual and the circumstances of the crime" (p. 2744). What the *Zant* decision does, then, is to allow the capital jury to consider virtually *any* factor in aggravation (that would be properly before it) once it has found a statutory aggravating factor.[6] The only function served by a statutory aggravating circumstance is to push a case from the second to the third level of the pyramid. Once a case reaches this third level, the designation of a circumstance as a statutory aggravating one (valid or not) is of no importance. The ultimate effect of *Zant* is to provide for the prosecution essentially the same opportunity to present evidence in aggravation that *Lockett* did for the defense and mitigating testimony.[7] The penalty phase of a capital trial virtually becomes, then, an information free-for-all.

In the second of these cases, the defendant, Elwood Barclay, was sentenced to death by a Florida trial court judge who overrode the jury's recommendation of a life sentence. In sentencing Barclay to death against the recommendation of the jury the trial judge noted that several aggravating circumstances were present. One of these "aggravating circumstances" found by the judge, that Barclay had a significant history of criminal convictions,[8] *was not* an aggravating circumstance listed in the Florida statute (see Chapter 2, Table 2–2), and could not, therefore, be considered as such. The judge's characterization of Barclay's criminal history as a statutory aggravating factor was nothing less than an error of state law.[9] The issue before the Supreme Court was, then, could a sentence of death rest upon both valid and invalid aggravating circumstances? A majority of the Court in *Barclay* held that yes it could.

It would seem that once the Court provided its explanation of the role of aggravating circumstances in *Zant,* it would have resolved the question in *Barclay.* Florida's capital statute is, however, more formal than Georgia's in that the jury is explicitly instructed to weigh aggravating against mitigating circumstances. In the weighing process the designation of a factor as a *statutory* aggravating one may, therefore, have been more consequential for Barclay than for the defendant in *Zant* who was tried under Georgia law. Such, however, was not to be the case.

In his opinion for a plurality of the Court, Justice Rehnquist provides only a bare-bones explanation of the Court's reasoning in rejecting Barclay's claim. He simply agrees with the Florida Supreme Court's characterization of the use of a nonstatutory aggravating circumstance in Barclay's case as "harmless error"— an error not prejudicial enough to have affected the outcome. In coming to this conclusion, Justice Rehnquist seems to be acceding to the view of Justice Harlan in *McGautha* that the penalty phase of a capital trial involves an awesome moral decision which is influenced by numerous subjective considerations not easily constrained by legal rules.[10] Rehnquist's view was that there are so many factors to consider during a penalty phase that the improper designation of one (or more) would hardly be prejudicial to the defendant.

On the same day that the *Barclay* case was decided, the Supreme Court announced its decision in another death penalty case, *Barefoot v. Estelle,* 103 S.Ct. 3383 (1983). The *Barefoot* case is particularly interesting in that it dealt with both a substantive issue concerning Texas' death penalty statute, and a procedural issue that concerned the federal court's handling of death penalty appeals. The Court's response to both issues further indicated that it might back away from a strict regulation of state death penalty trials. First, the substantive issue.

Thomas Barefoot was convicted and sentenced to death by a Texas jury pursuant to its post-*Furman* revised capital punishment statute where it had to decide if he was likely to commit acts of criminal violence in the future.[11] The jury unanimously agreed that he was so likely, at least in part because of the testimony of two prosecution psychiatrists, Drs. Holbrook and Grigson.[12] Neither of these two psychiatrists actually interviewed Barefoot. Their prediction as to his future dangerousness was in response to hypothetical questions. Dr. Holbrook concluded that "within reasonable psychiatric certainty" Barefoot would commit criminal acts of violence in the future and would constitute a continuing threat to society. Dr. Grigson was more emphatic in his testimony. He put Barefoot in the "most severe category" of sociopaths and that on a one-to-ten scale of sociopathy, Barefoot was "above ten." His ultimate conclusion was that there was a "one hundred percent and absolute" certainty that the defendant would be dangerous in the future. After deliberating for one hour the jury sentenced Barefoot to death.

What is substantively interesting about the Barefoot case is precisely the accuracy of this psychiatric testimony regarding future dangerousness. While Dr. Grigson testified that he could predict with one hundred percent certainty, and Dr. Holbrook with only somewhat less optimism, that the defendant Barefoot would commit acts of criminal violence in the future, the American Psychiatric Association (APA) submitted an *amicus curiae* brief in the case which reviewed the empirical literature on predicting dangerousness and concluded that *in two out of three instances a psychiatrist's prediction of dangerousness is wrong.* The APA brief also noted that psychiatrists as a class simply have no special expertise in predicting future dangerousness, that a lay person could do just as well or better, and that psychiatrists consistently overpredict future dangerousness when called upon to do so.

In his brief before the U.S. Supreme Court, Barefoot contended that since "expert" predictions about future dangerousness are so inaccurate (66% of the time), it injects unreliable testimony into the penalty determination. But the Court rejected his claim. Why would information of this type, which is recognized by the practicing community's professional association as generally erroneous, be allowed to be presented to a jury entrusted with determining life or death? The Court's answer to this question is interesting if at times seemingly disingenuous. Writing for a majority of the Court, Justice White acknowledged that psychiatric testimony about future dangerousness is often incorrect, but dismissed the importance of this by noting that psychiatrists are not wrong all of the time, simply "most of the time" (p. 3398). He also remarked that this campaign of misinformation on the part of the state's psychiatrists does not have to be one-sided; the defense could easily offer its own expert witnesses who could testify that they are equally convinced that the defendant is unlikely to be dangerous in the future. What about the poor jurors, who may be hearing equally confident but conflicting expert testimony regarding the defendant's likely conduct in the future? The solution is already available, Justice White concludes, in federal and state rules of evidence. Both parties to this psychiatric free-for-all can be cross-examined and impeached and the jury can determine for itself which is fact and which fiction. Rather than regulate what the capital jury hears, the *Zant, Barclay,* and *Barefoot* Courts seem to be saying that the jury should hear as much as possible and that it should be allowed to sort out the mess (see Weisberg 1984).

Barefoot also dealt with a politically charged procedural issue—the length of time it takes to litigate death penalty appeals. Thomas Barefoot was convicted and sentenced to death in November of 1978, some five years before the Court's decision in his case. In his majority opinion, Justice White could scarcely conceal his anger at the delays in state death penalty cases, noting that unlike a term of years which a defendant must begin serving while tending his appeals, the state is frustrated in carrying out death sentences until all reasonable appeals are fairly resolved.[13] In its decision, the *Barefoot* Court held that federal courts may now expedite death penalty appeals and speed the defendant toward a final resolution of his case. Specifically, it held that when a capital defendant tenders an appeal to a federal circuit court on a district court's denial of *habeas corpus,* the circuit court can hear arguments on both the merits of the legal claim and the request for a stay of execution and make a single summary decision of both. It does not have to first grant a stay of execution and then follow with a full hearing on the merits of the claim.[14] Ironically, the practical effect of the expedited federal review procedures announced in *Barefoot* is to give capital defendants *less time* to prepare their *habeas* appeals than those not fighting for their lives. As Mello (1988, 547–548) has recently noted, defense counsel in noncapital felony cases have ten days in which to file a notice of appeal and forty days more to prepare a brief after a federal district court's judgment. The defense also has two weeks to respond to the state's own brief and usually has at least a month before oral arguments are held. Compared with this, some post-*Barefoot* federal courts have implemented new procedures whereby the time between the district court's decision and the appeal court's ruling in a capital case can be less than one day.[15] The hectic pace of federal appeals of death penalty cases prompted by *Barefoot,* compared with the more considered judgment allowed in noncapital cases, led one prominent death penalty lawyer, Anthony Amsterdam (1987, 889–890) to observe that

> . . . a death-sentenced appellant who has obtained a certificate of probable cause can have his appeal decided on the merits under guise of denying a stay of execution *without* the full time for briefing, argument and judicial deliberation that would be permitted in a five-dollar tax case or a two-dollar social security case.

One final case needs to be discussed here. As part of the aftermath of *Gregg v. Georgia, Pulley v. Harris,* 465 U.S. 37 (1984) reflects the Supreme Court's reluctance to strictly regulate state death penalty systems. The issue in this case concerns one of the procedural protections the *Gregg* Court thought would protect state capital sentencing schemes from the arbitrary sentencing patterns condemned in *Furman*—the protection of comparative proportionality review of death sentences. Under the Georgia death penalty statute approved in *Gregg,* the Georgia Supreme Court is required to compare the death sentence under review with the sentence imposed in comparable cases in order to determine if it is excessive or disproportionate. The purpose of this practice is to ensure that no death sentence is arbitrarily imposed: "Proportionality review substantially eliminates the possibility that a person will be sentenced to die by the action of an aberrant jury" [*Gregg v. Georgia,* 428 U.S. 153 (1976) at p. 206].

While the intention of the Georgia Supreme Court's proportionality review is to ensure the evenhandedness of imposed death sentences, it was not clear how important the *Gregg* Court thought that protection was. The constitutionality of the Georgia statute was approved as a whole and it is not certain which elements (if any) were required, bifurcated hearings, statutory guidelines for the sentencer, or comparative proportionality review. The *Gregg* Court gave no indication that it found any one of these procedural protections constitutionally indispensable. Most important, it did not find comparative proportionality review so critical that without it the Georgia statute would have been constitutionally invalid.[16] The Court did seem to suggest, however, that with the protection of comparative review available to capital defendants many of the most lawless death sentences under previous sentencing schemes would be remedied by state court action.[17]

In spite of the apparent importance of comparative proportionality review in ferreting out that which was most consistently condemned in *Furman,* the aberrant death sentence, the U.S. Supreme Court had not held nor even suggested that it was required of a constitutionally valid death sentencing system. It decided that issue in 1984 in *Pulley v. Harris.* The defendant in *Pulley,* Robert Harris, was sentenced to death under the California statute that provides for an automatic appeal of the factual validity of each death sentence but does not require the state supreme court to conduct a comparative proportionality review.[18] The question before the Court in *Pulley* was whether or not *Furman* and its progeny required comparative proportionality review as a constitutionally indispensable element in a state death penalty scheme in order to ensure the consistent application of imposed death sentences. In a 7–2 decision, it ruled that it did not.

Writing for a majority of the Court, Justice White concluded that none of its previous death penalty cases could stand for the proposition that comparative sentence review was a constitutional requirement. While acknowledging that the Georgia and Florida statutes which had provisions for proportionality review were found to pass constitutional muster, White noted that the Court did not find such review to be so critical that the statutes would have been invalid without it. He noted further that the Court approved the Texas scheme in *Jurek* which contained no explicit provision nor established case law for comparative proportionality review. What is required of any constitutionally valid capital punishment scheme is a procedure to meaningfully narrow the range of cases eligible for the death penalty, which, Justice White says, California's provision of "special circumstances" does. Conceding that such schemes "may occasionally produce aberrational outcomes," Justice White nonetheless concludes that "[s]uch inconsistencies are a far cry from the major systemic defects identified in *Furman*" (p. 54).

Additional Reform of State Death Penalty Law

Regulating What the Sentencer Hears

We began this chapter with a discussion of the Supreme Court's *Lockett* decision. In holding that to meet constitutional requirements, "a death penalty statute must not preclude consideration of relevant mitigating factors" (p. 608), the *Lockett* Court stated that the defense must be able to present to the sentencing authority all aspects of the offender's character and record, and the circumstances of the offense, in its argument for a sentence less than death. The Court's holding in *Lockett* is consistent with its earlier *Woodson* decision, that capital sentences must be individualized and reflect the unique culpability of particular capital defendants. *Woodson* and *Lockett*, then, stand for the proposition that in a constitutionally valid capital punishment scheme the sentencer must be able to consider a broad range of mitigating testimony. Although as suggested earlier the U.S. Supreme Court may have backed away somewhat from strict regulation of state death penalty practices, it has continued to be active in regulating the kind of testimony it will allow a capital sentencing authority to hear.

In *Eddings v. Oklahoma*, 455 U.S. 104 (1982), the Court heard a case involving a death sentence imposed on a defendant who was only sixteen years old when he committed the offense. During the course of the penalty hearing Eddings presented testimony to the Court relating to his unhappy upbringing and previous emotional disturbance. The Court's *Lockett* decision required that the sentencing authority, in this case the trial judge, hear this evidence in mitigation. At the conclusion of the penalty phase, however, the judge in sentencing Eddings to death noted that the only mitigating factor he weighed was the defendant's youth. It was clear from the record that the judge had not found the totality of mitigating evidence wanting when compared with aggravating factors, he simply did not consider the other mitigating testimony offered by Eddings's defense counsel in affixing penalty.[19] In applying the principle adopted by the plurality in *Lockett*, a majority of the U.S. Supreme Court vacated Eddings's death sentence, pronouncing that no limitations should be placed on the relevant mitigating circumstances considered by a capital sentencing authority: "The state courts must consider all relevant mitigating evidence and weigh it against the evidence of the aggravating circumstances" (p. 117). Both *Lockett* and *Eddings* are important defense victories in that they require the capital sentencing authority to hear and give independent weight to all relevant mitigating evidence.

The Court is still not clear, however, on the appropriate *content* of the respective mitigating and aggravating evidence. In this regard, the Court has been active over the years in defining the kind of evidence that the capital sentencing authority is required or entitled to hear. For example, in *California v. Ramos,* 103 S.Ct. 3446 (1983), the Court held that it was constitutional for California judges to inform capital juries that the governor could commute a sentence of life imprisonment without the possibility of parole to a lesser sentence that included the possibility of parole. The Court noted that such information was both accurate and relevant to the jury's concern for the future dangerousness of the defendant. Although juries may be informed as to the factual accuracy of a "life-without-possibility-of-parole" sentence and therefore speculate as to the offender's future propensity for violence, the state cannot attempt to diminish the jury's responsibility for its sentencing decision. In *Caldwell v. Mississippi,* 105 S.Ct. 2633 (1985), the Court vacated a death sentence because the prosecutor had informed the jury that it should not view its decision as the final determination of sentence since every death sentence is reviewed for correctness by the Mississippi Supreme Court. The *Caldwell* Court noted that such information had the effect of minimizing the jury's sense of responsibility in determining whether or not a capital defendant should live or die.

The Court has also placed other restrictions and given other liberties as to what capital juries may hear during the penalty phase of a capital trial. For example, in *Skipper v. South Carolina,* 106 S.Ct. 1669 (1986), it held that the sentencing authority may consider as mitigating evidence the postoffense behavior of a capital defendant. In the *Skipper* case, the evidence consisted of the good behavior of the defendant while incarcerated pending and during his trial. The defense wanted to offer Skipper's experience of institutional adjustment as evidence that he was redeemable, constituted no threat or danger to other inmates or correctional staff, and could rehabilitate himself if given a life sentence. In *Hitchcock v. Dugger,* 107 S.Ct. 1821 (1987), a unanimous Court declared invalid a Florida death sentence because the advisory jury and sentencing judge did not consider nonstatutory mitigating factors in its decision. In line with *Lockett, Eddings,* and *Skipper* the Court in *Hitchcock* affirmed the position that the capital jury should hear any and all relevant testimony relative to the appropriateness of a sentence of death.[20]

A question may be raised now concerning the prosecution's equal "*Lockett/Eddings*"-type right. If the defense may proffer virtually any evidence in mitigation of penalty, may the state be granted an equally broad right in presenting aggravating testimony? In *Zant* the Supreme Court held that evidence in support of a death sentence properly presented may be considered by the jury once at least one legitimate aggravating circumstance is found, even if that evidence improperly bears the imprimatur of a statutory aggravating circumstance. Furthermore, the Court in *Ramos* allowed California juries to be informed about the future parole possibility of a capital defendant. Although the Supreme Court has been generous in allowing the defense great latitude in presenting evidence in mitigation, it has been more reluctant to grant the state the same amount of license.

For example, in *Booth v. Maryland,* 107 S.Ct. 2529 (1987) it disallowed the use of "victim impact statements" during the penalty phase of a capital trial. A victim impact statement was a written statement describing the personal attributes of the victim, the emotional impact of the murder on the victim's surviving family members, and the family members' opinions about the victim, the defendant, the crime, and the appropriate punishment. In Booth's case, family members also personally testified for the state during the penalty phase to relate to the jury the impact of the crime on their lives and the great loss suffered by the death of the victim. The Court stated that such considerations deflect the jury's attention away from the circumstances of the crime and the offender, and inject an arbitrary element into the jury's sentencing consideration. The reasoning of the Court was that the victim's personal characteristics are not directed at the defendant's own culpability but to factors about which the offender would be unaware. Essentially, then, *Booth* stands for the proposition that statements by family members about the emotional impact of a crime on their lives have no place in capital sentencing. This position was reaffirmed and given a broad interpretation in *South Carolina v. Gathers,* 109 S.Ct. 2207 (1989), where the Court held that not only written and personally rendered victim impact assessments by family members, but also prosecutors' comments concerning the personal characteristics of the victim, were invalid sentencing considerations which could not be presented to the jury.[21] In both cases a majority of the Court thought that capital juries should not hear or consider information that pertains solely to the victim's personal characteristics.

In sum, it would appear that the Court has given defense counsel wide latitude in the presentation of mitigating testimony to the capital sentencing authority in its argument for a sentence less than death. The capital defendant may present, and the sentencer must give weight to: personal characteristics concerning motivation and extenuating circumstances at the time of the crime; background characteristics, which may provide some explanation of the defendant's conduct; testimony from family members, relatives, and friends about the defendant's good character; and both pre- and postoffense information pertaining to the capacity of the defendant to be rehabilitated. Although state trial courts have not always been cooperative, the U.S. Supreme Court has taken seriously the commands of *Lockett* and *Eddings* that the penalty phase ought to be used to allow the sentencer full access to mitigating testimony in an effort to reliably determine the defendant's own culpability. The Court has not, however, been as liberal with the state's presentation of aggravating testimony at the penalty phase. It has for the most part scrupulously adhered to the policy of excluding what it sees to be irrelevant and inflammatory information, that which may divert the attention of the jury from the characteristics of the offender, offense, or offender's record. At least for now, then, the Court seems reluctant to grant to prosecutors the same freedom to present information to the jury as they have to defense counsel.

Competency of Counsel in Capital Cases

Long before it was recognized in noncapital cases, the Supreme Court has held that a defendant on trial for his life must be afforded counsel.[22] The need for the right to counsel for capital defendants today can hardly be disputed. The reasons for this include the fact that a very high proportion of defendants accused of capital murder are indigent,[23] most are not sufficiently competent to conduct their own defense,[24] and capital defense law is exceedingly complicated jurisprudence for even the most seasoned attorney.[25] While the need for representation by counsel in capital cases has been acknowledged, the issue of the *quality* of such representation has been troubling. In comments before the Judicial Conference of the United States Court of Appeals for the Second Circuit, Justice Marshall (1986) stated:

> [C]apital defendants frequently suffer the consequences of having trial counsel who are ill-equipped to handle capital cases. Death penalty litigation has become a specialized field of practice. . . . And even the most well-intentioned attorneys often are unable to recognize and preserve and defend their clients' rights. . . . Though acting in good faith, they often make serious mistakes.[26]

Although capital defendants are afforded counsel as a matter of constitutional right, the competency of provided counsel has often been less than admirable. A few examples will establish this point with greater force.

In *Goodwin v. Balkcom,* 684 F. 2d 794 (1982) the defendant, Terry Goodwin, was represented by court-appointed counsel Henry Austin, who along with co-counsel Michael Jones alerted the jury both during opening argument and at the penalty phase of Goodwin's trial that the only reason they were representing him was because as court appointed they had to. Defense counsel's displeasure with having to represent Goodwin, and their general racial attitude, was made clear to the jury:

> Well, if you decide to impose the death penalty today and you decide to sentence him to the electric chair, historically speaking, you have got a very likely candidate. He is a little old nigger boy, he would not weigh 150 pounds. He had got two court-appointed attorneys appointed by this court to represent him to do the very best we can for him. He is poor. He is broke. He is probably mentally retarded. I dare say he has not got an I.Q. of over 70. He is uneducated. Probably just unwanted. This is the kind of people that we have historically put to death here in Georgia. (p. 805, note 13)

The jury agreed with defense counsel's assessments and sentenced Goodwin to death. Neither the state supreme court nor federal district court found Goodwin's attorneys ineffective. Only the Eleventh Circuit Court of Appeals found the representation constitutionally lacking and remanded the sentence.

Hengstler (1987, 59) provides an even more chilling example of ineffective counsel in a capital case and the difficulty of winning a subsequent ineffective counsel claim. In 1975 John Young was convicted of the murder of three elderly Georgia women and sentenced to death. Young was represented by Charles Marchman, Jr., who one year after Young's trial removed himself from the practice of law and in 1985 filed an affidavit in one of Young's *habeas corpus* appeals admitting that he was ineffective in defending Young. In his affidavit before the Eleventh Circuit Court of Appeals, Marchman admitted that he failed to prepare for the case because at the time of Young's trial his marriage was breaking up, he was involved in a homosexual relationship, and he was using drugs. The Eleventh Circuit refused to consider Marchman's affidavit and Young was executed on March 20, 1985.

Other instances of inadequate performance by counsel include the case of Gibbs Hyman in South Carolina, whose defense counsel had not yet read the state death penalty statute at the time of his trial; Kevin Osborn's counsel who described him and his codefendants to the jury as "sharks feeding in the ocean in a frenzy"; Charles Young's counsel who was unaware that Georgia had a bifurcated proceeding in capital cases and had to be informed of such fact by the court only after first making a plea for mercy during the guilt phase, thus conceding Young's guilt of first-degree murder. Then there are Jack House's trial lawyers, Dorothy and Ben Atkins, who were real estate attorneys and had never before represented a defendant in a capital case. Both failed to interview any witnesses personally; Dorothy Atkins failed to obtain documents from the prosecution during discovery because she was "too busy"; Ben Atkins was absent from court because he was parking his car and did not hear the testimony from a key hostile witness, was absent a second time for approximately one half of the prosecutor's closing argument, and failed to introduce physical evidence that would have substantiated House's claim of innocence. Eddie Spraggins arrested for murder and rape in Georgia in 1977 was represented by one Vernon Belcher, a court-appointed attorney. Although Spraggins pled not guilty and took the stand during the guilt phase of his trial to deny any involvement in the crimes of which he was accused, Belcher stated to the jury during the guilt phase of the capital trial his personal belief that Spraggins had in fact committed the murder but deserved to receive a life sentence.[27]

These are but a few of the examples of the quality of representation received by some capital defendants who are more likely than not dependent upon overworked public defenders, court-appointed lawyers, or volunteers for the defense of their lives. It was suggested above that capital defendants have the constitutional right to counsel. They have more than this, however, for the Supreme Court has held that the Sixth Amendment right to counsel means more than the simple presence of a lawyer at trial alongside the defendant, it means that "the right to counsel is the right to the *effective assistance* of counsel" [*McMann v. Richardson*, 397 U.S. 759, 771, note 14 (1970), emphasis added]. Although proclaiming that capital defendants have the right not just to counsel but to the effective assistance of counsel, prior to 1984 the Court had not provided any guidelines as to when counsel may become ineffective. It examined that issue in *Strickland v. Washington*, 466 U.S. 668 (1984).

David Washington pled guilty in Florida to three murders and associated crimes, waived his right to an advisory sentencing recommendation by the jury, and chose instead to be sentenced by the trial judge. In preparing for the sentencing hearing before the judge, Washington's attorney, who was described in the record as experiencing a sense of hopelessness about the case because of the confessions, spoke with Washington about his background and on the telephone with Washington's wife and mother. Defense counsel did not, however, meet personally with either of these two latter potential character witnesses, giving up after one unsuccessful effort to meet with them. Counsel did not pursue the possibility of other character witnesses who could speak on his client's behalf, nor did he request a psychiatric examination for Washington. Washington's counsel abandoned any effort to seek out evidence of his client's character or emotional state at the time of the crime; he did, however, move to exclude from the penalty hearing some evidence he thought would be potentially damaging. At the penalty phase, counsel called no witnesses and instead relied on argument as to the defendant's remorse, cooperation with law enforcement authorities, and acceptance of responsibility for the crimes committed. The trial judge was unpersuaded by the offered mitigating testimony and sentenced Washington to death. The Florida Supreme Court affirmed both the conviction and sentences on appeal and Washington sought relief from the U.S. Supreme Court claiming that his counsel was ineffective and that he was entitled to a new sentencing hearing.

The Supreme Court was not sympathetic to Washington's plight nor apparently to the plight of many other condemned persons with claims of ineffective counsel. In *Strickland v. Washington*, (466 U.S. 668 (1984),) the Court rejected the defendant's contention that counsel was ineffective in his specific case, and set up a two-pronged test which established the standards for determining a defendant's claim that counsel provided ineffective assistance at either the guilt or penalty phase of a capital trial. The first prong of the test is that a defendant making a claim of ineffective counsel must demonstrate that the performance of counsel was deficient under "prevailing professional norms."[28] In making a determination that counsel's performance may have fallen below a professional standard, the Court admonished that a strong presumption about effective assistance should be maintained with the burden of proof on the complaining defendant.[29] In essence, the *Strickland* Court is simply requiring that counsel in capital cases behave like a reasonably competent attorney.

The second prong of the *Strickland* test poses an even more crippling burden of proof on those capital defendants who wish to make a claim of ineffective counsel. This second element holds that even if a defendant is able to show that counsel's performance fell below professional standards of competence, it must be further shown that the substandard performance prejudiced the outcome of the trial. This part of the test requires that a court reviewing an attorney's performance for effectiveness must, with hindsight, determine if the outcome of the trial would have been different had counsel not been incompetent. The simple question is, would it have made any difference in the result if counsel had been more effective? This is a demanding burden of proof because the *Strickland* test almost requires that defendants, before they can win an ineffective counsel claim, must be able to conclusively demonstrate that they would have been found not guilty or would have been sentenced to life had it not been for counsel's course of action.[30] Since court records are generally rich with information about what defense counsel did and the reasons and explanations for such action, it is easy for a reviewing court to put together a scenario suggesting that the actions taken were "reasonable" and that it is unlikely that the outcome would have been altered with a different course of action. The *Strickland* test requires such reviewing courts to make retrospective judgments about the probability of alternative outcomes with little basis for making such speculation. The difficulty of this task is precisely what Justice Marshall pointed out in his dissent from *Strickland*:

> [I]t is often very difficult to tell whether a defendant convicted after a trial in which he was ineffectively represented would have fared better if his lawyer had been competent. Seemingly impregnable cases can sometimes be dismantled by good defense counsel. On the basis of a cold record, it may be impossible for a

reviewing court confidently to ascertain how the government's evidence and arguments would have stood up against rebuttal and cross-examination by a shrewd, well prepared lawyer. [*Strickland v. Washington*, 466 U.S. 668 (1984): 710]

With *Strickland v. Washington,* then, the Court seems to be suggesting that the Constitution does not require that defense counsel in a capital case be effective, only that the lawyer not be ineffective. The prevailing standard is that a person on trial for their life should not have a legally ineffective lawyer. The distinction between a capital defendant having an effective counsel and not having an ineffective counsel was recently made with chilling clarity by Circuit Judge Alvin B. Rubin of the Fifth Federal Circuit in *Riles v. McCotter,* 799 F. 2d 947 (5th Cir. 1986). In this case the defendant was sentenced to death after defense counsel failed to raise on direct appeal the possible improper exclusion of two potential jurors during *voir dire,* failed to object to the trial court's prejudicial conduct during *voir dire,* and failed to object to the state's introduction during the penalty phase of psychiatric evidence concerning Riles's future dangerousness. In his appeal Riles claimed that counsel was ineffective in his defense, but the Fifth Circuit Court of Appeals denied his claim under the *Strickland* standard. In concurring with the court's decision, however, Judge Rubin noted that to say that counsel was not ineffective was not at all to say that Riles's lawyer was competent or that he provided the kind of counsel that should be afforded when a person's life is at stake. The difference, Judge Rubin concurred in *Riles,* is nothing less than the difference between life and death:

> The Constitution, as interpreted by the courts, does not require that the accused, even in a capital case, be represented by able or effective counsel. It requires representation only by a lawyer who is not ineffective under the standard set by *Strickland v. Washington.* Proof that the lawyer was ineffective requires proof not only that the lawyer bungled but also that his errors likely affected the result. . . . Consequently, accused persons who are represented by "not-legally-ineffective" lawyers may be condemned to die when the same accused, if represented by *effective* counsel, would receive at least the clemency of a life sentence. (p. 955)

Two final points need to be addressed here. First, a good case could be made that the Supreme Court has been less than sympathetic to the plight of the poorly represented capital defendant. The *Strickland* test is a demanding one and when judging the claim of ineffectiveness counsel is afforded a strong presumption of competence. When this is combined with the expedited postconviction procedures approved of by the Court in *Barefoot v. Estelle,* the result can be a rush to judgment of a defendant not afforded the quality of counsel we would expect to see in a capital case, with sometimes fatal consequences. A good example of this combination of events is *Taylor v. Maggio*, 727 F. 2d 341 (5th Cir. 1984). At his death penalty trial, Taylor's attorney failed to offer any resistance to the impaneling of an all-white jury (Taylor was black); failed to call any character witnesses to speak in Taylor's behalf during the penalty phase; and in fact failed to present any evidence in mitigation during the penalty phase. He did not even argue that Taylor did not deserve a death sentence. Perhaps not surprisingly, the jury sentenced Taylor to death. Taylor had new, volunteer counsel to handle his post conviction appeals, a lawyer who was still in his first year of practice, and who had less than two weeks to file a claim of ineffective assistance of counsel in four different courts. Two days after his unsuccessful hearing on this issue in the federal court of appeals, and two weeks after obtaining his new lawyer, Taylor was put to death.[31]

The case of *Taylor v. Maggio* brings up a second and final issue regarding the adequate representation of capital defendants. Since *Gregg v. Georgia* the constitutional right to counsel in capital cases has meant the right to have counsel at trial and for the first direct appeal. Prior to 1989 there was no clear constitutional right to counsel in the labyrinthine network of state and federal postconviction remedies, in spite of the fact that such postconviction litigation is among the most complex law to practice. Judge John C. Godbold of the federal court of appeals for the Eleventh Circuit calls federal postconviction law "the most complex area of the law I deal with" (1987, 23–24). Moreover, this state and federal postconviction process is of no small concern to capital defendants. Michael Mello cites evidence that success rates for federal *habeas corpus* petitions is approximately 70 percent in capital cases, while only 6.5 percent in noncapital cases (Mello 1988, 520–521). He further notes that in one of the busiest federal circuits for death penalty cases, the Eleventh Circuit, in one half of the fifty-six *habeas* appeals ruled on between 1976 and 1983 the court decided in favor of the capital defendant. This success rate is after both a state trial court and an appeals court, as well as state postconviction courts and the U.S. Supreme Court, have examined and rejected the defendant's claims (see Amsterdam 1987).

It may appear at first, then, that given the complexity and importance of state and federal postconviction relief, capital defendants would be afforded a constitutional right to counsel during these processes as well as at the original trial and direct appeal. This issue was directly confronted by the U.S. Supreme Court in 1989 in *Murray v. Giarratano*, 109 S.Ct. 2765 (1989). *Giarratano* was a class action case brought before the Court by Joseph Giarratano on behalf of indigent Virginia death row inmates who were unrepresented in their postconviction hearings. The essential argument was that given the complexity of postconviction death penalty appeals and the poverty of death row inmates, the constitutional requirement of meaningful access to the courts requires the appointment of counsel for those unable to afford it.

In a plurality opinion written by Chief Justice Rehnquist, the Court in

Giarratano rejected this claim holding that the Constitution *does not* require states to provide counsel to death row inmates pursuing their postconviction remedies. Rehnquist noted that state postconviction proceedings are not themselves constitutionally required and that the procedural safeguards applied by the Court in its previous cases at the trial stage, where the jury can hear testimony and evidence and sift through such information and determine the questions of guilt and punishment, are sufficient to assure the reliability of imposed death sentences.

The Execution of Special Groups of Capital Defendants

In addition to pursuing various procedural reforms of death penalty law, the Supreme Court has also addressed important substantive issues. In this section we deal briefly with the issue of the execution of special groups of defendants (those who have killed a police officer, those who are currently serving a life sentence, the insane, the mentally retarded, the young). In the next section we will examine in more detail the issue of the appropriateness of capital punishment for offenses not involving the killing of another person.

Mandatory Death Sentences for Narrow Categories of Murderers. In *Woodson v. North Carolina* and *S. Roberts v. Louisiana* the Supreme Court struck down mandatory death sentences for the offense of first-degree murder. They did not, however, rule out the possibility that death could be a mandatory punishment for a more narrowly defined crime, such as the murder of a police officer or murder committed by a prison inmate serving a life sentence.[32] These issues appeared in the cases of *H. Roberts v. Louisiana,* 431 U.S. 633 (1977) and *Sumner v. Shuman,* 483 U.S. 66 (1987). In *H. Roberts* the Court struck down a mandatory death penalty for those who murdered police officers. In remaining faithful to its principle established in *Woodson* and *Lockett* that death sentences should be individualized to the unique culpability of defendants, the Court held that the sentencing authority is required to consider the unique features of each case: "The fundamental respect for humanity underlying the Eighth Amendment . . . requires consideration of the character and record of the individual offender and circumstances of the particular offense as a constitutionally indispensable part of the process of inflicting the penalty of death" (p. 636). The Court followed a similar rationale in *Sumner v. Shuman.*

Raymond Shuman was convicted in Nevada of first-degree murder in 1958 and sentenced to life imprisonment without the possibility of parole. In 1975 while serving that sentence Shuman killed another inmate. Existing Nevada law stipulated that murder committed by a person serving a life sentence is a capital murder and that all capital murderers shall be punished by death. Shuman was sentenced to death under that law for the second murder. The U.S. Supreme Court affirmed the federal district court and the Ninth Circuit Court of Appeals judgment that Sumner's death sentence was invalid because the Nevada mandatory statute violated the Eighth and Fourteenth Amendments. Basing its decision on the *Lockett/Eddings* principle, the Court held that the need to ensure that death sentences are individualized to the offender's own unique culpability requires the capital sentencer to hear any and all mitigating circumstances. It was not that Nevada, or any other state, could not put to death inmates serving life sentences who kill again, it is that they could not summarily do so. Any legitimate state interest in executing these persons (deterrence, retribution) could be satisfied through a guided discretion statute that affords individualized sentencing.

Execution of the Mentally Ill and Retarded. One of the recognized problems on death rows throughout the United States is the precarious mental condition of those who occupy them. For example, Lewis et al. (1986, 840–841) clinically evaluated fifteen death row inmates who were close to the date of their execution. She and her colleagues reported that five of the fifteen had "major neurological impairments," including "seizures, paralysis, and cortical atrophy"; six death row inmates were evaluated to be chronically psychotic; and three others were "episodically psychotic." In a later study, Lewis and her colleagues (1988) examined the mental condition of fourteen juveniles on death rows (40% of the total juvenile population then on death row). They reported that nine of these fourteen had serious neurological abnormalities, seven were psychotic, and twelve of the fourteen had IQ scores lower than 90. In addition to these clinical data are interview data from occupants of death rows (Johnson 1981). As a result of their long stay on death row with little to do, and under virtually twenty-four-hours-a-day lockup while living under the grim shadow of their impending death, many inmates demonstrate symptoms of mental illness. A pragmatic question arises, then, as to the constitutionality of executing those who go insane after their crime has been committed while under a sentence of death.[33] This question came to the Court's attention in the case of *Ford v. Wainwright,* 477 U.S. 399 (1986).

Alvin Ford was convicted of murder in 1974 in a Florida court and sentenced to death. There was no indication either at the time of his offense or during his trial that Ford was mentally ill. However, during his long stay on death row, over ten years, he began to exhibit bizarre behavior, including delusions and feelings of paranoia and persecution. By 1983 Ford's delusions reached the point where he began to refer to himself as "Pope John Paul III" and believed that 135 of his friends and family were being held hostage in the prison and that he was their only salvation. When interviewed by a psychiatrist, Dr. Harold Kaufman, Ford, while acknowledging the existence of the death penalty, denied that he would ever be executed because he owned the prisons and controlled the governor of Florida through mental telepathy. Subsequent to this interview Ford became almost completely incomprehensible, speaking only in a bizarre, codelike language.

Following Florida law, a panel of three psychiatrists appointed by the governor examined Ford for twenty-five minutes. While differing in their diagnoses, all three did agree that Ford understood why he was going to be executed and was therefore sane enough to be put to death. On April 30, 1984 the governor of Florida signed Ford's death warrant, and the state of Florida prepared to execute him. Ford's counsel sought a stay of execution and an evidentiary hearing on the question of Ford's fitness to be executed. The U.S. Supreme Court agreed to hear Ford's claim that the Eighth Amendment's prohibition against cruel and unusual punishment prohibits the execution of the insane.

Writing for the majority of the Ford Court, which held that the execution of the insane is unconstitutional, Justice Marshall noted that the common law has long forbidden the execution of mentally ill defendants, and this prohibition is no less commanding today than in the past. He further stated that in addition to constituting an affront to human decency and humanity, executing the insane would further no legitimate state interest such as deterrence or retribution. In dissenting from the *Ford* majority, Justice Rehnquist and Chief Justice Burger would have allowed Ford's execution under the theory that the determination of mental "fitness" or sanity for execution is an executive duty. They believed that when the governor of Florida signed Ford's death warrant after presumably examining the reports of the panel of psychiatrists, Ford was declared sane enough to be put to death and the state of Florida should have been permitted to carry out that sentence.

Related to the execution of those defendants who become mentally ill while on death row is the issue of the constitutionality of putting to death the mentally retarded.[34] The American Association on Mental Retardation (AAMR) defines mental retardation as significantly below average general intellectual functioning (Ellis and Luckasson 1985). Subaverage general intellectual functioning is understood as an IQ score below 70 on a standardized intelligence test (with a mean score of 100). There are, of course, variations within this range. Mildly retarded persons have IQ scores which range from 70 to 50–55; moderate retardation is defined as those with IQ scores from 50–55 to 35–40, severely retarded from 35–40 to 20–25, and profoundly retarded are those with IQ scores below 20–25.

In relation to mental retardation and the criminal justice system, Ellis and Luckasson (1985) have noted that courts have been reluctant to hold that mental retardation results in complete exculpation from criminal responsibility. With regard to capital sentencing, the Supreme Court's ruling (in *Lockett* and *Eddings*) would only seem to require that the sentencing authority take the mental capacity of the defendant into account as a mitigating circumstance in its sentencing decision, it does not preclude the execution of the mentally retarded defendant. In fact, in recent years capital defendants of subnormal intelligence have been put to death. For example, Reid (1987) notes that James Henry executed in 1984 had an IQ in the low 70's, Ivan Stanley also executed that year had an IQ that measured 61 as an adolescent and 81 at the time of his trial, Morris Mason put to death in 1985 had an IQ of 66, Jerome Bowden executed in 1986 had an IQ that ranged from 59 to 65, and James Roach executed in 1985 had an IQ score that ranged from 69 to the low 70's. In none of these cases did the United States Supreme Court halt the execution because of the diminished mental capacity of the defendant. It directly addressed the issue as to whether or not the Eighth Amendment forbids the execution of a capital defendant who is mentally retarded in 1989 in *Penry v. Lynaugh,* 109 S.Ct. 2934 (1989).

Johnny Paul Penry was convicted and sentenced to death in Texas in 1979 of the rape and murder of Pamela Carpenter. Before her death Pamela Carpenter gave the police a description of her attacker, and the police were led to suspect Penry, who had recently been paroled from a previous conviction for rape. During police interrogation, Penry confessed to the crime. At a competency hearing before his trial was to begin, Penry was examined by a clinical psychologist, Dr. Jerome Brown, who testified that Penry was mentally retarded. Dr. Brown stated that his testing of Penry's intelligence indicated that Penry had an IQ of 54, with the mental age of a child six and one-half years old and the social maturity of a nine or ten year old. The jury at the competency hearing found Penry competent to stand trial. At his trial for capital murder, Penry's confessions were deemed to be voluntarily given and were introduced into evidence. The jury rejected Penry's insanity defense and convicted him of capital murder. During the penalty phase clinical evidence was introduced concerning Penry's mental retardation; in addition, his mother testified that he was unable to learn in school and never finished the first grade. After hearing all evidence regarding penalty, Penry's jury answered all three questions under Texas' capital punishment law in the affirmative and Penry was sentenced to death. The Texas Court of Criminal Appeals affirmed his conviction and sentence holding that Penry's mental retardation did not prohibit the imposition of the death penalty.

Penry's case went through the federal postconviction process and the Supreme Court granted *certiorari* in part to determine whether or not it was "cruel and unusual" under the Eighth Amendment to execute a mentally retarded person who possesses Penry's diminished intellectual abilities. In his brief before the Court, Penry argued that because of their diminished moral culpability it would be cruel and unusual punishment to execute mentally retarded persons who have mental ages like himself of 7 or lower. In addition, citing public opinion polls which show little support for the execution of the mentally retarded, Penry argued that to do so would go against a prevailing national consensus against it. Although remanding Penry's death sentence on other grounds,[35] the Supreme Court rejected his contention that the Eighth Amendment to the Constitution forbids the execution of a capital defendant with a mental age of 7. The question is, why would the Court countenance the execution of a defendant with such a diminished mental age?

In the first place, the *Penry* Court rejected the claim that there is a national consensus against the execution of mentally retarded defendants. The evidence that the Court refers to, however, is not public opinion polls, but legislation, which indicates that only one state explicitly prohibits the execution of the retarded. In relation to Penry's claim that capital defendants with a mental age of 7 do not possess sufficient moral culpability to be punished by death, the Court claims that mildly to moderately retarded persons vary a great deal in their mental capacities and reasoning ability so that a general rule excluding them from criminal responsibility is unwarranted. The majority noted that defendants with an even greater mental deficiency than Penry, the severely and profoundly retarded, would not reach the stage of capital trial because the normal rule of an insanity defense would exclude them. Rather than create a general rule for all capital defendants based upon Penry's diminished mental age, the Court noted that mental capacity should simply be regarded as one of a number of mitigating factors to be duly considered by the capital sentencing authority.

The Execution of Juveniles. There have been relatively few executions of capital defendants who were under the age of eighteen when they committed their offense. Since 1930, when official records of executions were initiated, until the end of May 1990, less than 3 percent of the 3,971 executions were of juvenile offenders. From the resumption of capital punishment in 1977 until September of 1990, there have been 140 executions, of which four involved juveniles: Charles Rumbaugh, James Terry Roach, Jay Kelly Pinkerton, and Dalton Prejean.[36] In addition, juvenile offenders continue to be placed on death rows across the United States. At the end of September 1990, 32 of 2,393 persons under a state sentence of death (31 males and 1 female) were under the age of eighteen at the time of their offense.[37]

In the past, states have executed offenders who were younger than seventeen years old at the time of their crime and the time of their execution. For example, James Lewis, Jr. was fourteen years old at the time of his conviction and only fifteen when he was executed by the state of Mississippi on July 23, 1947. Lewis's codefendant, Charles Trudell, was also only fourteen when the offense was committed and was sixteen when executed on the same day as Lewis. Perhaps the most dramatic execution of a juvenile since 1930, however, was the case of George Junis Stinney, Jr. Stinney, a black South Carolina youth, was arrested at age fourteen for the rape and murder of two white girls. After forty minutes of questioning following his arrest Stinney confessed to the crimes. Stinney's trial began on April 24, 1944 before an all-white jury. The prosecution took less than thirty minutes to present its case, and the defense, while raising the issue of Stinney's youth, called no witnesses and presented no evidence in his behalf. The jury received its final instructions around 4:55 that afternoon and ten minutes later returned its verdict of guilty without mercy, sentencing Stinney to death. On June 16th, 1944, approximately three months after his arrest, George Stinney, who was fourteen years old, five feet one inch tall and weighing less than one hundred pounds, was strapped into South Carolina's electric chair and put to death.[38]

Although state trial courts have consistently considered the defendant's age when making its sentencing decision in capital cases, up until recently there was never an explicit prohibition against the execution of someone who was a minor at the time of their offense. Since giving its approval to capital punishment under some sentencing schemes in 1976, the United States Supreme Court has, however, shown an interest in regarding age as a special status in capital cases. In three 1976 cases the Court explicitly referred to the defendant's age as an important factor in determining a defendant's appropriate sentence. In *Gregg v. Georgia,* although the Georgia statute did not explicitly list factors in mitigation of penalty (such as age), the Court read the statutory requirement that mitigating factors be considered to include the age of the defendant: ". . . the jury's attention is focused on the characteristics of the person who committed the crime . . . his youth . . ." (p. 197). The Florida statute approved in *Proffitt* included the following as one of the statutory enumerated mitigating circumstances: "The age of the defendant at the time of the crime" [Florida Statutes Ann. Section 921.141 (6) (Supp. 1976–1977)]. Finally, in *Jurek,* although the Texas statute did not provide for either statutory aggravating or mitigating circumstances, the Court approved it, noting that Texas juries would consider the age of the defendant when making a determination as to the defendant's likelihood of offending in the future, one of the "special conditions" under Texas law.[39]

Several times after *Gregg* the Supreme Court has directly had before it the issue of the constitutionality of executing juvenile offenders. In the case of *Bell v. Ohio,* 438 U.S. 637 (1978), the companion case to *Lockett v. Ohio,* the defendant was sixteen years old at the time of the offense for which he was convicted and sentenced to death. On appeal, Bell's attorney claimed that under Ohio law the sentencing authority was not entitled to treat Bell's age as a mitigating circumstance,[40] and that the execution of a defendant who was sixteen years old at the time of the crime was constitutionally forbidden by the Eighth Amendment. The Ohio Supreme Court affirmed Bell's death sentence, finding that Ohio's restriction of mitigating circumstances was valid and that the death penalty could be imposed upon a defendant who was sixteen years old at the time of the offense. In Bell's case the Supreme Court of the United States declined to rule on the constitutionality of executing one who committed a capital crime as a juvenile, but did remand it for resentencing based on its holding in *Lockett* that the trial court should not be restricted from hearing relevant mitigating evidence.

A few years after *Bell,* in 1982, the U.S. Supreme Court did agree to hear a case for the purpose of determining whether the Constitution prohibited the execution of one who was sixteen years old at the time of their offense. In *Eddings v. Oklahoma* the defendant, Monty Lee Eddings, was convicted of the first-degree murder of a police officer and sentenced to death. At his penalty phase hearing, the state alleged three aggravating circumstances: (1) that the murder was especially heinous, atrocious, or cruel; (2) that the murder was committed for the purpose of avoiding a lawful arrest; and (3) that there was a probability that the defendant would constitute a continuing threat to society. On his behalf, Eddings introduced as mitigating evidence the circumstances of his troubled youth, which included a broken home and substantial physical abuse, and testimony from a sociologist who testified that Eddings was treatable, a state psychologist who stated that Eddings had an antisocial personality which he could possibly mature out of, and a psychiatrist who testified that Eddings could be successfully rehabilitated over a fifteen- to twenty-year period. At the end of the penalty phase the trial court judge sentenced Eddings to death. He stated that he found all three of the state's aggravating circumstances, but found only one mitigating factor—Eddings's youth. The judge stated that he could not consider Eddings's troubled childhood or emotional disturbance as proper mitigating circumstances. The Oklahoma Court of Criminal Appeals affirmed the conviction and sentence.

The U.S. Supreme Court originally granted *certiorari* on the issue as to whether the Eighth Amendment prohibits the death penalty from being inflicted on one who committed a capital crime at age sixteen. The Court did not decide Eddings's case on this ground, however; it chose instead to avoid this new constitutional issue and vacated his death sentence because the trial judge's refusal to hear and consider all relevant evidence in mitigation was a violation of the Court's earlier *Lockett* decision. In a dissenting opinion, Chief Justice Burger, joined by Justices White, Blackmun, and Rehnquist, essentially criticized the majority for its failure of nerve in accepting an "11th-hour claim"[41] and would have found no constitutional impediment to the execution of sixteen-year-old offenders like Eddings.

After *Eddings* the Court was repeatedly petitioned to decide the constitutional issue of a lower age limit for the execution of criminal defendants but declined to do so.[42] As a result, the Supreme Court had left the minimum age requirement for executions at the discretion of state legislatures. In 1987, of the thirty-seven states that allow for the death penalty, nineteen have no minimum age at which it would be unconstitutional to put a capital defendant to death. In the eighteen death penalty states that have enacted legislation placing a minimum age for the imposition of capital punishment, all of them require that the defendant be at least sixteen years old at the time of the offense. After ignoring the constitutional issue regarding the execution of juveniles for several years, in 1988 the U.S. Supreme Court finally moved in the direction of resolving it. The first attempt in this effort was *Thompson v. Oklahoma,* 108 S.Ct. 2687 (1988).

William Thompson was fifteen years old when he and several accomplices brutally murdered his former brother-in-law on January 23, 1983. Thompson's case was waived from juvenile to adult court where he was tried, convicted, and sentenced to death. The Oklahoma Court of Criminal Appeals affirmed both the conviction and sentence. The U.S. Supreme Court granted *certiorari* to consider the narrow question as to ". . . whether a sentence of death is cruel and unusual punishment for a crime committed by a 15-year-old child. . . ." The *Thompson* Court held in a 5–3 decision (Justice Kennedy took no part in the decision) that the execution of someone who was fifteen years old at the time of the offense was constitutionally forbidden by the Eighth Amendment's "cruel and unusual punishments" clause.

There was a four-justice plurality opinion written in *Thompson* by Justice Stevens (joined by Justices Brennan, Marshall, and Blackmun) which concluded that there was a national consensus against the execution of one who was fifteen when the capital offense was committed. The plurality noted that among those states that have included a minimum death-eligibility age in their capital punishment statutes, all of them require that the defendant be at least sixteen years old at the time of the offense. In concluding that the execution of a fifteen-year-old offender would be offensive to contemporary standards of decency, the plurality also noted the fact that the international community has virtually abandoned the execution of juveniles, and juries in the United States have traditionally been reluctant to impose death sentences on offenders who were fifteen years of age. Finally, noting the diminished culpability of young offenders, the plurality concluded that two legitimate state interests served by capital punishment, deterrence and retribution, would not be furthered by the execution of a fifteen year old.

The fifth and critical vote in *Thompson* came from Justice O'Connor who concurred with the judgment of the plurality that fifteen-year-old offenders cannot constitutionally be executed, but did so on much more narrow legal grounds. Justice O'Connor did not accept the plurality's conclusion that a national consensus existed that railed against the execution of fifteen-year-old offenders. Instead, she would forbid states like Oklahoma from executing those who were fifteen years old at the time of their offense under a statute that did not directly specify a minimum age for death-eligibility. Oklahoma was one of the nineteen states whose capital punishment statute provided no minimum age barrier for the death penalty, although it did authorize juveniles to be transferred from juvenile to adult court where they could face a death sentence. Justice O'Connor's opinion essentially asserted that states, like Oklahoma, that did not establish a minimum death-eligibility age did not give the issue the careful attention that it deserves. Until they do, she concludes, they cannot put fifteen-year-old capital offenders to death.

In a dissenting opinion to *Thompson,* Justice Scalia, writing for himself, Chief Justice Rehnquist, and Justice White, concluded that there was nothing in the Constitution that precluded states from executing those who were fifteen years old at the time of their offense. Scalia first notes that there was nothing in the intent of the Framers of the Eighth Amendment to preclude the execution of juvenile offenders. He also disagrees with the plurality's assessment of the national mood regarding the execution of young offenders. He claims that since most state legislatures that have decided to retain some form of capital punishment have theoretically allowed for the possibility of executing fifteen-year-old defendants, it can hardly be argued that there is national sentiment against the practice. In addition, while the plurality interpreted the infrequency of the execution of juveniles as indicative of the capriciousness of the death penalty, Justice Scalia countered that this simply reflects careful selectivity on the part of discerning jurors reluctant to sentence most young capital defendants to death.

With the decision in *Thompson,* then, there were at least three Justices (Scalia, Rehnquist, and White) who held the opinion that the Eighth Amendment to the Constitution did not prohibit states from executing fifteen-year-old murder defendants who were deemed to be responsible enough to be tried as adults and who were sentenced to death after an individualized consideration of all the facts of their case including the fact that they were of tender years when the offense was committed. The fractured *Thompson* decision reflects a Court divided on the issue of the constitutionality of the execution of juveniles, however, with a bare majority holding to the position that fifteen-year-old defendants cannot be executed without careful and deliberate consideration of that issue by the state's legislature.

Thompson v. Oklahoma was not the last word from the United States Supreme Court on the constitutionality of executing juvenile capital defendants. In its very next term, the Court decided two other cases, *Stanford v. Kentucky* and *Wilkins v. Missouri,* 109 S.Ct. 2969 (1989) where the issue was the constitutionality of death sentences for capital defendants who were sixteen (Wilkins) or seventeen (Stanford) years old at the time of their offense. Both of these cases involved gruesome murders, and as in *Thompson,* in deciding whether or not it is constitutionally acceptable to execute sixteen- and seventeen-year-old defendants, the Court looked to legislative authorizations and the behavior of capital juries as indicators of the acceptability of executing offenders of these ages. The decision in *Stanford* was as fractured as that in *Thompson,* with one critical difference. In *Stanford* a four-justice plurality (Scalia, Rehnquist, White, and Kennedy) was joined by a narrow concurring vote from Justice O'Connor in holding that the Constitution *does not* prohibit the execution of capital defendants who were sixteen or seventeen years old when they committed their crime.

In his opinion for the plurality, Justice Scalia notes that of thirty-seven states that permit capital punishment, only fifteen (41%) decline to impose it on sixteen-year-old offenders and only twelve (32%) decline to impose it on seventeen-year-old offenders. The absence of a legislative rejection of capital punishment for sixteen- and seventeen-year-old offenders is interpreted by Scalia as evidence that contemporary standards of decency would not find such executions abhorrent. In terms of the number of death sentences meted out and actually imposed on sixteen- and seventeen-year-old capital offenders, he reaffirms his dissenting view in *Thompson* that this merely reflects the opinion of juries that death sentences for minors should *rarely* be imposed, not that they should *never* be imposed. In Justice O'Connor's pivotal concurring opinion (of no more than one and one-half pages) she concludes that the Eighth Amendment does not prohibit the execution of sixteen- and seventeen-year-old offenders because there is no clear national consensus against it. She is led to this conclusion by the fact that when state legislatures have set a minimum age for death eligibility every one has fixed the age at sixteen years or above.

The Constitutionality of the Death Penalty for Nonmurderers

In its *Gregg* opinion, the United States Supreme Court held that capital punishment *for the crime of murder* is not unconstitutional under some sentencing schemes.[43] In *Gregg* and its companion cases, however, the Court said nothing about the constitutionality of capital punishment for other kinds of crimes. We saw in Chapter 1 that historically, executions have been carried out as the authorized punishment for a number of different offenses, including murder, kidnapping, treason, rape, carnal knowledge, robbery, perjury in a capital case, burglary, and arson. The two most frequent offenses for which the penalty of death was imposed were murder and rape. Of the approximately 3,800 persons executed from 1930 to 1967 (before the modern moratorium on executions), only about 14 percent were for nonhomicide offenses, and of these approximately 85 percent were for rape.

In addition to murder, the Georgia statute approved in *Gregg* included five offenses as potentially capital ones: kidnapping for ransom or where the victim is harmed, armed robbery, rape, treason, and aircraft hijacking. The U.S. Supreme Court reviewed the constitutionality of capital punishment for the rape of an adult woman in the 1977 case of *Coker v. Georgia*, 433 U.S. 584 (1977). In a 6–2–1 decision (Justice Powell concurred in part and dissented in part, Chief Justice Burger and Justice Rehnquist dissented), the Court held that capital punishment for the offense of the rape of an adult woman was unconstitutional because it was excessive and disproportionate: ". . . a sentence of death is grossly disproportionate and excessive punishment for the crime of rape and is therefore forbidden by the Eighth Amendment as cruel and unusual punishment" (p. 592). In announcing its decision, the plurality stated that in order to determine whether or not a punishment is excessive and therefore unconstitutional in relation to a given crime, it was employing a two-pronged test: (1) "if it makes no measurable contribution to acceptable goals of punishment and hence is nothing more than the purposeless and needless imposition of pain and suffering; or (2) is grossly out of proportion to the severity of the crime" (p. 592).

One objective indicator as to the excessiveness of a punishment can be found in how willing states are to employ it for a particular offense. Examining existing state death penalty statutes, Justice White reported that of all the states that decided to retain the death penalty after *Furman,* only Georgia authorizes a sentence of death for the nonfatal rape of an adult woman. As further evidence of the fact that it is generally thought excessive, White notes that Georgia juries have sentenced rapists to death only six times from 1973 to 1977. Having examined these objective indicators, White then writes that it is ultimately the Court's own judgment that must be exercised to determine the excessiveness of a given punishment:

> These recent events evidencing the attitude of state legislatures and sentencing juries do not wholly determine this controversy, for the Constitution contemplates that in the end our own judgment will be brought to bear on the question of the acceptability of the death penalty under the Eighth Amendment. (p. 584)

While not depreciating the egregiousness of a rape,[44] the Court's own judgment in this matter is that the death penalty is a disproportionate penalty. It is excessive, because while deserving of a severe penalty, rape is a less serious offense than murder. Rape is less serious, the Court notes, because "[t]he murderer kills; the rapist, if not more than that, does not" (p. 598).

The importance of the *Coker* case, then, is that it concerns more than a holding that death is an excessive penalty for the nonfatal rape of an adult woman. The majority in *Coker* provide a two-pronged test for determining whether or not a particular punishment is excessive and therefore impermissibly cruel and unusual. A punishment is excessive if it fails to further a legitimate state interest such as deterrence or rehabilitation, or if it is flagrantly out of proportion to the seriousness of the crime. Applying this test to the penalty of death for rape, the Court determined that it is an excessive penalty because the crime of rape, however harrowing for the victim and society, does not involve the actual taking of a human life. In this regard, then, the Court in *Coker* appeared to be adopting the position that death is an impermissibly excessive penalty to impose on a defendant who did not him/herself take a life. This interpretation is given some credence in that immediately after it was decided the Court used the *Coker* rationale to strike down as "cruel and unusual" the imposition of the death penalty for the offense of kidnapping where there was no loss of life [*Eberheart v. Georgia*, 433 U.S. 917 (1977)].

In addition to rape and kidnapping, the Court has ventured with its proportionality theory into other substantive areas, importantly in the realm of extending the felony-murder rule to include aiders and abettors (nontriggermen) of a homicide. Under a felony-murder rule, if a defendant commits a homicide (even unintentionally) during the commission of a felony, that homicide is considered first-degree murder. The malice aforethought necessary to establish first-degree murder is implied from the offender's intent to commit the felony. One who aids and abets an offense is one who actively and knowingly facilitates another in the commission of a crime. These issues, and their relevance to the death penalty, came together in *Enmund v. Florida*, 458 U.S. 782 (1982).

In April of 1975 Earl Enmund participated in a robbery with two accomplices, Jeanette and Sampson Armstrong. While Enmund waited in a getaway car some 200 yards from the scene of the robbery, his two accomplices robbed and fatally shot an elderly couple.[45] All three offenders were charged with first-degree murder and robbery. Enmund and Sampson Armstrong were tried together, at which time the prosecutor asserted that Sampson was the one who fired the fatal shots at the Kerseys. The jury found Enmund and Armstrong guilty of two counts of first-degree murder and one count of robbery and advised the trial judge that the sentence should be death. The judge agreed, sentencing both defendants to death, and the Florida Supreme Court affirmed noting that Enmund was equally responsible for the actions of his accomplice, Sampson Armstrong. Enmund appealed and the U.S. Supreme Court granted *certiorari* on the question as to whether the Eighth Amendment prohibits the imposition of capital punishment on one who did not take, attempt to take, or intend to take a life.

In coming to its decision that the death penalty imposed upon Enmund and others like him was excessive and therefore prohibited by the Eighth Amendment, the Court utilized its *Coker* test for determining the disproportionality between an offense and its punishment. Examining legislative enactments, the Court noted that there were very few states that authorized the death penalty for defendants like Enmund who had a minor participation in a robbery during which a murder was committed. As additional evidence of societal rejection of the death penalty for a nontriggerman convicted of felony murder, the Court pointed to the general reluctance of juries to sentence such defendants to death. Finally, recognizing that ultimately the Court's own judgment about excessiveness must be brought to bear on the problem, it stated that although robbery is a serious offense deserving of a serious punishment, it is not comparable to the offense of murder. When examining Enmund's own culpability, divorced from that of Sampson, his codefendant, the Court concluded that death is an excessive punishment for one whose participation in the offense is minor and who merely aids and abets a felony during the commission of which a murder is committed.

There are two things that the Court actually established in *Enmund:* first, that the Eighth Amendment prohibits the imposition of the death penalty for that subgroup of felony-murder defendants whose participation in the crime is minor and who did not take, attempt to take, nor intend to take a life; second, that the Eighth Amendment does not prohibit the death penalty for defendants, like Sampson Armstrong, who actually kill, attempt to kill, or intend to kill. *Enmund* does not bear, however, on the constitutionality of the death penalty for other defendants in between these two groups who may not have taken a life or have intended to take a life but whose participation in the offense was substantially more than minor. The permissibility of capital punishment for defendants in this category was addressed by the Court in *Tison v. Arizona,* 107 S.Ct. 1676 (1987).

On July 30, 1978 Ricky, Raymond, and Donald Tison smuggled guns into the Arizona State Prison in order to assist in the escape of their father, Gary, who was serving a life sentence for the killing of a prison guard during a previous escape attempt. After making good on their prison escape the Tisons drove through the Arizona desert on their way to Flagstaff. During the course of this journey they had a flat tire and a passing motorist stopped to render assistance. After commandeering this vehicle (a Mazda) and its four occupants, Gary Tison told Raymond to move their own car (a Lincoln) into the desert while he and a fellow escapee held the four occupants (a Mr. and Mrs. Lyons, their two-year-old son, and a fifteen-year-old niece) at gunpoint. After the four captives were ordered out into the desert to stand by the Lincoln, the Tison brothers were instructed to go back to the Mazda and get some water, presumably for the captives to have while stranded in the desert. While the Tison brothers were at the second car they heard gunshots and all four people were killed. The escape continued until stopped by a police roadblock, at which time Donald Tison was killed, Gary escaped into the desert where he died of exposure, and Raymond and Ricky Tison and the other escapee were captured. All three were tried for the crimes, and Raymond and Ricky, though not the triggermen, were convicted under a felony-murder statute and sentenced to death.

In reviewing their case, a majority of the Court took pains to differentiate the participation and culpability of the Tisons from that of Enmund in *Enmund v. Florida.* While acknowledging that the Tisons neither killed nor intended to kill anyone, the Court did adopt the position that the participation of the Tisons in the series of crimes was major rather than minor and that in carrying weapons into the prison in order to effect the escape of their father, and in failing to protect or assist the victims in any conceivable way, they demonstrated a reckless disregard for human life. This, the Court held, is sufficient to establish their culpability as fundamentally different from the defendant in *Enmund,* and as one deserving a sentence of death. The Court in *Tison,* then, proclaimed that although the death penalty cannot be imposed on defendants whose participation in a felony-murder is minor and who do not take, attempt to, or intend to take life, it is constitutionally permissible to do so for that group of felony-murderers whose participation in the crimes are major and who demonstrate a reckless indifference for human life. There are some nontriggermen who deserve to die, the *Tison* Court declared, and those states that choose to do so may put them to death.

Summary and Conclusions

In its 1976 *Gregg* decision the Supreme Court held that, at least for the offense of murder, procedurally reformed guided discretion death penalty statutes were constitutional. This decision simply approved a general form that an acceptable death penalty law could take, it said nothing about what was constitutionally required. The Court did not, therefore, end its involvement in the death penalty business with this case. In fact, *Gregg* merely marked the beginning of the Court's long and arduous journey into death penalty jurisprudence. In every term since *Gregg* the Supreme Court has handed down major decisions in its attempt to regulate the manner in which the states administer the death penalty.

Some of these decisions redefined what was constitutionally required of a state death penalty scheme. For example, in *Zant v. Stephens,* the Court declared that the purpose of an aggravated circumstance is not to guide and direct the discretion of the jury, but merely to narrow the range of the cases that are death eligible. Once a valid statutory aggravating circumstance was found, the capital jury may hear evidence with regard to other nonstatutory factors, even if they are improperly labeled statutory aggravating factors (*Zant v. Stephens, Barclay v. Florida*), and even if the reliability of the information heard is of dubious quality (*Barefoot v. Estelle*). The Court has also held that in spite of the importance given to comparative proportionality review in its *Gregg* decision, it is not a constitutional requirement of a valid death penalty scheme (*Pulley v. Harris*).

In other cases the Court has sought to define what the jury may and may not hear during the penalty phase of a capital trial. In *Lockett v. Ohio* it decided that the sentencer may not be precluded from hearing and giving independent weight to any mitigating evidence proffered by the defense in its argument for a sentence less than death. This mitigating evidence may include information about the defendant's character, involvement in the offense, and behavior *after* the offense has been committed (*Skipper v. South Carolina*). The Court has also restricted the kind of information that the sentencer may hear. If any general rule can be articulated, it would appear that the Court will not look favorably upon any evidence that diverts the sentencer's attention away from the offender or offense, such as any information that suggests that the sentencer's decision is not final (*Caldwell v. Mississippi*), information about the victim's personal characteristics (*South Carolina v. Gathers*), or information about the impact of the victim's death on family members (*Booth v. Maryland*).

One of the problems in ensuring the fair administration of capital punishment is the quality of legal representation given defendants as they move from trial to execution. In spite of the difficulty and importance of death penalty lawyering, there is abundant evidence that suggests that defense counsel in capital cases is not always as effective as it could be. The Court indicated that it was concerned with the quality of representation in capital cases by examining the issue in *Strickland v. Washington,* although in its decision it did not create a very exacting standard for competent counsel. In *Strickland* the Court held that capital defendants are not entitled to effective counsel, only that they are allowed "not ineffective" counsel. Under the *Strickland* standard, in order to demonstrate ineffective counsel, a capital defendant would have to show both that counsel's performance fell below "prevailing professional norms" and that counsel's subprofessional performance prejudiced the outcome of the trial. Although states are required to provide counsel for those accused of capital crimes up to and including their direct appeal, the Court has also determined that counsel is not required for the postconviction process (*Murray v. Giarratano*).

Finally, the Court has ventured into the area of the appropriateness of executing certain "special" groups of people. Consistent with its rejection of a mandatory death penalty for the general offense of murder in *Woodson v. North Carolina,* the Court rejected mandatory death sentences for more narrowly drawn offenses, such as the murder of a police officer (*H. Roberts v. Louisiana*) and murder committed by one already serving a life sentence (*Sumner v. Shuman*). The Court did not say that such killers could not be executed, just that the sentencer had to have the opportunity to hear and consider all factors that might argue for a lesser sentence. When it reviewed the constitutionality of executing the mentally retarded (*Penry v. Lynaugh*) and the insane (*Ford v. Wainwright*), the Court determined that while the latter could not be executed the retarded could be. The diminished mental capacity of the defendant would simply be a mitigating factor to be considered in the sentencer's determination of the appropriate penalty.

Other "special" groups of capital offenders have been given attention by the Supreme Court in their attempt to regulate state death penalty statutes. The constitutionality of executing juveniles was reviewed by the Court in *Thompson v. Oklahoma, Wilkins v. Missouri,* and *Stanford v. Kentucky* where the defendants were fifteen, sixteen, and seventeen years old respectively. In the *Thompson* decision, the Court did not automatically preclude the execution of fifteen-year-old offenders, though it did so in Thompson's specific case because the state of Oklahoma did not explicitly provide for the execution of offenders so young in its capital statute. In *Wilkins* and *Stanford,* the Court concluded that the Eighth Amendment does not preclude the execution of sixteen- and seventeen-year-old offenders. The Court has also determined that the death penalty is an unconstitutionally excessive punishment for those offenders who do not take life, attempt to take life, or intend to take life (*Enmund v. Florida*). It has, however, permitted the state to execute those offenders who may not themselves have killed but whose participation in a murder was major and who demonstrated a reckless disregard for human life.

Although we have reviewed many cases and examined a multitude of legal issues regarding capital punishment in this chapter, it should not be concluded that we have reviewed all of the issues or that the Supreme Court has discontinued its involvement in capital jurisprudence. There are numerous legal issues that are left unexamined by this chapter simply because they are too arcane for our more general review. In addition, as in the past, each term the Supreme Court continues to review and rule on death penalty cases and is rapidly adding to the body of already labyrinthine capital punishment law.

Notes

1. In the Court's plurality opinion in *Gregg,* Justice Stewart expressed the sentiment that the Georgia death penalty scheme was but one general form that a constitutionally valid state capital punishment scheme could take:

> We do not intend to suggest that only the above described procedures would be permissible under *Furman* or that any sentencing system constructed along these general lines would inevitably satisfy the concerns of *Furman.* . . . Rather, we have embarked upon this general exposition to make clear that it is possible to construct capital-sentencing systems capable of meeting *Furman's* constitutional concerns.

2. Under Ohio law at the time of Lockett's trial, the jury could hear only mitigating testimony directed to one or more of three issues: (1) that the victim had induced or facilitated the offense; (2) that it was unlikely the offense would have been committed if the defendant were not under duress, coercion, or strong provocation; (3) the offense was primarily the product of the defendant's psychosis or mental deficiency [Ohio Rev. Code Ann. Sec. 2929.03–2929.04 (B) (1975)]. Since the fact that Lockett had only a minor role in the murder does not directly address any of the three issues above, the trial judge did not allow her to introduce that fact as a mitigating circumstance.

3. This was precisely Justice White's point in his acerbic dissent from this part of the *Lockett* opinion:

> The Court has now completed its about-face since *Furman v. Georgia.* . . . Today it is held . . . that the sentencer may constitutionally impose the death penalty only as an exercise of its unguided discretion after being presented with all the circumstances which the defendant might believe to be conceivably relevant to the appropriateness of the penalty for the individual offender. (p. 622)

4. For a detailed accounting of this, see Weisberg's (1984) essay "Deregulating Death."

5. Under Georgia law, evidence of a defendant's prior convictions could legitimately be put before and considered by the jury; the issue was whether its designation as an "aggravating circumstance" was prejudicial.

6. Writing for the Court, Justice Stevens's opinion provides an interpretation of the Court's *Gregg* position regarding the purpose of statutory aggravating circumstances under a guided discretion capital sentencing scheme:

> . . . statutory aggravating circumstances play a constitutionally necessary function at the stage of legislative definition: they circumscribe the class of persons eligible for the death penalty. But the Constitution does not require the jury to ignore other possible

aggravating factors in the process of selecting, from among that class, those defendants who will actually be sentenced to death. What is important at the selection stage is an *individualized* determination on the basis of the character of the individual and the circumstances of the crime. (p. 2744)

7. The difference is that *Zant* requires the finding of at least one statutory aggravating factor; *Lockett* does not require the finding of a statutory mitigating factor before nonstatutory mitigating factors may be considered by the jury.

8. The most serious of Barclay's prior crimes was breaking and entering with intent to commit grand larceny.

9. Under Florida's statute the absence of a prior criminal history was a statutory mitigating factor. This was not the only error at Barclay's trial. Weisberg (1984, 356) correctly describes Barclay's penalty phase hearing as "a farce of errors." In overriding the jury's recommendation of a life sentence, the trial court judge, Judge Olliff, found several other aggravating circumstances that had little or no basis in either the facts of the case or state law. For example, Judge Olliff found as an aggravating circumstance the fact that Barclay's crime committed a great risk of death to more than one person, even though state law had restricted this circumstance to instances of terrorist bombings or plane hijackings, instances having nothing to do with Barclay's fact pattern. Judge Olliff also found as an aggravating circumstance the fact that Barclay was under a sentence of imprisonment at the time of the murder, determination that had no basis in fact in Barclay's case.

10. This is consistent with Justice Rehnquist's concurring opinion in *Zant v. Stephens* where he makes repeated references to the moral complexity of capital sentencing. For example, he states that during the penalty phase of a capital trial a jury hears evidence "on literally countless subjects" (p. 2755), that an aggravating circumstance is "simply one of the countless considerations weighed by the jury" (p. 2755), and that sentencing decisions rest on "countless facts and circumstances" (p. 2756).

11. See note 41, Chapter 2.

12. The state also submitted to the jury evidence of Barefoot's prior convictions and his "reputation for lawlessness." His criminal history consisted of two convictions for drug offenses and two convictions for the unlawful possession of a firearm. The state also introduced at the guilt phase of his hearing the fact that at the time of the murder Barefoot had escaped from a New Mexico jail where he was being held on charges of statutory rape. As regards his reputation for lawlessness, the state called several witnesses from towns in five states. These witnesses, without recalling specific instances of his conduct, testified that Barefoot had a bad reputation in their community.

13. Justice White in his majority opinion in *Barefoot,* joined by Justices Burger, Powell, Rehnquist, and O'Connor, described the limited role of federal review of state death sentences:

When the process of direct review . . . comes to an end, a presumption of finality and legality attaches to the conviction and sentence. The role of federal habeas proceedings, while important in assuring that constitutional rights are observed, is secondary and limited. Federal courts are not forums in which to relitigate state trials. Even less is federal habeas corpus a means by which a defendant is entitled to delay an execution indefinitely. (pp. 3391–3392)

Other Supreme Court justices have expressed similar outrage over the length of the appeals process. In a dissent from a stay of execution in 1983, Justice Powell (1989) expressed frustration in the delays caused by what he believes is frivolous litigation: "Once again . . . a typically 'last minute' flurry of activity is resulting in additional delay of the imposition of a sentence imposed almost a decade ago" [*Stephens v. Kemp,* 464 U.S. 1027 (1983) at p. 1032]. In a speech before the Criminal Justice Section of the American Bar Association on August 7, 1988, Justice Powell continued to be highly critical of the currrent system of capital appeals: ". . . our present system of multi-layered appeals has led to excessively repetitious litigation and years of delay between sentencing and execution. This delay undermines the deterrent effect of capital punishment and reduces public confidence in the criminal justice system" [published remarks (p. 1035) in the *Harvard Law Review* 102: 1035–1046 (1989)].

In concurring in a denial of *certiorari* and a request for a stay of execution in two different cases, Chief Justice Burger expressed a similar sentiment: "This case illustrates a recent pattern of calculated efforts to frustrate valid judgments after painstaking judicial review over a number of years . . ." [*Gray v. Lucas,* 463 U.S. 1237 (1983) at p. 1240]; "The argument so often advanced by the dissenters that capital punishment is cruel and unusual punishment is dwarfed by the cruelty of 10 years on death row inflicted upon this guilty defendant by lawyers seeking to turn the administration of justice into the sporting contest that Roscoe Pound denounced three-quarters of a century ago" [*Sullivan v. Wainwright,* 464 U.S. 109 (1963) at p. 112].

14. Thomas Barefoot was executed by the state of Texas on October 30, 1984, a year and three months after the Supreme Court decided his case.

15. Mello (1988, 548) cites as an example the case of Johnny Taylor, sentenced to death in Louisiana. Under the Fifth Circuit's rules Taylor had his *habeas* appeal heard and denied by the federal circuit court, on the same day he was denied relief in district court and only three days after losing in a state post-conviction proceeding.

16. The Court gave a mixed message about the indispensability of comparative proportionality review in its two other decisions that gave constitutional approval to state death penalty schemes, *Proffitt v. Florida* and *Jurek v. Texas.* Although the Florida statute approved in *Proffitt* provided for the automatic review of all imposed death sentences by the state supreme court, it did not specify the parameters of that review. In its own case law, the Florida Supreme Court did define its function as including a type of comparative review of death sentences similar to the Georgia court. In *State v. Dixon,* 283 So. 2d 1, 10 (1973) the Florida court said that it would review a particular death sentence "in light of the other decisions and determine whether or not the punishment is too great."

In *Jurek,* however, the Court approved the Texas statute which did not explicitly provide for proportionality review of death sentences, nor was it established in Texas case law. The statute does call for the direct appeal of all death sentences to the Texas Court of Criminal Appeals, a court with statewide jurisdiction, but the Texas court has not consistently defined one of its functions as comparative proportionality review. The U.S. Supreme Court did suggest in *Jurek* that the Texas court would ensure the consistency of death sentences: "By providing prompt judicial review of the jury's decision in a court with statewide jurisdiction, Texas has provided a means to promote evenhanded, rational, and consistent application of death sentences under law" [*Jurek v. Texas,* 428 U.S. 262 (1976) at 276].

17. Justice Powell's plurality opinion in *Gregg* concluded that "The review function of the Supreme Court of Georgia affords additional assurance that the concerns that prompted our decision in *Furman* are not present to any significant degree in the Georgia procedure applied here" (p. 207). Justice White's concurring opinion in *Gregg* expressed

similar confidence that state supreme court review would remedy the most gross injustices: "[I]f the Georgia Supreme Court properly performs the task assigned to it under the Georgia statute, death sentences imposed for discriminatory reasons or wantonly or freakishly for any given category of crime will be set aside" (p. 224). Finally, in accepting the "threshold theory" of statutory aggravating circumstances, Justice Stevens in his majority opinion in *Zant v. Stephens* alluded to the additional protection afforded by comparative proportionality review: "Our decision in this case depends in part on the existence of an important procedural safeguard, the mandatory appellate review of each death sentence by the Georgia Supreme Court to avoid arbitrariness and to assure proportionality" [*Zant v. Stephens*, 103 S.Ct. 2733 (1983) at 2749].

18. Under California law a capital jury first decides if the defendant is guilty of first-degree murder and if any of the "special circumstances" enumerated in the statute are present beyond a reasonable doubt (an example of a special circumstance is the act of murder during the commission of an armed robbery). If the jury finds the defendant guilty of first-degree murder and finds at least one special circumstance, the trial moves to a penalty phase. At this penalty phase hearing the jury hears evidence in aggravation and mitigation and determines whether the penalty should be death or life imprisonment without parole. If a death sentence is imposed the defendant moves to modify the verdict. The trial judge then renders an independent review of the jury's findings and whether or not the weight of the evidence supports those findings. If the judge denies the motion to modify the sentence there is an automatic appeal to the state supreme court. Regarding the parameters of this review, the statute simply states that if the trial judge does not modify the death sentence it "shall be reviewed." California case law has established that this review is of the factual validity of the evidence relied on by the trial court [*People v. Frierson*, Sup., 158 Cal. Rptr. 281 (1979)].

19. The judge noted that as a matter of state law he could not consider Eddings's home life and emotional problems as mitigating evidence, presumably because it had no probative value regarding his responsibility for the slaying of which he was convicted. In affirming the trial court's sentence, the Oklahoma Court of Criminal Appeals also found the presented (but ignored) mitigating evidence as irrelevant, because it did not provide a legal excuse from criminal responsibility.

20. Although trial courts generally give the defense wide liberty with respect to the kinds and quantity of evidence they may present in mitigation, the *Locket/Eddings* decisions do not give defense counsel the right to present *any evidence whatsoever* in mitigation. These two cases essentially stand for the principle that capital defendants have the constitutional right to present and have the sentencing authority give independent weight to any aspect of the crime or their character, background, or record that may call for a penalty less than death.

21. In his closing remarks to the jury, the prosecutor in *Gathers* read from some religious pamphlets the victim carried with him when killed, and made extensive comments to the jury about the victim's character: "He wasn't blessed with fame or fortune . . . he took things as they came along" (p. 2210).

22. While the right to counsel in capital cases was secured in 1932 in *Powell v. Alabama*, 287 U.S. 45 (1932), a similar constitutional right for indigent, noncapital felony defendants was established over three decades later in *Gideon v. Wainwright*, 372 U.S. 334 (1962).

23. Steven Raikin, staff director of the American Bar Association's Section on

Individual Rights and Responsibilities, has estimated that 99 percent of the defendants on death row who could not afford the cost of legal representation were indigent (Hengstler, 1987), "Attorneys for the Damned").

24. See, for example, Lewis 1979, "Killing the Killers." Lewis reports that the mean educational level of Florida's death row population was approximately the ninth grade, and that 15 percent had an IQ of less than 90. For a more general discussion of the competency of death row inmates, see Mello 1988, "Facing Death Alone."

25. See Godbold 1987, "You Don't Have to Be a Bleeding Heart." Judge John C. Godbold, a former chief judge for the United States Court of Appeals for the Eleventh Circuit (one of the busiest for death penalty law), noted that "[capital litigation] is the most complex area of the law I deal with."

26. See Marshall 1986, "Remarks on the Death Penalty Made at the Judicial Conference of the Second Circuit."

27. See *Young v. Kemp*, 758 F. 2d 514 (1985); *Hyman v. Aiken*, 824 F. 2d 1405 (4th Cir. 1987); *Osborn v. Shillinger*, 861 F. 2d 612 (1988); *Young v. Zant*, 677 F. 2d 792 (11th Cir. 1982); *House v. Balkcom*, 725 F. 2d 608 (11th Cir.), *cert. denied*, 469 U.S. 870 (1984); *Francis V. Spraggins*, 720 F. 2d 1190 (1983). For a more complete discussion of the effective assistance of counsel in capital cases, see Goodpaster 1983, "The Trial for Life"; Goodpaster 1986, "The Adversary System"; and Tabak 1986, "The Death of Fairness."

28. The Court in *Strickland* noted that

[w]hen a convicted defendant complains of the ineffectiveness of counsel's assistance, the defendant must show that counsel's representation fell below an objective standard of reasonableness . . . The proper measure of attorney performance remains simply reasonableness under prevailing professional norms. (p. 687)

29. The *Strickland* Court cautioned:

Judicial scrutiny of counsel's performance must be highly differential. . . . Because of the difficulties inherent in making the evaluation, a court must indulge in a strong presumption that counsel's conduct falls within the wide range of reasonable professional assistance; that is, the defendant must overcome the presumption that, under the circumstances, the challenged action "might be considered sound trial strategy." (p. 689).

30. This is not to say that capital defendants have not made successful ineffective assistance of counsel claims under the *Strickland* standard. One such case was *Thomas v. Kemp*, 796 F. 2d 1322 (11th Cir. 1986). Donald Thomas was sentenced to death by a Georgia jury for the murder of a nine-year-old boy. Thomas's attorney made very little effort in preparing for the penalty phase of the trial. The lawyer interviewed Thomas's mother but did not call her as a witness during the penalty hearing, and no attempt was made to contact other possible witnesses who could present mitigating testimony in his behalf. The defense side of the penalty phase was conducted in virtual silence. The Georgia Supreme Court affirmed both the conviction and sentence, but a federal district court vacated the sentence on the grounds that Taylor's counsel was ineffective. Counsel's failure to even examine the possibility of any witnesses to speak in mitigation was determined to fall below an objective standard of reasonableness—the first prong of the *Strickland* test. In determining whether or not the failure to present any defense witnesses was prejudicial—the second of the *Strickland* prongs—the district court examined the record and noted that several witnesses would have given evidence relevant to Thomas's previous mental and physical abuse, his mother's alcoholism, and other factors which would have constituted mitigating factors. Thomas prevailed on his ineffective counsel claim and his death sentence was vacated.

31. See Tabak 1986, "The Death of Fairness."

32. In his plurality *Woodson* opinion, Justice Stewart noted:

This case does not involve a mandatory death penalty statute limited to an extremely narrow category of homicide, such as murder by a prisoner serving a life sentence, defined in large part in terms of the character or record of the offender. We thus express no opinion regarding the constitutionality of such a statute (p. 287, note 7).

33. Those murderers who were mentally ill at the time of their crime could, of course, raise an insanity defense. Under a successful insanity defense defendants lack responsibility for their actions and cannot be punished by the criminal justice system.

34. See Blume and Bruck 1988, "Sentencing the Mentally Retarded to Death."

35. The Court remanded Penry's case for resentencing because the jury was not given explicit instructions that it could consider and give weight to the mitigating evidence of his diminished mental capacity by declining to impose the death penalty even though it found all three of the Texas statute's "special conditions." In the summer of 1990, Johnny Paul Penry was resentenced to death.

36. For a detailed account of the history of capital punishment for juvenile offenders, see 1987, *Death Penalty for Juveniles*.

37. NAACP Legal Defense and Education Fund, 1990 *Death Row, U.S.A.*

38. See 1987.

39. See *Jurek v. Texas*, 428 U.S. 262 (1976) at pp. 271–273.

40. As was true for Sandra Lockett, who could not introduce her minor involvement in the crime as a mitigating circumstance, Bell was prohibited from introducing his age. Existing Ohio law only permitted the jury to hear evidence on three statutory mitigating circumstances: (1) that the victim had induced or facilitated the offense; (2) that it was unlikely the offense would have been committed but for the fact that the defendant was under duress, coercion, or strong provocation; and (3) that the offense was primarily the product of the defendant's psychosis or mental deficiency [Ohio State Rev. Code Sec. 2929.03–2929–04 (B) (1975)].

41. The claim the majority ruled in favor of, that the judge's failure to consider all mitigating factors was unconstitutional in view of *Lockett*, was not raised by Eddings's counsel either in its brief to the Oklahoma Court of Criminal Appeals or to the U.S. Supreme Court in its petition for *certiorari*.

42. *Roach v. Martin*, 757 F. 2d 1463 (4th Cir. 1985), *cert. denied*, 106 S.Ct. 645 (1986); *Trimble v. State*, 300 Md. 387, 478 A. 2d 1143 (Md. 1983), *cert. denied*, 105 S.Ct. 1231 (1985); *Cannaday v. State*, 455 So. 2d 713 (Miss. 1984), *cert. denied*, 105 S.Ct. 1209 (1985); *High v. Zant*, 250 Ga. 693,300 S.E. 2d 654 (1983), *cert. denied*, 104 S.Ct. 2669 (1984); *Tokman v. State*, 435 So. 2d 664 (Miss. 1983), *cert. denied*, 104 S.Ct. 3574 (1984).

43. In *Gregg v. Georgia*, 428 U.S. 153 (1976), Justice Stewart, writing for a plurality of the Court, noted that

. . . we are concerned here only with the imposition of capital punishment for the crime of murder, and when a life has been taken deliberately by the offender, we cannot say that the punishment is invariably disproportionate to the crime. It is an extreme sanction, suitable to the most extreme of crimes.

In his concurring *Gregg* opinion (joined by Chief Justice Burger and Justice Rehnquist), Justice White similarly noted that the Court's decision pertains only to the validity of capital punishment for the offense of murder: "The issue in this case is whether the death penalty imposed for murder on petitioner Gregg under the new Georgia statutory scheme may constitutionally be carried out. I agree that it may."

44. In a rather poignant commentary, Justice White states:

We do not discount the seriousness of rape as a crime. It is highly reprehensible, both in a moral sense and in its almost total contempt for the personal integrity and autonomy of the female victim and for the latter's privilege of choosing those with whom intimate relationships are to be established. (p. 597)

45. The crime was perpetrated as follows: The Armstrongs approached the back door of the victim's home requesting water for an overheated car. When one of the victims, Mr. Kersey, came out of the house, Sampson Armstrong pointed a gun at him and told Jeanette to take his money. Mr. Kersey called out for help and his wife appeared with a gun, shooting and wounding Jeanette Armstrong. Sampson Armstrong (and perhaps Jeanette, the record is not clear) then shot and killed both of the Kerseys.

III
The Fair and Rational Imposition of the Death Penalty

4

Racial Discrimination and the Death Penalty

In Chapters 2 and 3 we reviewed some important features of the pre- and post-*Furman* death penalty statutes under which capital defendants have been sentenced to death. One of the most prominent features of these laws is that a sentence of death has almost never been the mandatory penalty for all defendants convicted of a given crime. Pre-*Furman* capital statutes gave the sentencing authority a great deal of discretion in the determination of the penalty in a potentially capital case. Under such statutes the jury was essentially instructed to use its own judgment in its penalty deliberation. Under post-*Furman* schemes, some degree of discretion is constitutionally required in capital cases. State capital punishment schemes must allow the defense wide latitude in presenting information to the sentencer that supports a sentence less than death, and such schemes must provide the sentencing authority the discretion to impose either the death penalty or a prison sentence on death-eligible defendants.

The evidence seems to indicate that both past and present capital juries frequently exercise their discretion not to sentence capital defendants to death. Under earlier, pre-*Furman* capital statutes, evidence reported by Sellin (1980, 69–74) revealed that less than 30 percent of all convicted murder defendants were sentenced to death (see also Johnson 1957; Kleck 1981, 794–795), and that in most states the proportion sentenced to death was much lower than that. More recent studies have shown that under procedurally reformed post-*Furman* capital punishment statutes, death sentences are imposed in fewer than one half of the cases where the defendant was convicted of first-degree murder and was, therefore, eligible to be sentenced to death (Arkin 1980; Zeisel 1981; Radelet 1981; Baldus et al. 1983, 1985, 1990; Nakell and Hardy 1987; Paternoster and Kazyaka 1988; Gross and Mauro 1989; Vito and Keil 1988).

Since juries may, but often do not, sentence a defendant to death even when they are convicted of a capital crime, a question arises as to what it is that distinguishes those who are condemned to die from those whose lives are spared. It is quite likely that part of this difference in sentence reflects distinctions in the offense or the offender. For example, capital sentencers have been shown to be more likely to impose a death sentence when a homocide involves another felony such as rape, armed robbery, or kidnapping, when it involves more than one victim or the slaying of a stranger rather than an acquaintance, when the homicide was conducted in a particularly brutal manner, or when the offender has a previous history of convictions for violent crimes (see the reviews by Nakell and Hardy 1987; Gross and Mauro 1989; Paternoster and Kazyaka 1988; and Bienen et al. 1988).

It is also conceivable that in some instances the imposition of a death sentence is influenced by nonlegal considerations, such as the race of the offender and/or victim. More specifically, when deciding which capital defendants should die and whose life should be spared, juries may be more inclined to sentence to death black than white offenders, particularly those black offenders who cross racial boundaries and slay a white person. Given the history of racial animus in the United States, both in society generally and in the criminal justice system, as well as the emotionally volatile nature of both capital crimes and capital punishment, it is reasonable to believe that the administration of the death penalty has in the past and may continue to be tainted with racial discrimination.

The purpose of this chapter is to review the relationship between race and the administration of capital punishment in the United States. In this effort we will study both historical and contemporary examples of racial bias in the administration of the death penalty. We will first examine early attempts by state legislatures to control their black population through obviously discriminatory Slave and Black Codes. We will then examine more specifically the treatment of black defendants under both pre- and post-*Furman* capital statutes. Where possible we will examine the effect of race at three critical decision-making points in the capital sentencing process: the decision of the prosecutor to charge or indict a defendant on a capital murder charge, the decision of the jury to impose a death sentence on a capital defendant, and the decisions of postconviction courts to overturn death sentences and state executives to commute them. We will end the chapter with a review of how the courts have dealt with the issue of racial discrimination through the exposition of two important death penalty cases, *Maxwell v. Bishop* and *McCleskey v. Kemp*.

Early Evidence of Racial Discrimination in the Legal System

It should come as a surprise to no one who is familiar with U.S. legal history that the enforcement of criminal laws in general and the imposition of capital punishment in particular may be plagued by racial discrimination. Throughout our history black Americans have disproportionately been the target of hostile treatment by the law, by both judicial and law enforcement systems. The Slave Codes enacted during the 1660s in the American colonies and both revised and extended during the late 1800s in the antebellum South in the form of Black

Codes were ways for the white population to control the conduct and lives of the black slave and free person.

Early Slave Codes defined the status of slavery as a life-long condition, that slaves could be inherited like any other form of property, that a child born to a slave mother was to carry her slave status, and that Christian baptism did not change the social or legal position of the child. As Kenneth Stampp (1956, 192–236) describes them, a characteristic feature of every Slave Code was that blacks were required to show deference and respect to all whites while expecting little or nothing in return. A slave could not strike, raise his hand, or use abusive language against his master and had to move out of the way when approached by whites, thus allowing their passage. Slave Codes did more than require a particular deferential demeanor from blacks, however; they regulated their every movement. Slaves were not to be outside of their master's property without a pass, nor could they congregate in numbers or be out on the streets after curfew; with rare exceptions they could not sell their free time or seek employment, neither could they learn to read or write. In most southern slave states slaves were not permitted to possess liquor, own animals, gamble, or raise certain crops such as cotton.[1]

The subordinate position in which these Slave Codes placed and ensured the placement of blacks was also characteristic of the criminal law, though perhaps with greater ruthlessness there. In *The Peculiar Institution* Stampp (1956, 210) describes antebellum southern Slave Codes in the following way:

> State criminal codes dealth more severely with slaves and free Negroes than with whites. In the first place, they made certain acts felonies when committed by Negroes but not when committed by whites; and in the second place, they assigned heavier penalties to Negroes than whites convicted of the same offense.

Potentially capital crimes abounded for blacks as virtually every slave state had a substantial number of crimes punishable by death if committed by blacks and lesser penalties if perpetrated by whites.[2] For example, a pre–Civil War Georgia statute provided that whites convicted of rape would be punished by imprisonment while slaves or free blacks could be put to death for any crime (White 1984, 70). In 1816 this law was amended so that the maximum term of imprisonment for a white convicted of a rape was set at twenty years while the punishment for blacks was death.

White males in the South were particularly careful in guarding the gentility of whites (see Cash 1941; Myrdal 1944; Genovese 1974), and this "rape complex" (Cash 1941, 116–120) was transferred to the criminal law. Antebellum criminal codes stipulated that blacks (slave and free) convicted of raping white women be either castrated or put to death (Berger et al. 1989, 441). There was not such mandatory penalty for whites, nor did many states criminalize the rape of a black woman (Genovese 1974). In addition to murder and rape, blacks could also be put to death for attempted murder and manslaughter, for the attempted rape of a white woman, for assaulting a white person (Stampp 1956, 210), and for various property offenses, such as arson and burglary.[3] In the laws of the antebellum states of Virginia, Louisiana, Tennessee, and Alabama, both slaves and free blacks could be and were sentenced to death for burglary, arson, and destruction of property, while whites who committed the same offenses received a short prison sentence or had to recompense the owner for the lost property (Berger et al. 1989, 441).

In addition to the fact that the laws of slave states criminalized more of the conduct of black persons than white and punished violations with greater severity, there were numerous procedural restrictions against blacks in the criminal justice system (Berger et al. 1989, 443). In all but a few states, for example, blacks, both slave and free, could not testify in court against whites, nor could a slave ever serve on a jury no matter what the race of the defendant.

Although many of the aforementioned examples concern the treatment of slave and free blacks in the antebellum South, discrimination against blacks did not end with the Civil War in 1865 and the passage of the Thirteenth Amendment (which abolished slavery) in that same year. Responding to the problem of newly freed black labor and the need to exert control over free blacks, southern states quickly passed (1865–1867) the nefarious Black Codes, an extension of the previous Slave Codes.[4] Like the Slave Codes before them, the purpose of the Black Codes was to enable the white population to maintain virtually total control over blacks.

There were several ways through which the Black Codes produced this result. Most southern states enacted vaguely constructed vagrancy statutes which gave local authorities the power to arrest, fine, and imprison poor men who did not have signed labor contracts. Those unable to pay their fine could, however, be contracted out to an employer who agreed to post bond in exchange for a labor contract. These labor contracts were rigidly enforced, most states making it a criminal offense to break them, and the offending party was returned to his former employer (Schmidt 1982a). An 1869 South Carolina law stipulated that any worker who failed to provide the work required of him or who refused to abide by the terms of the contract would be liable to a fine or imprisonment. To further tie black laborers to white employers, states also passed "labor enticement statutes" which made it a crime for one person to hire another already under contract (Cohen 1976). The practical effect of these Black Codes was to withhold from blacks the fruits of emancipation by recreating in only slightly altered legal form the master–slave relationship.

Perhaps the most striking indication of the extent to which blacks were historically discriminated against was the failure in the antebellum and post–Civil War South to protect the lives of blacks against vigilante justice. No discussion of race and capital punishment can ignore the role of nonofficial executions of blacks, primarily in the South, in the form of lynching. Bowers

(1984, 54) estimated that some 3,500 illegal executions by lynching have taken place in the United States since the 1880s. While many of these lynchings were the result of mob vigilante action, others received at least the tacit consent of the authorities. Belknap (1987, 8–9) relates the attitude of a Texas prosecutor in 1935 who described lynching as "an expression of the will of the people." Perhaps the most outspoken official advocate of lynching was South Carolina governor Cole Blease (1911–1915) who publicly stated that he would be willing to personally participate in the lynching of any black man who attacked a white woman (Belknap 1987, 9), and who pronounced at the 1912 Governor's Conference his desire to "wipe the inferior race from the face of the earth" (Schmidt 1982b). There can be little doubt that historically, white justice rarely served black interests, and as we will soon see, this would be no less true of capital punishment.

Racial Discrimination and Capital Punishment in the Pre-*Furman* Period

There are many decision-making points in the capital punishment process that could conceivably be affected by racial considerations, only three of which will be discussed herein. First there is the decision to charge or indict a defendant on a capital rather than a noncapital charge. After this, there is the decision of the judge or jury to convict a defendant of the capital charge or a lesser offense (or acquit), and whether or not to impose a sentence of death or a lesser punishment if convicted of a capital offense. The conclusion of the trial does not end the decision-making process; the condemned offender may not have the death sentence carried out because of a pardon or an act of executive clemency. Our review of racial discrimination in the capital punishment process will examine each of these decision-making points.

The Indictment and Charging Stage

In an early study of race and capital punishment, Harold Garfinkel (1949) examined the disposition of homicide indictments in ten North Carolina counties during the period 1930–1940. His data are summarized in Table 4–1. Garfinkel found that black defendants were only slightly more likely to be indicted for first-degree murder given a homicide indictment than were white defendants. Ninety-one percent of black defendants indicted for homicide were indicted for first-degree murder while 82 percent of white defendants were (column 6, panel A). There was even a smaller effect for the race of the victim. Eighty-six percent of those defendants who killed white victims were indicted for first-degree murder while 90 percent of those who killed blacks were (column 6, panel B). These small differences are also found when the proportion of first-degree murder charges given an indictment for first-degree murder are examined (column 7, panels A and B).

More pronounced racial differences are found, however, when the race of the offender and the race of the victim are considered in combination. For example, 73 percent of black offenders with white victims but only 58 percent of black offenders who killed black victims were charged with first-degree murder given a first-degree murder indictment (column 7, panel C). Although not definitive, because various legal factors distinguishing homicides were not considered, Garfinkel's data do suggest that the decision to indict and charge first-degree murder is affected by the racial characteristics of the parties involved.

The Conviction and Sentencing Stage

There is also some evidence to suggest that during the pre-*Furman* period race may have affected the decision to convict potential capital defendants. In one of the earliest studies, Brearley (1932) reported that from 1920 to 1926 white defendants accused of homicide were convicted 32 percent of the time while 64 percent of black defendants were convicted. These findings were corroborated by Sellin (1980, 55–68) who found that in South Carolina for the years 1923, 1927, and 1938 black male murder defendants were twice as likely to be convicted of murder compared with white males. Sellin also reported higher conviction rates for black compared with white murderers in Arkansas (1912–1916; 1921–1924).

Guy Johnson (1941) in his data from Richmond, Virginia (1930–1939), and five counties in North Carolina (1930–1940) found evidence that given a murder indictment blacks who killed whites were more likely to be convicted than any other racial combination.[5] Finally, a similar pattern was found in Garfinkel's (1949) North Carolina data.[6] He reported that 43 percent of black offenders who were charged with first-degree murder and killed white victims were convicted of first-degree murder compared with only 5 percent of black victims who killed other blacks (Table 4–1, column 8, panel C). In other words, blacks were almost nine times more likely to be convicted of first-degree murder rather than a lesser offense if they killed a white rather than a black. Also, 15 percent of white defendants charged with first-degree murder who killed other whites were convicted, and no white who killed a black during this time period was convicted.

It should be remembered that most pre-*Furman* capital statutes were structured in such a way that the sentencing authority had a substantial amount of discretion in deciding whether or not to impose a death sentence on convicted offenders. In exercising their discretion it is conceivable that capital sentencers were influenced by the offender's or victim's race. In his Richmond and North Carolina study discussed earlier, Guy Johnson's (1941) data indicates that race may have played a part in the decision to sentence an offender to death. White offenders convicted of murder were over twice as likely to be sentenced

Table 4-1
Number of Homicide Indictments, First-Degree Murder Indictments, Charges, Convictions, and Death Sentences for Ten North Carolina Counties: 1930–1940

	(1) Number of homicide indictments	First-Degree Murder			(5) Number of death sentences	(6) Percent indicted with 1st-degree murder given homicide indictment	(7) Percent charged with 1st-degree murder given 1st-degree indictment	(8) Percent sentenced to death given 1st-degree murder charge
		(2) Indictment	(3) Charge	(4) Conviction				
A. Race of Offender								
White	189	155	83	11	11	82	54	13
Black	632	578	342	30	30	91	59	9
B. Race of Victim								
White	216	186	108	26	26	86	54	24
Black	605	547	317	15	15	90	58	5
C. Race of Offender/Race of Victim								
Black kills White	51	48	35	15	15	94	73	43
White kills White	165	138	73	11	11	84	53	15
Black kills Black	581	530	307	15	15	91	58	5
White kills White	24	17	10	0	0	71	59	0

Sources: H. Garfinkel, "Research Note on Inter- and Intra-Racial Homicides," *Social Forces* 27(1949):369–380, Tables 2 and 3; W.J. Bowers, G.L. Pierce, and J.F. McDevitt, *Legal Homicide: Death as Punishment in America, 1864–1982 (Table 7-1, 208).* Copyright © 1974, 1984 by W.J. Bowers. Reprinted by permission of Northeastern University Press.

to death as black offenders (25% v. 9%). This finding is somewhat deceptive, however. Whites are more likely to be sentenced to death than blacks because white offenders are more likely to kill other whites, and any offender is more likely to be sentenced to death if they slay a white rather than a black. Johnson's Richmond data showed that almost one half (45%) of those who killed whites were sentenced to life imprisonment or death, while less than 6 percent of those who killed a black victim received life or death sentences. Killers of whites were eight times more likely to be sentenced to life or death than were killers of blacks. These findings were essentially duplicated in his North Carolina data set. Convicted offenders who killed a white were almost five times more likely to be sentenced to death given a conviction for murder than were killers of blacks, and black killers of whites were seven times more likely to be sentenced to death than blacks who killed other blacks.

Comparable results were reported by Garfinkel (1949) in his study of ten North Carolina counties over the years 1930–1940. Referring back to Table 4–1 it can be seen that compared with black offenders, white offenders were slightly more likely to be sentenced to death given a first-degree murder indictment (13% v. 9%). Again, this race differential obscures the fact that when they kill both white and black offenders are more likely to kill one of their own race, as well as the fact that death sentences are far more likely for those who slay whites. Of those charged with first-degree murder, 24 percent of those who killed whites were sentenced to death, while only 5 percent of those who killed blacks (column 8, panel B). This race-of-victim effect is even more dramatic when the race of the offender is simultaneously taken into account. Black offenders convicted of first-degree murder who killed white victims were over eight times more likely to be sentenced to death than blacks who killed other blacks (43% v. 5%).

Although many of these studies employ data from the 1930s and 1940s, a study by Zimring, Eigen, and O'Malley (1976) examined the disposition of the first 204 homicide cases reported to the Philadelphia police in 1970. They reported that 245 persons were arrested and 170 were eventually convicted of some charge. Although only three death sentences were imposed in these cases, Zimring et al. found that 65 percent of those defendants who killed a white received a life or a death sentence compared to only 25 percent of those who killed a black. They also found that black defendants who killed a white were twice as likely to be sentenced to death or life imprisonment as black offenders who killed black victims. All three death sentences were imposed in homicides where a black defendant killed a white victim.

In a more recent study, Kleck (1981, 798) reported evidence that during the period 1967–1978 black offenders were no more likely to be sentenced to death for homicide than white offenders. Calculating the number of death sentences per 1,000 homicide arrests, he found that the death sentencing rate was generally higher for white offenders. It should be kept in mind, however, that previous studies that found evidence of racial discrimination did so with data from southern states, and Kleck did not calculate the death sentencing rate separately by region of the country. Kleck also did not examine the influence of the race of the victim, which, we will discover, is a very important factor in understanding racial discrimination and the death penalty.

The Commutation Stage

Not all capital defendants sentenced to death are actually executed. Death sentences may be commuted to life sentences, as they have frequently been in the past, as a result of executive clemency; or reduced to a lesser sentence on the basis of a successful appeal. These decisions may also be influenced by racial factors. Mangum (1940, 369) reported evidence from nine states that indicated that in each state a higher percentage of black defendants were executed than white defendants. For example, in Florida during the period 1928–1938 56 percent of white defendants who were sentenced to death were ultimately executed, while nearly 75 percent of black defendants had their death sentences carried out. Guy Johnson (1941) examined the proportion of condemned offenders executed in North Carolina during the years 1933–1939. While there was no effect for the race of the offender, there was for the race of the victim. More offenders were executed who had killed white victims (74%) than who had killed black victims (65%), and those black offenders who crossed racial lines and killed white victims were the least likely to have their death sentences commuted (81% were executed).

Elmer Johnson (1957) examined the likelihood of execution among those persons sentenced to death for the offense of rape in North Carolina during the years 1909–1954. He reported 56 percent of black condemned rapists executed, and only 43 percent of whites. Even more troubling was his finding that while 64 percent of those who were convicted of raping white victims were ultimately executed, only 14 percent of those convicted of raping black women were. Additional evidence about rape execution risk comes from a study by Partington (1965). He reported that in the period 1908–1964 every rapist executed in Virginia was black, and that in four other southern states (Louisiana, Mississippi, Oklahoma, and West Virginia) blacks were the only rapists executed. Johnson's findings from North Carolina and Partington's from Virginia with regard to execution risk and rape are comparable to those reported by Koeninger (1969) with Texas homicide data from the years 1924–1968. He reports that there were 360 executions conducted in Texas during that period; an additional eighty five death sentences were commuted by the governor. Eighty-eight percent of all black offenders but only 76 percent of white offenders were ultimately executed.

Most of this pre-*Furman* execution risk research has been conducted in southern states where evidence of racial discrimination may not be surprising. There is some indication, however, that blacks in other parts of the country also fared less well than their white counterparts in the commutation/appeals process. Wolfgang, Kelly, and Nolde (1962) analyzed the fate of 439 persons sentenced to death in Pennsylvania during the period 1914–1958. They found that black offenders who committed a felony–type murder were substantially less likely to have their death sentences commuted than were whites (6.3% v. 17.4%); nearly three times as many whites were commuted as blacks.

Not all of the evidence supports the position that racial discrimination affects the decision to execute capital defendants, however. Bedau (1964; 1965) found no race-of-defendant effect in the commutation decision in either New Jersey (1907–1960) or Oregon (1903–1964). Kleck (1981, 793–795) reports data on the risk of homicide execution for the nation during the period 1930–1967. He found that the risk of execution was comparable for white and black offenders alike: 10.42 executions per 1,000 homicides for white offenders; 9.72 per 1,000 homicides for blacks. When these aggregate rates were broken down by region, however, a racial effect consistent with previous studies emerged. In the South execution rates were higher for black offenders than for whites, although this difference declined over time. For the rest of the United States white offenders had generally higher execution rates than blacks (p. 796). In addition, it should be noted that Kleck did not consider the effect that the race of the victim would have on race-of-offender discrimination. This is particularly important since previous studies have shown that black offenders who kill white victims fare less well than all other racial combinations at every decision-making point.

Summary of pre-Furman Research: The Search for Racial Effects in Capital Sentencing

Collectively, the findings from these research efforts paint a telling picture of our country's early experience with the imposition of capital punishment. With few exceptions, these data suggest that black offenders and those who victimize whites are more likely (1) to be indicted for a capital crime, (2) to be convicted of a capital crime, (3) to have the death penalty imposed, and (4) to have their death sentences carried out, than white offenders and those who victimize blacks. This pattern is particularly characteristic of capital punishment in the South and when there is a black offender and a white victim, and least likely to occur for black offenders with black victims.

We cannot conclude on the basis of these studies, however, that racial discrimination in the capital punishment process during the pre-Furman period has been definitively proved. This is because few of these studies controlled for legally relevant and racially neutral factors, which may account for the observed differential racial treatment. The observed differences in the legal treatment between black and white offenders or black and white victim cases may be due to legitimate differences in the offenses and offenders involved. Black offenders (and those who victimize whites) may have more extensive criminal records, they may commit more brutal crimes, or victimize more than one person, or commit other felonies during the commission of a murder or rape. Before it can be concluded that either the offender's or victim's race does have an effect on any of the capital sentencing decisions thus far examined, it will be necessary to consider these other factors.

This was the position of Gary Kleck (1981) after his extensive review of the capital punishment and race literature. He concluded that when adequate controls are made for such factors as the seriousness of the defendant's criminal record, social class, and the nature of the offense committed, evidence of racial discrimination disappears. To support his conclusion he cites one of the most methodologically sophisticated studies published up to that time, a 1969 research report that appeared in the *Stanford Law Review*. This study found no race-of-offender or race-of-victim effect when statistical controls were made for legally relevant characteristics of the offense, offender, and the trial (Judson et al. 1969). For three reasons, however, Kleck's conclusion should be viewed with some degree of skepticism.

First, the Stanford study does not show a complete absence of discrimination under California's capital sentencing law. Although no racial effect was found, there was a significant effect for the social class of the defendant, even when controlling for legally relevant factors. Blue-collar defendants were substantially more, and white-collar defendants substantially less likely to be sentenced to death by California juries. Second, the failure of the California study to find a race effect in comparison with previous research may also be due to jurisdictional differences. Perhaps racial discrimination is not as strong or is more subtle in states, such as California, without a legacy of racism and racial conflict. Third, there is evidence that suggests that race effects exist even when controls are made for racially neutral, legal factors that may affect case outcome.

Wolf (1964) examined the effect of race on the decision to sentence murder defendants to death in New Jersey during the period 1937–1961. Of 159 offenders 39 percent were sentenced to death; however, 48 percent of black defendants received a death sentence while only 30 percent of white offenders did. Wolf also separately controlled for three case-related characteristics (felony circumstance, type of weapon, and the defendant's age) and found that the race-of-offender effect did not disappear. In felony homicides, 60 percent of black offenders, while only 41 percent of white defendants, were sentenced to death; and in nongun homicides black offenders were more than twice as likely to be sentenced to death as white murderers. Although Wolf did not have complete data on the race of the victim, he did report that 72 percent of black offenders who killed a white were sentenced to death, 50 percent of black offenders who killed a black were sentenced to death, and only 32 percent of white offenders who killed a white were sentenced to death.

There was one very important study of southern capital sentencing that included even more extensive controls for offender, offense, and trial factors. Marvin Wolfgang and his colleagues collected data on over 3,000 rape convictions in 230 counties in eleven southern states that covered a twenty-year period. In addition to the final disposition of the case, Wolfgang collected information on offender characteristics (age, employment status, criminal record), victim characteristics (age, dependent children, reputation), the nature of the relationship between offender and victim, offense characteristics (use of weapon, nature and extent of injury, degree of force employed), and circumstances of the trial (appointed v. retained counsel, defense of consensual relations) (Wolfgang and Riedel 1973). In their published findings from this research, Wolfgang and Riedel (1973) found dramatic racial differences; blacks were six and one-half times more likely to be sentenced to death for rape than white offenders, and blacks who raped white women were eighteen times more likely to be sentenced to death than those rapes involving any other racial combination.

Wolfgang and Riedel also found that if the rape was committed along with another felony, defendants of both races were more likely to be sentenced to death, and that black rapists were more likely to commit another felony during the commission of the rape. Speculating that the commission of a contemporaneous offense might explain the observed racial difference, Wolfgang and Riedel examined the racial effect separately for those rapes involving another offense. The racial effect persisted, however. Among those rapes that involved the commission of another crime, while 39 percent of black offenders who raped white women were sentenced to death, only 2 percent of those in all other racial combinations of offender and victim were. Blacks with white victims in rapes not involving a contemporaneous felony were almost twenty times more likely to be sentenced to death than those offenders with other racial combinations. Not only did the presence of a contemporaneous felony fail to account for the large racial difference in the likelihood of receiving a death sentence in Wolfgang's data set, he and Riedel controlled separately for over two dozen other variables. In no case did the racial effect disappear, leading them to the conclusion (1973, 133) that southern rapes involving black offenders and white victims are substantially more likely to result in a sentence of death than other rapes, and that this disparate treatment cannot be accounted for by legally relevant differences among rapes or rapists:

> All the nonracial factors in each of the states analyzed "wash out," that is, they have no bearing on the imposition of the death penalty in disproportionate numbers upon blacks. The only variable of statistical significance that remains is race.

The Wolfgang and Riedel 1973 study is a particularly important one because they demonstrated that a large racial effect in capital sentencing could not be explained by a set of racially neutral factors such as prior criminal record and the presence of a contemporaneous offense, at least when these other variables are considered singly. It was still possible that several legally relevant variables considered simultaneously might account for the large racial differences in the southern rape data. This hypothesis was examined in a second Wolfgang and

Riedel (1975) study which examined 361 rape convictions from a sample of twenty-five Georgia counties over the period 1945–1965. Each rape conviction contained information about the victim, the offender, the relationship between victim and offender, the offense, and the trial. In a statistical analysis that controlled for fourteen legally relevant variables simultaneously, Wolfgang and Riedel found that the most important predictor of which among the 361 rapists would be sentenced to death was the racial combination of offender and victim. The race of neither the offender nor the victim had an independent effect; black offenders who raped white victims, however, were significantly more likely to be sentenced to death in comparision to rapes involving all other racial combinations.

The evidence thus far presented has suggested that under discretionary pre-*Furman* statutes various decision-making points in the capital sentencing process, from indictment to commutation, are influenced by the race of the offender and victim. At least two justices of the United States Supreme Court referred to such patterns of discrimination in striking down existing death penalty statutes. When the death penalty was resurrected in the United States in the mid-1970s, it was thought that procedurally reformed death penalty statutes, which restricted and guided the discretion of the jury, would eliminate much of the discrimination. The remaining question is whether the post-*Furman* reforms in state death penalty laws were actually effective in eliminating the vestiges of racial discrimination from the administration of the death penalty. It is to that literature that we now turn our attention. Like the pre-*Furman* studies, the post-*Furman* research will be reviewed according to the type of decision being made in the capital sentencing process.

Racial Discrimination and Capital Punishment in the Post-*Furman* Period

The Course of the Empirical Work

Our discussion of empirical work on racial discrimination in the capital punishment process during the post-*Furman* years will involve some fairly dense material. Before reviewing these studies, it will be helpful to first understand in a general sense the general development of this empirical work. The researchers conducting this work were interested in determining if race was an important factor in determining who is sentenced to death. As we have seen, the influence of race can be felt at many different points in the capital sentencing process, from the earliest decision to indict an offender for a capital crime to the later decision of the jury to impose a death sentence. Our task of understanding this process is made more difficult by the fact that the magnitude of the racial effect may not be the same at different decision points. Race may strongly influence the decision to indict capital offenders, for example, but may play a far less prominent role in determining who, among those having a penalty trial, are sentenced to death.

It should also be reiterated here that the attention of researchers is directed at a different form of racial discrimination in the post-*Furman* period. While many persons are now consciously aware of the inappropriateness of some racial attitudes, other, much more subtle, attitudes may go unnoticed. For example, in our society, most are aware that persons should not be judged on the basis of their skin color, and certainly that criminal offenders should not be afforded differential treatment on that basis. What people may be less aware of, however, is the attitude that they may harbor when one of their own race is criminally victimized. Whites may find the murder of a white much more shocking, brutal, and threatening than the comparable slaying of a black, particularly if the murder of the white was committed by a black. Such whites, when sitting on capital juries, may, therefore, be more inclined to impose death sentences when other whites are victimized. Anticipating this, prosecutors may be more inclined to seek a sentence of death against those who kill whites, especially if the offender is black. Although more blatant forms of racial discrimination, such as the exclusion of blacks from juries, may have receded, discrimination may not have been eliminated. The possible existence of race-of-victim discrimination would suggest that it has only changed its appearance and is now less flagrant, though no less real.

Finally, a word should be said about the nature of the empirical work itself. As was true of the pre-*Furman* studies, most of the research on post-*Furman* capital sentencing schemes was conducted in southern states. This was because southern states were the first to pass new death penalty statutes, the first to accumulate enough capital punishment cases for researchers to study, and historically the logical place for reseachers to find evidence of racial discrimination. The first few research studies were also rather methodologically simple. Researchers simply collected data from police reports of homicides (Supplementary Homicide Reports) which recorded the race of the offender and victim as well as a few descriptive characteristics of the homicide (e.g., type of weapon, if another felony was committed, if a relationship existed between the victim and offender). These studies reported that those who killed white persons were far more likely to be sentenced to death than those who killed blacks. A few of these studies did consider one or two legally relevant factors in their analyses. Later, more methodologically rigorous research considered a full range of aggravating and mitigating factors which would possibly explain any observed racial effect. In conducting these studies researchers were required to gather rather extensive data from police records, prosecutors' files, court transcripts and records, and sometimes cororners' reports and newspaper accounts of crimes. These more sophisticated studies not only collected more detailed information about each homicide, they also were able to investigate several different decision-making points in the capital sentencing process. It was increasingly possible, therefore, to be sure that a "true" racial effect was being observed, and of the magnitude of that effect (since more factors were considered), and at exactly what points racial influences were the strongest.

The Indictment and Charging Stage

Some of the first post-*Furman* studies to appear in the literature were examinations of one of the earliest decision-making points in the process, the decision to indict a defendant for first-degree/capital murder or some lesser offense. Bowers and Pierce (1980a) investigated the likelihood that an offender would be indicted for first-degree murder given a homicide charge in Florida from 1973 until the end of 1977. They report that for all homicides (over 700), black offenders who killed white victims were over twice as likely to be indicted for first-degree murder than black offenders who killed black victims. They further reported that when this was examined separately for felony–type murders, the observed racial effect persisted, and all black offender/white victim homicides resulted in an indictment for first-degree murder, while only 80 percent of those involving both black offenders and black victims did.

Another important study of the Florida capital indictment system was conducted by Radelet (1981). His data included over 600 homicide indictments in twenty Florida counties in 1976 and 1977. He reported that for homicides committed among strangers the probability of a first-degree homicide indictment for white defendants (.800) was higher than that for black defendants (.687). As we have seen before, however, white offenders are more likely to be indicted for first-degree murder because they are more likely to kill white victims than are black offenders, and killers of white victims in Radelet's data are far more likely to result in a first-degree murder indictment (.850) than are homicides involving black victims (.536). When Radelet examined the race of the offender and victim combination, striking racial differences appeared. Homicides involving black offenders and white victims are more likely to end in a first-degree murder indictment than those involving all other racial combinations. In fact, over 92 percent of black offender/white victim homicides resulted in a first-degree indictment, while only 70 percent of all other homicides did. In a statistical model that estimated the probability of a first-degree murder indictment among stranger homicides that included the victim's and offender's race, Radelet (1981, 923) concluded that "there is a tendency to indict defendants accused of killing whites for first-degree murder and to indict defendants accused of killing blacks for a less severe homicide charge".

In a later and more sophisticated study of prosecutorial discretion in the capital sentencing process in Florida, Bowers (1983) estimated a statistical model that included ten legally relevant factors that might have affected the decision to indict a homicide defendant for first-degree murder (e.g., number of offenders and victims, presence of another felony, age of victim, type of weapon), two variables reflecting the geographical location of the crime, and two variables reflecting the type of attorney. He found that even when important legally relevant factors were taken into account, race made a substantial difference in the indictment decision. Blacks who killed whites and whites who killed whites were significantly more likely to be indicted for first-degree murder rather than a lesser murder charge compared with murders involving black victims. In fact, he reported that the fact that a homicide involved a black defendant and a white victim was more important in predicting a first-degree murder indictment than all but one of the legally relevant factors of the case.

An additional and more extensive analysis of the role of race in the decision of Florida prosecutors to seek the death penalty was conducted by Radelet and Pierce (1985). They collected information on 1,382 homicide defendants for the years 1973–1977 including whether or not the defendant's act of homicide involved the commission of a felony. In most instances, if the police report noted that a felony occurred the prosecutor's charge reflected that fact. In a small number of cases (17%), however, the prosecutor's homicide charge included a felony that was not indicated in the police report (these cases were referred to as having been "upgraded" by the prosecutor), or the prosecutor's charge did not include the commission of a felony even though the police report indicated that one had been committed (these cases were "downgraded"). The upgrading of a homicide means that the prosecutor increases its seriousness in comparison to the police report, while a downgraded homicide is treated by the prosecutor with diminished seriousness. Whether or not a homicide was upgraded by the prosecutor had practical effects for the capital defendant as well, since it increased the probability of a death sentence by 22 percent.

Radelet and Pierce found that the prosecutor's decision to upgrade or downgrade a homicide was related to the victim's and offender's race. In a statistical model that controlled for offender, offense, and victim characteristics, they reported that prosecutors were more likely to upgrade white victim homicides than those involving a black victim (regardless of the race of the offender), and that homicides involving black offenders and white victims were less likely to be downgraded than those involving black offenders and black victims.

Florida is not the only state where there is some evidence to suggest that early decision-making points in the capital sentencing process may be affected by considerations of race. Paternoster (1983; Paternoster and Kazyaka 1988) examined the decision of local prosecutors in South Carolina to charge homicide defendants with capital murder, thus making them eligible for the death penalty. There was evidence that South Carolina prosecutors frequently exercised their discretion to charge or not charge a capital offense given the commission of a homicide. Of the approximately 1,800 homicides committed in the state during the years 1977–1981, 302 were identified as potentially capital murders in that there was at least one statutory aggravating circumstance present. Of these 302 potentially capital murders, prosecutors filed a notice to seek the death penalty, thus actually charging the defendant with capital murder, in only 114 (38%) cases. A preliminary inquiry revealed no race-of-

offender effect, but also showed that prosecutors were over twice as likely to seek a death sentence if the victim was white rather than black. In addition, black offenders who crossed racial lines and killed a white were almost four times more likely to be charged with capital murder than were blacks who killed other blacks.

Paternoster and Kazyaka (1988) also found that homicides involving white victims were more egregious than those involving blacks in that they were more likely to involve more than one victim, offenders with prior records, and two or more aggravating factors. The question that these findings compelled was whether or not the observed racial differences in the likelihood of a capital charge for killers of whites was due to these legally relevant factors rather than to racial discrimination. To answer this question, Paternoster (1983) and Paternoster and Kazyaka (1988) estimated a statistical model which predicted the probability of the prosecutor making a capital charge on the basis of legally relevant and racial variables. They found that the prior violent criminal record of the defendant, the overall brutality of the crime, the total number of statutory aggravating factors, and the number of contemporaneous felonies committed were important predictors of the prosecutor's charging decision. Even when these factors were simultaneously taken into account, however, the race of the victim had a statistically significant and important effect, that is, killers of whites were almost twice as likely to be charged with capital murder as were killers of blacks. In an elaboration of this analysis Paternoster and his colleague ranked each homicide according to how aggravated or serious it was, and estimated the effect of the race of the victim at comparable levels of homicide severity. They found that the effect of race was strongest at the lowest and middle levels of homicide aggravation. Homicides at the highest levels of seriousness were almost always charged as capital murders regardless of the race of the victim, while black victim homicides at the mid- and low levels were rarely so charged.

Results similar to the Paternoster study were found by Nakell and Hardy (1987) in their study of capital sentencing in North Carolina and by Vito and Keil (1988) in their examination of prosecutorial discretion under the Kentucky capital statute. Nakell and Hardy examined 489 cases of homicide that occurred from June 1, 1977 to May 21, 1978, the first year of the state's new death penalty statute, and collected detailed information about each. One of the decision-making points they studied was the likelihood of an indictment for first-degree murder, the only degree of murder that is a potentially capital crime under North Carolina law. They reported that the most important predictor of the decision to indict for first-degree murder was the quality of the evidence against the defendant; the race of neither the victim nor the offender had a stronger effect. They also examined the prosecutor's decision to bring the case to trial for first-degree murder, and found that for this discretionary decision the best predictors were the strength of the evidence and a factor reflecting how aggravated the offense was. There was also a significant effect for the race of the defendant under certain conditions.

Vito and Keil (1988) examined for the first twenty-two months of Kentucky's new capital statute all murder indictments that fit the statutory requirements of a death-eligible murder. They found that racial variables affected the likelihood that the prosecutor would empanel a capital jury, thereby making a given homicide eligible for the death penalty. Homicides involving white victims were over twice as likely to be treated as a capital murder as those that involved the killing of a black, and homicides where a black offender killed a white victim were three and one-half times more likely than those involving a black offender and black victim. This racial disparity persisted when the researchers simultaneously controlled for several factors in aggravation and mitigation.

It should finally be noted here that evidence of racial disparity in the capital charging decision is not restricted to southern or border states. Bienen and her colleagues (1988) conducted an extensive investigation of the capital sentencing system of New Jersey. Their data set consisted of all homicides (n=703) committed during the years 1982–1986. Of these homicides, 404 were death eligible in that there was a factual basis for the prosecutor to seek a death sentence, and a sentence of death was actually sought in 131 of these homicides. Bienen et al. reported that a slightly higher percentage of white defendants were charged with a capital offense (43%) than were either black (32%) or Hispanic (18%) offenders. There was a larger difference when the race of the victim was examined. Almost one half of those defendants who killed a white victim (43%), while less than a third in either black-victim (28%) or Hispanic-victim (19%) killings, were charged with capital homicide. There was also a strong effect observed when both the race of the victim and that of the defendant were considered. Prosecutors served a notice to seek the death penalty in one half of those homicides where a black defendant killed a white victim, but in less than a third of those where a black killed another black (28%), and in only 20 percent of the cases where a white killed a black. In a statistical model of the prosecutor's decision to seek a death sentence, they reported that even after controlling for several aggravating and mitigating factors, relevant characteristics of the offender and victim, and trial characteristics, race still had a determinative influence—killers of white victims were ten times more likely to have the death penalty sought than were killers of Hispanic victims. In a separate analysis, Bienen et al. reported that cross-racial slayings that involved a white victim were more likely to be treated as a capital homicide than intraracial killings. With relevant legal factors controlled, black and Hispanic offenders who killed whites were twice as likely to have the death penalty sought than black killers of blacks or white killers of other whites, and seven times more likely than Hispanic offenders who killed Hispanic victims.

The most detailed studies of prosecutorial discretion in death penalty cases were done by David Baldus and his colleagues (Baldus et al. 1983, 1985, 1990), who investigated the cases of 594 offenders who were tried for murder under the Georgia post-*Furman* statute during the period 1973–1978. One of the decision-making points examined by Baldus et al. was the decision of the prosecutor to seek the death penalty given a murder conviction. As is true of other states, Georgia prosecutors frequently exercise their discretion not to seek a death sentence. For example, of the 594 cases in this data set a death sentence was sought in only 190 (32%). One of the factors that Baldus et al. found to be an important determinant as to whether or not the death penalty would be sought by the prosecutor in a particular case was the race of the victim. Georgia prosecutors sought the death penalty in 44 percent of the cases that involved the slaying of a white victim but in only 15 percent of those where a black was killed, a factor of almost three to one (Baldus et al. 1983).

This disparity by the race of the victim persisted when Baldus et al. attempted to control for differences in the characteristics of the homicides. When they examined the proportion of death penalty trials in white victim and black victim cases controlling for the number of statutory aggravating factors, the rates were consistently higher among the former cases. For example, for those homicides that involved one statutory aggravating factor, prosecutors were almost three times more likely to seek the death penalty when a white was killed than when a black was killed; for those homicides that included four aggravating factors, prosecutors were almost four times more likely to seek a death sentence (Baldus et al. 1983). When they conducted a multivariate analysis that simultaneously controlled for over 150 aggravating and mitigating factors, the effect of the race of the victim persisted, with prosecutors more inclined to seek a death sentence if a white rather than a black was killed.

In a refined analysis of these data, Baldus et al. (1985) compared the likelihood that Georgia prosecutors would seek a death sentence in white and black victim cases of comparable seriousness. To this end they created a homicide aggravation/seriousness scale which ranged from a low score of 1 to a high of 6. There were 268 homicides at the lowest level of aggravation and a sentence of death was sought by prosecutors in only eight (3%) cases; there were 34 homicides at the highest level of aggravation and a death sentence was sought in every one of these cases. When the effect of the victim's race was examined for homicides of comparable seriousness, they found that the influence of race varied. Among those homicides that were the most serious white victim and black victim cases were treated similarly. That is, when a particular homicide was very brutal/serious Georgia prosecutors were likely to seek a death sentence, regardless of the race of the victim. Strong race-of-victim effects were found, however, for those homicides at the mid-range of seriousness. For example, at levels 2 and 3 of their 6-point scale Baldus et al. found that prosecutors were twice as likely to seek a death sentence in a homicide that involved a white victim (50 out of 120 cases, 42%) than in one that involved a black (only 13 of 71 cases, 18%). These findings suggest that when a given homicide crosses a threshold of seriousness or brutality it is likely to motivate the prosecutor to seek a sentence of death no matter what the color of the victim's skin. In other homicides that are less shocking, where perhaps there is greater opportunity for prosecutors to exercise their discretion because of the absence of a public outcry to "do something" about the offender who committed this crime, prosecutors do seem to be influenced by the race of the victim in their decision to seek a sentence of death.

Baldus and his colleagues have confirmed these findings in their most recent and refined analysis of their Georgia data (Baldus et al. 1990). They reported (1990, 164) that even after controlling for over twenty legally relevant factors, offenders who killed a white victim were over five times more likely to have the death penalty sought against them than those who killed blacks. They also found (1990, 168) that this racial disparity at the level of the local prosecutor was stronger for those cases and the mid- and low levels of aggravation. Prosecutors treated a black victim homicide as they would a white victim killing only for the most aggravated murders.

The Conviction and Sentencing Stage

An extensive analysis of capital sentencing during the first few years after *Furman* was conducted by William Bowers and Glenn Pierce (1980a). They examined the probability of a defendant receiving a death sentence in each of four states (Florida, Georgia, Texas, and Ohio). For all homicides, they found that black offenders who killed white victims in Florida were thirty-seven times more likely to receive a death sentence than blacks who killed other blacks, in Georgia they were thirty-three times more likely, in Texas eighty-seven times, and in Ohio they were fifteen times more likely to be sentenced to death. When Bowers and Pierce examined the effect of offender's and victim's race separately for felony–type homicides (those killings that also involve the commission of a contemporaneous felony offense), the racial difference was diminished but remained substantial. Blacks who murdered whites in Florida and Georgia were over seven times more likely to be sentenced to death than blacks who killed other blacks, in Texas they were almost ten times more likely to be sentenced to death.

Arkin (1980) conducted a study which followed 350 murder cases presented to the grand jury for a first-degree murder indictment in Dade County (Miami), Florida, during the first few years after the enactment of Florida's revised post-*Furman* capital statute (1973–1976). Arkin's data indicated that race did affect the disposition of these 350 cases. His study is important to note here because the data suggest that evidence of racial discrimination may appear at some but not all stages of the capital sentencing process. For example, when all homicides are considered, he reported that blacks who killed whites were over four times more likely to be convicted of first-degree murder than were blacks who killed other blacks, and killers of whites were over three times more likely to be convicted of first-degree murder than were those offenders who killed black victims. Arkin did note, however, that killings involving white victims were more likely to take place under felony circumstances, and were thus more serious homicides than black victim killings. He then reported a comparable analysis for felony–type homicides only. This analysis revealed smaller, though still consistent race effects. Of ten death sentences imposed in the 142 felony–type homicide cases, nine involved the slaying of a white victim. For all felony–type homicides, killers of whites were over twice as likely to be sentenced to death than were killers of blacks (8% v. 3%). When only those cases that resulted in a conviction for first-degree murder were examined, however, the death sentencing rates for white victim and black victim cases were quite comparable (.167% v. .176%). The difference between these two sets of findings was that killers of whites were over twice as likely to be convicted of first-degree murder by Florida juries than were killers of blacks (.45% v. 21%). Evidence of racial discrimination existing at an early stage in the capital sentencing process (conviction), then, did not persist at a later stage (sentencing).

Results comparable to Arkin's were reported by Radelet (1981) in a more general study of Florida homicide cases. While Arkin's data were restricted to Dade County, Radelet's examined those homicides committed in twenty Florida counties (1976–1977). In the previous section we reported that Radelet found that killers of whites were more likely to be indicted for first-degree murder than were those defendants who killed black victims; this was also true when the analysis was restricted to those homicides committed among strangers. In a related analysis, Radelet reported that among all homicide cases, while the race of the defendant had no statistically significant effect on the probability of being sentenced to death, the race of the victim did; killers of whites were significantly more likely to be sentenced to death than were killers of blacks. When only those cases that resulted in a first-degree murder indictment were examined, however, neither the race of the victim nor that of the defendant affected the likelihood of a death sentence. Radelet's findings are another indication that racial discrimination found at one point in the capital punishment system (indictment) may not spill over into subsequent decisions (sentencing).

Together, Arkin's and Radelet's examinations of Florida data indicated that the critical decision point in the capital sentencing process, at least as far as race is concerned, is the decision to indict and convict a defendant of first-degree murder. The evidence indicates that these decisions are affected by the race of the victim, but that once a defendant is indicted or convicted of first-degree murder, their race and the race of the victim may not play as important a role.

Although the research by Bowers and Pierce, Arkin, and Radelet strongly suggest the existence of discrimination in the form of race-of-victim effects in post-*Furman* capital sentencing practices, their data do not provide definitive proof. White-victim homicides may more likely result in a death sentence because they are committed by offenders with more extensive criminal records than those committed against blacks, or they may be more brutal slayings. Although Bowers and Pierce and Arkin controlled for the commission of another felony offense and Radelet for the relationship between the victim and offender, they did not consider the effect of other offense- or offender-related characteristics on the likelihood of a death sentence. Their studies were quite important, however, in that they led to other, more sophisticated research into the effect of race on the likelihood of a death sentence, which controlled for a greater number of factors.

One of these more rigorous studies of capital sentencing was conducted by Bowers (1983). He examined the effect of race on the likelihood of a defendant being sentenced to death with a sample of Florida homicide defendants who had been indicted for first-degree murder from 1973 to 1977. Bowers controlled for ten legally relevant factors, such as the existence of a felony, number of victims, number of offenders, age and sex of the victim, type of weapon, and age of the offender, as well as the location of the crime in the state and the type of defense attorney. He found that even with these factors controlled for, black killers of whites and white killers of whites were significantly more likely to be sentenced to death than were black killers of blacks.

Another comprehensive study of capital sentencing under post-*Furman* statutes was conducted by Gross and Mauro (1984; 1989); they examined the effect of race on the imposition of death sentences in Georgia (1976–1980), Florida (1976–1980), Illinois (1977–1980), and five other states. Consistent with previous research, Gross and Mauro found that for all homicides, both the race of the victim and the combination of victim's and offender's race had an effect on the likelihood that a defendant would be sentenced to death. In Georgia, killers of whites were almost ten times more likely to be sentenced to death than killers of blacks, in Florida they were almost eight times more likely, and in Illinois six times more likely to be sentenced to death. In a by now familiar pattern, black offenders were particularly likely to be sentenced to death if they killed a white rather than a black. Georgia juries were, for example, twenty-five times more likely to sentence to death a black defendant who crossed racial boundaries and killed a white person, in Florida black killers of whites were twenty times more likely, and in Illinois they were twelve times more likely to be sentenced to death than were black killers of other blacks.

Having found this pattern in three different states,[7] Gross and Mauro then examined the extent to which race was an important factor in determining who was sentenced to death after considering various characteristics of the homicide. These researchers controlled (one variable at a time) for the existence of a contemporaneous felony, the relationship between the victim and offender, and the number of victims, and found that the race-of-victim effect did not disappear. Defendants who killed whites were still more likely to be sentenced to death than those who killed blacks. They then estimated a statistical model of the death sentencing decision simultaneously controlling for several legally relevant variables and found persistent race-of-victim effects. When various characteristics of the homicide are controlled for, the killing of a white victim increased the defendant's odds of being sentenced to death by a factor of 7 in Georgia, almost 5 in Florida, and 4 in Illinois.

Evidence from other states is consistent with the Gross and Mauro findings.

Nakell and Hardy (1987) reported that during the first year of the new North Carolina capital statute (1977–1978), defendants who killed white victims were six times more likely to be convicted of first-degree murder than those who killed blacks, even after controlling for the quality of the evidence and the seriousness of the offense. There was, however, no race-of-victim effect for the decision to sentence convicted first-degree murderers to death, although there were only eight death sentences imposed during this period. In a comparable study of capital sentencing practices in Kentucky, Vito and Keil (1988) found that once appropriate legal factors were controlled, race had no effect on which defendants were sentenced to death, although as we discussed earlier in relation to other studies, they did report that race had a significant effect on the prosecutor's decision to treat a given homicide as a capital offense.

By far the most extensive analysis of post-*Furman* capital sentencing practices was conducted in Georgia by David Baldus, George Woodworth, and Charles Pulaski (Baldus et al. 1983, 1985, 1990). In the first of their analyses (Baldus et al. 1983), they examined the disposition of 594 post-*Furman* murder defendants in which there were 203 penalty trials and 113 death sentences imposed. They found that the likelihood that a defendant would be sentenced to death by a Georgia jury was related to the race of the victim who was killed, though this effect was not strong. Juries imposed a death sentence in 58 percent of the white-victim cases and 43 percent of those involving black victims. In a series of multivariate analyses that controlled for several aggravating and mitigating factors, Baldus and his colleagues reported persistent but small effects of the race of the victim on the likelihood that a Georgia defendant would be sentenced to death.

When the death sentencing rates in white- and black-victim cases were examined for all 594 homicides, not just the 203 that were advanced to a penalty trial, greater disparities were observed. A sentence of death was four times more likely to be imposed on a defendant who killed a white rather than a black victim. This effect persisted when Baldus et al. considered the seriousness of the homicide by controlling for the number of statutory aggravating factors and the predicted likelihood of a death sentence. While white-victim and black-victim cases were treated comparably at the lowest and highest levels of seriousness, race-of-victim disparities were quite large at the mid-range. The difference between the two sets of findings discussed above, a strong race-of-victim effect when all homicides are considered but a weak one when the analysis is restricted to only those that advanced to a penalty trial, can be accounted for by the fact that the strongest effect for race is to be found not in the jury's decision to impose a death sentence, but in the exercise of the prosecutor's discretion to seek one. Although noting the consistent (though weak) effect at the level of jury decision making, these findings led the researchers to conclude (Baldus et al. 1983, 710, note 131) that "[t]he leading source of the race-of-victim disparities in Georgia's death-sentencing system for defendants convicted of murder at trial is clearly the decision to advance the case to a penalty trial."

In 1985 Baldus, Pulaski, and Woodworth reported the results of a reanalysis of their Georgia data, focusing on the 606 sentencing decisions in the 594 homicide cases.[8] They again reported a strong race-of-victim effect within this sample of cases. Defendants were four times more likely to be sentenced to death if a white person was killed rather than a black. Recognizing that white-victim homicides were generally more egregious than those involving black victims, they attempted to control for this difference by creating a homicide aggravation scale and then estimating the effect of the victim's race on the likelihood of a death sentence for those homicides of comparable seriousness. This homicide aggravation scale ranged from a low score of 1 to a high score of 6. Defendants committing homicides at the lowest level of aggravation were not very likely to be sentenced to death (only 6 of 399, or 2%, were), while those committing the most serious homicides were almost certainly sentenced to death (59 out of 62, or 95%, of those at the two highest seriousness levels). Baldus et al. found that the race of the victim did make a difference in the likelihood of a death sentence but that this effect appeared most strongly in those homicide cases at the mid-range of aggravation. When a homicide was extremely brutal, defendants were regularly sentenced to death regardless of the race of the person killed. When a homicide was less aggravated, however, defendants who killed white victims were more likely to be sentenced to death than those who killed black victims.

These findings were corroborated in the most recent analysis of their Georgia data. Baldus et al. (1990, 164) found that juries were less sympathetic to offenders who killed a black. When they statistically controlled for over twenty legally important factors, offenders who killed whites were seven times more likely to be sentenced to death than those who killed blacks. As with prosecutorial discretion, this racial disparity was found to be greatest for those cases at the mid- and low levels of their homicide aggravation scale.

Evidence of Racial Discrimination before the Courts

In the preceding pages we reviewed most of the empirical evidence regarding racial discrimination under pre- and post-*Furman* capital sentencing schemes. The nature of the alleged racial bias has changed somewhat over the years. Although some studies did suggest that the race of the victim in combination with the offender's race was important, most of the pre-*Furman* literature was concerned with racial discrimination against black offenders. As we have seen, looking solely at the defendant's race can be misleading. The post-*Furman* literature, however, has been almost exclusively concerned with race-of-victim effects. Both of these bodies of literature strongly suggest that race is an important determining factor in who is sentenced to death and ultimately executed.

The empirical effort directed at uncovering the existence and direction of racial disparity in the administration of capital punishment has been prodigious. In this final section of the chapter we will examine the extent to which the courts have considered the claim that state capital sentencing statutes are unconstitutional because they are racially discriminatory. We will first examine the legal basis for any claim of racial discrimination, then we will examine how the courts have handled petitioners' claims that either their death sentences in particular or capital punishment in general is invalid because of racially discriminatory treatment. We will conduct this inquiry by following the legal course taken by two capital defendants, one during the pre-*Furman* years of capital sentencing, William Maxwell, and the second during the years after *Furman,* the case of Warren McCleskey. These cases were chosen both because they were the most important test cases at their respective times concerning impermissible racial factors in capital sentencing, and because of the similarity of the court's treatment of the evidence regarding the petitioners' claim of racial discrimination.

Two Legal Claims of Racial Discrimination

A Fourteenth Amendment Claim. A death sentence can be challenged by a capital defendant on the grounds of racial discrimination through the "equal protection" clause of the Fourteenth Amendment. This clause states that "[n]o State shall . . . deny to any person within its jurisdiction the equal protection of laws."[9] One of the practices that the Fourteenth Amendment sought to prohibit was the unequal enforcement of southern laws. Earlier in this chapter we noted that southern Black Codes called for different punishments for white and black offenders and more severe punishments when the victim was white. The Georgia Penal Code of 1861, for example, carried a penalty of two to twenty years in prison for the rape of a white woman by a white male but required the death penalty for black offenders, and carried a far less imposing sentence for offenders of either color if the victim were a black woman. Historically, the Fourteenth Amendment was passed by Congress to put an end to this disparity in legal treatment afforded white and black citizens. Pritchett (1984, 250) notes in this regard that

> [t]here can be no doubt that the equal protection clause was meant to end discrimination enforced upon blacks by the "Black Codes" of certain states which limited their right to hold property, specified criminal offenses for blacks only, and hampered their access to the courts in a variety of ways.

There were, then, at least two specific prohibitions of the Fourteenth Amendment. One of them, which is very clear, is that a state may not have two different punishments for an offense, one for white and one for black defendants. The Fourteenth Amendment, therefore, unambiguously forbids discrimination by the race of the offender.[10] Another way in which the Black Codes hampered the access of black citizens to the courts was the failure or reluctance on the part of legal officials to intervene, or to intervene with the full measure of the law, when the victim of a criminal offense was black. This would suggest that the Fourteenth Amendment also prohibits the practice of differentially prosecuting crimes committed against black and white victims.

There is historical support for such an inference. Gross and Mauro (1989, 119–120) noted that the Congressional Joint Committee on Reconstruction, which penned both the Civil Rights Act of 1866 and the Fourteenth Amendment, was aware of the fact that southern justice did not extend equally to white and black victims of crime, and expressed the belief that the Fourteenth Amendment would be one of the remedies. Pritchett (1984, 251), too, noted that the purpose of the Civil Rights Act of 1866 was to ensure that citizens of every color enjoy equal benefit in the security of their person and property, and that the Act was directed not only against abuses of state power but at cases where the state refused to exercise its power, as in instances when blacks were victimized:

> [T]he Civil Rights Act was based on an unquestioned assumption that Congress had plenary legislative power to enforce the protections of the Fourteenth Amendment, that its authority was as broad as was necessary to correct abuses that might be found, and that it could be invoked to punish acts of omission or failure to enforce the law, as well as affirmative discriminatory acts.

Gross and Mauro (1989, 119) emphasize that the protections afforded by the Fourteenth Amendment were specifically meant for victims of official *in*action: "The language of the Fourteenth Amendment itself, prohibiting the denial of 'equal protection of the law,' speaks, if anything, more clearly of victims than of defendants." There is evidence, then, that the Fourteenth Amendment's mandate for equal protection of the laws prohibits discrimination that is based either on the race of the offender or the race of the victim.[11]

The question to be addressed now is, how do defendants go about demonstrating that they have been denied equal treatment of the law, either on the basis of their race or the race of their victim, in violation of the Fourteenth Amendment? There is a great deal of established case law on this issue, and courts have insisted that only *purposeful* discrimination violates the "equal protection" clause.[12] This requirement of purposeful discrimination means that generally defendants must show that there was an intent of an official to discriminate in their individual case. At times this burden of proof is relatively easy to meet, as when, for example, a state statute directly discriminates against a group of persons. One such instance occurred in *Strauder v. West Virginia*, 100 U.S. 303 (1880) where a West Virginia statute that explicitly required that all juries include only white male citizens was declared unconstitutional under the Fourteenth Amendment. Generally, however, showing an intention to discriminate is difficult to prove since rarely do statutes contain direct racially discriminatory language, and seldom do officials express their discriminatory motives openly.

In recognition of both the difficulty of proving intent and the existence of unspoken racial animus, courts have been willing to infer discriminatory purpose from evidence of racially disparate impact. The Supreme Court has expressed both of these positions in *Village of Arlington Heights v. Metropolitan Hous. Dev. Corp.*, 429 U.S. 252, 264–265 (1977):

> Proof of racially discriminatory intent or purpose is required to show a violation of the Equal Protection Clause . . . in proving intent or purpose] . . . [s]ometimes a clear pattern, unexplainable on other grounds other than race, emerges from the effect of state action even when the governing legislation appears neutral on its face.

In the absence of any direct evidence that a law is racially discriminatory, courts, then, have inferred an intent to discriminate if there is a disparate impact associated with race that cannot be accounted for or explained by other factors. Under this Fourteenth Amendment analysis, what capital defendants would have to show in order to make a claim of racial discrimination is that decisions made in the administration of the state's death penalty statute (for example, prosecutors' decisions to seek a death sentence or juries' decisions to impose one) are more often than not unfavorable against black defendants (or those who killed whites), and that these unfavorable decisions cannot be accounted for by relevant legal factors such as criminal record, seriousness of the offense, or the existence of a contemporaneous felony.

An Eighth Amendment Claim. Defendants after *Furman* have another basis on which to make a racial discrimination claim against their death sentence—that it is the product of an arbitrary sentencing scheme. If nothing else, *Furman* stands for the proposition that the arbitrary imposition of the death penalty violates the Eighth Amendment's prohibition against cruel and unusual punishment. The imposition of the death penalty can be arbitrary if it is imposed randomly, with no disconcernible rational basis (the subject of Chapter 6), or if it is imposed on the basis of legally impermissible factors, such as race.

The opinions in *Furman* of Justices Stewart, White, and Brennan alluded to the first form of arbitrariness. Stewart referred to death sentences under *Furman*-like statutes as "cruel and unusual in the same way that being struck by lightning is cruel and unusual."[13] Brennan was no less charitable, remarking that such a statute "smacks of little more than a lottery system."[14] In describing the pattern of capital sentences prior to *Furman*, Justice White noted that "there is no *meaningful* basis for distinguishing the few cases in which it is imposed from the many cases in which it is not," suggesting that only irrational criteria separate condemned defendants from those whose life is spared.[15] The majority opinions of Justices Douglas and Marshall refer to the second form of arbitrariness. Douglas recounts the history of capital punishment in America as one where the penalty was directed against the poor and minority, and described discretionary statutes, such as the Georgia law reviewed in *Furman*, as "pregnant with discrimination." Justice Marshall referred to the racially disparate impact of death sentences as one contributing factor in persons' rejection of the death penalty.

It should also be mentioned that the evidence the Court had in *Furman* was not of a particularized instance of discrimination. There was, for example, no direct or indirect evidence that the petitioner Furman had been discriminated against in his case by any particular decision maker. Rather, the Court had systemic evidence that the prevailing scheme for the imposition of capital punishment was operating in an arbitrary manner. Patterns of life and death sentences indicated that few (and not the worst) defendants were actually sentenced to death, although a great many were death eligible, and that "if any basis can be discerned for the selection of these few to be sentenced to die, it is the constitutionally impermissible basis of race."[16] After *Furman* was decided, then, defendants could attempt to show that their death sentences were invalid under the Eighth Amendment because they were imposed under a sentencing scheme that failed to "minimize the risk of wholly arbitrary and capricious action."[17]

The issue to be addressed now is how the courts have dealt with the question of proof of racial discrimination in the states' imposition of capital punishment as it has been presented to them by petitioners. We will first examine the different requirements of social scientific and legal proof, and then review the cases of William Maxwell and Warren McCleskey.

Social Scientific versus Legal "Proof" of Racial Discrimination

Up to this point we have examined the prodigious research literature which strongly suggest that procedurally reformed post-*Furman* statutes have not rid capital sentencing schemes of racial discrimination. The most rigorous of these studies show that the race of the victim plays a significant role in determining who is ultimately sentenced to death even when legally relevant factors are considered. However persuasive, these studies have not definitively proved that the capital sentencing schemes of these states are tainted with racial discrimination.

The nature of social scientific work is that it finds a relationship or correlation between one variable, the race of the victim or offender, and another variable, the decision of the prosecutor to charge a defendant with a capital offense. Since many other factors can influence the prosecutor's charging decision besides race, such as the brutality of the crime, the number of victims, or the presence of mitigating factors, social scientists attempt to measure these other factors and explicitly consider their influence. If the effect of race still persists after these other factors are considered, then, researchers are more sure that this is a "true" race effect, rather than one due to some other factor (say, for example, the type of attorney one has) which may be related to race. The more of these factors that researchers are able to consider (and the more they are able to consider the important ones), the more confident they can be in their conclusion that they have found a true race effect.

Given the nature of social scientific work, then, researchers cannot know for certain if they have considered all of the important "other factors." With their expert knowledge of the process they are examining, the accumulated work of previous researchers, and an understanding of relevant theory, they can in their research make sure that the most important factors are measured, and therefore considered. But there may be factors affecting the decision that they were not aware of or were unable to measure. If this is true then the race effect they have found may not be as pronounced as they think, or may even be nonexistent. What social scientific researchers find, then, is a relationship or correlation of some magnitude between race and some decision-making point in the capital sentencing system. Confidence in this race effect depends upon many things, including the number and type of other factors measured, but racial discrimination can never be definitively proved.

It should also be noted that what social scientific work investigates is the overall consequence of a state's capital sentencing scheme as a whole. For example, in their study of the Georgia capital sentencing system, Baldus and his colleagues (1990) collected information on what happened to over 500 defendants convicted of murder over a number of years. Based on aggregated data they drew their conclusion that Georgia prosecutors and Georgia juries discriminated against those defendants who killed white persons. What social scientific work *does not* investigate, at least in this body of literature, is whether or not a given individual was the victim of racial discrimination in their particular case. Nothing in the Baldus data would be helpful in determining if a given offender was discriminated against by her prosecutor or her jury. Social scientific work in capital punishment is directed at *patterns* in decision making, not the influences on any specific case.

Traditionally, legal proof is fundamentally different from social scientific evidence. Persons in the judicial system are concerned with such things as motivation and intentions, in addtion to individual defendants and how they are treated. As a result, for many years the law was unwilling to presume the existence of discrimination unless a defendant was able to prove that she was the intentional victim of racial bias. As we found in an earlier section, this required that those who wanted to make a claim of racial discrimination prove that *they* were specifically discriminated against (not that they could have been because a system had discriminatory consequences), and that the discrimination was intentional.

The requirement to show intentional discrimination in an individual case is a very crippling burden of proof for defendants to overcome. It would require those making a claim of racial discrimination to have judicial actors (prosecutors, judges, jury members) attest that they were influenced by racial considerations in their consideration of the case. We have seen in the previous section, however, that under some contexts courts have abandoned this very demanding burden of proof and have adopted the more social scientific one that defendants show a clear pattern of discrimination which cannot be explained on other (nonracial) grounds. It is from this clear pattern inexplicable by other factors that courts will infer a racially discriminatory intent. It should be remembered that in the *Furman* case the Supreme Court had before it only data about *patterns* of death sentences in different states, not information as to how individual defendants were being treated.

One of the problems we will encounter in our review of the *Maxwell* and *McCleskey* cases is that the Supreme Court will at times seem to hedge on its requirement that defendants making a claim of racially discriminatory treatment merely need to show a clear pattern of disparate treatment that cannot be explained on other grounds. As we shall soon see, social scientific evidence presented to the courts has demonstrated, at least by traditional social scientific standards, that race does significantly affect which capital defendants are ultimately sentenced to death. Courts have all too often dismissed the probative value of this statistical proof, however, claiming, among other things, that an insufficient number of other factors were controlled, that the magnitude of the observed racial disparity was not great enough, or, as in the *McCleskey* case, that social scientific data showing patterns of discrimination in a state's death sentencing system cannot ultimately "prove" that such discrimination exists.

A Specific Legal Claim of Racial Discrimination: The Pre-Furman Case of Maxwell v. Bishop

We learned a little about the *Maxwell* case in Chapter 2. William Maxwell was a twenty-four-year-old black male who was convicted of rape in Arkansas in 1962 and sentenced to death. His conviction and death sentence were affirmed by the Arkansas Supreme Court. Maxwell sought relief from his death sentence in federal district court claiming, among other things, that Arkansas' death penalty statute for rape was unconstitutional because it had been discriminatory in application, in violation of the equal protection clause of the Fourteenth Amendment. Maxwell claimed that black defendants who raped white women in Arkansas were more frequently sentenced to death than defendants who raped black women.

Maxwell's initial hearing on his equal protection claim occurred on May 6, 1962 in the United States District Court, Eastern District of Arkansas [*Maxwell v. Stephens*, 229 F. Supp. 205 (1964)]. The evidence that petitioner Maxwell presented to prove that Arkansas discriminated against black rapists was rather paltry. His information sources consisted of Arkansas State Penitentiary records of criminal executions from September 5, 1913 through October 28, 1960 and evidence from circuit court clerks, prosecuting attorneys, and the sheriffs of three Arkansas counties (Garland, Pulaski, and Jefferson) as to the number and disposition of rape prosecutions in these counties during the ten-year period from January 1, 1954 to January 1, 1964. The evidence from these sources indicated that (1) all but two of the men executed for rape since 1913 had been black, (2) all of those executed for raped white woman, and (3) in Garland, Pulaski, and Jefferson Counties from 1954 to 1964, of only three criminal charges made for white men who raped black women, one resulted in an acquittal and the other two in reduced charges. During the same period, seven blacks were arrested for raping white women, two of whom were sentenced to death and three to life imprisonment.

The reaction of the district court in Maxwell's first *habeas* petition was to be typical of later courts' efforts to respond to statistical evidence of racial discrimination. The court discredited the statistical evidence by noting that important variables were left out of the petitioner's analysis of rape prosecutions, such as the defense of consent in rape cases. The court reasoned that more blacks were convicted for raping white women because consent is not as likely in these instances of rape as they were in cases where black men raped black women. A second omitted factor was the role of the moral character of the victim. The court again reasoned that this would also explain the conviction differences since the moral character of white women would be more difficult to impeach in Arkansas trial courts than that of black women. The court ultimately concluded that the proof offered by the appellant was not good enough to establish an equal protections violation. In fact, it was characterized in the court opinion as "a rather naive attempt to ascertain why a rape conviction was sought in one case and yet not in another" [*Maxwell v. Stephens*, 229 F. Supp. 205 (1964) at 217].

This was not to be Maxwell's last attempt to present statistical evidence about the racially discriminatory administration of the Arkansas death penalty statute in rape cases, however. Although the district court rejected Maxwell's claim, it did continue to stay his scheduled execution and issued a petition for a certificate of probable cause, suggesting that the court saw some merit in the claims raised. Maxwell then appealed his denial of relief in federal district court to the United States Court of Appeals for the Eighth Circuit, and was heard on June 20, 1965. There was no new statistical evidence for the court of appeals to examine, and after reviewing the available information, it concluded that the statistical argument was not persuasive:

> These facts do not seem to us to establish a pattern or something specific or useful here, or to provide anything other than a weak basis for suspicion on the part of the defense. The figures certainly do not prove current discrimination in Arkansas . . ." [*Maxwell v. Stephens*, 348 F. 2d. 325 (1965) at p. 331]

Again, the court found that the statistical evidence was not convincing, mainly because the reported racial effects were not large enough to infer a consistent and striking pattern of racial discrimination, because there might be legally relevant factors which could explain the difference in prosecution and conviction probabilities between white victim and black victim rapes, and because although there may be historical evidence of racial discrimination in Arkansas these historical patterns "do not prove current discrimination."

After his petition was denied by the court of appeals and the U.S. Supreme Court denied *certiorari,* the governor of Arkansas scheduled the execution of Maxwell for July of 1966. That execution was stayed, however, and Maxwell returned to federal district court in a second *habeas corpus* proceeding [*Maxwell v. Bishop,* 257 F. Supp. 710 (1966)]. Among the issues raised in this round of appeals was the earlier question of the unconstitutionality of the Arkansas rape statute because of the discriminatory manner in which it was imposed against black men who rape white women. In this *habeas* proceeding, however, Maxwell had additional, far more detailed, information about the death sentencing practices of Arkansas juries in rape cases. This information was the result of an extensive empirical examination of capital sentencing in rape cases in a sample of counties from eleven southern states (Arkansas was one of these states) during the period 1945–1965. This study, conducted by Professor Marvin Wolfgang of the University of Pennsylvania, was discussed earlier in this chapter.

Professor Wolfgang personally testified at Maxwell's second *habeas* hearing, presenting evidence from a sample of nineteen Arkansas counties (Wolfgang 1974). During the years 1945–1965 there were 55 convictions for rape; 34 of these involved black defendants and 21 involved white defendants. Wolfgang testified that of the 34 black convicted rapists, 19 were convicted of raping white women; of these 9 (47%) were sentenced to death. Only 14 percent of those defendants in all other rape cases were sentenced to death. In addition, the data indicated that there was no known instance during the twenty-year study period of a white man being convicted for raping a black woman. Having found this racial disparity in the imposition of a death sentence, Professor Wolfgang then testified that he considered whether or not this difference was due to racially neutral and legally relevant characteristics of the case, such as the age of the defendant and victim, the extent of force used or injury inflicted, and the use of a weapon. He told the court that none of these factors could adequately explain the observed racial disparity in death sentences for rape and that the most important factor was whether or not the offense involved a black offender and a white victim.

Although presented with far more detailed information than in previous hearings, the district court again rejected Maxwell's claim that Arkansas juries imposed death sentences for rape in a discriminatory manner. The reasons for the court's decision were that (1) statistical proofs of general patterns of racial discrimination may not be probative as evidence of discrimination in the current case, and (2) the statistical evidence was neither valid nor strong enough. Before dealing with the specifics of the statistical evidence presented by the petitioner, however, the district court seemed to foreclose the possibility that any statistical evidence of racial discrimination is relevant because it says nothing about whether or not the petitioner at hand was intentionally discriminated against by his own particular jury: "Petitioner has made no effort here to show that the individual jury which tried and convicted him acted in his particular case with racial discrimination" [*Maxwell v. Bishop*, 257 F. Supp. 710 (1966) at p. 719]. The court seemed to be suggesting here that the requisite proof for a claim of racial discrimination is evidence that defendants were intentionally discriminated against in their particular case.

Regarding the validity of the statistical evidence, the district court concluded that the study presented by Professor Wolfgang was not complete:

> While the statistical evidence produced in this case is more extensive and sophisticated than has been produced heretofore, the Court is not convinced that it is sufficiently broad, accurate, or precise as to establish satisfactorily that Arkansas juries in general practice unconstitutional racial discrimination in rape cases . . . [*Maxwell v. Bishop*, 257 F. Supp. 710 (1966) at p. 719]

The court then engaged itself in a methodological critique of the Wolfgang study, noting that the data consists of only 55 rape convictions that occurred over a twenty-year period in only 19 Arkansas counties which comprise less than 50 percent of the state's population. It also noted that the 19 sampled counties were not representative of Arkansas counties but overrepresented the southern and eastern portions of the state. There counties, which did not include the one in which Maxwell committed his crime, were the areas of Arkansas with the highest concentration of blacks. The court went on to note that there were missing data on some of the variables in the study, and that some information which the court thought pertinent was simply not collected, such as the availability of a consent defense. The district court concluded by casting doubt on the ability of any statistical showing of proof of racial discrimination:

> As a matter of fact, the Court doubts that such discrimination, which is a highly subjective matter, can be detected accurately by a statistical analysis such as was undertaken here. Statistics are elusive things at best, and it is a truism that almost anything can be proved by them. [*Maxwell v. Bishop*, 257 F. Supp. 710 (1966) at p. 720]

The district court's ruling against Maxwell was again not the last word to be heard on his claim that Arkansas juries discriminated against black offenders who raped white women. The district court's denial of relief was reviewed by the Eighth Circuit Court of Appeals for a second time in *Maxwell v. Bishop*, 398 F. 2d 138 (1968).

The Eighth Circuit's opinion was written by Judge (later Supreme Court Justice) Blackmun. The court reviewed and independently weighed the statistical evidence presented by Professor Wolfgang and concluded that "the argument does not have validity and pertinent application in Maxwell's case." It rejected the general statistical proof of discrimination for two reasons: (1) the evidence itself is insufficiently valid, and (2) even if the statistical proof were valid it is not enough in itself to successfully make a claim of racially discriminatory treatment. Again, the *Maxwell* case is a particularly interesting and prescient one because the reasons given by this court for rejecting general statistical evidence of racial discrimination will appear in an important subsequent case raising much the same issue (*McCleskey v. Kemp*). We need, then, to briefly examine these reasons.

The Eighth Circuit's opinion noted that it doubted the validity of the statistical evidence because the research by Professor Wolfgang did not include in the sample the county where Maxwell committed his crime nor did it "take every variable into account" [*Maxwell v. Bishop*, 398 F. 2d 138 (1968) at p. 147]. The latter argument made here is that in order to make a credible case of racial discrimination a statistical study must have examined the influence of every conceivable racially neutral factor. The court is expressing the opinion that there may have been other factors, legally relevant ones, which could have produced the observed racial disparity in death sentences, and as long as these factors are not considered the court will be unwilling to view the pattern of death sentences as due to racial discrimination.

The other reasons offered for rejecting the value of the Wolfgang study, even if one were to assume its statistical validity, was that statistical evidence of racially disparate sentencing patterns provide no proof that the petitioner was the subject of particularized discrimination. That is, the court was suggesting that even though general patterns of death sentencing may show evidence of a racially disparate impact (against blacks who raped white women in this case), a successful claim of racial discrimination may require direct evidence that defendants were the victim of racial discrimination by actors in their particular case. The court concluded that the Wolfgang data "do not show that the petit jury which tried and convicted Maxwell acted in his case with racial discrimination" and that "[w]e are not ready to condemn and upset the result reached in every case of a negro rape defendant in the State of Arkansas on the basis of broad theories of social and statistical injustice" (at p. 147).

The Eighth Circuit, then, rejected Maxwell's statistical proof of racial discrimination because it doubted the validity of the study's results and because it thought that there was no evidence that the petitioner was discriminated against in his own case. The Eighth Circuit's denial of relief was then appealed to the United States Supreme Court. It would have been most interesting to see how the Supreme Court would have ruled on the discrimination issue, and the role that general statistical information may play in staking a claim of racial discrimination, but the Court ignored the issue and instead vacated Maxwell's death sentence on other grounds.

The Supreme Court would, in fact, eventually rule on the issue of racial discrimination in the imposition of capital punishment, but much later. Over fifteen years after it vacated Maxwell's death sentence the Court directly addressed the issue of whether or not death sentences were being imposed in a racially discriminatory manner, and the kind of evidence it required to make this determination. This case concerned the post-*Furman* death sentencing practices of Georgia, and in this instance the statistical evidence suggesting that death sentences were influenced by racial considerations was even more formidable than that offered in *Maxwell*.

A Specific Legal Claim of Racial Discrimination: The Post-Furman Case of McCleskey v. Kemp

Warren McCleskey, a black male, was convicted of two counts of armed robbery and one count of murder by a Georgia jury in 1978 stemming from the robbery of a furniture store which resulted in the death of a white police officer.[18] Pursuant to the Georgia death penalty statute approved in *Gregg*, the jury at a separate penalty phase hearing found no mitigating and two statutory aggravating circumstances, that the murder had been committed during the course of another felony (armed robbery) and that the murder had been committed upon a police officer during the commission of his duties, and sentenced McCleskey to death. McCleskey's death sentence was automatically appealed to the Georgia Supreme Court which affirmed both the conviction and sentence, and the U.S. Supreme Court denied the appeal of this decision. McCleskey next sought relief in the Georgia postconviction process and was denied. In 1981 he filed a petition for a writ of *habeas corpus* in U.S. District Court.[19]

Among the eighteen grounds for relief presented in his writ, McCleskey claimed that his death sentence was unconstitutional because he was being discriminated against on the basis of his race and the race of his victim. The evidence McCleskey presented to support his discrimination claim was in the form of an empirical study of the Georgia capital sentencing process conducted by Baldus, Woodworth, and Pulaski (1990) (herefter referred to as the Baldus study). Baldus and his colleagues conducted a study of over 2,000 Georgia offenders who had been convicted of murder or voluntary manslaughter from March 1973, when Georgia's new capital statute took effect, until 1978. They collected information on approximately 500 variables from each case, which included data on the offender, the victim, the nature of the crime, and the kind and quality of evidence and legal representation. It is safe to say that the statistical study presented by petitioner McCleskey in his case was far more sophisticated than that presented by Maxwell in his discrimination claim, and is probably the most extensive study conducted to date of the sentencing process, capital or noncapital.

As was reported in an earlier section of this chapter, the Baldus study found that during the years examined there was a large racial disparity in the imposition of the death penalty in Georgia on the basis of the victim's race, and a lesser disparity on the basis of the race of the offender. Baldus and his colleagues attempted to control for the effect of racially neutral, legally relevant variables by estimating a statistical model of the capital sentencing decision in Georgia. They found that with these factors controlled offenders who were charged with killing a white were 4.3 times more likely to be sentenced to death than those charged with killing a black, and black defendants were 1.1 times more likely to be sentenced to death than white defendants. They found that the strongest racial effect was in those homicide cases at the mid-level of aggravation, and determined that McCleskey's own murder fell within this mid-level. They also presented evidence that indicated that there was a racially disparate impact in Fulton County, Georgia, where McCleskey was convicted and sentenced to death. Both the race of the defendant and the race of the victim were significantly related to the decision to plea bargain a case and the prosecutor's decision to move a homicide case to a penalty trial. The question before the district court was whether or not this statistical evidence constituted enough proof that the Georgia capital sentencing scheme was unconstitutional because it was discriminatory.

McCleskey's specific claim was that this disparate impact rendered his death sentence, and the Georgia capital statute, unconstitutional under both the Fourteenth and Eighth Amendments. If killers of whites were being disproportionately sentenced to death, then, McCleskey claimed, the Georgia statute was invalid because it denied him (as a black offender who killed a white victim) equal protection (the Fourteenth Amendment claim). If there is a risk that an irrelevant factor (race) entered into his sentencing decision, then death sentences imposed under that scheme are being arbitrarily and capriciously applied in violation of *Furman* (the Eighth Amendment claim). McCleskey's essential argument was that the Georgia capital sentencing *system* was producing discriminatory results, and this violated his Fourteenth Amendment right to equal treatment before the law and his Eighth Amendment right to have his sentence imposed free of impermissible considerations.

Regarding McCleskey's Eighth Amendment claim, the district court thought that this was foreclosed by the Fifth Circuit's opinion in *Spinkellink v. Wainwright,* 578 F. 2d 582 (1978). In *Spinkellink* the court was presented with evidence that in Florida defendants who killed white victims were more likely to be sentenced to death than killers of blacks. The Fifth Circuit did not even entertain the Eighth Amendment claim, accepting the facial neutrality of the Georgia law; that is, it is assumed that as long as the procedural protections approved in *Gregg* were in place, then the sentences imposed were simply taken to be nonarbitrary: ". . . if a state follows a properly drawn statute in imposing the death penalty, then the arbitrariness and capriciousness—and therefore the racial discrimination—condemned in *Furman* have been conclusively removed" (at pp. 613–614).[20] The district court in *McCleskey*, then, simply concluded that any Eighth Amendment challenge was rendered null. It did, however, give considerable attention to McCleskey's Fourteenth Amendment claim, although it noted that the claim would best be pursued under the due process rather than the equal protection clause.[21]

In order to make out a successful Fourteenth Amendment claim, the district court noted that McCleskey would have to demonstrate that he was the intentional victim of racial discrimination. It stated that a statistical showing of a disparate racial impact is alone not sufficient to prove intentional discrimination unless it is "so strong that the only permissible inference is one of intentional discrimination" [*McCleskey v. Zant*, 580 F. Supp. 338 (1984) at p. 349]. With this as its backdrop the court then proceeded to evaluate the validity of the petitioner's proof of disparate impact—the Baldus study.

What the district court did at this point was to engage in a lengthy and extensive methodological evaluation of the social scientific validity of the Baldus study (see Baldus et al. 1990). The discussion of Judge Forrester, who wrote the opinion, cannot be reviewed at length here, but in rejecting McCleskey's Fourteenth Amendment claim he did conclude that the statistical evidence presented by Professor Baldus was not valid. The district court offered several specific statistical reasons for rejecting the validity of the Baldus study. One of these reasons was the familiar complaint that the study did not consider all of the relevant aggravating and mitigating evidence. Others included the fact that (1) the data base was too inaccurate because some of the questionnaires were miscoded, there were missing variables that were important, and the manner in which missing data were treated was inappropriate; (2) the models were flawed because they could not explain a large proportion of the variation in sentencing decisions; (3) many of the variables were so highly correlated (the statistical problem of multicollinearity) that the estimated models could not be correctly interpreted; and (4) the statistical technique used, multiple regression, is ill suited to provide proof of discrimination. In rejecting the validity of the proffered statistical evidence along with McCleskey's Fourteenth Amendment claim, the district court concluded that "[t]o the extent that McCleskey contends that he was denied either due process or equal protection of the law, his [Baldus's] methods fail to contribute anything of value to his cause" (at p. 373).

The district court's decision, along with the statistical argument of the Baldus study offered by petitioner McCleskey, was reviewed in 1985 by the Eleventh Circuit Court of Appeals in *McCleskey v. Kemp*, 753 F. 2d 877 (1985). The Eleventh Circuit did not take the same route of the district court in examining the Baldus study. Rather than reviewing the district court's treatment of the methodological issues and rendering a statistical critique of the social scientific evidence, the Eleventh Circuit essentially accepted the validity of the Baldus study and examined the legal merits of the case. That is, the court presumed that the statistical study was scientifically valid and that it showed that Georgia death sentences were being imposed in a manner that discriminated against defendants who killed white victims. The question that it addressed was whether or not the disparity that was found was sufficiently large enough to make a claim that the Georgia capital sentencing system was constitutionally suspect.[22]

In addressing the issue, the Eleventh circuit first concerned itself with the question of the kind and amount of proof that must be marshalled before a claim of discrimination may be successful under the Eighth or Fourteenth Amendment. Contrary to the district court's opinion, the Eleventh circuit court noted that the petitioner's Eighth Amendment challenge *was not* foreclosed by *Spinkellink* since the Supreme Court sustained an Eighth Amendment challenge to a Georgia death sentence in *Godfrey v. Georgia,* 446 U.S. 420 (1980). It did, however, observe that to prevail under the "cruel and unusual punishments" clause of the Eighth Amendment or either the "due process" or "equal protection" clause of the Fourteenth Amendment, the factual burden of proof was the same—petitioners must demonstrate intentional discrimination. With no direct evidence of a motive or intent to discriminate against a particular petitioner by particular decision makers, the Eleventh circuit noted that general statistical studies which show a disparate racial impact may constitute proof of intentional discrimination. The court quickly qualified this by stating that the *magnitude* of that disparate impact must be so large that the only reasonable explanation that could be drawn is one of purposeful discrimination:

> We, therefore, hold that proof of a disparate impact alone is insufficient to invalidate a capital sentencing system, unless that disparate impact is so great that it compels a conclusion that the system is unprincipled, irrational, arbitrary and capricious such that purposeful discrimination—i.e., race is intentionally being used as a factor in sentencing—can be presumed to permeate the system. [*McCleskey v. Kemp,* 753 F. 2d 877 (1985) at p. 892]

The above passage attests to the fact that the Eleventh Circuit was willing to accept general statistical evidence of disparate racial impact as proof of an intent to discriminate, but would require a particularly clear pattern of discrimination. The observed racial disparity must be so strong that the only conclusion could be that it was the product of purposeful discrimination.

The Eleventh Circuit Court of Appeals, then, accepted the methodological validity of the Baldus study and its substantive conclusion that there was a disparate racial impact, and was most concerned with the magnitude of that impact. In reviewing the Baldus study it made the following determinations: (1) that the results of Baldus's best statistical model indicated that homicides involving white victims are 6 percent more likely to result in a death sentence than a comparable black victim killing, (2) killers of whites in the state of Georgia are 4.3 times more likely to be sentenced to death than killers of blacks, and (3) for those cases (like McCleskey's) at the mid-level of aggravation the likelihood of a death sentence increases 20 percent for those who killed white victims.[23] Accepting these statistical findings are valid, the Eleventh Circuit also concluded, however, that they were not sufficiently large enough to compel the inference that the Georgia statute was operating in an unconstitutionally fashion. The court determined that some amount of sentencing disparity is inevitable in a system that constitutionally requires sentencers to exercise some discretion, "in any discretionary system, some imprecision must be tolerated," that the amount of disparity revealed by Baldus's analyses does not cross that threshold of constitutional acceptability, and that "[t]aking the 6% bottom line revealed in the Baldus figures as true, this figure is not sufficient to overcome the presumption that the statute is operating in a constitutional manner" (at p. 897). Regarding the larger racial disparity found for the moderately aggravated murders, the Eleventh Circuit concluded that this cannot be used to condemn the Georgia capital sentencing system as a whole.

The essence of the Eleventh Circuit opinion, then, was that since a constituitonally valid capital sentencing scheme requires that sentencers possess the discretion not to impose a sentence of death, some inconsistencies and irregularities will result. The unevenness found by the Baldus study in the Georgia death penalty system was simply too small to sustain a constitutional challenge. In fact, the court concluded that "[t]he evidence in the Baldus study seems to support the Georgia death penalty system as one operating in a rational manner" (at p. 987).

The issue of racial discrimination in the imposition of capital punishment came to a conclusion two years later. The United States Supreme Court reviewed the Court of Appeals' decision and, in a sharply divided and somewhat caustic 5–4 opinion in *McCleskey v. Kemp,* 107 S. Ct. 1756 (1987), upheld the Eleventh Circuit's rejection of McCleskey's constitutional claims. Justice Powell wrote the opinion for a majority of the Court and addressed McCleskey's Fourteenth and Eighth Amendment claims. In its decision the Court followed the lead of the Eleventh Circuit Court of Appeals in assuming the validity of the Baldus study and directly confronted the legal merits of the case.

Regarding McCleskey's Fourteenth Amendment challenge, Powell noted that a successful equal protection claim must prove purposeful discrimination. Absent direct evidence of intentional discrimination, Powell observed that the Court has accepted general statistical evidence of disproportionate racial impact in certain "limited contexts" (at p. 1767), such as the selection of a jury venire and employment discrimination. (Title VII) cases. He stated, however, that the nature of the capital sentencing decision is so fundamentally different from these other two contexts that general statistical evidence of racial disparity in death penalty cases is of little value. Justice Powell wrote that what makes the capital sentencing decision so unique as to render general statistical evidence of racial disparity in death penalty cases is of little value. Justice Powell wrote that what makes the capital sentencing decision so unique as to render general statistical proofs incompetent is that unlike jury venire and Title VII contexts, capital sentencing decisions are made by numerous and ever-changing bodies (the petit jury which is unique in its composition and changes with each case) that are required to consider a multitude of factors. Powell also noted that unlike jury venire and Title VII situations, there is no practical opportunity for the state to rebut a presumptive showing of discrimination. Finally, since McCleskey's complaint is directed at a fundamental requirement of capital sentencing discretion, Powell unequivocally stated that the Court would require exceptionally strong evidence of a disparate racial impact before it could conclude that the exercise of this discretion was infected with impermissible considerations of race. McCleskey's statistical offering in the form of the Baldus study did not make such a compelling case, and the Court rejected his Fourteenth Amendment claim.

In his opinion, Powell directed considerable attention to McCleskey's Eighth Amendment challenge. McCleskey's complaint was that his death sentence was influenced by his race and the race of his victim and that inbeing affected by these impermissible factors it was arbitrary. In replying to this claim the Supreme Court followed a line of analysis similar to the Eleventh Circuit's. Powell noted that the Baldus study does not *prove* that race entered into any Georgia capital defendant's sentencing decision, just that there was "a discrepancy that appears to correlate with race" (at p. 1777). In response to this demonstrated showing of some risk of racial discrimination, Powell noted that discretion was an indispensable element in any constitutionally acceptable capital sentencing system and that within such schemes a certain amount of unevenness is "inevitable" (p. 1777). In addition, Powell observed that the disparities unearthed by Baldus's empirical analyses were tolerable given that there is no perfect procedure for making the life–death determination and were in fact "a far cry from the major systemic defects identified in *Furman*" (p. 1777 citing *Pulley v. Harris*, 465 U.S. 37 (1984) at p. 54). Powell provided two other reasons for rejecting McCleskey's evidence of racial discrimination. First, if McCleskey was successful the Court could be faced with other claims of discrimination in both capital and noncapital cases based on other impermissible factors such as gender or physical appearance. Second, McCleskey's arguments are more suitably directed to state legislatures who are in a better position to weigh the statistical evidence within the context of local customs and history.

It is important here to briefly take stock of precisely what *McCleskey* did and did not say. The Court *did not* conclude that there was no racial discrimination under Georgia's new capital sentencing scheme. In fact, it explicitly noted that race did influence which Georgia defendants were sentenced to death. What the Court *did* conclude was that the racial disparity uncovered by Baldus and his colleagues' analysis of the Georgia system was not large enough, and, more importantly, that a finding of systemic discrimination could not be used to definitively prove that any particular defendant was the victim of racial animus. Here we witness a clear conflict between social scientific and legal "proof."

The social scientific evidence seems conclusive. The "bottom line" of the Baldus research, the most sophisticated and careful study of criminal sentencing yet conducted, was that because of the operation of the Georgia capital sentencing system, offenders who killed whites were significantly more likely (about four times more likely) to be sentenced to death than those who killed black victims. The Supreme Court, however, essentially said that this evidence was not strong enough for capital defendants who wanted to prove racial discrimination. It also concluded that such systemic evidence, which revealed patterns of discrimination, could not constitute sufficient legal proof in these cases, although it is appropriate for employment discrimination claims. To the members of the majority, McCleskey "only" demonstrated that as a whole Georgia prosecutors and juries discriminate on the basis of race, not that any one defendant was discriminated against. Defendants like McCleskey would have to demonstrate that *they* were the victims of particularized discrimination. Essentially, the Court concluded that criminal offenders on trial for their life must meet a more demanding burden of proof in making a claim of discriminatory treatment than one who questions an employment decision.

The reader who has reached the end of this chapter must now feel a certain confusion about the Supreme Court's attitude about racial discrimination and the death penalty. In 1972 the Court in *Furman* struck down existing death penalty statutes at least in part because of the possibility of racial discrimination. The *Furman Court, however, had very little empirical data before it when it made its decision that there is a risk that some offenders may be sentenced to death because of suspect factors such as race. Some fifteen years later, the McCleskey* Court had available a comprehensive social scientific study of one state's capital sentencing system that suggested that race played a very important role in which murderers were eventually sentenced to die. In spite of this evidence, it determined that there was only a "risk" of racial discrimination faced by some capital defendants (a risk that *Furman* appeared to condemn), and noted that such a risk is constitutionally acceptable because it is a small one.

The amount and strength of the evidence of racial discrimination was much stronger in *McCleskey* than in *Furman,* but the outcome was quite different. The difference may be due to two sources. The composition of the *McCleskey* Court was much different from *Furman's.* Ideologically, the *McCleskey* Court was a very conservative one. At least as it pertained to the rights of capital defendants, Justices Rehnquist, White, Powell, and Stewart constituted a solid conservative plurality not particularly inclined to be sensitive to claims of legal discrimination. Justice O'Connor has often joined this conservative group, as she did in the *McCleskey* decision. The prospect that the Supreme Court might become more responsive to these demands in the future, with the departure of Justices Powell and Stewart, seems very unlikely. These justices were replaced with equally, if not more conservative minded jurists, Justices Kennedy and

Scalia. In addition, one of the dissenting justices in *McCleskey* and a staunch death penalty opponent, Justice Brennan, has since been replaced by one more conservative, Justice Souter.

A second, and perhaps more critical, difference between the *Furman* and *McCleskey* decisions lies in the political climate of the country. In the years just before *Furman,* a majority of the public was not supportive of the death penalty for those convicted of murder. We also know that executions had come to a standstill. Such was decidedly not the case by the time *McCleskey* was decided. The *McCleskey* Court had ample data to indicate that the public mood had changed dramatically in favor of capital punishment: There was a flurry of legislative activity in response to *Furman* which reinstated the death penalty in a majority of states, juries were sentencing nearly three hundred offenders to death each year, and public approval of the death penalty was at an all-time high. Confronted with such overwhelming public support for capital punishment, the Court may have been reluctant to follow the logic of its previous *Furman* decision by striking down existing death penalty laws.

Summary and Conclusions

One of the most consistent historical characteristics about the death penalty in the United States is the disproportion with which it has been imposed on black offenders. Over the time period 1930–1967 (the pre-*Furman* years) 50 percent of those executed for murder and 89 percent of those executed for rape were black, even though black males have comprised less than 20 percent of the U.S. population. This has not changed much during the post-*Furman* period. About 40 percent of all those executed since 1977 have been black, and over 80 percent killed white victims. That racial variables may affect the capital punishment process should not be too surprising given the historical legacy of racism in the United States, particularly in the South. In this chapter we have reviewed the old Slave and Black Codes of the South which provided for more severe punishments for black offenders, particularly when committed against whites, and which often failed to protect the lives and property of blacks.

Social scientific research conducted over the years since the Slave Codes has suggested that black mistreatment in the criminal justice system did not end with emancipation. These studies indicated that black offenders, particularly black offenders who crossed racial boundaries and committed crimes against white victims, were particularly likely to be indicted for a capital crime, convicted of a capital crime, sentenced to death, and executed. This pattern was fairly consistent during the pre-*Furman* period (particularly for the offense of rape) when capital juries had ample opportunity to exercise feelings of racial prejudice because of their unchecked sentencing discretion. The question was whether or not the disparate racial impact of death sentencing reflected racial prejudice or genuine legal differences between types of crimes, and whether or not post-*Furman* procedural reforms of state death penalty statutes were effective in eliminating any vestiges of racial discrimination.

Much more sophisticated research on the racial discrimination question during the pre-*Furman* years was conducted by Marvin Wolfgang. Controlling for several racially neutral factors, he continued to find a strong racial effect in his southern rape study. Blacks who raped white women were several times more likely to be sentenced to death by southern juries than all other racial combinations. Wolfgang's and others' evidence seemed to suggest that if one factor distinguished those defendants condemned to death and those sentenced to life, it was the impermissible influence of race.

If racial discrimination infected the administration of capital punishment during the pre-*Furman* years, it was believed that the standardless jury was the chief culprit. In several of the majority opinions, the Court in *Furman* alluded to the problem of racial bias under capital statutes which allowed the jury such unrestrained discretion. It was believed by the *Gregg* Court, however, that guided discretion statutes would rid the capital sentencing system of both its arbitrariness and discrimination.

Studies conducted during the post-*Furman* years have suggested that the Court's faith in procedural reforms of the states' death penalty statutes may have been misplaced. This research has shown that, even with relevant legal variables controlled, offenders who kill whites are significantly more likely to be indicted and charged with capital murder, convicted of capital murder, and sentenced to death. In perhaps the most comprehensive sentencing study to date, David Baldus and his colleagues (1990) have found that the race of the victim is an important consideration in the Georgia death penalty scheme, particularly at the charging stage and in the prosecutor's decision to move a case to a penalty phase hearing. Baldus et al. (1990) controlled for over two hundred possible mitigating and aggravating factors, and still found that blacks who killed whites fared far worse than defendants of other racial combinations.

The Baldus research is the most detailed capital sentencing study to be published; it is also important because it was used to challenge the constitutionality of Georgia's death penalty statute. The courts have in the past reviewed claims of racial discrimination in capital punishment. For example, in *Maxwell v. Bishop* the Eighth Circuit Court of Appeals evaluated the Wolfgang data which suggested that in the South generally and Arkansas in particular, death sentences have been disproportionately imposed on blacks who raped white women. The Eighth Circuit's opinion, however, rejected Wolfgang's research primarily on the basis that it failed to take into account enough racially neutral variables which the court thought could have explained the apparent disparate racial impact.

The Baldus data, which was far more extensive than Wolfgang's earlier study, was before the U.S. Supreme Court in the case of *McCleskey v. Kemp* (1987). The Court rejected McCleskey's Fourteenth Amendment equal protection claim because he had failed to show purposeful discrimination in his own case. It also indicated that a statistical study such as Baldus's cannot readily be used to establish an equal protection violation. Regarding McCleskey's Eighth Amendment claim that his death sentence was influenced by an impermissible factor, race, the Court concluded that Baldus's study did not prove that race had any impact. What Baldus's research indicated, the Court concluded, was that there was some correlation with race but that it was not strong enough to invalidate the Georgia statute.

The *McCleskey* decision seems to have foreclosed any further consideration of the racial discrimination issue by the Supreme Court. It is doubtful if any other researcher will be able to conduct as methodologically sound a study as Baldus's, and even if one were conducted it would apparently have to show far more substantial racial discrimination before the Court would view it as intolerable. If arguments about racial discrimination are of any policy relevance anymore, and this is by no means certain, it is probably at the grass roots or legislative rather than the judicial level.

Notes

1. For detailed descriptions of these Slaves Codes and their function in creating racial discipline, see Stampp 1956, *The Peculiar Institution:* Higginbotham 1978, *In the Matter of Color;* Genovese 1974, *Roll Jordan Roll;* and Bowers 1984, *Legal Homicide.*

2. Antebellum Virginia law, for example, contained over seventy offenses that could result in the death penalty if committed by blacks; only three offenses were potentially capital crimes for whites [see Note 1972, "Capital Punishment in Virginia," pp. 97, 103–104].

3. Louisiana law during the antebellum period allowed juries to sentence to death slaves for "grievously wounding a white person, merely shedding the blood of the master, a member of his family, or the overseer, and for the third offense of striking a white" [see Flanigan 1987, *The Criminal Law of Slavery and Freedom, 1800–1868, p. 25*].

4. For an excellent discussion of both the Slave and Black Codes, see Flanigan 1987.

5. It is interesting to note that in Johnson's Richmond data, which covers the period 1930–1939, there was only *one* homicide indictment for a murder involving a white defendant and a black victim. In five North Carolina counties over the years 1930–1940 there were only three indictments where a white killed a black.

6. It should be noted, however, that part of this similarity in findings may be due to the fact that Garfinkel's and G. Johnson's North Carolina data overlap somewhat.

7. In an analysis of data from Oklahoma, North Carolina, and Mississippi, Gross and Mauro (1989, 88–94) found significant race-of-victim effects as well. Killers of whites were far more likely to be sentenced to death than were killers of blacks in these three other states, even after controlling for legally relevant factors. A similar effect for victim's race was also found in their Virginia and Arkansas data sets, but these racial differences did not reach statistical significance.

8. Of the 594 homicide cases in the original data set, twelve involved more than

one sentencing decision because the original conviction and/or sentence was vacated on appeal. Since the unit of analysis analyzed by Baldus et al. in this study is the sentencing decision, the size of the sample is 606, and the number of death sentences imposed was 113.

9. Fourteenth Amendment to the U.S. Constitution, Section 1.

10. See *Wayte v. United States,* 470 U.S. 598 (1985); *Oyler v. Boles,* 368 U.S. (1962); *Yick Wo v. Hopkins,* 118 U.S. 356. (1886). In *Pace v. Alabama,* 106 U.S. 583 (1882), the U.S. Supreme Court noted that equal protection under the law means that persons "shall not be subjected, for the same offense, to any greater or different punishment" (at p. 584).

11. For a contrary view of what the 14th Amendment does and does not forbid, see Berger 1982, *Death Penalties.*

12. See *Washington v. Davis,* 426 U.S. 229 (1976).

13. *Furman v. Georgia,* 408 U.S. 238 (1972) at p. 309.

14. Ibid., at p. 293.

15. Ibid., at p. 313 (emphasis added).

16. Ibid., at p. 310 (Stewart, J., majority opinion).

17. This was the characterization given of the requirements of *Furman* by the *Gregg* plurality:

> *Furman* mandates that where discretion is afforded a sentencing body on a matter so grave as the determination of whether a human life should be taken or spared, that discretion must be suitably directed and limited so as to minimize the risk of wholly arbitrary and capricious action. [*Gregg v. Georgia,* 428 U.S. 153 (1976) at p. 189].

18. For detailed examinations of McCleskey's trip through the courts, see Gross and Mauro 1989, *Death and Discrimination;* and Baldus et al. 1990, *Equal Justice and the Death Penalty.*

19. For more extensive discussions of the McCleskey case as it traveled through the federal court system, and its importance in the jurisprudence of capital punishment, see Baldus et al. 1990, *Equal Justice and the Death Penalty;* Gross and Mauro 1989, *Death and Discrimination;* Gross 1985, "Race and Death"; Kennedy 1988, "*McCleskey v. Kemp;* Bendremer et al., 1986, *McCleskey v. Kemp;* Bynam 1988, "Eighth and Fourteenth Amendments—The Death Penalty Survives."

20. The petitioner in *Spinkellink* also raised a Fourteenth Amendment equal protection claim on the basis of evidence that death sentences imposed in Florida were disproportionately imposed upon those who killed white victims. The statistical evidence reviewed by the *Spinkellink* court, however, was not particularly extensive (it controlled for far fewer of the important variables than the Baldus study did), and it rejected the equal protection claim because the evidence "could not prove racially discriminatory intent or purpose" [*Spinkellink v. Wainwright,* 578 F. 2d 582 (1978) at p. 616].

21. Although the district court makes a good argument for this, there is probably no practical difference for McCleskey.

22. The court noted that:

> We assume without deciding that the Baldus study is sufficient to show what it purports to reveal as to the application of the Georgia death penalty. Baldus concluded that his study showed that systematic and substantial disparities existed in the penalties imposed upon homicide defendants in Georgia based on race of the homicide victim, and the disparities existed at a less substantial rate in death sentencing based on race of defendants, and that the factors of race of the victim and defendant were at work in Fulton. County. [*McCleskey v. Kemp,* 753 F. 2d 877 (1985) at p. 895]

23. The 11th Circuit focused almost exclusively on this 6 percent disparity figure and found it to be so small as to be constitutionally tolerable. For an excellent discussion on how the court's opinion misunderstands the significance of this disparity and the evidence of discrimination in the Baldus study generally, see Gross and Mauro 1989, *Death and Discrimination*.

5

Arbitrariness in the Administration of Capital Statutes after *Furman v. Georgia*

In the last chapter we examined the issue of the role of race (both the offender's and victim's) in the administration of capital punishment. The extensive empirical literature we reviewed seemed to suggest that the victim's race is an important factor at several decision-making points in the capital punishment process. In addition to the brutality of the offense, the number of victims killed, the criminal history of the offender, and other offense/offender characteristics that either aggravate or mitigate a homicide, one of the factors that determine which first-degree murder defendants receive a death rather than a life sentence is race, particularly the race of the victim. Although the empirical evidence presented to the United States Supreme Court in *McCleskey v. Kemp* was not accepted by a majority, it is nonetheless true that racial discrimination if proven in capital sentencing is unconstitutional under the Eighth and Fourteenth Amendments.

Several members of the U.S. Supreme Court expressed some concern about the effect of race on the administration of capital punishment in *Furman v. Georgia*. At least two members of the *Furman* Court, however, also saw the problem of capital punishment in somewhat different terms. For Justices Stewart and White, the problem was that the death penalty was imposed in an irrational manner.[1] To these two justices, prevailing patterns of death sentences did not even bear the impress of being systematically imposed according to race. According to both Justice White and Justice Stewart, death sentences seemed to be imposed without regard to rhyme or reasons. Justice Stewart described the imposition of death sentences as "freakishly rare," "wanton," and comparable to "being struck by lightning." Justice White regarded death sentences as not only "rare" but so irrationally imposed that there is "no meaningful basis for distinguishing the few cases in which [the death penalty] is imposed from the many cases in which it is not" [*Furman v. Georgia*, 408 U.S. 238 (1972) at p. 313].

Arbitrariness by Infrequency and Arbitrariness by Irrelevance

Justices White's and Stewart's characterizations of the pattern of capital sentences are particularly instructive. They both allude to the fact that the number of capital crimes far exceeds the number of death sentences, making the imposed death sentence a "rare" event. There is a subtle difference between the two, however, in terms of what this infrequency suggests.

For Justice Stewart, the infrequency of death sentences means that the capital sentencing process is very much like a system of chance. It is as if the fate of capital defendants is determined by a diabolical roulette wheel, where every tenth or twentieth slot is reserved for a death sentence, and where there are no rules that influence who is to eventually land on the unlucky slot. The determination of which convicted offenders live and which die is, then, a matter of caprice and "blind luck" rather than any important characteristics of the offender (the extensiveness of her criminal history) or the offense (the brutality of the crime). Justice Stewart is concerned with the fact that the very infrequency of death sentences implies that only the unfortunate few, those "struck by lightning," are sentenced to death:

> These death sentences are cruel and unusual in the same way that being struck by lightning is cruel and unusual. For, of all the people convicted of rapes and murders in 1967 and 1968, many just as reprehensible as these, the petitioners are among a capriciously selected random handful upon whom the sentence of death has in fact been imposed. [*Furman v. Georgia*, 408 U.S. 238 (1972) at pp. 309–310]

Stewart's complaint is that within a group of capital offenders, all of whom have been convicted of a comparable offense, only a few may ever be sentenced to death. This is a kind of "unfairness" that would exist if out of all those students who were caught cheating on a college examination only every twelfth person was punished by school expulsion, the one who rolled a double-one with a throw of the dice. These unlucky persons would be punished by being dismissed from the university while all the others, who were equally guilty, would have been spared school suspension, and would instead have simply been required to write a short essay on cheating. It is in this sense that Justice Stewart believes that death sentences are arbitrary. We will refer to this kind of arbitrary death sentence as arbitrariness by infrequency.

Justice White would agree in principle with Justice Stewart's characterization of discretionary capital sentencing schemes as arbitrary because of the sheer infrequency of death sentences. White's somewhat different concern was that without frequent death sentences and executions the deterrent message of the death penalty would be eroded:

A major goal of the criminal law—to deter others by punishing the convicted criminal—would not be substantially served where the penalty is so seldom invoked that it ceases to be the credible threat essential to influence the conduct of others. [*Furman v. Georgia*, 408 U.S. 238 (1972) at p. 312]

Justice White also suggested that death sentences not only must be frequent, they must be based on *meaningful criteria*. He voted to strike down discretionary capital statutes in part because "there is no *meaningful basis* for distinguishing the few cases in which [the death penalty] is imposed from the many cases in which it is not" (p. 313, emphasis added). Those condemned to die and those whose lives are spared should be distinguished on important legally relevant factors, such as the brutality of the crime or the number of persons killed, not on meaningless characteristics such as hair color, the weight of the offender, or the location of the crime. Death sentences can be arbitrary in the sense that they can be based on factors that should not determine or influence which capital defendants are to live and which die. Some factors are simply irrelevant to what is literally a life and death decision. We will refer to this kind of arbitrary capital sentence as arbitrariness by irrelevance.

It was for these reasons that Justices White and Stewart voted to strike down existing death sentencing schemes in *Furman v. Georgia*. When state death penalty statutes were subsequently revised, Justices White and Stewart both voted to uphold the guided discretion type of statute, in large measure because they believed that under such a reformed scheme death sentences would no longer be imposed in the irrational manner in which they were imposed under discretionary pre-*Furman* statutes. In *Gregg* the Court held that under guided discretion capital sentencing schemes, "[n]o longer can a jury wantonly and freakishly impose the death sentence; it is always circumscribed by the legislative guidelines" [*Gregg v. Georgia*, 428 U.S. 153 (1976) at pp. 206–207]:[2]

With the procedural reforms of bifurcated trials, sentencing standards for juries, and appellate review in place, it was assumed that death sentences would no longer be as unprincipled as they were under pre-*Furman* statutes. For example, in approving the new Georgia death penalty statute Justice White concluded that it "would escape the infirmities which invalidated [Georgia's] previous system under *Furman*," in that under such a law "it can no longer be said that the [death] penalty is being imposed wantonly and freakishly" [*Gregg v. Georgia*, 428 U.S. 153 (1976) at p. 222].[3] Similarly, after reviewing and approving the Georgia statute, Justice Stewart was satisfied that "[n]o longer can a jury wantonly and freakishly impose the death sentence" [*Gregg v. Georgia*, 428 U.S. 153 (1976) at pp. 206–207].

The enactment of procedural reforms of a state statute does not, however, guarantee that the mischief which was its origin will inevitably be cured. Our discussion of the role of race in the imposition of capital punishment under post-*Furman* statutes should have convinced us to be skeptical of the curative power of reforms of procedure. Capital punishment is a very volatile and highly emotional issue, and our discussion in the previous chapter suggests that the influence of race has not been effectively purged from the administration of states' capital punishment statutes. We should be equally skeptical of the capacity of procedural reforms to rid the capital sentencing system of capriciousness and arbitrariness.

Just as we were able to empirically determine the extent to which race continued to influence the infliction of the death penalty under post-*Furman* capital statutes, we can also examine studies that have investigated the extent to which post-*Furman* capital sentences are arbitrarily imposed. This will be the sole issue of this chapter. We will first examine an important measurement issue, how do you go about determining whether or not death sentences are arbitrarily and capriciously imposed?

After this we will review the extant literature to see if either type of arbitrariness (infrequency and irrelevance) continues to exist under post-*Furman* reformed capital statutes.

Determining What Constitutes an Arbitrary Death Sentence

Arbitrariness by Infrequency

Precisely how does one go about determining if a death sentence is arbitrary or not? Let us first reexamine what this kind of a death sentence is. Not all defendants who are convicted of a capital crime are sentenced to death, in fact only a modest proportion of death-eligible offenders are. In their study of capital sentencing in Georgia, Baldus et al. (1990, 115) found that capital juries sentenced to death only 23 percent of death-eligible offenders (those involving a murder plus at least one statutory aggravating circumstance) and only one half of those offenders who were advanced to a penalty trial by the prosecutor. If death sentences are to avoid being arbitrary in the infrequency sense, then, they must be imposed with some regularity and consistency.

The infrequent infliction of a death sentence may, however, reflect the fact that juries are simply being very selective in when they decide to impose the state's ultimate sanction—taking the life of another human being. That is, the infrequency of a death sentence may simply be due to the fact that juries reserve their right to put to death one of their fellow citizens only in those instances where the offense is so shockingly brutal, or the offender so hopelessly irredeemable, that the only viable response is to permanently cast that person from the human community. The rarity of a death sentence, then, may not be due to caprice but may reflect reasoned *selectivity*, the careful selection of the death penalty for only the most egregious offenses and/or offenders. If juries sentence only 10 percent of all capital offenders to death, but sentence 100 percent of the worst offenders—the "top 10 percent," they are being selective rather than arbitrary. In order to determine whether a death sentence is arbitrary, then, we need to make sure that the infrequency we observe is not due to the fact that juries are simply being discerning in their use of the death penalty.

One way to separate selectivity from arbitrariness would be to group convicted capital offenders into rank-ordered categories depending upon how serious their offense was and how culpable or blameworthy they were. We know that offenders differ with respect to how serious/brutal their crime was and how much individual responsbility they bear for it. Factors related to the seriousness of the crime would consist of such things as the number of persons murdered, the brutality with which the victim was killed, or the commission of another felony (rape, armed robbery) along with the murder. The culpability of the offender is related to such factors as the extensiveness and seriousness of their criminal history, history of drug abuse or mental instability, and diminished mental capacity or age.

With this knowledge we can then categorize individual offender into distinguishable groups so that we can say with some reasonable degree of accuracy that some offenders and offenses are "comparable" or "alike" and that some are different (less or more serious). The group of "alike" crimes would involve offenses of generally comparable seriousness committed by similarly culpable offenders. Offenses and offenders within these rough groupings would be similar to one another, but they would be different from other offenses and offenders in different categories or groups. We could then order the groups of offenders in terms of how "serious" their crime was (considering both offense and offender characteristics). We could then say that this particular group is the most serious group of offenders and this group is the next most serious . . . and this group is the least serious group of offenders.

If the criteria we select for grouping these offenders are the ones that should be or are employed in actually sentencing capital defendants, then the proportion of offenders sentenced to death should be highest in the first (most serious) group and lowest in the last (least serious) group, where arguably there should be no death sentences. If offenders within a category of seriousness are all given the same sentence, then we would conclude that no sentence was arbitrary, since similar offenders were treated alike. An arbitrary or capricious death sentence could be identified, however, to the extent that it was one that was infrequently imposed, in comparison to the sentence given to other offenders in the same seriousness grouping. Quite simply, then, within a class of comparable offenders, an arbitrary sentence is an infrequent or rare one.

To illustrate the point, let us take the hypothetical example of state "X" in Table 5–1. The table shows that in this state there were 50 death sentences imposed out of a total of 400 capital offenders during the years 1977–1987. Death sentences were imposed, then, in about 12 percent of all death-eligible cases. A sentence of death is, then, an infrequent sentence since it is imposed on only one out of every 10 convicted offenders. The table also indicates, however, that death sentences are imposed more frequently as the seriousness of the homicide increases. At the highest level of homicide seriousness or aggravation, for example, all 10 offenders were sentenced to death, and at the next highest level 86 percent, or nearly 9 out of every 10 offenders were sentenced to death. At the two highest levels of homicide seriousness, then, a sentence of death is by far the most frequent sentence (it is given in 34 of 38 cases, or nearly 90 percent of the time), and cannot, therefore, be said to be arbitrarily imposed.

At the third or mid-level of homicide seriousness, however, death sentences become substantially more infrequent. Out of 65 offenders 57 were sentenced to life while only 8 (12%) were sentenced to death. Assuming that all cases at level 3 are roughly comparable in important ways, the difference in sentence received cannot be due to glaring differences among offenders or how the offense was committed. It would appear that in instances such as this, where approximately 9 out of every 10 similar offenders are sentenced to life, the one death sentence can be said to be capricious, or, in the words of Justices Stewart and White, "freakish" and "wanton."

An even stronger case of an arbitrary death sentence can be made for those at the fourth and fifth levels of homicide seriousness. In this hypothetical illustration, 112 offenders committed an offense that could be categorized at the fourth level of seriousness, but only 7 of these (6%) were sentenced to death. These 7 offenders could reasonably raise the objection that their death sentences were arbitrary and capricious because while the "usual" sentence for a homicide of that degree of seriousness is a life sentence (94% of all offenders in this category were sentenced to life), they were selected to be sentenced to death. Absent a "meaningful" way to distinguish these 7 death-sentenced cases from the 105 life cases at seriousness level 4, it could fairly be argued that they are arbitrary and capricious, and therefore invalid under the *Furman* theory that death sentences should be imposed in an evenhanded manner.

Table 5–1
Number and Percentage of Death Sentences Imposed in State "X" during the Years 1977–1987 by Seriousness Category

Seriousness Level	Number of Offenders	Number of Death Sentences	Percentage of Death Sentences
1 (highest)	10	10	100%
2	28	24	86%
3	65	8	12%
4	112	7	6%
5 (lowest)	185	1	1%

The case for arbitrariness becomes even stronger for the lone death sentence imposed at the lowest level of homicide seriousness. At this level only one out of 185 offenders was sentenced to death. Assuming that there was nothing extraordinary about this case (and we have assumed that we have considered all of the important case characteristics that should govern the penalty decision), the one death sentence at this level stands out markedly as an aberration, a random event akin to "being struck by lightning."

This illustration reveals how the arbitrary by infrequency death sentence can be identified if one is examining the patterning of death sentences in a given state. If an offender receives a death sentence in a type of case that "generally" results in a sentence of life imprisonment, that death sentence can be considered an arbitrary one.

The next important issue to be addressed here is how regularly must a sentence be imposed before we can conclude that it is the "generally" imposed sentence for that offense type (or seriousness). There are, unfortunately, no clear guides here. We can easily recognize and define both a nonarbitrary and an arbitrary sentence at the extremes. For example, in our illustration above a death sentence was imposed in 34 out of the 38 cases that fell at the two highest levels of homicide seriousnes. For homicides that are this serious, a sentence of death, is imposed approximately 90 percent of the time. It seems reasonable, therefore, to conclude that for homicides of this type death is the "generally" imposed sentence since it is imposed on 9 of every 10 offenders. At the other extreme, for homicides at the two lowest levels of homicide seriousness (levels 4 and 5), a sentence of life was imposed in 289 out of 297 cases. Where a life sentence is given in 97 percent of the cases, we can reasonably conclude that it is the "generally" imposed sentence for homicides of that seriousness. The 8 death sentences imposed at these two levels are, then, quite rare and can be thought of as arbitrary. Another way to look at this is to think that 8 offenders were sentenced to death for crimes that were usually (97% of the time) punished by life imprisonment. For a comparable offense, these 8 offenders were treated more severely than the 289 other offenders, and were, therefore, punished excessively.

As we move away from these easily defined extremes, however, the decision as to how to characterize a sentence as the one that is "generally" given is less clear. For example, if 60 percent of the cases in a group of comparable homicides result in a death sentence, is it true that death is the "generally" given sentence? What about if death sentences comprise only 30 percent of a given category of homicides? Would it be reasonable to characterize a death sentence imposed in three out of every ten cases as "rare" or "freakish"? At this juncture we simply have to recognize that a precise decision as to what constitutes a "generally" imposed sentence cannot be made. In reviewing the extant empirical literature on arbitrariness in capital sentencing, we will venture the conclusion, however, that if a death sentence is imposed in fewer than 20 percent of the cases, that is, if a sentence of life is given in eight out of every ten cases or more, a sentence of death will be said to be arbitrary.

Arbitrariness by Irrelevance

The next question to address is how does one determine if a death sentence is arbitrary because some extra legal and therefore irrelevant factor played a part in it? It was suggested in the section above that we can identify those important factors about an offense and offender that should influence the determination as to which convicted capital offenders should live and which die. Such factors as the number of victims, the brutality of the offense, the presence of other felonies, the criminal history, age, and mental capacity of the offender are all relevant considerations for the capital jury. What constitutes an irrelevant consideration would be a factor that is not pertinent to either the seriousness of the crime or the culpability of the offender. These irrelevant factors would include such things as where the crime was committed, the type of defense attorney, or which of the state's prosecutors handled the case.

One way to determine the extent to which some death sentences were arbitrary because they were based on irrelevant or meaningless criteria would be to first ascertain the extent to which legal factors influenced the decision to sentence defendants to death. Once the effects of these factors are determined we could then see if irrelevant considerations played any role in determining who was sentenced to death. If after all legal criteria were examined it was found that capital defendants in one section of the state were far more likely to be sentenced to death than those who committed similar crimes in a different area, we would have an empirical basis for concluding that some death sentences were arbitrarily imposed because they were based on an impermissible factor—in this case the region of the state.

Fortunately, there has been some research already conducted which has examined both infrequency and irrelevance arbitrariness under procedurally reformed, post-*Furman* capital statutes. It is to this literature that we will now turn our attention.

Evidence of Arbitrary Death Sentences under Post-*Furman* Statutes

Arbitrariness by Infrequency

Although the precise percentage varies by state, capital juries during the post-*Furman* years still impose a sentence of death with some infrequency. It was reported earlier that in their study of capital sentencing in Georgia, Baldus et al. (1990, 88–89) reported that of 606 defendants convicted of murder in a jury trial, only 112 (19%) were sentenced to death. Among those who were death eligible, because the jury found at least one statutory aggravating circumstance, only 23 percent (112/483) were sentenced to death, while one half of those who subsequently advanced to a jury trial were sentenced to death (Baldus et al. 1990, 72, 89, 115). Over a slightly different time period Gross and Mauro (1984) found that death sentences were imposed in only 24 percent of all felony–type homicides in Georgia, 22 percent in Florida, 6 percent in Illinois, 25 percent in Oklahoma, 11 percent in North Carolina, 21 percent in Mississippi, 11 percent in Virginia, and 8 percent in Arkansas.

As was suggested earlier in this chapter, however, the general infrequency of death sentences does not necessarily mean that all such sentences are arbitrary. The reluctance of juries to condemn most capital offenders to death may simply reflect reasoned selectivity rather than caprice. That is, juries may reserve their right to sentence a defendant to death in only the most egregious homicides. For these crimes they may regularly sentence defendants to death. They may also extend mercy to the majority of capital offenders who they feel deserve some severe punishment, but not death. If this is indeed the case, post-*Furman* reforms of capital statutes will have successfully rid the administration of capital punishment of a central infirmity condemned by the *Furman* Court. The research to date, however, suggests that the infrequency of death sentences cannot be attributed entirely to the selectivity of capital juries.

Gross and Mauro (1984) examined death sentencing practices in three states, Georgia, Florida, and Illinois, from 1976 to 1980.[4] In their analysis they created a homicide aggravation scale comprised of three factors they found to be the best predictors of which capital defendants would be sentenced to death: (1) whether or not a contemporaneous felony was committed (felony/nonfelony homicide); (2) the relationship between the victim and suspect (stranger/ acquaintance or family member); and (3) the number of victims (multiple victims/single victim). The commission of a felony, a murder committed on a victim who was not known by the offender, and the killing of more than one victim constituted aggravating factors because they increased the likelihood of a death sentence. Each homicide was scored one if the aggravating factor was present and zero if not. These scores were summed so that every homicide had a total aggravation score which ranged from a low of zero (which meant that none of the three factors were present) to a high of three (which meant that all three factors were present).

Gross and Mauro assumed that homicides that had the same score were roughly comparable, at least in terms of those three factors that were most strongly related to the imposition of a death sentence. After categorizing each homicide on this scale of aggravation, Gross and Mauro then calculated the percentage of homicides that resulted in a death sentence within each of the three categories. The results of this analysis are presented in Table 5–2, and provide some understanding of the presence of arbitrariness under post-*Furman* capital statutes.

The first thing to notice about Table 5–2 is that Gross and Mauro were fairly successful in creating a scale that captures the degree of aggravation/ seriousness present in a given homicide. At each level of aggravation the percentage of cases that result in a death sentence increases from the previous, less serious level. The second thing to notice is that while there is some frequency in the imposition of death sentences at the higher levels of aggravation, at lower levels of homicide seriousness death sentences are not consistently imposed, but appear to be quite rare events. There appears to be, then, a substantial amount of arbitrariness in the death sentences imposed in these two states.

Taking first the case of Georgia, it can be seen that at the highest level of homicide aggravation almost 60 percent of the cases result in a sentence of death. For the most serious of homicides, then, Georgia juries regularly sentence defendants to death. This is decidedly less true, however, when only two aggravating factors are present. When there are two aggravating factors, only about one in three capital offenders eventually gets sentenced to death (31.6%). We previously decided that such a proportion may be infrequent, but is not necessarily "rare" or "freakish." We do, however, find very infrequent death sentences at the two lowest levels of homicide aggravation in Georgia. When these two levels are combined there are nearly 1,974 offenders and only 32 death sentences. For the least aggravated homicides in Georgia, then, death sentences are imposed in only 2 percent of the cases. In other words, for these less serious homicides Georgia juries sentence defendants to life over 98 percent of the time. Given such a general tendency, the imposition of a death sentence in the 32 cases at these two aggravation levels appears to be freakishly rare and arbitrary when compared with the sentence that is imposed on other, similar offenders.

This same general pattern applies to Florida. Death sentences are applied with general consistency at the highest level of aggravation (44%), although even

Table 5–2
Percentage of Death Sentences by Level of Homicide Aggravation for Two Post-*Furman* Capital Punishment States

| | Number of Aggravating Circumstances | | | |
	0	*1*	*2*	*3*
Georgia	0.4%	7.7%	31.6%	57.1%
	(6/1635)	(26/339)	(43/136)	(4/7)
Florida	0.6%	4.7%	21.9%	44.0%
	(14/2295)	(41/874)	(62/283)	(11/25)

Source: Adapted from S.R. Gross and R. Mauro, "Patterns of Death: An Analysis of Radical Disparities in Capital Sentencing," *Stanford Law Review* 37 (1984): 71, Table 21. Reprinted by permission.

here most capital offenses do not result in a sentence of death. When just two aggravating factors are present only 20 percent of the offenders are sentenced to death. As was true for Georgia, at the two lowest levels of aggravation death sentences are imposed in less than 2 percent of the cases. Only 55 out of 3,169 offenders committing the least serious homicides were sentenced to death. We could reasonably consider that these death sentences are also aberrant or arbitrary.

These findings do not, of course, suggest that the capital sentencing systems of Georgia and Florida are completely arbitrary. In fact, Gross and Mauro's data summarized in Table 5–2 suggest that there is a great deal of rationality in both systems. For example, during the years of the Gross and Mauro study (1976–1980) 79 death sentences were imposed; 47 of these (59%) were imposed for homicides that were at the highest two levels of aggravation. During the same time period, 128 death sentences were imposed in Florida of which 73 (57%) were imposed for homicides at the highest two levels of aggravation, where death sentences were handed down with some degree of regularity. Almost 60 percent of the death sentences imposed in Georgia and Florida during this period, then, could not reasonably be called arbitrary, but were imposed with a fair degree of consistency and rationality.

The data in Table 5–2 clearly indicate, however, that arbitrary and irrational elements have remained, even after procedural reforms in the two states' death penalty statutes were put into place. For example, in Georgia 32 death sentences were imposed, and in Florida 55 death sentences were handed down for homicide cases where 98 percent of comparable other cases did not result in a death sentence. These death sentences, which comprise approximately 40 percent of the total number of death sentences in both Georgia and Florida, seem more reasonably the product not of selectivity but of caprice and arbitrariness.

A detailed analysis of arbitrary capital sentencing in the state of South Carolina, whose capital statute is very similar to Georgia's, was conducted by Paternoster and Kazyaka (1990). For the years 1979–1987, they estimated the proportion of defendants who were sentenced to life or death within groups of comparable homicide cases. Three different techniques were employed to measure the comparability or similarity of homicides. One of these was to match cases on the number of relevant, specific facts characterizing the homicide. For example, if a given homicide involved an armed robbery where two elderly victims were killed by gunshot in a nonbrutal manner (for example, the victims were not bound and gagged or were not forced to plea for their lives), cases were sought that contained four specific features: (1) a killing involving an armed robbery, (2) multiple victims, (3) elderly victims, (4) gun as a weapon. The researchers then calculated the percentage of life and death cases within this matched group of "factually similar cases."[5] The second and third approaches to identifying comparable cases was to measure the overall seriousness of an offense by two different methods and match cases on the level of general aggravation.

During the time of the study there were 26 death sentences imposed in South Carolina that had been affirmed by the state supreme court on direct review. When they used the specific-facts approach to case comparability, Paternoster and Kazyaka (1990, 124) found that in 17 of the 26 cases (65% of the total number of imposed death sentences) a death sentence was also handed down in the matched group of comparable cases at least 36 percent of the time. For these 17 defendants, then, their death sentences cannot be called "rare" or "freakish," since about 4 out of 10 defendants convicted of similar crimes were also sentenced to death.

There were, however, 9 defendants who were sentenced to death in South Carolina during this period (35% of the total number of death sentences) whose death sentences were probably arbitrary in that the infliction of capital punishment for an offense of their seriousness type was a rare event. For these 9 defendants who were sentenced to death, the offenders in the matched group of comparable cases were also sentenced to death in fewer than 3 out of 10 instances. Seven out of 10 times offenders committing a comparable offense were sentenced to life. These 9 death sentences, then, can be described as arbitrary and capricious in that the "generally" imposed sentence for a crime of that type was one less severe than death. When the comparability of the case was determined by the two methods of overall seriousness, over one half of the 26 death sentences were rare events in that about 7 out of 10 of the matched group of cases resulted in a life sentence rather than death (Paternoster and Kazyaka 1990, 147).

The most extensive and methodologically sophisticated analysis of the arbitrariness of capital sentencing under post-*Furman* statutes was conducted by David Baldus and his colleagues (Baldus et al. 1983, 1985, 1990). They examined the imposition of death sentences on over six hundred Georgia defendants who had been convicted of murder after a jury trial. Of these 606 defendants 483 involved a statutory aggravating circumstance and were, therefore, death eligible. Under the Georgia death penalty statute approved in *Gregg v. Georgia,* the decision to move a case to the penalty phase of a capital trial is a discretionary decision in the hands of the prosecutor. Baldus et al.'s data indicate that prosecutors regularly exercise their discretion not to have a penalty trial. Of these 483 death-eligible cases, only 206 (43%) were advanced by the prosecutor to a penalty trial.

Baldus and his colleagues developed a more sophisticated manner with which to measure the comparability or similarity of homicide cases than that employed by other researchers. Their scale of homicide aggravation consisted of those offense, offender, and case characteristics that were statistically related to the probability that any Georgia defendant would be sentenced to death. These factors included such things as the number of statutory aggravating circumstances, the number of victims, if the victim was a female, if the victim was kidnapped, if the offender had a prior conviction for murder or other violent personal crime, and if the murder was particularly bloody. Each factor was weighted in terms of its importance and each homicide offender was given a summed score to reflect his/her overall degree of culpability and the seriousness of the homicide that was committed.

Baldus and his collaborators then divided the 483 death-eligible homicides and the subset of 206 cases that advanced to a penalty trial into six culpability/homicide aggravation levels, which ranged from least culpable defendants/least aggravated homicides (level 1) to most culpable defendants/ most aggravated homicides (level 6) and calculated the percentage of offenders within each level who were sentenced to death. The results of this analysis are presented in Table 5–3, which reports the percentage of cases that resulted in a death sentence at each of the six aggravation/culpability levels.

During the years covered by the Baldus study there were 112 death sentences imposed on 483 death-eligible convicted murderers. Twenty-three percent of these Georgia murderers, then, were sentenced to death. The distribution of the 112 death sentences was not, however, random. The data summarized in Table 5–3 clearly indicate that the likelihood of a death sentence increases dramatically as the case culpability or seriousness of the homicide increases. When the case is highly aggravated, death sentences are almost always imposed by Georgia juries. At the highest level of seriousness all 34 convicted murderers were sentenced to death. At the next two highest levels 23 out of 27 (85%) and 22 of 34 (65%) offenders were sentenced to death. When these three levels are combined, the data indicate that when a homicide is above a certain level of seriousness Georgia juries are quite consistent in their decision to impose

Table 5–3

Percentage of Death Sentences within Levels of Aggravation for Georgia Offenders Convicted of Homicide

Case Aggravation Level	*Percentage of Death Sentences*
1 (lowest)	2% (6/276)
2	14% (9/65)
3	38% (18/47)
4	65% (22/34)
5	85% (23/27)
6 (highest)	100% (34/34)
Total	23% (112/483)

Source: Adapted from D.C. Baldus, G.G. Woodworth, and C.A. Pulaski, Jr., *Equal Justice and the Death Penalty: A Legal and Empirical Analysis* (Table 10, 92). Copyright © 1990 by D.C. Baldus, G.G. Woodworth, and C.A. Pulaski, Jr. Reprinted by permission of Northeastern University Press.

the death penalty. Out of 95 convicted murderers a death sentence was imposed almost 83 percent of the time (79 cases).

If Georgia juries exercise some selectivity in that they regularly impose the death penalty for the most serious homicide cases, they do not always reserve it only for these egregious kinds of killings. In fact, the data in Table 5–3 suggest that some juries hand down death sentences for death-eligible homicides where most Georgia juries did not. At the third or mid-level of aggravation, juries returned a sentence of death only in about one third of the cases. Within this level, 18 of 47 offenders were sentenced to death while the other 29 convicted offenders (62%), who committed comparably aggravated crimes, were sentenced to some term of imprisonment.

A few death sentences were also imposed for homicides that were at the lowest two levels of aggravation, where the imposition of capital punishment is a very rare event. Sixty-five homicides were committed at the second-lowest level of homicide aggravation, and only 9 of these (14%) resulted in a sentence of death. At the lowest level of aggravation, where there were 276 homicides, a death sentence was handed down only 2 percent of the time (6 cases). When these two levels are combined we can see that for low-aggravation homicides such as these the "typical" Georgia jury has determined that the appropriate penalty is a sentence other than death. They imposed nondeath sentences 96 percent of the time (326/341). Given the consistency with which nondeath sentences are imposed by Georgia juries for homicides of this type, the imposition of 15 death sentences (out of 341 cases) can reasonably be said to be "freakish" or "rare," and therefore arbitrary.

After their thorough analyses, Baldus et al. (1990, 131) concluded that the post-*Furman* capital sentencing system of Georgia, though perhaps an improvement over the discretionary statute struck down in *Furman,* continues to produce a considerable proportion of arbitrary death sentences: Even when viewed in the most favorable light, only 50 to 60 percent of Georgia's death sentence cases appear to be presumptively evenhanded, and nearly a third of them are presumptively excessive.

It is clear, then, that some death sentences imposed in Georgia do fit the definition of an arbitrary death sentence, although it must be recognized that the Georgia capital punishment system also possesses elements of rationality to it. During the time period studied by Baldus and his colleagues there were 112 death sentences imposed on 483 death-eligible convicted Georgia murderers. Fifty-seven of these death sentences were imposed for homicides where juries handed down a death sentence in a comparable case 93 percent (57/61) of the time. An additional 22 death sentences were imposed in homicide cases where the death sentencing rate was 65 percent (level 4). When homicides at the three highest levels are combined we see that for these 95 offenders a sentence of death was handed down in 79 cases (84%), and these 79 cases represent 70 percent of all of the Georgia death sentences imposed during this period. When death sentences are imposed in 84 percent of the eligible cases, as over two thirds of the Georgia death sentences were during these years, it cannot be argued that they are imposed arbitrarily. Finally, it must be reiterated once again that although the majority of Georgia death sentences do appear to be handed down in a rational manner, there remains considerable arbitrariness within its capital sentencing system. Some defendants (approximately 30%) continued to be sentenced to death by aberrant Georgia juries in cases that usually result in a life sentence. With Baldus's data we have identified at least 33 such cases (levels 1, 2, and 3), which comprise 30 percent of the total number of death sentences.

Arbitrariness by Irrelevance

Location of the Crime. In the above section we identified one form of arbitrary capital sentencing—arbitrariness by infrequency. We can, however, identify a second type of arbitrary capital sentence. It should be remembered that in our discussion of arbitrariness we noted that there must be a *"meaningful"* basis on which to distinguish those offenders sentenced to death from those whose lives are spared. This implies that even if we can identify a factor that clearly differentiates between those condemned to die and those sentenced to imprisonment, this factor must be meaningfully or rationally related to the goals of punishment, as would for instance such factors as the brutality of the offense or the violent criminal history of the offender. These two factors clearly are relevant sentencing considerations. A concern for retribution, giving murderers their "just deserts," might legitimate a death sentence, and it could be argued that capital punishment is rationally related to the punishment goals of deterrence and incapacitation. If a factor is identified that discriminates those sentenced to death from life-sentenced defendants but that bears no rational or relevant relation to the reason for punishing criminal offenders, then that factor is an irrelevant one and the imposed sentence an arbitrary one.

One such irrelevant factor is the location in the state where a homicide was committed. Since a death penalty statute is passed and enacted by the *state* legislature, it is expected that the law (indeed, any law) would be uniformly enforced throughout the state. That is, an offender who commits his capital crime in one part of the state should be given a similar sentence as another offender who commits a comparable crime in a different part.[6] It would seem reasonable to argue that a death penalty statute cannot be said to be applied with rationality if being sentenced to life or death depends upon where one commits the offense. The location of the state where the crime was committed cannot fairly be called a "meaningful" basis upon which to distinguish those capital offenders who deserve to live and those who deserve to die. To return to our earlier analogy, this is the same kind of arbitrariness that would occur if those who were caught cheating on a college examination in the even-numbered rooms at the university were punished far more severely than those caught cheating in the odd-numbered rooms.

As Gross and Mauro (1984, 68–69) have suggested, there is nothing in the Fourteenth Amendment's "equal protection" clause to forbid capital sentencing variation by geography. They do note, however, that it may violate the Eighth Amendment's special requirement that capital sentences be imposed in an evenhanded and uniform manner. It is clear that in its 1976 death penalty cases the U.S. Supreme Court thought that guided discretion statutes, which were approved as constitutional, would ensure that capital punishment statutes were consistently imposed throughout the state. In *Gregg v. Georgia,* for example, the Court noted with approval the Georgia Supreme Court's statement that "we view it to be our duty under the similarity standard to assure that no death sentence is affirmed unless in similar cases *throughout the state* the death penalty has been imposed generally . . ." [438 U.S. 153 (1976) at p. 205, citing *Moore v. State,* 233 Ga. 861,864 213 S.E. 22 829, 832 (1975), emphasis added].

There is some evidence to suggest that death sentences imposed under procedurally reformed post-*Furman* statutes do substantially vary by the location in the state where the crime was committed. Perhaps the first to investigate this kind of arbitrariness were Bowers and Pierce (1980), who examined death-sentencing rates in Florida and Georgia. They found that the likelihood that a homicide defendant would be sentenced to death was in part influenced by where in the state the killing occurred. Table 5–4 provides a summary of their results.

Bowers and Pierce (1980, 599) reported that 16 percent of all felony murders committed in Georgia and 19 percent of all felony murders committed in Florida resulted in a death sentence. Table 5–4 indicates that these statewide rates vary substantially by the area within the state where the homicide occurred. Within Georgia, for example, felony–type murderers are least likely

Table 5–4
Percentage of Felony–Type Murder Cases That Resulted in a Death Sentence in Geographical Areas of Georgia and Florida

State and Region	Percentage of Death Sentences
Georgia	
North	6%
Central	23%
Fulton County (Atlanta)	3%
Southwest	22%
Southeast	17%
Florida	
Panhandle	58%
North	14%
Central	27%
South	13%

Source: W.J. Bowers and G.L. Pierce, "Arbitrariness and Discrimination under Post-*Furman* Capital Statutes," *Crime and Delinquency* 26(1980a):604, Table 5. Reprinted by permission.

to be sentenced to death if they commit their offense in Fulton County (Atlanta) and the northern part of Georgia than anywhere else in the state. This variation by geographic region is quite striking. Felony–type murderers who kill their victims in the central or southeast region of Georgia are almost eight times more likely to be sentenced to death than one who kills in Fulton County.

Other data from Georgia confirm these findings. Baldus et al. (1990, 121) examined death sentencing rates in different regions of Georgia over the years 1973–1979. They reported death sentencing rates that varied from a high of 33 percent in north central Georgia to a low of 9 percent in northern Georgia and 13 percent in Fulton County. Defendants convicted of a capital murder in north central Georgia were almost four times more likely to be sentenced to death than those convicted in the more northern parts of the state. This geographical disparity existed even when Baldus and his colleagues (1990, 128) considered the severity/aggravation of the homicide. They did find that most defendants were sentenced to death at the highest levels of aggravation, no matter where in the state the crime was committed. For less serious offenses, however, considerable geographical disparity existed. At the two lowest levels of aggravation, offenders committing their crime in north central Georgia were over five times more likely to be sentenced to death than those in Fulton County, and over three times more likely than those in southwest Georgia.

Disparate capital sentencing by geographical area also characterizes Florida death sentences. Death sentencing rates vary from a high of approximately 60 percent to a low of 13 percent (see Table 5–4). Felony–type murderers in the panhandle of Florida are almost four and one half times more likely to be sentenced to death than those who kill in the southern or northern part of the state. In a later, and more refined, analysis of Florida data, Bowers (1983) found that murderers who committed their crime in the central part of Florida were more likely to be indicted and convicted for first-degree murder than offenders in other regions of the state, even after taking into consideration the different kinds of crimes committed in these different areas.

Gross and Mauro (1984, 64–65) also found geographical disparity in death sentencing rates in their study of Georgia, Florida, and Illinois. Rather than divide the three states into geographical regions, however, Gross and Mauro categorized each homicide as occurring in a rural or urban part of the state. They found that homicides committed in rural areas of Florida and Georgia (but not Illinois) were almost twice as likely to result in a death sentence as those homicides committed in an urban area. Gross and Mauro's finding, that homicide defendants who kill their victims in rural areas are more likely to be sentenced to death, was corroborated by Baldus et al.'s (1985, 1990) more sophisticated analysis of Georgia data. They (1990, 121) reported that 27 percent of the convicted murderers who committed their crime in rural Georgia were sentenced to death, while only 19 percent of urban murderers were. This was not a consistent pattern, however, and changed somewhat depending upon the seriousness of the homicide. Low aggravation/serious homicides were more likely to result in a death sentence if committed in an urban area of the state, while more serious homicides were more likely to end in a death sentence in rural areas of Georgia (1985, 1405).

Finally, although he did not examine the rural–urban distinction, Bowers (1983, 1084–1085) found that convicted first-degree murderers were significantly more likely to be sentenced to death in north Florida counties than in other parts of the state, even when controlling for several legally relevant factors.

The Existence of "Killer Prosecutors." The finding that offenders are more likely to be sentenced to death in certain parts of a state raises the important question, why would the geographical location of the crime make a difference? The answer may reside in local moral climates. Perhaps some areas of a state are more conservative than others; the citizens, and the capital juries that are selected from among them, are more intolerant of those who murder and punish them more severely. Such an explanation seems unlikely for some of the findings, however, unless the cultural climate within a state changes dramatically within a short distance. Bowers and Pierce found a substantial difference in the percentage of felony–type murder cases that resulted in a death sentence between Fulton County (Atlanta) and nearby counties in central Georgia (see Table 5–4). There must be more than geographical variations in "culture climate" at work here since it is doubtful if the "cultural climate" changed substantially by crossing contiguous county lines.

It may not be the moral climate of the community that best explains these geographical variations but the moral attitudes of actors within the capital punishment system itself. For example, juries cannot impose death sentences unless prosecutors make the initial decision to charge defendants with a capital offense. For a comparably serious crime, some prosecutors may be more inclined to charge a murder as a capital offense than another prosecutor in a different jurisdiction. A prosecutor's inclination to charge a capital offense may be due to her own moral attitude, the fact that the community was recently victimized by a brutal murder, or the fact that the prosecutor is facing a reelection. If there are such "killer prosecutors," and for whatever reason, then perhaps much of the observed geographical disparity is due to the selection of cases by different prosecutors. In any event, if this is true, the likelihood that any defendant will be sentenced to death is influenced by which prosecutor they happen to have in charge of their case—an arbitrary consideration that should not influence who lives and who dies.

There is some evidence to suggest that capital defendants are in fact at the mercy of which prosecutor they face. Bowers (1983, 1079) found that the likelihood that a Florida defendant would be indicted for first-degree murder was also a function of where in the state the crime was committed. Even when legally relevant differences in the kinds of murders that were committed were considered, homicide defendants perpetrating their offense in central Florida were more likely to be indicted for first-degree murder than those in other parts of the state.

Paternoster (1983, 779) reported comparable findings from another state. He found that in South Carolina the prosecutor's discretionary decision to charge a homicide as a capital murder was related to the particular judicial district within which the case was tried. Table 5–5 reports the probability that the prosecutor requested a death sentence in each of the sixteen judicial circuits of South Carolina. Prosecutors in some South Carolina judicial circuits entered a charge of capital murder for 80 to 90 percent of their death-eligible cases while in others less than 20 percent of those who committed a capital offense were charged with a capital crime. Defendants who committed their murder in South Carolina's Fifteenth Judicial Circuit were over five times more likely to be charged with capital murder than those in the Fourth or Fifth Circuit. When the sixteen judicial circuits were categorized into either urban or rural districts, Paternoster (1983, 780) reported that rural prosecutors were almost twice as likely to charge a defendant with capital murder as their urban counterparts, even though rural murders were no more serious or aggravated than urban ones.

South Carolina is not the only state where such variation by judicial circuit can be found. Nakell and Hardy (1987, 125–130) found that the probability of a first-degree murder indictment was related to the judicial district within which the crime was tried. While for the state of North Carolina as a whole

Table 5–5
Number of Capital Murders, Number of Death Penalty Requests, and Percent of Cases Resulting in a Death-Penalty Request by Judicial Circuit

Judicial Circuit	Number of Murders	Number of Death-Penalty Requests	Percent of Cases with a Death Request
First	9	4	44%
Second	15	4	27%
Third	14	6	43%
Fourth	12	2	17%
Fifth	30	6	20%
Sixth	5	2	40%
Seventh	10	7	70%
Eighth	9	4	44%
Ninth	45	11	24%
Tenth	5	4	80%
Eleventh	15	12	80%
Twelfth	14	4	29%
Thirteenth	30	7	30%
Fourteenth	17	10	59%
Fifteenth	15	13	87%
Sixteenth	16	9	56%

Source: R. Paternoster, "Race of Victim and Location of Crime: The Decision to Seek the Death Penalty in South Carolina," *Journal of Criminal Law and Criminology* 74(1983):779, Table 6. Reprinted by special permission of Northwestern University, School of Law.

approximately 70 percent of capital murders resulted in a first-degree murder indictment, in the Fifth Judicial District 100 percent of the murders resulted in a first-degree indictment and 90 percent in the Twenty-Sixth Circuit. The probability that a defendant would be indicted for first-degree murder was over twice as high in these two circuits than in North Carolina's Twelfth Judicial Circuit, where only 38 percent faced a first-degree murder indictment. The Fifth Judicial Circuit of North Carolina was a "killer circuit" for other reasons. Prosecutors in this circuit were also more likely to move first-degree indictments to a first-degree murder trial. In fact, Nakell and Hardy (1987, 136) reported that even after considering the legal evidence in the case, defendants in the Fifth Circuit were 158 times more likely to stand trial for first-degree murder than a similar defendant in other circuits.

An extensive study of the capital sentencing system of New Jersey by Bienen et al. (1988, 178–184) documents extensive variability under that state's relatively new death penalty statute. They reported that in some New Jersey counties approximately two thirds of all death-eligible defendants were sentenced to death (Camden and Mercer Counties) while in others fewer than one third were (Passaic and Monmouth Counties). They also identified the existence of "killer prosecutors" in two counties in New Jersey, Monmouth and Mercer Counties. Murder defendants in Mercer County were almost fifty times more likely to go to trial than comparable defendants in Camden County, New Jersey (Bienen et al. 1988, 231–232). Defendants in Monmouth County were over thirteen times more likely to face a capital trial than those in Camden County. It would appear, then, that in North Carolina and New Jersey, like South Carolina, it makes a significant difference which prosecutor a murderer has to face.

Other Kinds of Irrelevant Factors

Death sentences can be affected by other irrelevant considerations in addition to the location of the crime and the particular prosecutor handling the case, considerations which should not reasonably affect which capital defendants live and which die. One of these other irrelevant considerations is the kind of defense counsel a defendant has. It seems a basic precept of justice that when defendants are on trial for their life they should be afforded the best possible legal assistance. As we have seen in Chapter 3, however, defense counsel in capital cases often leaves a lot to be desired. Although there was anecdotal evidence to suggest that capital defendants are adversely affected by the type of counsel they have, is there any social scientific data to suggest that a defendant's fate is tied to her attorney?

One such piece of social scientific evidence comes from a study by William Bowers, who investigated several decision-making points in the Florida capital sentencing system. He found (1983, 1086) that the type of attorney a defendant had was one of the single most important factors determining the sentence received by those convicted of first-degree murder. Bowers's study showed that having a public defender or a court-appointed counsel significantly increased a defendant's chance of a death sentence. Those able to afford their own retained lawyer fared far better at the penalty phase of a Florida capital trial. In fact, Bowers found that having a court-appointed lawyer was as damaging to a defendant's chance of avoiding Florida's electric chair as committing a felony-related murder.

Further evidence that the fate of a capital defendant often depends upon the quality of her counsel, which in many cases may be quite poor, comes from a study conducted by the *National Law Journal* (Coyle et al. 1990, 44). They reported that in the six states that have performed 80 percent of the post-*Furman* executions (Alabama, Georgia, Florida, Louisiana, Mississippi, and Texas), trial lawyers representing capital defendants are disbarred, suspended from practice, or otherwise professionally disciplined at a substantially higher rate than the state average. For example, capital defense counsel in Louisiana are professionally censured at a rate forty-seven times higher than other lawyers in the state; in Mississippi capital counsel are disciplined thirty-six times more frequently than other lawyers in the state. This is not to suggest that these lawyers were disciplined because of their incompetent performance in a specific capital case. More likely, it reflects the selection of lawyers to defend capital defendants in these states. Without a well-organized and well-developed capital defense bar most defendants are given court-appointed counsel. The data collected by the *National Law Journal* suggest that, at least in these states, court-appointed counsel in death penalty cases may come from the lower stratum of the legal profession. These findings suggest that no matter how procedurally reformed state death penalty statutes are *in the law,* they mean little or nothing to capital defendants who have ineffectual counsel. With an inept lawyer even a procedurally reformed capital sentencing system may easily become a crapshoot.

Bowers's Florida study also gives us a clue as to the importance of these extralegal considerations which may influence a capital defendant's case. He reported (1983, 1075–1078) the results of interviews with Florida judges, prosecutors, and defense attorneys. Prosecutors stated that among the factors that influenced their decision to charge a case or bring it to a trial were the publicity surrounding the case, pressure from the police or from superiors, and the prosecutor's relationship with the defense attorney. Bowers found that extralegal considerations such as the prosecutors' personal values, political and situational influences, and social pressure from the community were mentioned more often than legal considerations (facts of the case, strength of the evidence) as factors that influenced the course of a case through the capital sentencing system. Although there has been little research to date, these preliminary findings suggest that the fate of capital defendants is affected by other than strictly legal considerations, factors that are irrelevant to the seriousness of the offense they committed or their own personal culpability.

Summary and Conclusions

In the decision of *Furman v. Georgia,* which invalidated existing state death penalty statutes, the Supreme Court maintained that death sentences could not be imposed in an arbitrary and capricious manner. We have suggested in this chapter that there are two related kinds of arbitrary death sentence. First, a death sentence is arbitrary if it is not the generally imposed penalty for a given homicide type, that is, if it is excessive when compared to the penalty given similarly situated offenders. This was referred to as arbitrariness by infrequency. A second type of arbitrary death sentence occurs when a capital defendant's fate is influenced by extralegal or immaterial considerations, such as the location of the crime. This was referred to arbitrariness by irrelevance. Although arbitrary death sentences characterized the capital statutes that were reviewed and rejected in *Furman,* post-*Furman* procedurally reformed capital statutes promised to be different.

We have examined research evidence suggesting that current death penalty statutes have not been successful in ridding arbitrariness completely from the capital sentencing system of most states. This research did indicate that when a homicide is particularly aggravated a death sentence is consistently requested by the prosecutor and imposed by the jury. There is, then, some careful selectivity under these statutes. The death penalty is frequently imposed on the most egregious and culpable offenders. This is not at all to say, however, that capital punishment is reserved *only* for the most serious offenses.

Research in several states has shown that some death sentences are irregularly imposed for homicides that are only of moderate or low aggravation. For these types of homicides, life sentences are the most frequent penalty, although some offenders are sentenced to death by an occasional jury. These aberrant death sentences, which may comprise as much as one third of the total number of death sentences that are imposed in a state, constitute the same kind of arbitrary sentence that was condemned in *Furman.* There is evidence, then, that selectivity and arbitrariness are not mutually exclusive characteristics, and may exist side by side under current capital sentencing schemes.

In addition to arbitrariness by infrequency, we also examined the existence of arbitrariness by irrelevance. We discovered that the fate of many capital defendants is influenced by where in the state they committed their crime. In an early analysis, Bowers and Pierce (1980) found that offenders who committed their homicides in one part of Georgia were over seven times more likely to be sentenced to death than those who committed theirs in another area. They reported a similar pattern in Florida, and their Georgia findings were corroborated by Baldus et al.'s research (1990). All of these findings are consistent with the work of Gross and Mauro (1984), who found that defendants who killed their victims in rural areas of a state were substantially more likely to be sentenced to death than those who killed in urban areas.

In addition to the influence of geography, the fate of some capital defendants is also affected by the particular prosecutor who tries their case. In a study of the prosecutors' decision to charge a capital offense in South Carolina, Paternoster (1983) found considerable variation by judicial circuit. A defendant who committed a homicide in one judicial circuit was five times more likely to be charged with capital murder than those in a different circuit within the same state. There were some "killer prosecutors" who charged most of their death-eligible offenders with capital murders, while others charged a much smaller percentage. Nakell and Hardy (1987) found that some judicial circuits in North Carolina were particularly severe on capital defendants. Independent of the facts of the case, defendants in one particular circuit were more likely to be indicted and tried for first-degree murder than offenders in other judicial circuits. Finally, Bowers (1983) reported evidence suggesting that those defendants who could afford to retain their own counsel were less likely to be sentenced to death than those with court-appointed or public defenders. He also found that the prosecutor's decisions in a capital case were more likely to be affected by extralegal considerations than by the particular facts of the case.

Together these data paint a rather bleak picture of post-*Furman* capital sentencing schemes. Although these statutes promised to eliminate arbitrary and capricious death sentences, research suggests that for some capital defendants today, being sentenced to death is the result of a process that may be no more rational than being struck by lightning.

Notes

1. Although Justice Douglas grounded his objection to prevailing capital sentencing schemes on racial discrimination (such statutes were "pregnant with discrimination" [*Furman v. Georgia*, 408 U.S. 238 (1972) at p. 257]), he also expressed concern that some death sentences were imposed in a capricious, unprincipled manner: "Under these laws no standards govern the selection of the penalty . . . People live or die, dependent upon the whim of one man or 12" (at p. 253).

2. At the time the Court decided in *Gregg* that guided discretion capital statutes were constitutionally acceptable, it rejected mandatory death statutes as a cure for standardless juries because such mandatory schemes only "papered over" the problem of discretion and could not, therefore, correct for the "arbitrary and wanton jury discretion" that was condemned by *Furman* [*Woodson v. North Carolina*, 428 U.S. 280 (1976) at p. 303 (plurality opinion)].

3. *Gregg v. Georgia*, 428 U.S. 153 (1976) at p. 222 (White, J. concurring).

4. Illinois' post-*Furman* capital statute became effective in July of 1977, so the Gross and Mauro data for this state covers the period between July 1977 and December 1980.

5. Obviously, these cases were not matched on all features of the homicide, but on the few that were deemed most relevant for sentencing purposes.

6. This equality of treatment would not have to extend to noncapital prison terms. For example, it would be permissible for burglars in one part of the state to be sentenced for longer prison terms (say, on average, four years) than those burglars convicted in another part (on average, two years). Since death is such a qualitatively different punishment than life imprisonment, however, and not just different in degree, geographical disparity would not be tolerated for capital sentencing.

IV
Arguments For and Against the Death Penalty

6

The Cost of Life and Death

In this chapter we will examine one of the arguments that may be made in support of the death penalty—the fact that capital punishment may be a far less costly penalty for the public to bear than life imprisonment. We will call this the economic benefits argument. This is indeed a very pervasive belief. In their research on public opinion and the death penalty, Ellsworth and Ross (1983, 142) found that 73 percent of their respondents thought that the death penalty would cost the taxpayer less than life imprisonment. Among those who initially expressed support for capital punishment, almost 80 percent believed it was less costly. Since cost seems to be a very important consideration for the public generally and in particular for those who support capital punishment, we will examine the details of this argument and determine whether or not it is supported by the evidence.

The Economic Benefits Argument

The economic benefits argument states that the death penalty is a far less costly punishment for the state (and its taxpayers) to bear than life imprisonment for its murderers. Those who argue this position would claim either that citizens are already burdened with taxes that are high enough or that the limited amount of tax dollars collected should go to more "worthy" state programs. In either form, the argument suggests that life imprisonment is a more costly alternative than the death penalty because convicted murderers must be confined for long periods of time in state penal institutions, and that these penal institutions are both already overcrowded and extremely expensive to construct and maintain. Much money would be saved, it is suggested, if convicted murderers were simply put to death.

There can be little doubt that executing convicted murderers would be far more cost efficient than an alternative of life imprisonment if capital murder trials were conducted in much the same manner as noncapital trials and if the executions took place immediately or soon after a conviction was secured. However, it may not be more cost efficient to maintain a *system* of capital punishment where capital defendants are entitled to procedural protections from the courts. Those who oppose capital punishment on these grounds would claim that a constitutionally acceptable system of capital punishment is in fact far more costly than a system of criminal justice that includes life imprisonment (or a very long period of confinement) as the only available punishment for murder. They would further argue that there are far more cost effective ways to severely punish those who murder, assist the families of homicide victims, and reduce the homicide rate.

The belief that life imprisonment is less costly than the death penalty may at first blush seem counterintuitive. How could it possibly be cheaper to keep someone in prison, either for a long period of time (say, thirty to forty years) or for the remainder of his natural life, than to hold a "normal" trial and execute the offender, if convicted, soon after? The answer to this question is that capital murder trials are not in any sense tried as if they were "normal" trials, nor do we or could we execute murderers soon after their convictions were secured. Proponents of the death penalty note the cost savings that would accrue if capital punishment were to simply replace life imprisonment as the punishment for murder without any other changes in the system. Opponents, however, compare the cost of capital punishment incurred by an overall system of justice that includes capital punishment with one that excludes the death penalty. Opponents also base their cost considerations on how much it costs the *current system* of capital punishment to operate.

In this chapter we will examine what it is about our prevailing, constitutionally acceptable, death penalty schemes that make them costly to operate, so expensive in fact that it is more economical to imprison someone for life. We will learn that a system of life imprisonment is considerably less expensive than one that includes capital punishment, largely because (1) capital trials are far more expensive for the state to prosecute and for the defendant to defend than noncapital trials because there are more and more complex legal issues to contend with, (2) capital trials are really two separate trials (a guilt and a penalty phase) which require far more preparation resources than noncapital cases, and (3) the appeals process in capital cases is so complex and lengthy that large sums of money are required to bring them to a final legal determination. Before we examine each of these specific arguments, a more general comment is in order about the special nature of capital trials which may make them in the end more costly to prosecute to finality than noncapital trials.

The Doctrine That "Death Is Different" and the Requirement of "Super Due Process"

Under the Fourteenth Amendment to the United States Constitution, criminal defendants are entitled to "due process" protections: ". . . nor shall any State deprive any person of life, liberty, or property, without due process of law." The requirement of "due process" is a rather vague one, but over the years as a result of Supreme Court rulings it has been determined that criminal defendants are guaranteed such things as protection against unreasonable search and seizure, warnings of their right to remain silent upon being arrested, the right to effective assistance of counsel, the right to a jury from a representative cross-section of the community, and the right to counsel at a sentencing hearing.

These rights of criminal defendants have been established because of the belief that they are necessary to protect fundamental interests of individuals in our society. These interests (which include "life, liberty, and property") are at stake in any criminal prosecution where the defendant may, as a result of state action, be denied life (the death penalty), liberty (a term of confinement), or property (a fine). Since these interests are so important they need to be protected when the state attempts to take them away as a result of a criminal prosecution. Recognizing that there is a substantial imbalance of power between lone individuals and the agents of the state, extensions of the Fourteenth Amendment afford protections to the individual in numerous ways: providing individuals with a skilled advocate to advance their interests (effective counsel at pretrial, trial, and sentencing), ensuring that the state make its case not behind closed doors but in a public and unbiased forum (jury trial), and protections should the state pursue its case too aggressively (search and seizure protections and evidence rules).

Due process protections are provided to criminal defendants, then, because of the necessity to protect fundamental interests which may be jeopardized as a result of a successful state prosecution. Not all interests are equal, however. The most important interest individuals may have to protect is their right to life. Life is the *sine qua non* of all other rights; without life an individual can exercise no other rights. The Supreme Court has repeatedly recognized the importance of legally protecting the lives of capital defendants in their pronouncements that "death is different" from all other penalties. For example, this belief was expressed in *Furman v. Georgia* by Justice Brennan:

> Death is a unique punishment in the United States . . . The only explanation for the uniqueness of death is its extreme severity. Death is today an unusually severe punishment, unusual in its pain and its finality, and in its enormity. [408 U.S. 238 (1972) at p. 287]

and by Justice Stewart:

> The penalty of death differs from all other forms of criminal punishment, not in degree but in kind. It is unique in its total irrevocability. It is unique in its

rejection of rehabilitation of the convict as a basic purpose of criminal justice. And it is unique, finally, in its absolute renunciation of all that is embodied in our concept of humanity. [408 U.S. 238 (1972) at p. 306]

These individual expressions that "death is different" were accepted by the Court's plurality in *Gregg v. Georgia:* "There is no question that death as a punishment is unique in its severity and irrevocability" [428 U.S. 153 (1975) at p. 187 (opinion of Justices Stewart, Powell, and Stevens and Justice Marshall in his dissent]. In *Gardner v. Florida* it was recognized that a majority of the Court now embraced that view:

> Five Members of the Court have now expressly recognized that death is a different kind of punishment from any other which may be imposed in this country [citations omitted]. From the point of view of the defendant, it is different in both its severity and its finality. From the point of view of society, the action of the sovereign in taking the life of one of its citizens also differs dramatically from any other legitimate state action. [*Gardner v. Florida,* 430 U.S. 349 (1977) at pp. 357-358]

It was its recognition that capital punishment was different from all other criminal penalties in terms of its severity and irrevocability that led the Supreme Court to procedurally reform state death penalty statutes in order to ensure that those sentenced to death are those truly deserving of the ultimate sanction. The position of the Court, that heightened due process considerations are due capital defendants because of the uniqueness of the death penalty, was summarized by Justice O'Connor in *Thompson v. Oklahoma:*

> Under the Eighth Amendment, the death penalty has been treated differently from all other punishments. Among the most important and consistent themes in this Court's death penalty jurisprudence is the need for special care and deliberation in decisions that may lead to the imposition of that sanction. The Court has accordingly imposed a series of unique substantive and procedural restrictions designed to ensure that capital punishment is not imposed without the serious and calm reflection that ought to precede any decision of such gravity and finality. [*Thompson v. Oklahoma,* 487 U.S. 815 (1988) at p. 856]

As we saw in Chapters 2 and 3, these reforms include, among other things, a bifurcated trial process, an enhanced opportunity to present evidence in mitigation of penalty to the sentencing authority, the provision of psychiatric assistance if the defendant's sanity is likely to be an issue, and direct appellate review of both the conviction and penalty. The Court, then, has provided additional due process protections to capital defendants because death "calls for a greater degree of reliability" [*Lockett v. Ohio*, 438 U.S. 586 (1977) at p. 604] than noncapital sentencing.

Because of the unique nature of the life/death decision, then, those on trial for their life have been afforded heightened due process protections, or "super due process."[1] There are two implications of this requirement for "super due process" in death penalty cases. First, the heightened due process protections provide defense counsel many opportunities to raise legal issues and pursue avenues of defense not generally available to noncapital defendants. There quite simply are many more possible procedural means for capital counsel to exhaust in order to prevent their clients from being executed.[2] Second, the number of avenues of appeal are numerous in death penalty cases and the courts have generally scrutinized capital cases with great care, leading to a time-consuming appellate process.

The Cost and Process of a Capital Trial

In this section we will explore the special nature of the death penalty trial and the costs that may accrue during the course of a capital case. It should be kept in mind at the outset that a precise financial accounting of operating each state's capital punishment system is not available. Although there have been attempts to estimate the overall cost of state capital punishment systems,[3] we are generally limited in our study of this issue to cost estimates from a small number of cases in a few states. The problem is that not only do costs vary from state to state, but within each state each case is different, so that the expense of one capital trial (even if accurate cost information were collected) may differ markedly from another. Much of the literature concerning the cost of capital punishment comprise either cost estimates or the funds that were actually expended in a particular state for one specific case. With these caveats in mind, we can now begin to examine the issue of the cost of trying a capital case.

PreTrial Costs

In assessing the cost of prosecuting and defending a capital case, we must include those costs that occur prior to the trial itself. These include, first of all, investigation costs. In order for defense counsel in capital cases to effectively serve their clients, they should be able to investigate every aspect of the crime and offender. For lawyers working in noncapital law, this work is generally undertaken by highly paid and trained investigators.[4] The investigation will include not only the circumstances of the offense and the involvement of the defendant, but the locating and interviewing of witnesses to appear at the trial. When done properly, this generally requires a large number of labor hours and extensive travel costs. It has been estimated that this kind of witness investigation takes three to five times longer in a capital case than it does in a noncapital trial and may require as much as two years in preparation (Garey 1985).

There are at least two reasons why the pretrial investigation is so time-consuming and therefore costly in capital trials. One is that defense counsel naturally pursues every conceivable lead in a death penalty case, however remote,[5] and this is probably particularly true at the pretrial stage when investigative information is critical both for pretrial motions and the general defense preparation of the case.

The second, and more important, reason is that the pretrial investigation is actually needed for two separate occasions, the trial itself, where the guilt/innocence of the client is determined, and the penalty phase. One of the most costly and time-consuming components of an investigator's task is the investigation of the defendant's background in preparation for the penalty phase of the capital trial. This investigation normally includes locating and interviewing the defendant's parents, siblings, relatives, wife and children, employers, teachers, work associates, neighbors, and clergy, virtually any person who could be called as a witness to attest to the defendant's good character, as possible mitigating evidence during the penalty phase.[6] The background investigation may require the investigator to examine the past ten or twenty years of the defendant's life and will, therefore, require countless hours of the investigator's time in marshalling the evidence and more hours for the defense team in preparing the testimony for presentation. In constructing an explanation of the crime to the sentencer, counsel requires information into the defendant's early childhood experiences, any traumas, psychological history, educational and occupational experiences, and friendships and current personality.

The investigation of the defendant's background is substantially more difficult in death penalty cases than noncapital ones because the latter do not have penalty phase trials. The importance of this pretrial background investigation, however, cannot be minimized; not only is it directly important in counsel's construction of the defendant as a human being before the sentencing body, experienced capital counsel have observed that it also affects the conduct of jury selection, and the nature of the defense strategy at trial (Goodpaster 1983).

Related to the cost of the background investigation is the employment of experts during the pretrial stage. One such expert is a mental health professional (psychiatric social worker, psychologist, psychiatrist). These experts would be helpful in providing valuable information to defense counsel in virtually all capital cases, not in just those cases involving an insanity defense. At the penalty phase of a capital trial, defendants are allowed to present mitigating testimony related to any previous history of mental or emotional distress, their mental state at the time of the offense, and current psychological and mental condition. The expertise of mental health experts, then, is critical in fashioning a mitigation defense around diminished responsibility. In addition, the defendant may present evidence to the sentencer during the penalty phase of a capital trial related to his diminished mental capacity due to chronic alcoholism or drug addiction. The role of experts in investigating and presenting this information is of vital importance to defense counsel.[7]

Other experts in addition to psychiatrists and psychologists are often useful during the pretrial preparation of a capital case. These include forensic scientists to examine the validity of the physical evidence and offer any alternative theories, polygraph experts, and jury selection specialists who would assist counsel is selecting a group of jurors that would be receptive to their case. The estimated fees for these kinds of experts typically range from $500 to $1,000 per day.[8]

In addition to the necessity of securing the assistance of experts, pretrial costs in a capital case are elevated above those of noncapital cases because of the number and complexity of pretrial motions. These motions include general constitutional attacks on the state's death penalty statute, motions for the appointment of expert witnesses, investigators, and mental health professionals, motions for a change of venue, for individual *voir dire,* and sequestration of jurors during *voir dire.* Although many of these motions would also be filed in noncapital cases, those who have experience in these matters note that in death penalty cases the motions are more complex and raise more evidentiary issues (Garey 1985). Pretrial motions also take far longer to prepare than comparable motions in a noncapital case, not only because they have greater ramifications but also because the pretrial motions are part of an overall defense strategy to avoid the death penalty; hence, a great deal of work goes into motions to render the case a noncapital one from the very beginning.

Not only are these pretrial motions lengthier and more complex than motions in noncapital cases, they are more numerous when the defendant's life is at stake. Garey (1985, 1248) reports that the number of pretrial defense motions in capital cases is from twice to five or six times the number in a noncapital case, and the number filed by the prosecution is twice the number filed in noncapital cases. In their report on the cost of the death penalty, the New York State Defenders' Association (1982, 12) estimated that the average number of pretrial motions in a noncapital case ranged from five to seven, while in a death penalty case the number of motions ranged between ten and twenty-five.[9] It should also be remembered that the prosecution files its own pretrial motions and must respond to those filed by the defense, thus raising the pretrial cost of a capital case even further.

As it relates to events that occur at the pretrial stage, a final reason for the higher cost of a capital case in comparison to a noncapital one is that there is far less plea bargaining in capital cases. It has been estimated that about 85 to 90 percent of noncapital cases that reach the stage of arraignment are disposed of by a plea of guilty, thereby obviating the need for a jury trial (Reynolds 1981; Vorenberg 1981; Nakell 1978). This saves the state a considerable amount of money and court time and prevents the judicial system from being overloaded. There is far less incentive for the defense to plea-bargain in a death penalty case, however. The nature of the plea bargain is that the defendant agrees to plead guilty in exchange for a reduced charge or sentence. In death penalty cases there is less room for the prosecution to maneuver, because if the charge were reduced, or a promise of a more lenient sentence offered, it would render the case a noncapital one. In those cases that are genuinely capital ones the prosecutor has nothing to offer the defendant in exchange for a plea of guilty; as a result, far fewer guilty pleas are entered in capital cases. This is not to say that every first-degree murder case results in a full-blown, bifurcated murder trial. There is charge reduction in capital cases since prosecutors charge a capital offense in only about one third of the capital-eligible homicides (Paternoster and Kazyaka 1988). In addition, Baldus et al. (1983, 721) reported that in Georgia among those defendants convicted of capital murder (and who are, therefore, death eligible), only 40 percent are moved along to the penalty phase. The number of jury trials is, however, greater in capital than noncapital cases. Nakell (1978, 71) has estimated that capital cases result in jury trials about ten times more often than noncapital cases.

These various costs accruing to the defense during the pretrial stage of a capital case must also be borne by the prosecution. Prosecutors must also pay for investigators, forensic professionals, psychologists and psychiatrists, polygraph authorities, medical examiners, and other experts. We have alluded to the fact that prosecutors must also prepare for and respond to the flurry of pretrial motions filed by the defense. Prosecution costs also include court time and court personnel used to conduct pretrial hearings. A report by the Judicial Council of California (1985) has estimated that these court costs run over $2,000 per day. In fact, however considerable the costs are to defend someone accused of a capital offense, the costs to prosecute the case are probably much higher (Garey 1985, 1254).

Although the data are sporadic, available cost estimates suggest that the pretrial defense costs in a capital case are quite high, much higher than that expended in a noncapital case, and that however high the dollars expended by the defense, the costs for the prosecution are at least as high or higher.

Trial Costs

Voir Dire. One of the most expensive components of a capital trial is the selection of potential jurors, called *voir dire*. Theoretically, the goal of *voir dire* is to select a fair and unbiased jury, one that favors neither the prosecution nor the defense. During the *voir dire* potential jurors are extensively questioned by counsel for both prosecution and defense and in many instances by the trial judge. This query includes general qualification questions, such as if the potential juror harbors any prejudice or predisposition that would prevent an impartial hearing of the case, or if they or any family member has been a victim of crime or a witness in a criminal case. During *voir dire* the jurors are also asked other, more specific questions concerning their opinions and attitudes about the case and whether or not they have formed and fixed an opinion about it that would be unaffected by the evidence.

As alluded to above, the purpose of conducting a *voir dire* examination is to provide both the prosecution and the defense with the information they need to select a jury favorable to their side. Neither side intends to have completely neutral jurors; each wants the jury to be sympathetic to their version of the case. With the information obtained during *voir dire*, however, any prospective juror who is felt by either party to be biased against them could be asked to be removed from jury service in that case. There are two ways that a potential juror could be dismissed, for *cause* and for *peremptory challenge*. In challenging a juror for cause, the party making the challenge must specify to the presiding judge the precise reason for believing that the potential juror is biased and partial (e.g., they are related to the victim, defendant, prosecutor, or defense attorney); if they are successful, the court would then excuse the juror from service. Both the prosecution and defense have an unlimited number of these "for cause" challenges.

In exercising a peremptory challenge, no reason for dismissal need be given by either the prosecution or defense. There is, however, a limited number of such challenges. The importance of the *voir dire*, then, is that it provides both the prosecution and defense with the information they need to select an "indifferent" jury by arguing for the dismissal of some potential jurors "for cause" or in order to intelligently exercise a peremptory challenge.

For several reasons, the *voir dire* in a capital case often takes much longer and is far more expensive to conduct than in a noncapital trial. First of all, the time it takes to question jurors in capital cases is much longer than it is in noncapital cases. In addition to general qualification questions, jurors in a capital case are generally "death qualified." In the process of "death qualification," jurors are asked their opinions and beliefs about the death penalty, their willingness to impose it, and if the possibility of a death sentence would prevent them from being impartial. In *Witherspoon v. Illinois,* 391 U.S. 510 (1968) the U.S. Supreme Court held that a prospective juror could not be excused for cause unless they make it unmistakably clear that they would vote against the death penalty in any case or that their opposition to the death penalty was so great it would affect their decision on the defendant's guilt. This *"Witherspoon rule"* was clarified by the Court in *Wainwright v. Witt,* 105 S.Ct. 844 (1985) when it held that the prosecution may challenge potential jurors for cause if they state that their doubts about the death penalty could impair the performance of their duties as a juror.

Even if a juror at first admitted that they were strongly opposed to the death penalty or that it could possibly affect their performance as a juror, they would not automatically be dismissed for cause. The defense could attempt to "rehabilitate" the prospective juror by finding out if they could vote for the death penalty under some circumstances and that their general apprehension about the penalty would not hinder the performance of their duties.

This "death qualification" process, then, means that the *voir dire* will take much more time since individual prospective jurors are questioned at length about their opinions and attitudes, and it means that with additional and more detailed information at their disposal as a result of this extensive examination, both the prosecution and defense will be able to exercise more dismissals for cause and more potential jurors will have to be questioned.

There are other reasons why a capital *voir dire* takes longer and is therefore more costly than a noncapital one. Generally in a capital case both the prosecution and defense are allotted more peremptory challenges.[10] This ensures a longer *voir dire*. In addition, in capital cases trial courts have allowed both sides greater leniency in questioning prospective jurors, making the *voir dire* more time-consuming and making it more likely that information pertaining to a successful "for cause" challenge will be found (Goodpaster 1983), leading to a questioning of more potential jurors. The U.S. Supreme Court has held that in capital cases potential jurors may also be questioned about the possibility of racial bias when the defendant and victim are of different races [*Turner v. Murray*, 106 S.Ct. 1683 (1986)]. In extending the range of questioning during *voir dire*, questions about racial bias also increase its length and the probability that a juror will eventually be excused.

Voir dire in capital cases is more time-consuming than in noncapital cases because prospective jurors are more closely scrutinized by both sides: extensive questioning will lead to a more efficacious use of challenges, and the jury is being selected for two tasks, the determination of guilt and the determination of penalty. Defense counsel (and prosecution) will want to ensure that the prospective juror is not unfavorably disposed toward either issue, and is instead favorably disposed toward the unique features of the case at hand (Goodpaster 1983).

Finally, the conduct of *voir dire* in capital cases will be more expensive than in noncapital cases because of the procedure by which prospective jurors are questioned. In noncapital cases the questioning of prospective jurors can be done all at once as a group, saving both time and money. In many states, however, jurors in capital cases are required to be questioned individually, or individual *voir dire* is permitted at the request of the defense. In individual *voir dire* prospective jurors are questioned one at a time while the other prospective jurors are sequestered. Individual, sequestered *voir dire* is more expensive because the state must bear the expense of feeding and housing prospective jurors during the many days (or weeks) taken by *voir dire*. Individual, sequestered *voir dire* is seen by the defense to be particularly critical in capital cases since the questioning of one juror about their views on capital punishment in the presence of others may easily prejudice those awaiting questioning. One experienced capital attorney has claimed that "[n]othing, repeat nothing, is more important in a death case, than individual, sequestered *voir dire*" (Balske 1979, 341–342), and has discussed some of the pitfalls of collective juror questioning in capital cases:

> Group *voir dire* regarding capital punishment will lead to the exclusion of jurors ambivalent toward the death penalty, because jurors wishing to be excused will learn how to answer . . . questions to gain disqualification. That is, they will see other persons being excused for conscientious opposition to the death, and, although their belief may not meet the test, they will mimic the previous jurors' responses in order to be excused, either out of a sense of duty or simply to escape being chosen as a juror. Finally, collective *voir dire* will preclude the candor and honesty which is necessary in order for counsel to intelligently exercise statutory peremptory challenges.

In addition to the problems of jurors wishing to get out of jury service and candor, it is conceivable that questioning one juror about the death penalty in a group of prospective jurors may bias the attitudes of those listening (see Nietzel and Dillehay 1982). Haney (1984) found that the process of questioning jurors about their own attitudes toward capital punishment before the trial suggested to them that the defendant was guilty. This effect may "spill over" to those witnessing the questioning.

There are, then, numerous reasons to expect the *voir dire* in a capital case to be a very expensive process, and far more expensive than it would be in a comparable noncapital case. Kaplan (1983, 571) has reported that in a survey of twenty California murder trials jury selection was the most expensive part of a capital trial. In a direct comparison, *voir dire* averaged three days in the ten noncapital cases while jury selection averaged thirteen days in the capital cases. Garey (1985, 1257) has reported that jury selection in a capital case takes five times longer to complete than in a noncapital case, and that the difference in courtroom time alone between a capital and noncapital *voir dire* was approximately $87,000.

Guilt and Penalty Phase. Under post-*Furman* death penalty statutes, a capital trial is actually two trials in one. First there is the guilt phase to determine the guilt/innocence of the defendant. If the state secures a conviction at this stage it may advance the case on to a second trial, the penalty phase, where the sentencer determines whether or not the defendant will be sentenced to death or life imprisonment. We have already seen that the Supreme Court's concern for greater reliability in death penalty cases has resulted in a requirement of heightened due process protections for capital defendants, "super due process." The requirement of enhanced due process must be satisfied at both the guilt and penalty phase of a capital trial [*Gardner v. Florida*, 430 U.S. 349 (1976)]. Because of the additional due process requirements and the fact that it involves two discrete but related phases, the capital trial is far more expensive for both the defense and prosecution to conduct than a comparable noncapital case. In addition, because the defendant may ultimately be put to death, most defense counsel (and prosecution counsel) naturally work with greater diligence in preparing for both phases of a capital case.

In preparing for the guilt phase of a capital case, defense counsel must investigate and prepare not only for the first-degree murder charge but also for any additional charges that the prosecution may have filed as evidence of aggravating circumstances (such as armed robbery, rape, or kidnapping). This combined defense effort requires countless hours of attorney time, of investigators' time, of time to locate witnesses and bring them to court, and interviewing expert witnesses and paying their fees and expenses. Since this is a capital case, defense will likely prepare and present as many witnesses as they can (and, of course, can afford), making both the preparation time and trial time itself more lengthy than in a noncapital case. In many instances, because of the amount of work and complexity involved, more than one counsel is assigned to defend a capital case. This not only multiplies the cost of the guilt phase, but requires the public defender's office (or someone else) to pay for an additional attorney to do the work that would have been done by the second attorney assigned to the capital case. For similar reasons, the prosecution also usually has more than one attorney trying a capital case (Kaplan 1983; Garey 1985). In addition, as experienced capital attorneys have remarked, lawyers preparing for the guilt phase of a capital case must marshall a guilt phase strategy that can be integrated with the penalty phase strategy, even though the two are distinct (Goodpaster 1983; Weisberg 1984).[11] For these reasons, Kaplan (1983, 571) has estimated that the guilt phase of a capital trial is ten to twenty times more time-consuming than a comparable noncapital case.

The single greatest cost inflator of a capital trial is not, however, its guilt phase; it is the penalty phase. In noncapital cases most of the effort of the defense and prosecution is devoted to establishing the guilt/innocence of the defendant. This is so because neither party has much to contribute to the determination of penalty, which is made by the trial court in consultation with a presentence report or existing mandatory sentencing schemes (Goodpaster 1983; Garey 1985). In a capital case, however, the guilt of the defendant is not always at issue since the prosecution's evidence is at times overwhelming. In most cases, then, defense counsel is simply fighting for the life of their client. The penalty phase of a capital case, therefore, looms important for both the defense and prosecution.

The penalty phase of a capital case can be thought of as a separate, second trial, where the center of attention is not the factual issue of the guilt or innocence of the defendant but the moral issue as to whether or not they deserve to be put to death or imprisoned for life (Weisberg 1984). As we have learned in this and previous chapters, scrupulous attention to due process must be given at the penalty phase as well as the guilt phase [*Gardner v. Florida*, 430 U.S. 349 (1976)], and the defense is given very wide latitude in the presentation of mitigating evidence [*Lockett v. Ohio*, 438 U.S. 586 (1978)] at the penalty hearing. For these reasons, then, we would expect the penalty phase of a capital trial both to involve a great deal of preparation and to be lengthy, generally taking substantially longer to conduct than the guilt phase.

In adequately preparing for the penalty phase of a capital trial, Goodpaster (1983, 334–339) notes that defense counsel should be striving to achieve four objectives: (1) to convey to the sentencer that the defendant is a member of the community of human beings, with redeeming attributes; (2) to endeavor to demonstrate to the sentencer that the defendant's heinous crime, while perhaps not forgivable, is at least understandable given the defendant's immediate past and problems experienced in the formative years of life; (3) to attempt to put the death penalty on trial itself by arguing that it is generally inappropriate or inappropriate in the current case; and (4) to effectively rebut the prosecution's evidence of aggravating factors that weigh in favor of a death sentence (see also Mello 1988). It is in the defense counsel's attempt to successfully attain these objectives that the penalty phase of a capital trial becomes so costly.

In their attempt to "humanize" capital defendants, good defense lawyers will have to expend a considerable amount of time and money investigating their entire background and preparing a convincing picture that their clients are redeemable human beings. As suggested in the earlier discussion of investigation costs, this requires locating, interviewing, and presenting as witnesses the defendant's immediate and past family, neighbors, employers, ministers, friends, and any relevant professionals such as psychologists, psychiatrists, and social workers. One component of the penalty phase of a capital trial, then, is the appearance of a plethora of character witnesses who will testify that in spite of the egregious offense, the defendant is basically a good person. Again, this requires a great deal of time and expense in ferreting out this information and an equal amount of time in preparing a coherent strategy and presenting it to the sentencer. Complementary to this effort, of course, is the prosecution's time and expense in casting the defendant before the sentencer in contrary terms, as the consummate uncaring and inhuman killer, unlikely to change and not deserving of its mercy.

Defense counsel must, however, do more than paint a portrait of the defendant as a human being. The egregious nature of most capital murders is an all-too-vivid contradiction of that portrayal, so defense counsel must also present to the jury an explanation for the crime that makes it understandable (but not forgivable). In making the offense comprehensible, counsel often attempts to demonstrate that the crime was the end-result of years of neglect, abuse, or frustration by the defendant, or that it was an aberrant act that was completely out of character. In this effort, counsel attempts to strike a chord of compassion within the sentencer by arguing that breakdowns in child rearing or other traumatic past events have deformed the defendant's otherwise normal qualities. Counsel would also attempt to convince the jury that the defendant is redeemable, and that in spite of the crime there is a potential for rehabilitation.

The presentation of this case would require a thorough investigation of the defendant's distant past; for example, evidence of child abuse or childhood trauma (neglect, the death of a parent, excessive beatings, extreme economic hardships) would be instrumental in making the current offense understandable. Any past or current history of mental or emotional disturbance, or of drug or alcohol dependence, would also have to be uncovered. In addition to the extensive investigative effort this task would entail, and the consequent cost, a credible presentation to the jury would require the assistance of medical and mental health experts in order to make a convincing connection between such past events and the current offense. Weisberg (1984, 361) offers an excellent description of this task confronting defense counsel at the penalty phase: "The overall goal of the defense is to present a human narrative, an explanation of the defendant's apparently malignant violence as in some way rooted in understandable aspects of the human condition, so the jury will be less inclined to cast him out of the human circle." Again, the prosecution will attempt to negate the effect of these efforts with its own background investigation and panel of experts by relating its side of the story.

Where the law allowed it, defense counsel could also put the death penalty itself on trial by arguing that it would be inappropriate to impose. There are two forms this argument could take: (1) Counsel could argue that the death penalty is generally inappropriate because it is imposed in a discriminatory fashion, and/or (2) counsel could argue that it is inappropriate in this specific case because other defendants who committed crimes just as or more egregious than the defendant's were sentenced to life imprisonment. The defense may also have the opportunity to argue that the death penalty is no more of a deterrent to murder than life imprisonment, that those sentenced to life in prison make a successful adjustment and do not pose a threat either to correctional staff or other inmates, that the death penalty is contrary to religious principles, or that it is simply a cruel and painful punishment. To credibly argue any of these points, defense counsel would require the assistance of experts, as would the prosecution in their attempt to rebut the arguments.

Finally, it the defense counsel's task to attempt to rebut the prosecution's case that this particular defendant is irredeemable, and a good candidate for the death penalty. The prosecution will make its case through the presentation of aggravating circumstances, both statutory and nonstatutory, and lay and expert witnesses of its own. As Weisberg (1984, 361) relates, the prosecution's purpose during the penalty phase is the flip side of the defense's character portrait:

> A prosecutor demanding the death penalty wants to convey and reinforce the most damning facts about the crime for which the penalty is sought. He wants to bring out the criminal record of the defendant to paint a portrait of an irredeemably evil person. Where there is evidence of good character, he wants to stress the crime, and where there is evidence of bad character, he wants to stress that.

To effectively argue their case for life imprisonment, the defense must devise a strategy to blunt these arguments, which may be perceived by the sentencer as all the more credible in view of the defendant's actions.

As we have just seen, the preparation and conduct of both the guilt and penalty phase of a capital murder trial is a long, arduous ordeal that compels the investment of considerable expenditures. The question is, how much more time and money does a capital trial take? There are various answers to this question, most of them estimates. Spangenberg and Walsh (1989, 53) and Garey (1985, 1258), for example, report that capital trials can take over three times as long to complete as a comparable noncapital trial. The cost of conducting a capital trial can vary from state to state and case to case within one state, but the following are some reported cost estimates:

1. The New York State Defender's Association (1982, 19) estimated that if the death penalty were to be reinstated in New York it would cost nearly $750,000 for the guilt phase and an additional $750,000 for the penalty phase of each capital trial.

2. Garey (1985, 1258) reports that in California it takes on average thirty days longer to try a capital than a comparable noncapital case, and that the additional cost (heating, lights, etc., not personnel time) for the courtroom alone is over $65,000.

3. Based on documentation from other states, Garey (1985, 1261–1262) reports that New Jersey estimated that it would cost the state $16 million a year, Ohio's estimated expenditure was $1.5 million per year, while California budgets over $4 million annually just to reimburse county costs for the defense side of a capital trial.[12]

These cost estimates and actual expenditures would suggest that the total dollar outlay for the guilt and penalty phase of a capital trial is enormously high, and much higher than the costs for a noncapital case. There is no easy way to reduce these costs either, since a bifurcated capital trial is probably a constitutional requirement, and the gravity of the penalty dictates that both the defense and prosecution put forth the greatest effort in trying their cases.

Appeals of Capital Convictions. However time-consuming and expensive it is to conduct a capital trial, whether in absolute amounts or relative to a noncapital case, the trial phase of a capital case is not where the greatest costs are incurred. It is in fact at the appeals stage where the costs of a system of capital punishment become exorbitant. Since the process of appellate review is unique in capital cases, it is substantially more costly than a noncapital appeals system. The appeals process in a capital case is unique in that unlike a noncapital case, there is an automatic appeal to a state appellate court in all instances where the death penalty has been imposed. In addition, capital defendants have available a complex and multileveled system of both state and federal appellate review. The course of appeals in a death penalty case is shown in Figure 6–1. This is a general description of the postconviction appeals route in capital cases and differs in particular states. We will first examine the different routes of appealing a death case, and then discuss how this process is both extremely time-consuming and expensive.

Capital defendants have what is called a dual system of collateral review. They may contest their conviction and/or sentence through both state postconviction proceedings and federal *habeas corpus* petitions. The first feature of the capital postconviction process is that there is an automatic appeal of both the conviction and death sentence to a state appeals court. This direct appeal is automatic, although it may be waived by a defendant who wishes to forgo his appeals.[13] The nature of this direct appeal varies by state. In California, for example, the statute does not specify the parameters of the review or the nature of the direct appeal, only that the judge's decision not to modify the death sentence "shall be reviewed."[14] The California Supreme Court has not understood the nature of the direct appeal to include a proportionality review, and has restricted its focus to the factual validity of the death sentence. The Georgia statute is more explicit in what is required of its Supreme Court for its direct review. The Georgia Supreme Court is instructed to consider whether the death sentence was imposed "under the influence of passion, prejudice, or any other arbitrary factor," if the evidence supports the jury's finding of aggravating circumstance(s), and if the death sentence imposed is disproportionate to that imposed in similar cases. Whatever the precise form of the review, however, the first step in the capital appellate process is this direct appeal to a state court of appeals.

At this first step, the state court of appeals can do one of three things: (1) vacate the conviction (and therefore the sentence) and remand the case for a retrial, (2) affirm the conviction and remand the case for resentencing, and (3) affirm both the conviction and sentence. One of the reasons for the expense of a system of capital punishment is that a significant number of these direct appeals result in the vacating of either the defendant's conviction or his death sentence. For example, Dix (1979, 111) reported that during the time period from April 4, 1974 until March 6, 1979, the Georgia Supreme Court reversed 5 percent of the capital convictions they reviewed on direct appeal and almost 25 percent of the sentences. The Florida Supreme Court reversed almost one half of the capital cases (either sentence or conviction) they reviewed on direct appeal during a comparable period (November 4, 1974 to February 22, 1979). Radelet and Vandiver (1983) examined the decisions of the Florida Supreme Court in the direct appeal of 145 death penalty cases from 1973 to 1981. Of these 145 cases, 70 (48%) resulted in a reversal of either the conviction or sentence. Over half of these reversals resulted in either a new penalty hearing or a new trial (1983, 919). In their study, Baldus et al. (1990, 214) found that the Georgia Supreme Court reversed about 20 percent of the cases they reviewed on direct appeal. Finally, Pasternoster and Kazyaka (1990, 120) found that during the period 1979–1987

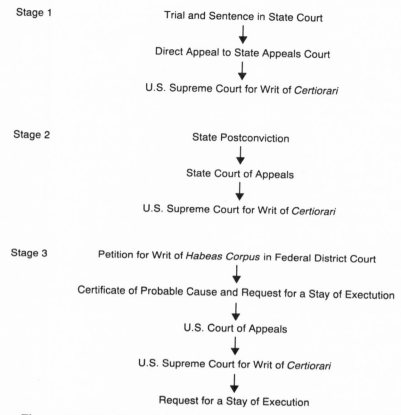

Figure 6-1. The General Appeals Process in a Death Penalty Case

the South Carolina Supreme Court reversed 29 percent of the convictions and 37 percent of the sentences in the death penalty cases that it reviewed on direct appeal. In total it reversed 55 percent of the death penalty cases it reviewed. The reversal of a conviction or sentence makes the capital sentencing system an expensive one, since it often requires either a new trial or a new sentencing hearing, with the attendant additional costs to both the defense and prosecution.

If the defendant's conviction and death sentence are both affirmed, he may petition the U.S. Supreme Court for a review. If this round of appeals is unsuccessful, the capital defendant can then proceed into state postconviction proceedings. It is at this point that the greatest cost difference between capital and noncapital cases begin to emerge, for unlike their noncapital counterparts who are imprisoned during their appeals and are petitioning the courts for their release, capital defendants are awaiting execution and are literally fighting for their lives. They are more inclined, therefore, to file as many *habeas corpus* petitions, raising as many issues, as possible (Kaplan 1983, 573).

These state postconviction remedies provide another way for both the conviction and capital sentence to be challenged, and issues may be raised that could not have been or were not made on the direct appeal. The issues raised in these appeals could include the quality of the representation and the fairness of the guilt and penalty phase hearings as well as more general constitutional claims.

As Figure 6-1 shows, an unsuccessful state postconviction claim may be appealed to the state's appellate court and following failure there, a petition for a writ of *certiorari* may be made to the U.S. Supreme Court. The review of capital sentences follows a dual system, however, for unsuccessful *habeas corpus* claims made in state postconviction procedures may be litigated again in federal district court,[15] and, if denied, to the relevant circuit court of appeals. A third appeal may be made to the U.S. Supreme Court.

As can be easily seen, the capital appeals process is quite extensive as death penalty cases are given great scrutiny. The question remains, however, how much time and money goes into this part of the death sentencing process? Although precise financial data are not available, we can examine some estimates of just how time-consuming and costly this process of capital review is. Following this we will examine why these appeals costs are so high and what can and cannot be done to attempt to reduce those costs.

A report by the New York State Defender's Association (1982, 21) estimated that were the state of New York to reinstate the death penalty the cost of a direct appeal of a death sentence to the New York State Court of Appeals would be approximately $160,000 per case. It also estimated (p. 22) that to prepare and argue a case before the U.S. Supreme Court it would cost an additional $170,000 per case. Garey (1985, 1263) reported that the direct appeal in California capital cases takes an estimated 80-100 hours of defense attorney time and, at the rate of $60 for a court-appointed lawyer, would cost $48,000-$60,000. This estimate did not include, however, defense expenses for travel or investigation, the prosecution's costs, nor the court's costs.

Estimates of the cost of the complete appeals process, of course, go much higher.[16] Spangenberg and Walsh (1989, 55) have reported that to litigate a Florida state postconviction claim would take an estimated 800 hours of attorney time and an additional 900 hours at the federal postconviction level. Even at a conservative estimate of $100 per hour of attorney time, it would cost approximately $170,000 to appeal each Florida death sentence. Garey (1985, 1265) provided expense data incurred by one legal firm that handled four capital appeals. The out-of-pocket expenses for each case averaged over $44,000, and the cost for attorney hours expended was on average $175,000 per case. The average cost to appeal these four death penalty cases was, then, close to a quarter of a million dollars, and these were only the defense costs.

Mello (1988, 554–563) provides more detailed data on the number of hours required to appeal a death penalty case, and the costs involved. He reports that a 1986 survey of lawyers involved in postconviction death penalty work by the American Bar Association (ABA) estimated that it takes on average 600 hours to litigate the appeal in state courts and an additional 65 hours in the U.S. Supreme Court in appeals from state court decisions. In the federal postconviction process it was estimated on average to take 305 hours per case at the district court level, 320 hours at the circuit court of appeals level, and 180 hours for a U.S. Supreme Court appeal from unfavorable federal appeals. If a death penalty case were to go through all avenues of appeal (and many are), it would consume approximately 1,470 hours of preparation by the defense. There was also an estimated average of 660 hours of support staff time for both state and federal appeals.

These time expenditures were, however, only estimates. A smaller sample of the lawyers surveyed by the ABA kept documented (actual) hours in their cases. These lawyers reported spending on average 963 hours litigating at the state postconviction level and 1,037 at the federal level for a total of 2,000 hours per case spent on death penalty appeals (Mello 1988, 557). Even at very conservative per-hour cost rates, the litigation of a death penalty appeal requires the expenditure of a great deal of money.

The questions to be addressed now are, why is the capital appeals process so time-consuming, and what has and can be done to streamline and thereby economize it?

The simplest explanation for the amount of time to prepare and litigate a death penalty appeal is that capital jurisprudence is among the most intricate and arcane body of law in the United States today. Judge John C. Godbold (1987), the former chief judge of the United States Court of Appeals for the Eleventh Circuit, the federal circuit that has perhaps the most experience in dealing with death penalty appeals, has called postconviction capital litigation "the most complex area of the law I deal with." What makes capital *habeas* litigation so complex, one experienced lawyer noted, is that Supreme Court holdings in capital cases are often confusing and inconsistent, and "its habeas corpus jurisprudence is Byzantine" (Mello 1988, 534).

In addition to the sheer complexity of the law, what makes capital postconviction procedures so time-consuming is that capital trials are so complex that there are numerous issues to be raised on appeal, and numerous avenues to press those claims (see Figure 6–1). Death row defendants have every incentive to present as many claims as possible in their appeals, for several reasons (see Mello 1988 and Kaplan 1983). One, to be examined in more detail below, is that postconviction litigation is very successful for the capital defendant, resulting in a large percentage of both conviction reversals and remands for resentencing (Greenberg 1982). While the appeals process is ongoing the capital defendant is alive, to the extent successful stays of execution are granted pending resolution of the appeals. It is therefore in the capital defendant's best interest to press as many legal claims in as many avenues as possible. It also takes a great deal of time to prepare a capital appeal because the trials themselves are so long and complicated; long transcripts (often several thousand pages) of both the guilt and penalty phase must be carefully examined for possible legal error. Mello (1988: 544–546) who has several death row clients in Florida, provides a very good description of the task confronting the postconviction litigator:

> Effective post-conviction litigation requires a complete reinvestigation of the case, with a focus on material *not* in the trial transcript. What evidence was *not* presented and why? What evidence was *not* investigated and why? The trial transcript provides clues, but those clues mark only the beginning of the post-conviction litigator's task . . . The person litigating the post-conviction case must review the trial docket sheets, files, and records that are maintained in the trial court, including physical evidence, exhibits, and notes of the court clerk about proceedings not designated as part of the formal record on direct appeal. Witnesses must be located and interviewed, including co-defendants and prior counsel. Records of proceedings relevant to co-defendants must be obtained and reviewed. Media coverage must be gathered and reviewed. Often collateral litigation must be initiated to obtain discovery of these matters. In most cases a post-conviction psychiatric examination must be arranged and efforts must be made to ensure that such examination is conducted properly. Any prior conviction that played a role at trial or penalty phase must also be reinvestigated for validity . . . the post-conviction investigation requires not only an informed evaluation of trial counsel's performance, but also a complete background investigation of the inmate's life, literally from embryo to death row.

A very clear reason why capital appeals are so long and costly, therefore, is that the enormity of the penalty, the complexity of capital jurisprudence, and the availability of many avenues of appeal conspire to produce a long and delayed system of capital punishment.

Both those who criticize the appeals process and proponents of capital punishment, however, will have by now realized an easy solution to this extensive delay and cost problem. If a system of capital punishment is so costly in large part because of the length of the appeals process, the necessary solution would be to shorten that process by limiting the scope, number, and avenues of appeal in death cases.

To some extent, there has already been a streamlining of the capital appeals process. In *Barefoot v. Estelle*, 463 U.S. 880 (1983) the United States Supreme Court attempted to expedite the federal review of state death cases when it held that a federal circuit court may decide the merits of an appeal together with a petition for a stay of execution rather than first granting the stay and conducting a full hearing on the merits of the appeal.

Mello (1988, 548) has reported that in response to *Barefoot* some federal courts devised new rules wherein the circuit court of appeal's decision in a capital case could be less than one day after a disposition was rendered in federal district court.[17] In *Saffle v. Parks*, 110 S.Ct. 1257 (1990) decided in the 1989 term, the Court restricted a capital defendant's use of *habeas corpus* by holding that the petitioner is not entitled to relief if his claim would require the application of a "new rule."[18] In *Clemons v. Mississippi*, 110 S.Ct. 1441 (1990) also decided in the 1989 term, the Court determined that rather than remand for resentencing (sending a case back to state court for an entirely new penalty hearing), an appellate court may itself reweigh the aggravating and mitigating evidence to determine the appropriateness of a death sentence in those instances where the jury based its death sentence on an invalid or improperly defined aggravating circumstance.

Those who argue that the appeals process in capital cases could be shortened at a considerable savings of money would point to these efforts at expediting death penalty appeals and argue for additional hastening. It is not at all clear, however, how much more streamlined the process could be. There are two stumbling blocks to further reduction through either the different avenues of appeals or the care with which death penalty appeals are heard. One of these is the previously discussed "death is different" doctrine.

It appears safe to say that because of the enormity of the penalty involved, the complexity of the law, and the overwhelming desire to avoid the execution of innocent or undeserving defendants, both state and federal courts will carefully scrutinize death penalty appeals and be more likely to grant relief in such cases.[19] In addition, capital defender projects such as Team Defense, the Southern Prisoners' Defense Committee, and the Legal Defense Fund, as well as organized defender associations within particular states, will ensure that the postconviction rights of capital defendants are conscientiously observed. Two means of preventing a shortened review of capital cases, therefore, is the willingness of both state and federal courts (but especially the latter) to carefully review death sentences because of the nature of the penalty, and the existence of capital defendant "protector groups" who will ensure that all due consideration is given each inmate's case.

Even if it is assumed that the length of time it takes to appeal a death case could be shortened, and as we have seen it may not be possible to do so, there is perhaps an even more compelling reason that should be considered before any additional efforts are made to further curtail or streamline the appeals process in capital cases. It could be argued that in some way it would be reasonable to take the position that the capital appeals process should be shortened and/or limited if capital defendants were raising frivolous issues in their appeals which, while being quickly dismissed, did, nonetheless, take up a great deal of courts' limited time and resources. If, however, state trial courts were making serious errors in death penalty cases, errors sufficiently perilous to question the validity of either the conviction or the imposed death sentence, then the wisdom (or morality) of limiting a capital defendant's appeals would be questionable.

The position here, therefore, is that if state and federal appeals courts are dealing with insignificant issues with the result that most capital appeals are dismissed without relief, then we may have grounds to question the necessity of a multilayered, prolonged system of review. If critical legal errors are frequently being made in state capital trials, errors that go uncorrected at the level of the first direct appeal to the state's supreme court, then the argument for a careful system of state and federal postconviction relief appears to be a much stronger one.

The record clearly shows that capital defendants frequently are not raising only frivolous appeals that have no legal merit and which serve only to thwart the state's legitimate attempt to carry out the sentence and make the entire capital punishment system a long and expensive one. The evidence thus far collected demonstrates that capital defendants are not raising trivial issues on appeal, because a large proportion of these appeals are successful, and capital appeals are far more successful than other criminal appeals.

Greenberg (1982, 918) has reported that while 1,533 defendants had been sentenced to death under approved post-*Furman* capital statutes, only 596 remained on death row as of December 20, 1980. Over 60 percent (937) of those capital defendants sentenced to death before 1981, therefore, had either their conviction or sentenced reversed. While it is true that a large proportion of these defendants were not innocent and are still in prison, and some may have even been resentenced to death, this 60 percent reversal rate in capital cases was about ten times higher than that for federal criminal cases (Greenberg 1982, 918). This would suggest that frequent errors are made in state capital trials, errors that are important enough to warrant reversal and are not being corrected on direct appeal. Mello (1988, 520–521) reports that while the reversal rate in noncapital federal *habeas corpus* petitions is low (he provides estimates that range from less than 1% to 7%), the reversal rate in capital *habeas* petitions was 60–75 percent as of 1982, 70 percent as of 1983, and 60 percent as of 1986. He further reports (1988, 521) that between 1976 and 1983 federal appellate courts ruled in favor of the capital defendant in 73 percent of the *habeas* petitions heard while relief was granted in only 6 percent of noncapital cases, and that in the Eleventh Circuit Court of Appeals capital inmates were granted relief half of the time in their *habeas* appeals.

It would appear, then, that capital defendants are successful in having their convictions and/or sentences reversed on postconviction relief. Given the careful scrutiny by the courts that capital cases are afforded, this should not be too surprising. What may be more surprising, however, is that this level of success in federal *habeas corpus* petitions occurs *after* the state's supreme court has affirmed the case, thereby rejecting the defendant's claims, and *after* the U.S. Supreme Court has denied *certiorari* (Amsterdam 1987). In addition, the reasons for these numerous reversals have rarely involved what might be thought of as "mere legal technicalities." This high reversal rate in capital cases has resulted from such fundamental constitutional errors as ineffective assistance of counsel, prosecutors' reference to defendants who refuse to testify, denial of the right to an impartial jury, and problems of tainted evidence and coerced confessions (Greenberg 1982; Mello 1988).

Given the high reversal rate in capital cases, then, and the fact that these reversals are for important constitutional errors that are generally corrected only at federal postconviction proceedings, it would appear to be unwise at this time to streamline the system of capital appeals too far.

The Cost of Life Imprisonment

Thus far we have only considered the cost of defending and at times prosecuting a death penalty case. In the course of this discussion we have discovered that the price of maintaining a system of criminal justice that includes capital punishment is a very high one. The contention of the economic benefits argument, however, is that the price of confining a convicted murderer in prison for a long period of time is substantially more than the expense of maintaining a system of capital punishment. The costs of incarcerating a defendant for life include the initial construction costs of a maximum security prison cell plus the annual operating costs borne by the state to maintain inmates sentenced to life. We need now to consider approximately how much it will cost the state to keep a convicted capital murderer in prison under a life sentence.

In a recent study involving a cost-benefit analysis of imprisonment and alternative sanctions conducted for the National Institute of Justice, Cavanagh and Kleiman (1990, 12–14) estimated that the average construction cost for a maximum security prison cell was approximately $63,000. This included the cost of the actual construction and additional expenses like architects' fees, furnishing costs, and cost overruns.[20] In addition to these direct costs, Cavanagh and Kleiman also considered the annual interest costs to the state to finance the construction of the prison. These interest costs were estimated to be approximately $204,692 over the fifty-year life span of the institution. When construction and financing costs are amortized over the fifty-year life period of the prison, the annualized costs are approximately $5,000.

To this initial cost of constructing a maximum security prison cell must be added the annual costs of operating the cell. Cavanagh and Kleiman (1990, 14) have estimated these costs to be approximately $20,000. This $20,000 annual cost estimate is comparable to the $15,000 annual cost figure used by Zedlewski (1987) in his calculation of the custody costs of incarceration. The discrepancy between Cavanagh and Kleiman's estimate of $20,000 and Zedlewski's estimate of $15,000 for annual operating costs is that the latter estimate is for a medium security rather than a maximum security institution. Since convicted murderers serving life terms of imprisonment are almost invariably confined in maximum rather than medium security institutions, we will use the Cavanagh and Kleiman estimate of $20,000. In addition to the annual operating costs are the annual costs to the state in constructing and financing the prison, which we estimated above to be $5,000. We then come to the estimate of building and operating a maximum security prison cell of approximately $25,000 per year.[21]

At an estimated annual cost of $25,000, we can estimate that it would cost a state approximately $500,000 to incarcerate an offender for twenty years, $750,000 to incarcerate an offender over a thirty-year period, and $1,000,000 over a forty-year period. Since the approximate average age of a homicide offender in 1988 was twenty-eight years,[22] a forty-year term of imprisonment would confine a convicted murderer until the age of sixty-eight. The average life expectancy of a male born in the United States in 1988 is approximately seventy-two years,[23] so that a convicted capital offender could be sentenced to life without parole at age twenty-eight and would on average spend forty years in prison before his death. If states instituted parole plans for convicted capital murderers such that they would spend twenty or thirty years of a life sentence before being released, some cost savings would accrue in comparison to a forty-year life sentence.

Assuming for the moment that capital punishment was replaced with life imprisonment, and that this implied an average length of confinement of thirty years for each sentenced capital murderer, it would cost the state approximately seven hundred and fifty thousand dollars. Even at this estimate, for a thirty-year life term, one third of which we would have to spend for ten years on death row before execution, this cost is less than the costs of maintaining a system of criminal justice that includes capital punishment. Keeping in mind the fact that it is very difficult to obtain an accurate estimate of the total cost of trying and appealing a capital case, and the fact that this cost is quite variable across cases, the cost estimates discussed earlier in this chapter suggest that it generally costs more than one million dollars to bring a capital case to its conclusion. Garey (1985) has estimated that it costs a *minimum* of $600,000 for each death penalty case in California, the New York State Defender's Association (1982) has estimated that it would cost on average almost two million dollars for each death penalty case, the Kansas Legislative Research Department (1987) has estimated the cost at about one million dollars, and Von Drehle (1988) estimated that it costs the state of Florida almost six times as much to execute a convicted capital offender as it would to imprison them for the rest of their life.

Thus far in this section, we have only discussed the cost of life imprisonment. Offenders serving life without parole terms are, and could more extensively, be employed in the institution itself or in prison industries. Inmates working in the prison could perform many of the requisite maintenance and custodial duties, thus reducing employment costs of the prison. Other inmates could be employed in prison industries producing a commodity. These inmates are not paid the full value of their labor so that the institution earns a profit from their work. This directly helps to reduce the cost of the prison. In addition, inmates serving life terms who work could have a portion of their wages deducted and used to provide restitution for the families of their victims. In many ways, then, murderers sentenced to life terms could help defray the cost of their own imprisonment.

Although difficult to pinpoint with precision, it appears that when the entire system of criminal justice is considered, the cost savings of capital punishment in comparison to life imprisonment are often illusory. This does not mean that if shown that capital punishment is a more expensive system of criminal justice to maintain than one based on life imprisonment, proponents of the death penalty would then shift their allegiance and favor its abolition. It is probably safe to say that most people do not favor the death penalty *only* because of economic reasons. Such persons would probably assert that even if it is more costly than life imprisonment, defendants convicted of first-degree murder should, nonetheless, be put to death, because (1) capital punishment is a more effective deterrent to homicide than life imprisonment, and/or (2) those who take a life deserve to have their own life taken. These issues will be taken up in the next two chapters.

Summary and Conclusions

One prevalent belief about the death penalty is that it is a less expensive punishment than life imprisonment. It is relatively easy to consider the costs of life imprisonment; they are immediate and clear—the price of constructing the cell, clothing and feeding the inmate for life, providing for their medical needs, and providing for some vocational and/or leisure requirements. The final price tag for this appears to be quite high, and far more expensive than it would be to simply try an accused for first-degree murder, convict and sentence her, and provide for her execution within a reasonable amount of time after the trial. The simple fact of the matter is that if capital trials were brief and uncomplicated, and if executions took place soon after the sentence were handed down, then capital punishment would be a far less sanction for the taxpayer to bear than would life imprisonment.

An accurate assessment of the costs involved, however, required us to move beyond this direct and simplistic understanding. In this chapter we examined the cost of maintaining a *system* of criminal justice that included capital punishment and compared it to a system that included only life imprisonment. We concluded that a capital punishment system probably costs more than one that excludes the possibility of the death penalty.

There were several reasons to account for the high cost of maintaining a system of capital punishment. One of these was high pretrial costs. The major expenses during the pretrial phase of a capital trial were investigation costs and the costs of preparing and arguing pretrial motions. Investigation costs were found to be particularly high because both the defense and prosecution must prepare for two separate trials, the guilt phase and the penalty phase of a capital trial. The investigator must thoroughly investigate all aspects of the offense and the offender, and must locate and interview all witnesses who will appear in the trial. This requires a great deal of labor and expense, and is often as long as two years in preparation. This background work is particularly important in a death penalty case because it contains most of the information that will be used during the penalty phase of the trial, which is unique to capital cases. Much time is spent in this background investigation because with the information gathered, the defense hopes to uncover and prepare for the sentencer some kind of rationale for the crime, while the prosecution hopes to paint a portrait of a irredeemable killer. In addition to investigation costs, many more pretrial motions are filed in capital than in noncapital murder trials. This is generally because in fighting for the life of their client, defense counsel will do any and everything to ensure a favorable hearing. Not only are there more pretrial motions filed in capital than noncapital cases, because of the complexity of death penalty law these motions are also more time-consuming to prepare and argue.

Trial costs are also higher in death than in nondeath cases. One of the reasons for this we found was the time-consuming process of selecting a jury in a death penalty case. Jury selection or *voir dire* in a capital case is more time-consuming and therefore more costly because potential jurors are questioned in greater detail and about a more diverse range of issues than in noncapital cases. Potential jurors in a capital case must be "death qualified," and may be questioned about any racial animus they may feel. Because of the extensive questioning there is more opportunity for both the defense and the prosecution to strike a potential juror "for cause" as a result of this detailed *voir dire*. In addition, *voir dire* may be more costly in death penalty cases because potential jurors may be individually sequestered and both the defense and prosecution are given more peremptory challenges.

The second reason for high trial costs in capital cases is that only in a death penalty case is there a separate penalty phase hearing. The penalty phase is a very time-consuming ordeal, both to prepare for and to conduct. This is the only opportunity for the defense to convince the sentencer that the defendant's life should be spared. In order to do this the defense interviews, prepares, and presents as witnesses the defendant's family, friends, employers, and neighbors, as well as expert witnesses such as psychologists and psychiatrists. The testimony of these witnesses takes a great deal of time to present, and there is additional time for the prosecution to cross-examine the defense witnesses and present its own.

Perhaps the most expensive part of the capital sentencing system, however, is the appeals process. This is not to say that noncapital cases are not appealed; they, of course, are, but the capital appeals process involves more complex issues, which take more time both to prepare and to respond to. In addition, lawyers for defendants who may be put to death generally pursue every conceivable avenue of appeal with every conceivable legal issue, and both the issues and avenues of appeal are more numerous in capital than noncapital cases. Attempts to restrict the appeals process, thereby resulting in some cost savings, on the grounds that the appeals of most capital defendants are trivial and based on mere "technicalities," cannot reasonably be done. The Supreme Court has already established in its death penalty case law the principle that "death is different," in that defendants who may be put to death are given additional, "super due process" and are entitled to greater scrutiny of their cases than noncapital defendants. In addition, most capital appeals are not based on "mere technicalities." We have seen in this chapter that lawyers for the state are making fundamental errors in prosecuting death penalty cases, errors that require appellate courts to reverse a high proportion of convictions and sentences in death penalty cases.

Compared with the cost of life imprisonment, the cost of maintaining a system of capital punishment seems to be at least as high and probably substantially higher.

Notes

1. For a more detailed discussion of this issue, see Radin 1980, "Cruel Punishment and Respect for Persons."

2. There are, of course, substantive challenges that could be litigated: for example, that the death penalty is an excessive punishment in comparison to the crime [*Coker v. Georgia,* 433 U.S. 586 (1978); *Tison v. Arizona,* 107 S.Ct. 1676 (1987); that the punishment would further no legitimate state interest [*Ford v. Wainwright,* 106 S.Ct. 2595 (1986)]; and that provisions of the death penalty statute are unconstitutionally vague [*Godfrey v. Georgia,* 446 U.S. 420 (1980)].

3. For example, the New York State Defenders Association (1982) attempted to estimate what it would cost the state of New York if it were to reinstate the death penalty. A similar study was conducted by the Kansas Legislative Research Department. Perhaps the best overview of the general cost of the death penalty is Spangenberg and Walsh 1989, *Capital Punishment or Life Imprisonment? Some Cost Considerations.*

4. In an examination of the projected costs of reinstating the death penalty, a published report by the New York State Defenders Association (1982, 13) noted that

investigators' fees, in our survey, range from $500 to $1,500 per day. Hourly rates for experienced investigators were reported to range between $75 and $200. The Office of the State Public Defender in California has found the cost for investigators at trial in some death penalty cases to have been in excess of $40,000. Similar amounts were reported by private attorneys. The national College for Criminal Defense in Houston found that the bare minimum needed for investigation is $10,000, and this figure only represents the investigation required for the trial phase.

5. In terms of the general penchant of defense counsel to aggressively defend a death penalty case, Justice Marshall observed that "defense counsel will reasonably exhaust every possible means to save his client from execution" [*Furman v. Georgia,* 408 U.S. 238 (1972) at p. 358].

6. Goodpaster (1983, 321) describes the awesome task of the pretrial investigation in the following terms:

Counsel will have to explore the defendant's past, upbringing and youth, relationships, treatment by adults, traumatic experiences, and other formative influences. Counsel will have to uncover witnesses from a possibly distant past, not only relatives, but childhood friends, teachers, ministers, neighbors, all of whom may be scattered like a diaspora of leaves along the tracks of defendant's travels.

7. The costs of retaining a psychiatrist are generally the responsibility of the defendant. In a very limited context the state must bear the financial burden. In 1985 the U.S. Supreme Court held that due process requires that a state provide an indigent defendant access to a psychiatrist's assistance if the defendant's sanity at the time of the crime is likely to be an issue at the trial [*Ake v. Oklahoma,* 105 S.Ct. 1087 (1985)]. *Ake* does not require the state to provide the defendant with all the expert assistance he might desire in psychiatric matters. The due process requirement is met by providing defense with the assistance of a single psychiatrist selected by the court.

8. See New York State Defenders' Association, 1982, *Capital Losses.* Total just investigation and expert witness costs can be quite high in a capital case. Spangenberg and Walsh (1989, 50) report that the average California pretrial cost for 1984–1985 was $12,000 and the average cost for capital trial preparation for Maryland was approximately $10,000.

9. See also Southern Poverty Law Center 1981, *Motions for Capital Cases.*

10. For example, in California both the prosecution and defense are allowed ten peremptory challenges in a noncapital case and twenty-six in a capital case (Garey 1985, 1256, note 167).

11. Goodpaster (1983, 329) describes the strategy as follows:

In a death penalty case . . . the possible punishment is so extraordinary that the defense attorney must consider from the outset the impact that the guilt phase defense may have on sentencing. Since the capital case defense attorney may have to be an advocate both for acquittal and for life, she should not frame a defense case for acquittal which will preclude or handicap effective advocacy for life. Indeed, in cases where a severe conflict or inconsistency between advocacy for acquittal and advocacy for life exists, the defense attorney will be forced to make the difficult decision of preferring one over the other.

12. Garey (1985, 1261) reported that in one California case the County Board of Supervisors refused to provide any defense funds for the retrial of a murder case because the projected cost was too prohibitive. Because of this the superior court judge determined that the prosecutor could not seek the death penalty.

The state of Kansas estimated that it would cost the state $10 million annually to try its death penalty cases, and an additional $2 million to fund the appeals (see Kansas Legislative Research Department 1987), *Costs of Implementing the Death Penalty, House Bill 2062).* The projected excessive cost of the death penalty was one factor in the legislature's decision not to reinstate the death penalty in Kansas.

13. Some states do not require a mandatory appeal in all death penalty cases. In Arkansas, for example, a convicted capital defendant may waive his direct appeal if after a competency hearing it has been determined that the waiver was done knowingly and intelligently. In *Pulley v. Harris,* 465 U.S. 37 (1984), while holding that the Constitution does not require comparative proportionality review, the court did concede that *Gregg* "suggested that some form of meaningful appellate review was required" [*Pulley v. Harris,* at p. 45, citing *Gregg v. Georgia,* 428 U.S. 153 (1976) at pp. 198, 204–206 (joint opinion of Stewart, Powell, and Stevens)]. The Supreme Court in 1990 decided that it was constitutionally permissible for Arkansas to execute a man who had waived his right to a direct appellate of his death sentence. It did not, however, provide an answer to the claim whether a state must provide some form of appellate review in a capital case [*Whitmore v. Arkansas,* 110 S.Ct. 1717 (1990)].

14. See California Penal Code Ann. Sec. 190(e) (West Supp. 1983).

15. With the availability of state and federal *habeas* procedures, there is a dual system of collateral review in death penalty cases. Virtually all states have mechanisms of collateral review, and there is *habeas corpus* review by federal courts when federal questions of law are presented. In deciding that arbitrary and capricious death sentences violated the 8th Amendment, *Furman* essentially federalized state death penalty practices so that federal claims can be raised in practically all state death penalty cases.

16. As will be detailed below, a large number of attorney hours are required to conduct a death penalty appeal. Since most capital defendants are indigent (Mello 1989), this cost must be borne either by the state or by individual lawyers doing *pro bono* work. At the level of the direct appeal to the state supreme court, states are required to provide counsel for the capital defendant. At the state and federal post-conviction stage, however, states are not required to provide counsel for the petitioner [see *Murray v. Giarratano,* 109 S.Ct. 2765 (1989)]. As Mello (1989, 54) notes, however, about one half of the death penalty states require by statute the provision of counsel upon request while others provide counsel at the discretion of the court or public defender's office. In these instances the state bears the defense costs.

17. For example, the U.S. Fifth Circuit Court of Appeal's Local Rule 8 adopted in 1983 after the *Barefoot* decision permits the appeals court to decide a request for a stay of execution almost immediately after it was denied by the federal district court [Local Rule 8 (5th Cir. 1983)]. In one case, a capital defendant had his appeal and request for a stay of execution denied by the Fifth Circuit Court of Appeals the same day that his *habeas corpus* relief was denied in federal district court [*Taylor v. Maggio,* 727 F. 2d 341 (5th Cir.), stay and cert. of probable cause denied, 104 S.Ct. 1432 (1984)].

18. In *Saffle,* the capital defendant, Robyn Parks, was convicted and sentenced to death by an Oklahoma jury. In instructing the jury the trial judge informed them that they could not be persuaded by sympathy for the defendant. In his post-conviction claim, Parks contended that the instruction to avoid being influenced by sympathy in effect told the jury to disregard the mitigating evidence in the case in violation of the 8th Amendment. In addressing Parks's claim, the U.S. Supreme Court had first to determine if the relief sought by Parks would constitute a "new rule." In *Teague v. Lane,* 109 S.Ct. 1060 (1989) the Court defined a "new rule" as one that "breaks new ground," "imposes a new obligation on the States or the Federal Government," or was not "dictated by precedent existing at the time the defendant's conviction became final." The "new rule" that the Court held Parks was creating pertained to how the jury must consider the mitigating evidence.

19. In *Beck v. Alabama,* 447 U.S. 625 (1980) at p. 637, the Court noted that imposing an undeservedly severe sentence on a defendant who might not deserve it "cannot be tolerated in a case in which the defendant's life is at stake. . . . As we have often stated, there is a significant constitutional difference between the death penalty and lesser punishments."

20. Cavanagh and Kleiman estimated the range of such costs to be between $62,000 and $64,000; the estimate of $63,000 used here is the midpoint of that range.

21. Cavanagh and Kleiman (1990, 14–16) include in their estimate of the costs of incarceration the cost of lost employment to inmates and the welfare costs to the inmate's dependents. Since these costs are incurred regardless of whether the defendant is

executed or sentenced to life imprisonment, they are not included in the annual operating costs estimated here.

22. This is the estimated average age of an offender who was arrested for murder and non-negligent manslaughter in 1988. The 1988 *Uniform Crime Reports* (1988, 178–179) provides the age for each offender arrested for homicide. The UCR does not provide information on those eventually convicted for capital murder. In addition, some of these ages are reported as age ranges, such as 25–29; in these cases the midpoint of the range was used. The age of very young and very old homicide offenders was also reported as a range, under ten years of age and sixty-five years and older. In the first instance the age of ten was selected in calculating the average age, while sixty-five was taken as the representative age in the oldest category.

23. *World Almanac 1990.*

7

Public Protection and the Death Penalty

In the last chapter we saw that one of the arguments proponents of the death penalty frequently use to support their position is that capital punishment is less costly than life imprisonment. We also saw that this argument did not seem to be a tenable one a *system* of capital punishment may be more costly than one based on life imprisonment. But the possible cost savings that accrue from capital punishment is not, of course, the only argument that could be and has been raised in the defense of the death penalty. Nor does this economic benefits argument seem to be the most important reason for persons' approval of capital punishment. In a 1985 Gallup poll (Gallup 1986) only 11 percent of those who supported capital punishment did so because they thought life imprisonment more costly. This would suggest that death penalty proponents may believe that capital punishment is a less expensive sanction than life imprisonment, but it is not the most critical factor upon which they base their approval.

Another argument that could be raised to support a belief in the death penalty is that it is needed in order to protect public safety. This position stipulates that the public needs to be protected both from those would-be murderers who are contemplating the commission of an offense, and from those who have already killed and who may commit another murder. The need for public protection is a very important and very real concern. Homicide rates in the United States are higher than in any Western country. In 1986–1987 the homicide rate per 100,000 population (males 15–24 years of age) in the United States (21.9) was over seven times higher than that in Canada (2.9), fifteen times higher than in France (1.4), eighteen times higher than in England and Wales (1.2), and almost twenty-two times higher than in West Germany (1.0) (Fingerhut and Kleinman 1990, 3293). The rates of homicide in California, Texas, New York, Arizona, Florida, Tennessee, Colorado, and Illinois are all about ten times higher than that found in most Western European countries (Fingerhut and Kleinman 1990, 3294). Reflecting this very real danger, public perception in the United States is that violent crime is endemic. For example, nearly two thirds of the public believe that crime is going to get worse in the United States in the next ten years, over one half report that they are afraid to walk alone at night in their neighborhood, and over 80 percent believe that there is more crime in the United States now than there was a year ago (Flanagan and Maguire 1990, 143, 155, 142).

As suggested in the paragraph above, the public protection argument actually takes two forms. One form of this argument is that capital punishment is needed in order to threaten would-be murderers with an extremely severe penalty which would prevent them from committing their crimes. The implicit extension of this argument is that other punishments, such as life imprisonment, do not constitute a severe enough sanction to keep those who would murder from offending. Preventing murders by threatening would-be offenders with the death penalty is referred to as general deterrence. The second form of the argument is that in not executing those who have already murdered we run the risk of them committing another murder either while imprisoned or if someday released back into the community. This argument holds that the only way to prevent convicted murderers from committing another homicide is to take their life. Preventing murders by denying convicted killers the opportunity to commit another homicide is referred to as incapacitation. We need capital punishment, the public protection argument alleges, in order to prevent new murders from being committed either through general deterrence or incapacitation, and only the execution of murderers can ensure this protection.

As was true of the economic benefits argument, there is a widespread belief among the lay public that capital punishment is more effective as a general deterrent to murder and can more effectively incapacitate convicted murderers than life imprisonment. Unlike the cost argument, however, a belief in deterrence is widespread and a very important reason for those who express support for the death penalty. In the 1986 Gallup survey, 61 percent of all respondents thought that capital punishment was a deterrent to crime. Among those who approved of the death penalty, 77 percent thought it was a deterrent. As an indication of how important a consideration the deterrence argument is, a 1985 Gallup survey reported that 40 percent of those respondents who favored the death penalty thought that capital punishment was necessary to keep others from killing, to keep murderers from killing again, and to keep murderers out of the community. These general deterrence– and incapacitation-based justifications were the most frequently expressed reasons for the approval of death penalty proponents. In view of its importance, therefore, it is necessary to examine the public protection argument in some detail.

The General Deterrence Argument

The Philosophy of Deterrence

The idea of deterring criminal behavior is grounded in eighteenth-century rational moral philosophy. Utilitarian philosophers such as Jeremy Bentham and

Cesare Beccaria asserted that crime was the product of a rational and calculating mind. In this utilitarian understanding of crime, offenses are committed because would-be offenders have estimated the benefits to be gained from crime and the costs to be incurred, and have found that the former outweigh the latter. One of the cost components to be considered by those contemplating committing an offense is the likelihood that they would be caught and the gravity of the punishment they would receive. Utilitarians would claim that the way to reduce the motivation to commit crimes, therefore, is to make the cost of punishment high enough to outweigh the benefits. The relevant dimensions of punishment in this regard are its certainty, severity, and celerity. Certainty refers to the likelihood or chance that an offender will be apprehended and punished. Severity refers to the intensity or harshness of the punishment imposed for a particular offense, while celerity reflects the swiftness with which punishment follows the commission of an act. Utilitarian philosophers would contend that if a punishment is made certain enough to convince would-be offenders that there is a good chance that they would be caught and punished, and severe enough such that the imposed penalty is credible and constitutes an undesirable cost to be avoided, and swift enough so that the association between the act and the punishment is unambiguously made, then persons would be deterred from committing offenses.

The basic general deterrence argument, then, is that persons will refrain from committing offenses if they perceive that they are certain to be punished, with a severe penalty, and soon after the offense has been committed. As it pertains to capital punishment, those who adhere to the deterrence argument would attest that other things being equal the death penalty is a more effective deterrent to murder than life imprisonment because it is a more severe sanction. Deterrence-influenced proponents of capital punishment would claim that when would-be offenders consider the costs involved they would be more likely to refrain from committing murder if they thought that they could be put to death if arrested and convicted than if the most severe penalty they could receive was life imprisonment.

The deterrence argument regarding capital punishment is one, like the economic benefits argument, where empirical data can shed some light. That is, just as we have examined estimates as to how much it costs to maintain a system of capital punishment as opposed to one based on life imprisonment, so too can we empirically investigate how effective capital punishment is in deterring homicide relative to life imprisonment.

The Empirical Literature on General Deterrence

The belief that capital punishment has a general deterrent effect, that executing some offenders keeps other would-be offenders from committing their crimes, is an old one. In the past, capital offenders have been put to death in both a visibly cruel and public manner, such as crucifixion, "drawing and quartering," and being burned alive, in order to maximize the deterrent effect. In 1864 Sir James Fitzjames Stephen (1864:753) wrote that "[n]o other punishment deters men so effectively from committing crimes as the punishment of death." This sentiment was expressed in virtually identical form by the Solicitor General of the United States when he argued in favor of the death penalty in 1974 before the U.S. Supreme Court: "The efforts of most criminals to avoid detection and to escape after being caught, show very clearly that they are sensitive to a calculus of pains and pleasures."[1] As we saw in the first pages of this chapter, a belief in the deterrent power of the death penalty is also part of the public's consciousness.[2]

As suggested above, whether or not the death penalty is a more effective general deterrent to murder than life imprisonment is an assertion that can be put to an indirect empirical test. We will now state the general deterrence argument as an informal hypothesis: Capital punishment is a more effective general deterrent if persons contemplating the commission of murder refrain from committing homicide because they fear the penalty of death but would have committed the act had they only been subjected to the penalty of life imprisonment. From this we can derive a number of more specific hypotheses, which, if true, would establish the relative deterrent superiority of capital punishment: (1) Do those states that have capital punishment as a penalty for murder have lower homicide rates than comparable states that punish homicide with life imprisonment? (2) Do states that had historical periods when capital punishment was available (retentionist periods) and other periods when it was abolished (abolitionist periods) have lower homicide rates during the former than the latter? (3) Is the immediate short-term effect of an execution a reduction in the number of homicides committed in the jurisdiction in which the execution took place? The proof of the pudding regarding the relative deterrent effect of capital punishment hinges on an affirmative answer to the three hypotheses above. There has been a great deal of empirical research on each of these questions, and it is to this research literature that we now turn our attention.[3]

Homicide Rates in Death Penalty and Non-Death Penalty States

State by State Comparisons

If capital punishment is a more effective deterrent to homicide than life imprisonment, then we can hypothesize that, all other things being equal, the level of homicide in a death penalty state should be lower than that in a life imprisonment state. The important phrase in this hypothesis is "all other things being equal." We will not have an accurate test of the general deterrence hypothesis if we compare the homicide rates in two states that are vastly different in ways other than the penalty they employ for homicide. For example, for much of its history Georgia has been a death penalty state while Maine abolished it in 1883 and has not reinstated it. The homicide rate, however, has consistently been higher in Georgia than in Maine. In spite of this difference, we cannot attribute the higher homicide rate in Georgia relative to Maine as due to the lack of any deterrent effect of the death penalty. This is because Georgia and Maine differ in so many other ways that may affect the states' homicide rate besides the kind of penalty they employ. Region of the country is one obvious such variable as are various indicators of poverty (unemployment, per capita income). Homicide rates are higher in the southern United States than they are in New England, and they are also influenced by how poor a state's population is (see Klein et al. 1978).

A fair test of the relative deterrent effectiveness of capital punishment and life imprisonment would entail a comparison of states that are comparable to each other in important ways, differing only in terms of their penalty for homicide. This does not mean, however, that the death penalty and life imprisonment states that are being compared have to be similar in *every possible way*, but only alike as to those factors that are related to the homicide rate. One way to ensure this rough comparability is to take states that are geographically contiguous, that is, next to each other. Such contiguous states will likely share many historical, cultural, and economic factors, ones that have traditionally influenced the commission of criminal homicide.

Thorsten Sellin was one of the first social scientists to conduct research along these lines (Sellin 1959; 1967, 135–138). Table 7–1 is an adaptation of Sellin's 1959 published data. It provides a comparison of homicide rates from groups of matched states that differ in terms of whether or not they are a death penalty state or a life imprisonment state. If capital punishment is a more effective deterrent to homicide than life imprisonment, then death penalty states should generally have lower homicide rates than life imprisonment states. An examination of Table 7–1, however, does not provide much evidence for the greater deterrent power of capital punishment.

In the first set of contiguous states, Michigan, Indiana, and Ohio, the highest homicide rate was in a death penalty state (Ohio), while Michigan, a non–death penalty state, and Indiana, a death penalty state, had identical homicide rates over the recorded time period. In the second set of contiguous states, the state with the death penalty has the lowest annual homicide rate (Iowa with 1.7 per 100,000), but this is not much different from that found in Wisconsin, a non–death penalty state (1.8 per 100,000). In the third set of states, North Dakota, a non–death penalty state, has a lower level of homicide than both death penalty states. In the two sets of contiguous New England states there is no evidence that capital punishment is a superior deterrent to homicide than life imprisonment. Maine, a non–death penalty state, had a slightly higher annual homicide rate than two contiguous death penalty states, New Hampshire

Table 7-1
Homicide Rates in Contiguous Death Penalty and Life Imprisonment States: 1920–1955
(Annual rate per 100,000)

Midwestern United States

	Contiguous States Set No. 1			Contiguous States Set No. 2			Contiguous States Set No. 3		
State	*State*	*Homicide Penalty*	*Homicide Rate*	*State*	*Homicide Penalty*	*Homicide Rate*	*State*	*Homicide Penalty*	*Homicide Rate*
	Michigan	Life	4.8	Minnesota	Life	2.2	North Dakota[b]	Life	1.4
	Indiana	Death	4.8	Wisconsin	Life	1.8	South Dakota[c]	Death	1.6
	Ohio	Death	6.1	Iowa[a]	Death	1.7	Nebraska	Death	2.7

New England States

	Contiguous States Set No. 4			Contiguous States Set No. 5		
State	*State*	*Homicide Penalty*	*Homicide Rate*	*State*	*Homicide Penalty*	*Homicide Rate*
	Maine	Life	1.6	Rhode Island	Life	1.7
	New Hampshire	Death	1.3	Massachusetts	Death	1.7
	Vermont	Death	1.2	Connecticut	Death	2.3

Source: Adapted from D.C. Baldus and J.W.L. Cole, "Statistical Evidence on the Deterrent Effect of Capital Punishment: A Comparison of the Work of Thorsten Sellin and Isaac Ehrlich on the Deterrent Effect of Capital Punishment," *Yale Law Journal* 85(1975):171, note 11. Reprinted by permission of The Yale Law Journal Company and Fred B. Rothman & Company.

[a] 1923–1955; [b] 1924–1955; [c] 1930–1955.

and Vermont, but Rhode Island's, a non-death penalty state, is lower than Connecticut's, a death penalty state.

As can be seen from Table 7–1, Sellin's research covers only the pre-*Furman* period (1920–1955). One of the promised products of the procedural reform of state death penalty statutes subsequent to the *Furman* decision was a greater consistency and regularity to death sentences. It is conceivable that the guided discretion statutes approved in *Gregg v. Georgia* and its companion cases brought about a greater certainty of capital punishment, and hence, a more powerful general deterrent effect. In addition, if the deterrent effect of a sanction threat is partly a function of how widely known that sanction is, the amount of media attention in the wake of these decisions that restored the death penalty in the United States should have increased the deterrent power of capital punishment.

Peterson and Bailey (1988, 784–785) examined the average annual homicide rates in death penalty and abolitionist states and all states during the post-*Furman* period (1973–1984). If capital punishment is a more effective general deterrent than a noncapital penalty, homicide rates should be lower in death penalty states. Peterson and Bailey found no evidence of a superior deterrent effect for the death penalty. For each year in the twelve-year time period the average annual homicide rate in the death penalty states was higher than the rate in both the abolitionist states and the national average. The twelve-year average annual homicide rate was 8.46 per 100,000 population in death penalty states, 5.35 in abolitionist states, and 7.61 for the United States as a whole. They also failed to find a relationship between the death penalty and changes in homicide rates over time.

Peterson and Bailey (1988, 786–788) then conducted a Sellin–like contiguous-state comparison in order to control for differences between death penalty and non–death penalty states. There was no more support for a greater deterrent effect of capital punishment in these analyses. They reported that the homicide rates in the abolitionist states of Maine and Vermont were the same as those in New Hampshire, which had the death penalty for eleven of the twelve study years. Homicide rates were consistently higher in Virginia which provided for the death penalty over the years 1973–1984 than in West Virginia, which was a noncapital state over the same time. Only one abolitionist state (Michigan) had a higher annual homicide rate than its comparable death penalty states (Ohio and Indiana). The homicide rate in Michigan is, however, governed by the rate in one city (Detroit). When the homicide rate in Detroit is excluded from the Michigan data its homicide rate is no different from the two death penalty states of Ohio and Indiana.

It would appear from these findings of Sellin and Peterson and Bailey, then, that the homicide rate is not consistently lower in those states that had capital punishment compared with similar states that did not have it as a legislatively prescribed sanction. As was suggested earlier, the validity of this hypothesis test depends upon the extent to which the life and death penalty states are truly comparable. If they differ on those factors that affect the number of homicides committed in a state (as did our earlier example of Maine and Georgia), the comparison is invalid since different kinds of states are being compared ("apples and oranges"), not just states that differ only in terms of their penalty for criminal homicide. It could be argued that although contiguous states are somewhat similar in geography and perhaps regional culture, mere physical proximity is not enough to ensure that they are sufficiently alike to permit an accurate comparison of annual homicide rates.

Sellin's work was subject to just this criticism (Ehrlich 1975). Many years after his published research, however, Baldus and Cole (1975, 177–182) compared Sellin's groups of contiguous states on such characteristics as the probability of apprehension and conviction, labor force participation, unemployment rate, population aged 15–24, per-capita income, percent nonwhite population, per-capita government expenditures, and per-capita police expenditures. Each of these factors was thought to be related to the homicide rate. Baldus and Cole found that the contiguous life and death penalty states selected by Sellin were very similar in terms of these factors. Their findings strengthened Sellin's assertion that the contiguous state comparison was methodologically sound and that the substantive conclusion of the research, that capital punishment is a no better general deterrent to murder than life imprisonment, was valid.

Initial doubts about Sellin's matching technique, however, led to the introduction of another attempt to control for differences between death penalty and life imprisonment states—statistical controls. In addition, doubts about the validity of using the offense of willful homicide (which includes both murder and non-negligent manslaughter) to measure a more specific category of homicide, capital murder, led to some refinements in the measurement of murder in deterrence research. We will briefly explore each of these issues.

Statistical Analyses of Homicide Rates and Punishment

As discussed above, the selection and comparison of contiguous death penalty and non–death penalty states is based upon the assumption that neighboring states are comparable in ways that are related to the homicide rate with the exception of the type of penalty that may be imposed. In comparing contiguous states, deterrence researchers are "holding constant" other variables that may affect each state's homicide rate (such as the unemployment rate or percent of the population that lives in poverty), so that any differences in the number of homicides can more unambiguously be attributed to the kind of punishment employed (death or life imprisonment). Isaac Ehrlich, an economist, was one of the first to criticize this approach.[4] Ehrlich (1975) criticized Sellin's method because he thought contiguous-state comparisons failed to adequately control for other factors that might affect the homicide rate in a state, and because a comparison of a death and non-death penalty state sheds no light on the effect of the risk or likelihood of execution (the certainty of punishment) on the homicide rate.

In his approach, Ehrlich used a statistical technique called multiple regression analysis to examine the simultaneous effect of several causal factors on the rate of homicide. Rather than look at the effect of capital punishment on homicide rates within individual states, however, Ehrlich aggregated his data and focused on this effect within the United States as a whole during the years 1933 to 1969. Although his regression equation contained several influences on the nation's homicide rate, such as the arrest and conviction rate for murder, labor force participation rate, unemployment rate, the population between the ages of fourteen and twenty-four, and per-capita income, Ehrlich's main interest was in the effect of what he called "execution risk."

The execution risk variable was measured as the ratio of the number of executions in the United States to convictions for murder during the selected time period. If capital punishment is an effective general deterrent to murder, then, when other influences are controlled for, the effect of this execution risk variable should be negative (the higher the risk of execution the lower the homicide rate). This is precisely what Ehrlich found. He reported (1975, 410) that there was a significant deterrent effect for the risk of execution. More specifically, he found that a one percent increase in the risk of execution could produce a six percent decrease in the national homicide rate. Ehrlich (1975, 414) stated his results even more dramatically: "An additional execution per year over the period in question [1933–1969] may have resulted, on average, in 7 or 8 fewer murders."

Ehrlich's conclusion, that each execution may have prevented seven or eight homicides by deterring would-be murderers, was rather striking. His was virtually the only research up to that time to find any empirical documentation for the general deterrent effect of capital punishment, and so it flew in the face of virtually all previous deterrence research, particularly the work of Sellin.[5] Ehrlich's research was also to have important policy implications. The Solicitor General of the United States included a draft of Ehrlich's paper in the government's brief before the United States Supreme Court in the case of *Fowler v. North Carolina,* 96 S.Ct. 3212 (1976) which argued in favor of capital punishment. The Court did put off its decision until the next term when it decided the *Gregg* case. It is significant, however, that in his *Gregg* opinion, Justice Stewart noted that the empirical evidence with respect to the general deterrent capability of capital punishment was "inconclusive" [*Gregg v. Georgia,* 428 U.S. 153 (1976) at p. 185], although the only study cited that shows that capital punishment deters more effectively than life imprisonment was Ehrlich's.

Ehrlich's 1975 paper promoted more than debate within the chambers of the Supreme Court. Immediately after his article was published (in a leading economics journal), reanalyses and criticisms of his work began to appear. A large number of scientific papers were published that were directed at attempting to reproduce Ehrlich's deterrent effect. Since this literature is abundant and quite technical we will simply review some of the more telling objections.[6]

One observation made about Ehrlich's deterrent effect for the execution risk variable was that it disappeared when the last few years (after 1962) were removed from the analysis (Passell and Taylor 1977; Bowers and Pierce 1975). This would suggest that the deterrent effect for capital punishment reported by Ehrlich was somewhat of an artifact, existing only during the mid-to late 1960s when the number and likelihood of executions in the United States was declining to zero and homicide rates were generally increasing. In fact, when the more recent years were deleted from the time series, the effect of execution risk on homicide rates was *positive* rather than negative. This positive effect would suggest that executions may actually increase the number of homicides in a state—a "brutalization" rather than a deterrent effect.[7]

Other critics of Ehrlich's work suggested that he omitted crucial variables from his analysis, such as private gun ownership (Kleck 1979), the rate of rural to urban migration (Baldus and Cole 1975), and the level of violent offending in the United States (Klein et al. 1978), variables which could have biased his estimated deterrent effect. When these other variables are included, they have noted, the deterrent effect of capital punishment no longer exists. One of the most important variables which Ehrlich failed to consider was a measure of the length of prison sentences for convicted murderers (Lempert 1981). Ehrlich's analysis only considers the possible deterrent effect of executions on the homicide rate, it *does not* allow one to compare the deterrent effect of capital punishment with that of confinement for life. The latter issue concerns the most important policy question, which is whether capital punishment is a more effective deterrent than life imprisonment. There is, however, no way to answer that critical question from Ehrlich's analyses.

The confusion over the meaning to be derived from Ehrlich's research, and the failure of other researchers to fully replicate his findings, led the National Academy of Sciences Panel on Deterrence and Incapacitation to commission a paper to specifically examine the Ehrlich data. This investigation was headed by the Nobel Prize–winning economist Lawrence Klein. Klein and his colleagues (1978) assessed Ehrlich's analyses with his own data set and noted several of the methodological problems we have just reviewed.[8] After extensive work with Ehrlich's data, their conclusion (1978, 358) was that "we see too many plausible explanations for his finding a deterrent effect other than the theory that capital punishment deters murder. . . . [his] results cannot be used at this time to pass judgment on the use of the death penalty."

Ehrlich's claim that capital punishment deters would-be murderers is further questioned by the failure of others to find such an effect with different data sets. Kleck (1979) failed to find a deterrent effect for executions on homicide rates over the period 1947–1973. Neither Forst (1977) who examined the effect of executions on homicide rates in 1960 and 1970 nor Knorr (1979) who conducted a similar analysis for the years 1955 and 1960 found a general deterrent effect for capital punishment. Finally, Bailey found that executions have a small and insignificant effect on the homicide rates in California (Bailey 1979a), North Carolina (Bailey 1978a), Oregon (Bailey 1979b), Ohio (Bailey 1979c), and Utah (Bailey 1978b).

It would appear from this vast and statistically sophisticated literature, then, that the earlier conclusion of Sellin remains intact: capital punishment does not seem to have a general deterrent effect on the level of general homicide. It is still possible, however, that the measures of homicide employed in this research are too insensitive to detect a deterrent effect, and that the latter would emerge with a more specific subtype of homicide. It is to this possibility that we now turn our attention.

Capital Punishment, Life Imprisonment, and Police Killings

One of the criticisms directed against early deterrence work was its employment of a general homicide measure, willful homicide, which included both capital and noncapital murder. If capital punishment deters, it is argued, it will only deter capital murder and any marginal deterrent effect may be obscured when a general homicide measure is used in deterrence research. Unfortunately, most official record sources, such as the FBI's *Uniform Crime Reports,* do not separately report capital and noncapital murders. One type of capital murder is, however, recorded separately, the killing of a police officer, and this capital offense can be used to determine the deterrent effect of capital punishment.

In addition to the fact that the killing of a police officer is a more refined and perhaps sensitive measure of capital homicide than willful homicide, there is an important substantive reason to examine the effect of the death penalty on police killings. It has frequently been argued by proponents of the death penalty that it is only the threat of capital punishment that prevents offenders from killing the law enforcement officers attempting to apprehend them (van den Haag 1983, 234): "[w]ithout the death penalty an offender having committed a crime that leads to imprisonment for life has nothing to lose if he murders the arresting officer." For these proponents, capital punishment is vital in protecting the lives of law enforcement officers in the performance of their duties; without it they would be at greater risk of being killed.

Sellin (1967, 138–154) was one of the first to examine whether or not the death penalty offers police officers better protection than life imprisonment. He compared the police homicide rate for cities of comparable size within death penalty and non–death penalty states. He found that the rate of police killings was no lower for those cities in death penalty states. He also compared the police homicide rate in death penalty and non–death penalty states as a whole. His findings from this analysis are reported in Table 7–2. It can be seen that the rate of police killings is no lower in death penalty states than it is in non–death penalty states, a finding that is contrary to the argument that capital punishment makes policing less perilous.

Sellin (1967, 152–153) also reported that during 1961–1963 the annual number of police killings in six non–death penalty states was 1.312 per 10,000 police officers while it was 1.328 in nine contiguous death penalty states. The existence of the death penalty, then, did not lower the risk that a police officer would be killed. In an updated analysis of the effect of the death penalty on police homicides, Sellin (1980) compared the rate of police killings in death penalty and non–death penalty states in 1975. He reported that police officers had a *higher risk* of being killed in those states that employed the death penalty than in nearby non–capital punishment states (with the exception of one abolitionist state).

As was true with Sellin's other work on capital punishment, which compared neighboring death and non–death penalty states, his research related to capital punishment and the deterrence of police killings has been criticized because of its failure to control for a wide range of other factors that may affect the rate of police killings (Bailey and Peterson 1987). Bailey (1982; Bailey and Peterson 1987) has tried to improve upon this research by examining the effect of two death penalty variables, the legal status of the death penalty (death penalty versus non–death penalty state) and the risk or certainty of execution, on the rate of police killings. In the first of his research reports, Bailey (1982) found that even after taking into account four other variables thought to be related to police killings, percent poverty, nonwhite population, unemployment rate, and percent urban, neither the legal possibility of the death penalty nor the

Table 7–2
Rate of Police Homicides in Selected Death Penalty and Non–Death Penalty States: 1919–1954

Midwestern United States			
Non–Death Penalty States		*Death Penalty States*	
North Dakota	1.9	Iowa	2.0
Minnesota	1.5	Illinois	1.1
Michigan	1.3	Indiana	2.3
Wisconsin	1.2	Ohio	2.2
Eastern United States			
Non–Death Penalty States		*Death Penalty States*	
Maine	0.0	New Hampshire	0.5
Rhode Island	0.6	Massachusetts	0.8
		Connecticut	0.5
		New York	0.9

Source: T. Sellin, *Capital Punishment* (New York: Harper & Row, 1967), 147. Copyright © 1967 by T. Sellin. Reprinted by permission of HarperCollins Publishers.

certainty of its infliction affected the number of police homicides during the period 1961–1971.

As Bailey correctly noted, however, his findings cannot be taken as unequivocal evidence of a lack of deterrent effect for the death penalty since it occurred at a time in history when the death penalty was rarely used (there were no executions in the United States between 1968 and 1976). In a reexamination of this issue, Bailey and Peterson (1987) investigated the relationship between capital punishment and the rate of police killings during the post-*Furman* period, 1973–1984. In their analysis, Bailey and Peterson took into account the percent black in the state's population, the region of the country, the percent of families below the poverty line, the percent between the ages of fifteen and thirty-four, and the gender ratio. They concluded from their analysis that contrary to the deterrence argument, death penalty states had no lower a rate of police homicides than non–death penalty states, nor was the rate of police killings related to the *use* of the death penalty since police homicides were not affected by the number of death sentences that were imposed in a death penalty state. It would appear, then, from the research of both Sellin and Bailey that law enforcement personnel are no safer in jurisdictions that retain and use the death penalty to punish those who deliberately kill police officers than in those who impose some other penalty.

The Short-Term General Deterrent Effect of Executions: The Effect of Execution Publicity

Both Sellin's contiguous state comparisons and the more recent multiple regression approaches have presumed that the deterrent effect of executions is felt over a long period of time (a year or more). It may be that the failure of these studies to find any evidence of a substantial deterrent effect is that if executions do deter homicides the preventive effect may be restricted to only a very brief period immediately after an execution has occurred. It is also possible that the key deterrence variable is not the actual performance of an execution but the publicity surrounding it. Since a general deterrent effect depends upon the communication of a threat message, that murderers are put to death for their offenses, it seems reasonable to presume that the more this message is conveyed to the public (the greater the publicity given to an execution) the stronger the deterrent effect will be. This argument would suggest that if we could compare the number of homicides that take place immediately before and after an execution and if we could measure the amount of publicity given to different executions we would be able to find a strong deterrent effect. The reason why previous studies have failed to find this effect is that it may diminish and eventually disappear over time as the vividness of the execution recedes in the memories of would-be killers.

Several researchers have advanced and tested this hypothesis. One of the first studies was by Dann (1935), who examined the number of homicides in the sixty days immediately before and after five highly publicized executions (one in 1927, 1929, 1930, 1931, and 1932). Dann found, contrary to the deterrence doctrine, that homicides *increased* after each execution. In 1956 Graves examined the number of homicides committed in the days just before and after an execution. In California during the time Graves was collecting his data virtually all executions took place on Friday. He compared the homicide rates on the days just before and after "execution Fridays" with the homicides committed on the same days that did not include an execution Friday. Graves found only partial support for a deterrent effect. Although there were fewer homicides on the Saturdays and Sundays after an execution Friday, there were more homicides on Thursday and Friday than during a nonexecution week. Graves's study indicated that the post-execution deterrent effect was cancelled by a pre-execution brutalization effect. In a reanalysis of the Graves data, Bowers (1988, 67) found that the brutalization effect was stronger and that "one out of four executions stimulates a homicide by the end of the following week."

Evidence of this short-term brutalization rather than deterrent effect of executions was also found in data collected by Savitz (1958), who examined the number of homicides that were committed during an eight-week period before and after four well-publicized murder trials in Philadelphia which resulted in the imposition of death sentences (one in 1944 and 1947 and two in 1946). Savitz originally found that there were forty-one murders in the period after these trials, two less than the number that occurred in the eight-week pretrial period. When these weekly rates were adjusted for seasonal variations in homicides (because some months have a higher number of average homicides than others), Bowers (1988) found that there was *one additional* homicide committed for each death sentence imposed.

There are three other studies that have examined the effect of executions on statewide homicide rates, all of which found some evidence of a brutalization rather than a deterrent effect. In one of these, King (1978) investigated the impact of twenty executions in South Carolina that occurred during the years 1951–1962 and were given coverage in the state's newspaper that had the largest circulation. He compared the number of homicides that were committed in the month of and month after the execution story with those that were committed during the same months in the previous and subsequent years. King found that there were on average 0.6 fewer homicides committed during the month an execution article was run in the newspaper and an increase of 1.8 homicides in the month after an execution story. Contrary to the deterrence hypothesis, there was, then, an overall increase of 1.2 homicides. Bowers and Pierce (1980b) investigated the relationship between executions and monthly homicide rates in New York State during the period 1906–1963 and found that there was on average 1.7 more homicides in the first month after an execution took place and 1.3 additional homicides in the second month after. Finally, Bailey (1983) examined the impact of executions on monthly first-degree homicide rates in

Chicago during the years 1915–1921 and found that there were three more first-degree murders than expected in the month following an execution.

Virtually all of the research on the short-term effect of capital punishment and the publicity accompanying executions has shown no evidence of a general deterrent effect. In fact, this literature suggests instead that by executing its offenders the state may actually encourage the commission of additional homicides. As in the case of Ehrlich's long-term impact studies, there have been a few studies that have reportedly found that execution publicity has a significant short-term deterrent effect.

One of these studies was conducted by David Phillips (1980), who identified twenty-two murderers executed in London between 1864 and 1921 and measured the attendant publicity of each execution by the number of newspaper column inches devoted to it. Phillips reported that for fifteen of the twenty-two cases the number of homicides committed during the week of the execution was substantially below the average number of homicides committed, and that the greater the newspaper coverage given the execution the more substantial the reduction in the number of weekly homicides.

Phillips's study created almost as much controversy as did Ehrlich's.[9] There is some suspicion that any deterrent effect that existed in Phillips's London data may be either short-lived or nonexistent. For example, Phillips reported that although the number of homicides in the week during which an execution took place and in the first week after was below the pre-execution weekly average, homicides *increased* in the next three weeks. As a result (Phillips 1980, 146), "within five or six weeks of a publicized execution, the drop in homicides is canceled by an equally large rise in homicides." The reported deterrent effect in Phillips's data may, therefore, have lasted for no longer than one or two weeks.

Bowers (1988, 72–79) conducted a detailed reanalysis of the Phillips data and concluded that Phillips's short-term deterrent effect may be due to errors in the data and analysis. Bowers extended Phillips's data to include a ten-week period before and after each London execution. In this analysis he found that the number of homicides after a publicized execution was substantially *higher* than that before, evidence of a brutalization rather than a deterrent effect. In addition, Bowers reported that this brutalization effect was enhanced the more publicity there was surrounding an execution. Contrary to Phillips's original claim, Bowers's study led him to the conclusion that executions have the effect of increasing the number of homicides, and the more they are publicized the greater this brutalization effect is.

It may be that even the very short-term deterrent effect reported by Phillips in London may not be true for the United States. McFarland (1983) examined the effect of the first four post-*Furman* executions, each of which was highly publicized (Gary Gilmore, John Spinkellink, Jesse Bishop, and Steven Judy), on weekly U.S. homicide rates. His results do not support Phillips's finding of even a very short-term general deterrent effect. He found that weekly homicide rates were unaffected by the executions of Spinkellink, Bishop, and Judy. While homicides did decline following the execution of Gary Gilmore (the most highly publicized execution), McFarland's analysis indicated that this decline was probably attributable to severe local weather conditions which kept the homicide rate down, rather than deterrence.

Another researcher, Stack (1987), however, challenges McFarland's research and offers evidence in support of Phillips's original finding that execution publicity has a short-term deterrent effect. He investigated the effect of sixteen publicized executions that occurred during the years 1951–1979 on monthly U.S. homicide rates and found that each execution story resulted in a decline of thirty homicides during the month of the story. He concluded that these sixteen highly publicized executions may have prevented as many as 480 additional homicides, a substantial deterrent effect.

As was true of Phillips's study, however, the deterrent effect reported by Stack appears to disappear when subjected to a more detailed and rigorous analysis. Bailey and Peterson (1989) analyzed Stack's contention that execution publicity prevented the loss of innocent life over the years 1940–1986. After noting several methodological shortcomings in Stack's study, Bailey and Peterson conducted several analyses and failed to find any deterrent effect for execution publicity. In attempting to replicate Stack's original deterrence findings, Bailey and Peterson concluded (1989, 731) that they were the result of technical errors in his analysis and not a genuine deterrent effect.

In a subsequent study, Bailey (1990) examined the effect of television publicity given to executions and homicide rates during the post-*Furman* period 1976–1987. After taking into consideration other factors that could influence the homicide rate in the United States during this time period, Bailey found that television publicity had neither a brutalization nor a deterrent effect on homicide rates. Neither the amount nor the type of television coverage of an execution was related to the national homicide rate.

Homicide Rates in Retentionist and Abolitionist Periods: "Before–After" Studies.

There have been some states that have inadvertently conducted a kind of natural experiment with the death penalty. These states have had the death penalty as the legislatively prescribed penalty for capital crimes during some periods of their history, but during other periods that penalty was abolished and replaced with life imprisonment or some other term of years only to have the death penalty reinstated at a later time. If the death penalty deters capital offenses better than life imprisonment, the rate of capital offending should be higher during those times it was abolished, all other things being equal.

Thorsten Sellin (1967) has conducted some research on the level of homicides during abolitionist and retentionist periods, and his findings are summarized in Table 7–3. The results of Sellin's research do not provide much support for the greater deterrent power of capital punishment. For example, during the years 1915–1916 the state of Arizona had the death penalty as its statutory penalty for murder, abolished capital punishment during the years 1917–1918, and reintroduced it in 1919–1920. Forty-one murderers were convicted of homicide during the preabolitionist period; the number increased to forty-six during the abolitionist period, but stayed approximately the same during the subsequent year when the death penalty was reinstated. If homicides were increasing during the 1917–1918 abolitionist period because there was no effective deterrent, it should have declined considerably when the death penalty was reinstated in 1919; but in fact, the rate stayed at approximately the 1918 level. Whatever factors were responsible for increasing the number of homicides during the abolitionist period in Arizona (1917–1918), they continued to operate for at least one more year.

A critic of these results could argue, however, that the one-year interval, following abolition in Arizona, during which the death penalty was reinstated (1919–1920) was not a sufficient time period for the deterrent effect to be established. That is, it may have taken Arizona citizens more than one year to get the message that life imprisonment has been replaced with capital punishment. The data from Missouri is informative on this point. The homicide rate during the preabolitionist period was 9.2 per 100,000. Consistent with the greater deterrent effect of capital punishment it increased to 10.7 during the abolitionist period 1917–1919. Contrary to the deterrence hypothesis, however, the homicide rate in Missouri stayed virtually the same (11.0 homicides per 100,000) during the next four years after the death penalty was reinstated (1920–1924). The postabolitionist period reported for Colorado is even longer (five years), and there is no sign of a deterrent effect after the reinstatement of the death penalty. The homicide rate in the five-year period after the death penalty. The homicide rate in the five-year period after the death penalty was brought back into effect was slightly *higher* than that during abolition (19.0 v. 18.0 homicides per 100,000). In fact, the general pattern in Table 7.3 is that homicide rates increase during a period of abolition but seldom decline when the death penalty is subsequently reinstated. This would suggest that both increases and decreases in the homicide rate over time are influenced by factors other than the existence or nonexistence of the death penalty.[10]

This early research by Sellin has been replicated, for different time periods, by Lempert (1983) and Peterson and Bailey (1988). Lempert analyzed the relationship between the frequency of executions and homicide rates in several groups of states over the years 1920–1955. He hypothesized that if capital punishment is an effective deterrent then a state should have a lower homicide rate during those years when it executes more offenders. Lempert found that whether or not a state executed frequently, infrequently, or not at all had no systematic effect on its homicide rate. He concluded (1983, 114) that this finding

Table 7-3
Number of Murder Convictions or Homicide Rates during Death Penalty Periods and during Abolitionist Periods

State	Homicide Measure	Death Penalty Period		Abolitionist Period		Death Penalty Period	
		Number	(Years)	Number	(Years)	Number	(Years)
Arizona	Murder convictions (total number)	41.0	(1915–1916)	46.0	(1917–1918)	45.0	(1919–1920)
Colorado	Murder convictions (average)	15.4	(1891–1896)	18.0	(1897–1901)	19.0	(1902–1907)
Iowa	Murder convictions (average)	2.6	(1864–1871)	8.8	(1872–1878)	13.1	(1879–1966)
Missouri	Homicide rate (per 100,000)	9.2	(1911–1916)	10.7	(1917–1919)	11.0	(1920–1924)
Washington	Homicide rate (per 100,000)	6.5	(1908–1912)	6.8	(1913–1918)	5.4	(1920–1924)

Source: T. Sellin, *Capital Punishment* (New York: Harper & Row, 1967), 122–124. Copyright © 1967 by T. Sellin. Reprinted by permission of HarperCollins Publishers.

"provides further evidence that within historically given parameters the death penalty in general and executions in particular do not deter homicide."

The research of both Sellin and Lempert concerned the effect of executions on state homicide rates during the pre-*Furman* period. It was suggested in the previous section that the certainty of capital punishment may have been enhanced by both the procedural changes in new guided-discretion capital statutes and the publicity attendant to the restoration of the death penalty in the mid-1970s. The restoration of the death penalty by the *Gregg* decision and the resumption of executions in 1977, then, provide a natural experiment regarding the effect of executions on homicides. If capital punishment is a more effective general deterrent than noncapital penalties, homicide rates in post-*Furman* death penalty states should be lower after the death penalty was reinstated than in the years before.

Peterson and Bailey (1988, 784) report homicide rates for the years 1973–1984 in death penalty and abolition states and for all states. Since executions resumed in the United States in 1977 we can examine the homicide rate in death penalty states (those states that enacted new death penalty statutes, sentenced offenders to death, and in a few states performed executions) and abolition states in non–death penalty (1973–1976) and death penalty (1977–1984) years. Peterson and Bailey's data show that the homicide rate in death penalty states during non–death penalty years was on average no different from the years after executions were resumed (8.75 per 100,000 in non-death years v. 8.31 after 1977). Homicide rates in states that did not have the death penalty over the years 1973–1984 were not substantially different pre- and post-1977 (5.2 v. 5.4 per 100,000), nor were those for the United States as a whole. Contrary to the deterrence hypothesis, there was no evidence in Peterson and Bailey's data to suggest that the restoration of executions in some states lowered their homicide rates.

The Incapacitation Argument

The Philosophy of Incapacitation

In the previous sections of this chapter we have considered the notion of public protection from the perspective of general deterrence. Although we have discovered that capital punishment may be no more an effective general deterrent to murder than noncapital punishment, deterrence is only one process through which the death penalty may protect the public. Some proponents of capital punishment have argued that murderers constitute a particularly dangerous group of violent offenders, those who have shown by their behavior that they are incapable of abiding by the laws of society. It is further believed that murderers will commit another heinous crime if they are given the opportunity to do so. The only way to ensure that murderers do not kill again, either while confined in prison or if released back into the community, is to execute them. This is the incapacitative function of capital punishment. By executing convicted murderers we guarantee that they will commit no other killings.

The empirical issue may appear quite clear. Capital punishment is obviously effective in incapacitating those who have previously murdered. If capital defendants are themselves killed they are effectively denied the opportunity every to murder again. But those who argue for the death penalty from the perspective of incapacitation would contend that the death penalty is the *only* *way* to protect ourselves from murderers who would commit another homicide if given the chance to do so. They would argue that a noncapital sanction does not offer sufficient public protection against murderers, who may kill correctional staff or other inmates while in prison or innocent citizens if ever put out on parole.

The argument that opponents of capital punishment would raise, however, is that convicted murderers serving long prison sentences are very unlikely to commit another murder, either while confined or when released back into the community, so that the greater deterrent effect alleged for capital punishment is a very small one, and one that does not outweigh its disadvantages. The incapacitation argument in favor of capital punishment, therefore, seems to hinge on the extent to which convicted capital defendants are prone to commit homicide either while confined or if released. There has been some empirical research studies directed at this important issue.

Empirical Research on Incapacitating Murderers

In 1982, Sellin (1982) reported the results of a 1965 survey which was sent to state and federal prison administrators requesting information on all homicides that occurred in their prison during 1964. Responses were received from 41 of the 50 states, the Federal Bureau of Prisons, and the District of Columbia. Combined, a total of 31 homicides were committed in these prisons. All of the victims were inmates, and very few of those homicides were committed by former murderers. Thirty-two inmates were implicated in these killings, of whom 5 (16%) were serving time for some type of homicide while 16 (50%) were serving sentences for property crimes. Sellin repeated his survey to cover prison homicides committed in 1965. In that year 52 victims were killed in prison, and 59 inmates were identified as the murderer. Of these 59 assailants, 11 (19%) were in prison for capital murder, 16 (27%) were serving time for some lesser type of murder, and 19 (32%) were serving time for armed robbery and 11 (19%) for theft or burglary.

These data on the prison behavior of convicted murderers is not current, but it does shed some light on the institutional violence of convicted murderers and other inmates confined for nonhomicide offenses. Sellin's data suggest that while some inmates who are serving time for murder do commit another homicide while imprisoned, the largest proportion of prison killings are committed by those in prison for some other offense. In fact, Sellin's 1965 survey indicates that inmates serving time for murder are no more likely to commit a homicide while in prison than those serving time for a property offense.

One of the limitations of Sellin's work for our purposes is that he was unable to differentiate between capital and noncapital confined murderers. More specific data come from a recent study of Texas capital prisoners by Marquart and Sorensen (1988). They had the opportunity to study the institutional behavior of former death row inmates who were released into the general prison population when their death sentences were commuted to life by the *Furman* decision. They compared the number and seriousness of violations of prison rules and regulations of a group of 47 capital inmates released from death row by *Furman* with a comparable comparison group of 156 inmates who were convicted of murder and rape (the same offenses for which the *Furman* inmates were sentenced to death) and received life sentences. Marquart and Sorensen reported that the former death row inmates were no more violent when released into the prison population than those similar offenders serving life sentences.

During the years 1973–1986 approximately 75 percent of the Texas *Furman*-released inmates and 70 percent of the control group life imprisonment inmates did not commit a serious prison infraction, and no inmate from either group committed a homicide. The 46 *Furman* inmates committed a total of 21 serious rule infractions, an average of .45 per inmate, while the 156 life sentence inmates committed 116, for an average of .74 per inmate, almost twice that of the former death row group. These *Furman*-released inmates, then, did not constitute a danger to either fellow inmates or correctional staff, nor were their prison violations more serious or more frequent than the comparable group of offenders serving a life sentence. Had the state of Texas executed these 47 capital defendants whose sentences were commuted by the *Furman* decision, it would have prevented no additional prison homicides and fewer institutional violations than those committed by offenders sentenced to life.

In a second study, Marquart and Sorensen (1989) extended this research by examining the institutional behavior of 533 inmates from thirty-one states whose death sentences for either murder (453 inmates) or rape (80 inmates) were commuted by *Furman* in 1972. These inmates were all on death row awaiting execution at the time of the *Furman* decision. Marquart and Sorensen reported that of the 453 convicted murderers only 6 (1%) committed another murder while incarcerated (none of the rapists committed a murder). In four of these killings the victim was another inmate while in the other two homicides a correctional officer was killed. Only 38 of the 533 former death row inmates (7%) were involved in armed but nonlethal assaults on other prisoners or staff. In fact, over a fifteen-year period less than one third of these condemned offenders committed a serious violation of prison rules; most inmates committed only one serious rule violation.

Proponents of capital punishment would argue in response to these findings of Sellin and Marquart and Sorensen that even if convicted murderers make an adequate adjustment while incarcerated, once they are released on parole or pardoned, and leave the very controlled environment afforded by prison life, they are likely to commit another murder in the community. To protect innocent citizens, then, these supporters of capital punishment would contend that murderers should be completely incapacitated by being put to death.

To address this concern, that is, to determine how likely they are as a group to commit another killing, we need to examine empirical information concerning the postrelease behavior of former capital defendants who have been let out of prison by some means (parole, commutation, or pardon). Stanton (1969) reported on the postrelease criminal activity of paroled murderers in New York State. He found that during the years 1958 and 1959 65 murderers and 7,305 offenders convicted of other offenses were paroled into the community. During a three-year follow-up period, 6 percent of the paroled murderers had been rearrested, while 18 percent of the nonmurderers were arrested for a new offense. Those originally serving time for an offense other than murder, then, were three times more likely to be arrested after being paroled than a group of released murderers. Stanton further reported that during the years 1948–1957 336 offenders convicted of first- or second-degree murder and 28,788 persons convicted of crimes other than murder were released on parole and followed up for a four-and-a-half-year period. Almost four times as many nonmurderers (8.2%) as murderers (2.4%) were arrested for committing a new offense on parole.

Sellin (1982) examined the subsequent criminal activity of a group of 56,265 inmates who were released on parole during 1969, 1970, and 1972 and followed up over a three-year period. Approximately 6,800 of these released offenders had been serving time for willful homicide (there was no distinction made between those serving time for capital murder and those who committed some lesser type of homicide). Sellin reported that of the 6,835 inmates who had served time for homicide, 310 (4.5%) had committed a new offense at some time during the three-year follow-up period and were returned to prison. Only 21 of the 6,835 (.31%) had committed a new homicide. The likelihood that any released offender who had been serving a sentence for homicide would commit another killing upon release was, then, quite small. In fact, Sellin's report indicated that the homicide rate per 1,000 paroled offenders was lower for those who had previously served time for homicide (3.6 per 1,000) than it was for those who had been incarcerated for armed robbery (6.2 per 1,000), aggravated assault (4.8 per 1,000), or forcible rape (4.0 per 1,000).

It would appear from the data reported by Stanton and Sellin that offenders who have served time for homicide do at times commit other offenses or repeat their offense and commit another killing when released.[11] It also is apparent, however, that they commit very few additional killings and are far less likely to commit a murder than those who have previously committed other violent offenses, such as assault, armed robbery, and rape. The one limitation of Sellin's analysis is that he does not report the postrelease homicide rate separately for those homicide offenders who were in prison for capital homicide in death penalty jurisdictions. We would like to know the answer to a more specific question: are those offenders who were originally sentenced to death but had their sentences reversed and were released at some time back into the community likely to commit another homicide? There are three studies that address this important question.

In his 1969 analysis Stanton does separate out those inmates who had served time for first-degree murder. He reports that during the period 1930–1961 New York released 63 inmates on parole who had been convicted and served time for first-degree murder. Of these 63 murderers, 61 had been sentenced to death, but their death sentences had been commuted to life. The postrelease behavior of this group was quite good. Only three of the 63 had their parole revoked, two for technical parole rule violations and one for committing a new offense, burglary.

Bedau (1964, 1965) examined the community behavior of former capital offenders from New Jersey and Oregon who were released either by clemency or by judicial decision. Thirty-one former condemned offenders were released on parole in New Jersey from 1907 to 1960. Of these none committed murder and only one had his parole revoked (once for sodomy and later for robbery). Of fifteen former death row inmates released in Oregon from 1903 to 1964, three had their parole revoked for either a technical parole violation or a new offense. None committed a murder while released.

More complete data on the post-release behavior of capital murderers were reported by Marquart and Sorensen (1988, 1989, 1990) and Vito and Wilson (1988). Both studies followed up a group of capital offenders whose death sentences were commuted to life imprisonment by the *Furman* decision. Marquart and Sorensen's data compares 47 Texas death row inmates, 28 of whom were eventually paroled into the community, with the parole behavior of 109 comparable inmates convicted of murder and rape who had served terms of a life sentence. They report that 1 of the *Furman* releasees committed a murder when released on parole while none of the life-sentenced inmates did, and that 4 (14%) of the *Furman* parolees committed a new offense while 6 (6%) of the non-*Furman* group did. The postrelease behavior of these former death row Texas offenders suggests, then, that released capital offenders are fairly good risks if sent back into the community. Had the state of Texas executed all 28 death row inmates it would have prevented the commission of only one murder and three other felony offenses (one rape and two burglaries).[12]

In their 1989 study, Marquart and Sorensen examined the postrelease behavior of 239 convicted murderers and rapists from around the country whose death sentences were commuted by *Furman* and who were released back into the community. Of these 239 inmates, fifty-one (21%) were returned to prison either for technical parole violations or for new offenses. Marquart and

Sorensen (1959, 23–24) reported that these released offenders, who were condemned to death, lived an average of five years during the study period and were involved in only twelve offenses. Only one murder was committed. Those who would argue for the death penalty from a public protection standpoint would have to insist that 239 convicted capital offenders be put to death in order to prevent seven murders (six committed while in prison, one in the community).

Vito and Wilson (1988) report the results of a comparable study of 23 former death row inmates in Kentucky whose death sentences were commuted to life by the *Furman* decision. Seventeen of these 23 inmates who were originally sentenced to death were eventually released on parole and followed up in the community for an average of forty-two months. Four (24%) of these released offenders committed and were convicted of new crimes, but none committed an additional murder; two were convicted of armed robbery, one for burglary and one for drug possession. Vito and Wilson do not report on the parole success rate of a comparable comparison group, one that had not been sentenced to death but that served time on death row. Their finding that 24 percent of the Kentucky *Furman* releasees committed a new offense while on parole is, however, comparable to the 14 percent success rate for the Texas *Furman* group reported by Marquart and Sorensen (1988), and the 27 percent success rate (new offenses and technical parole violations) found by Donnelly and Bala (1984) in their study of a five-year follow-up of sixty-six New York murderers released on parole.

Although a great deal of research has not been done on the institutional and parole adjustments of former death row inmates, the few studies that have been conducted do not indicate that offenders who had been sentenced to death are highly prone to commit another murder or another offense either in the confines of the prison or if released into the community. Those who have been sentenced to death are not likely to commit serious or assaultive offenses while in prison, nor are they likely to commit homicide or a violent offense when released on parole. In fact, it would appear from these data that former capital defendants constitute somewhat *less* of a risk to fellow prisoners, prison staff members, and the general public than incarcerated property offenders. Since few serious offenses and far fewer homicides are likely to be prevented by the execution of capital offenders, the argument in favor of incapacitation seems to be very questionable.

Summary and Conclusions

One of the reasons people seem to support capital punishment is that they believe that although it is a very severe sanction it is necessary in order to protect the lives of innocent persons. Those who believe in the need for capital punishment for public protection make two specific claims: that (1) executing those who have already killed is the only way to keep those who are contemplating murder from acting on their desires, and (2) executing those who have already killed is the only way to keep them from killing again. The first argument is referred to as general deterrence while the second is based on incapacitation. In this chapter we reviewed a great deal of empirical research which explicitly examines the deterrence and incapacitation question. It would appear from this review of the literature that capital punishment is no better at deterring would-be murderers than a prolonged period of confinement.

After years of research with different methodologies and statistical approaches, the empirical evidence seems to clearly suggest that capital punishment is not a superior general deterrent. Sellin's early work with states that experimented with the abolition and retention of the death penalty indicated that homicide rates over time were not affected by the type of punishment used to sanction murderers. Sellin's and Peterson and Bailey's (1988) work with contiguous death and non–death penalty states seemed also to indicate that those states that had capital punishment had no lower homicide rates than those without it. Both of these sets of findings were contrary to the general deterrence claim for capital punishment.

Critics of Sellin's contiguous state comparisons claimed that this approach could not control for all of the relevant differences between states being compared, which could account for observed homicide rates. One critic, Ehrlich (1975), conducted a multiple regression analysis which examined the simultaneous effect of several variables and reported that capital punishment did indeed have a substantial deterrent effect, preventing eight murders for each execution. Other researchers attempted to replicate Ehrlich's startling results but found that his deterrent effect (the homicide preventing effect of capital punishment) turned into a brutalization effect (the homicide producing effect of capital punishment) when the last few years of his time series were excluded. There were other critical methodological and statistical flaws that were noted in Ehrlich's research, and a National Academy of Sciences panel concluded that there was no evidence to suggest that capital punishment was a better general deterrent than a prison term.

Other attempts to examine the deterrent efficacy of capital punishment produced no better results. Bailey's (Bailey 1982; Bailey and Peterson 1987) work with the death penalty and police killings suggested that police killings suggested that police officers were no safer because the jurisdictions within which they worked chose to execute their capital offenders rather than imprison them. Other research on the short-term deterrent effect of capital punishment produced more equivocal results. While some researchers reported a short-term deterrent effect for highly publicized executions (Phillips 1980; Stack 1987), others found that any short-term deterrent effect is brief, and is quickly cancelled by an increase in the number of homicides (Bowers 1988; Bailey and Peterson 1989; Bailey 1990).

This research on the general deterrent effect of the death penalty seems to go against our intuitive notions. The extinction of life should be perceived to be a very severe, and perhaps painful, penalty. When contemplating committing a murder, then, we certainly should be affected by the possibility that we may as a consequence be put to death. Why does capital punishment not seem to deter?

There are several possible answers to this question. One may be that the question, and therefore the answer, is misunderstood. The empirical literature to date does not demonstrate that capital punishment is not an effective general deterrent, only that it is no more a deterrent than a noncapital punishment. This suggests that persons may find the possibility of a long prison term as frightening and painful as the possibility of being executed. But surely, it may be asked, death is more painful than long-term imprisonment. Perhaps not. Imprisonment with other dangerous offenders, in grossly overcrowded prisons, for a long period of time with few of the creature comforts of life is a very painful existence. Prison for long-term inmates is a very harsh place, and is made to be harsh. When the severity of lengthy confinement is considered, it may be seen as a long and slow way to die, certainly no less painful than execution. The punishments of death and long-term confinement may, therefore, be comparably severe penalties with one no more likely to deter than the other.

A second reason for these null findings from general deterrence research may be that capital punishment sends the wrong message. In executing convicted murderers, the state is attempting to communicate the idea that human life is sacred. Life is so sacrosanct that when one person takes the life of an innocent other the state must condemn that action by denying the offender the right to live. In deliberately taking the life of the convicted murderer, however, the message that the state may actually be delivering is that human life is cheap and that violence (even state-sponsored violence via an execution) is an acceptable action. The state's message may be that it is acceptable to treat other human beings in a brutal manner. The evidence of a brutalization effect for executions found in some studies seems to suggest that this message is being effectively communicated to the public.

A final reason which may account for the fact that capital punishment is no more of a deterrent than imprisonment is that the general deterrence process perhaps involves a highly untenable assumption. In order for punishment to deter a would-be offender it must be taken into consideration when the decision to offend is being made. It is entirely possible, however, that those who eventually murder do not actually consider the likelihood that they would be caught, convicted, and sentenced to death. Many murders do not start out as deliberately planned killings. They begin as an armed robbery (say, of a convenience store) where panic sets in by both offender and victim or things do not go according to plan and eventually escalate to lethal violence. This point was made by Albert Camus (1974) in his essay, "Reflections on the Guillotine":

> . . . capital punishment could not intimidate the man who doesn't know that he is going to kill, who makes up his mind to it in a flash and commits his crime

in a state of frenzy or obsession, nor the man who, going to an appointment to have it out with someone, takes along a weapon to frighten the faithless one or the opponent and uses it although he didn't want to or didn't think he wanted to.

Capital punishment may fail as a deterrent, therefore, because most murderers are not the completely rational, calculative offender posited by deterrence theory. Offenders (and victims) are scared, poorly prepared for their crime, and may not have deliberated long or hard over the consequences of their possible actions. Under such more realistic human conditions, it is perhaps not surprising that the death penalty does not intimidate.

A good deal of the research to date also indicates that capital offenders are unlikely to repeat their crimes either while in prison or if released into the community. Recent research by Marquart and Sorensen (1988, 1989) and Vito and Wilson (1988) indicates that those defendants who had originally been sentenced to death but whose sentences were commuted to life because of the *Furman* decision were no more likely to commit murder while in prison than a matched group of offenders serving life terms. Many of these offenders were released back into the community, and Marquart and Sorensen's research indicated that they did not constitute a danger to other citizens. Had these offenders been sentenced to life terms without parole only a few murders would have been committed. As an alternative sanction, life imprisonment without the possibility of parole seems to offer as much public protection as capital punishment.

Notes

1. Robert H. Bork et al., *Brief for the United States as Amicus Curiae* in the case of *Fowler v. North Carolina*, Supreme Court of the United States, October Term 1974 at p. 34.

2. McGarrell and Flanagan, eds., 1985, *Source Book of Criminal Justice Statistics—1984*. In a 1973 Harris Survey respondents were asked whether they believed the death penalty was a more effective deterrent to crime than life imprisonment. Fifty-six percent of the respondents thought that it was, while only 32 percent believed that it was not. Among those who expressed approval for capital punishment, 76 percent thought that it was a better deterrent than life imprisonment; only 29 percent of those who opposed capital punishment thought that it was more effective (Vidmar and Ellsworth 1974).

3. There are a number of excellent discussions of the general deterrence literature as it pertains to capital punishment. See, for example, Zimring and Hawkins (1973), Gibbs (1975), Baldus and Cole (1975), Zeisel (1976), Lempert (1981), and Zimring and Hawkins (1986).

4. Sellin (1967, 135) was critical of previous deterrence research in the area of capital punishment and was himself well aware of the need to consider other influences

on the homicide rate. This concern led to his attempt to control for these influences by examining the homicide rates in neighboring death penalty and non–death penalty states.

5. Ehrlich is not the only one to claim to have found a deterrent effect for capital punishment. Subsequent to the publication of his article a few others appeared which were based on similar regression procedures. One year after Ehrlich's paper appeared, another economist, Yunker (1976), reported that each execution prevented 156 murders. Cloninger (1977) found that the risk of execution during the period 1955–1959 had a deterrent effect on the 1960 homicide rate in thirty-two nonsouthern but not in sixteen southern states. Lempert (1981, 1218) has noted that one of the less plausible conclusions of Cloninger's analysis is that the number of homicides in Ohio would have been reduced by over 250 if one more murderer had been executed during the period 1955–1959. Ehrlich (1977) also published a later paper which examined the effect of executions on the murder rate across states for the years 1940 and 1950. This analysis led him to reaffirm his earlier conclusion that capital punishment does have a deterrent effect on the homicide rate, with each execution preventing from twenty to twenty-four homicides. In an update of Ehrlich's work, Layson (1985) examined the effect of execution risk on homicides in the United States up to 1977. In a regression equation which controlled for ten factors thought to be related to the homicide rate, Layson reported that each execution may have deterred eighteen murders. A recent analysis of Layson's research, however, has revealed some fundamental methodological flaws which make his conclusion of a deterrent effect for executions highly suspect (Fox and Radelet 1989).

6. For reanalyses and criticisms of Ehrlich's study, see Baldus and Cole (1975), Barnett (1978, 1981), Lempert (1981, 1983), Passell (1975), Passell and Taylor (1977), Bowers and Pierce (1975), Peck (1976), Zeisel (1976), Klein, Forst, and Filatove (1978), Forst (1977), and Knorr (1979). For Ehrlich's response to his critics, see Ehrlich (1975, 1977) and Ehrlich and Gibbons (1977).

7. This positive effect of executions on homicides has been termed a "brutalization effect" by Bowers and Pierce (1980b). The observation that the state by executing its offenders may actually be encouraging additional homicides by conveying the message that it is permissible to kill was noted many years ago by Cesare Beccaria (1985, 50):

> The death penalty cannot be useful, because of the example of barbarity it gives men. If the passions or the necessities of war have taught the shedding of human blood, the laws, moderators of the conduct of men, should not extend the beastly example, which becomes more pernicious since the inflicting of legal death is attended with much study and formality.

8. Other problems with Ehrlich's analyses reported by Klein et al., some of which had been noted by previous researchers, were: that the observed deterrent effect was present when the variables in the regression equation were in logged but not their natural form; that there was measurement error in the execution risk variable which biased its estimated effect in a negative (deterrent) direction; and that his estimated model failed to consider the fact that the crime variables may have a "feedback" effect on the economic variables included in his model. In addition, both Baldus and Cole (1975, 182) and Lempert (1981, 1210–1211) have observed that even if Ehrlich's deterrent effect for executions is a genuine one it is substantially weaker than the deterrent effect found for the certainly of conviction for homicide. Since increases in the probability of execution may reduce the certainty of conviction for a capital offense, any deterrent effect brought about by a rise in the number of executions may be reduced by a decrease in the conviction rate.

9. For critiques of Phillips's study, see Kobbervig et al. (1982), Zeisel (1982), Baron and Reiss (1985), and Bowers (1988). For responses to these critics, see Phillips (1982a, 1982b).

10. It could, of course, also be argued that the lack of a deterrent effect for capital punishment observed in these and other data to be discussed is due to the fact that the *frequency* of executions was so low. The key deterrence variable may be, then, not the statutory possibility of the death penalty being imposed but its actual use. This point was in fact raised by one of Sellin's critics: Ehrlich (1975, 415) noted that "the actual enforcement of the death penalty may be a far more important factor affecting offenders' behavior than the legal status of the penalty." As Baldus and Cole (1975, 174) point out in their comparison of the deterrence research of Sellin and Ehrlich, however, if one is interested in the comparative deterrent effect of capital punishment with respect to life imprisonment, the essential test is the effect on a state's homicide rate from its changing from an abolitionist state to a retentionist one.

11. For other studies of the institutional and postrelease behavior of those convicted of homicide, see Giardini and Farrow (1952), Bedau (1982)and Wolfson (1982).

12. Some proponents of capital punishment would argue that even if one murder were prevented because of the execution of convicted murderers the utility of capital punishment would have been established. Van den Haag (1978, 59), for example, has implied that the burden of proof is squarely on the shoulders of those who would claim that there is no deterrent effect for capital punishment: "It seems immoral to let convicted murderers survive at the probable—or even at the merely possible—expense of the lives of innocent victims had the murderer been executed."

8
Death as Deserved Punishment

T he most widespread argument in favor of the death penalty is that capital punishment is the only morally justified punishment for those who deliberately take the life of another. There is certainly evidence to suggest that Americans' current approval of the death penalty is not entirely due to their belief that it is an effective deterrent to crime. For example, in one 1986 Gallup poll (Gallup 1986), of those persons who initially expressed support for the death penalty, 73 percent said that they would still favor capital punishment for those who murder even if evidence indicated that it had no deterrent effect. A disbelief in deterrence is also not the sole reason for those who are opposed to capital punishment. In that same Gallup poll, 71 percent of those respondents who initially reported that they were not in favor of the death penalty for those who murder reported that they would continue to oppose capital punishment even if new evidence indicated that it would effectively save lives through deterrence.

It is clear from evidence such as this that while deterrence is an important consideration for those who support and those who oppose capital punishment,[1] it is not the only, nor even perhaps the most important, reason for their belief. What is the most important consideration for both proponents and opponents of capital punishment is the issue of deserved punishment.

In the 1985 Gallup poll (Gallup 1985), those persons (72 percent of the overall sample) who expressed support for the death penalty for murder were asked the reasons for their approval. Thirty percent of them reported that they were in favor of the death penalty for murder because of their belief in the notion of an "eye for an eye," and another 18 percent reported that murderers deserved that punishment. When opponents of the death penalty were asked to state their reasons, 40 percent said they opposed capital punishment because they believed it was wrong to take a life, 14 percent said that errors could be made and innocent people could be executed, and 15 percent reported that they thought that punishment should be left to God. This public opinion information is useful in that it indicates that behind current support for and opposition to the death penalty is some notion as to what punishment convicted murderers deserve.

Those who do believe that the death penalty is the only appropriate punishment for those who intentionally kill an innocent person—and that they, therefore, deserve to be executed—can offer several justifications for their position. It can be asserted that by deliberately taking the life of another the murderer has forfeited all of his rights including the right to live in a peaceful community. It can also be claimed that by taking the life of the murderer the community strengthens its moral solidarity. In this view, murderers deserve death because any lesser penalty could not convey the sense of community outrage at the injury it has suffered. Another common view among those who assert that murderers deserve to be executed is the belief that the murderer "has it coming to him," that the offender should be "paid back" equally for the suffering that has been inflicted on the murder victim. These persons adopt a principle of punishment which would assert a strict "eye for an eye," and would claim that the only injury morally equivalent to murder is the execution of the murderer.

Opponents of the death penalty have, of course, an entirely different view of the morality of capital punishment. Some would assert that it is morally wrong for the state to deliberately and willfully take the life even of a convicted capital offender, because it is morally wrong for anyone to intentionally take a life. These opponents of the death penalty adopt the position that in deliberately taking the life of the convicted killer the state is committing its own act of intentional murder which cannot be justified. Others would argue that there is no moral principle that *requires* the execution of convicted murderers since the doctrine of *lex talionis* ("an eye for an eye") is not strictly enforced with respect to other crimes. These critics would assert that one can be faithful to the idea of retributive punishment, giving murderers what they deserve, without exactly duplicating through punishment (execution) the injury the murderer inflicted (an intentional killing) so long as such offenders are punished severely. It has also been argued that the imposition of the death penalty at times produces mistakes, and that the execution of innocents or those who do not deserve to be put to death is a moral tragedy that can be avoided by abolishing capital punishment.

In this chapter we will examine the issue of the morality of the death penalty from both points of view. We will review the idea of death as just retribution for murderers and build an argument that would support such a position. We will then examine the rationale against the morality of capital punishment. At this point we will entertain three main ideas: (1) that the execution of convicted offenders is unnecessary from a retributive position and is therefore not the only morally justified punishment for murder so long as murderers are given a severe enough sanction so as not to trivialize the suffering and injury of the victim; (2) even if one assumes that death is the only deserved punishment for those who kill this means only that the state *can* execute such offenders, not that it *should* or *must* execute them; and (3) the idea of determining moral desert—the amount of punishment "due" an offender—is either an impossible task given the limitations of human knowledge and understanding or is so difficult to do even under guided discretion capital statutes that the task had best be abandoned.

The Death Penalty as Just Retribution for Murder

Those who would argue that capital punishment is the morally appropriate response to those who have murdered adopt the position that murderers *deserve to die*. The invocation of the idea of death as deserved punishment connotes the notion that the only "just desert" for one convicted of murder is to be executed him or herself. Contrary to the argument in the previous chapter, which asserted that capital punishment is justified because it has a utility—it deters murders and therefore saves lives, this desert-based argument is a nonutilitarian one. The desert argument contends that punishment for crimes committed is a morally required action that needs no further justification. Murderers deserve to be put to death even if it prevented no other homicides. This is the philosophy of retribution, and the argument is best described in the works of the German moral philosopher Immanuel Kant (1724–1804).

Punishment as Retribution

According to Kant, government or civil authority exists in order to expand human freedom. In a state of nature, where one would think that freedom is maximized, human freedom is limited because our lives and our possessions are in constant danger from other persons. Government is established wherein persons give up some freedoms (certain things are forbidden, such as theft, rape, and murder) in order to enjoy the security of others. Under a constituted civil authority, then, certain rights are lost (laws must be obeyed) and certain benefits enjoyed (the protection of government). Persons living under such civil authority derive certain benefits from the law because others are forced to obey, but they have the corollary duty of obedience to the same laws. Kant would argue from this that we have a moral obligation to obey the law because we enjoy the benefits of government and have thereby consented to it. Government, then, expands my freedom because it allows me to enjoy things that I could not enjoy in a state of nature, such as the security of my life and possessions. The price of this, however, is that in promising to obey the laws some limitation is placed on my own freedom.

Those who violate the laws constituted by civil authority have committed a moral transgression. They derive benefits from the laws (because others obey them) but refuse to sacrifice their freedom in the form of their own obedience to the law. They have therefore gained an unfair advantage over their fellow citizens. Punishment, as a form of coercive activity on the part of government, is morally justified, then, because it attempts to readjust the moral advantage taken by the criminal. Kant would assert that by not sacrificing his freedom in the form of obedience to the law, the criminal has chosen to make a sacrifice in a different way—by being punished. In this view, punishment becomes a debt to be paid by the criminal, who does so by submitting to punishment.

Although we have discovered through Kant the retributive justification for the state to punish in the first place, we have not uncovered any notion as to *how much* the state may morally punish. Kant (1965, 101–102) does provide some guidance on the quantity of punishment an offender deserves to receive. He refers to this guiding principle as the "principle of equality" and ties it directly to the death penalty:

> What kind and what degree of punishment does public legal justice adopt as its principle and standard? None other than the principle of equality (illustrated by the pointer on the scales of justice), that is, the principle of not treating one side more favorably than the other. Accordingly, any undeserved evil that you inflict on someone else among the people is one that you do to yourself. Only the Law of retribution (*jus talionis*) can determine exactly the kind and degree of punishment . . .
>
> If, however, he has committed a murder, he must die. In this case, there is no substitute that will satisfy the requirements of legal justice. There is no sameness of kind between death and remaining alive even under the most miserable conditions, and consequently there is also no equality between the crime and the retribution unless the criminal is judicially put to death.

As a statement of retributive punishment, the principle of equality requires that the amount and type of punishment directly reflect the crime. The *jus talionis* referred to by Kant, the notion of "an eye for an eye," would *require* that those who have taken a life to be put to death. Kant is unmistakably clear about this requirement of retributive justice in the second paragraph quoted above. Steven Nathanson 1987, 79–80) describes this kind of retributive punishment as "payback" retributivism; criminals must directly and exactly be "paid back" for what they have done.

Retribution Is Not Naked Vengeance

It should be made clear at this point that retributive punishment is not the same thing as revenge or vengeance. Revenge is the desire that a private person or persons may have to inflict harm on another person for real or imagined injuries suffered either by themselves or a third party. For example, if someone commits an assault on our parents or children, we, and our siblings and friends, may wish to physically injure the assaulter—we wish to give him what he "has coming to him." The reason for our action is that the assaulter has intentionally injured someone for no good reason or provocation and therefore "deserves" to be retaliated against. This example may make it seem that revenge or vengeance is similar to retributive justice, but there are important differences between them.

In the first place, retributive punishment is an injury that is imposed by duly constituted authority under the rule of law. Retribution is, then, not a private act but a public demonstration of censure and reprobation—it is the community that has been wronged, and the community that responds with legal punishment. Private acts of retaliation are not what is meant here by retributive punishment. Kant (1965, 101) himself clearly differentiated retributive punishment from revenge in noting that the former is a function of government: "[o]nly the Law of retribution (*jus talionis*) can determine exactly the kind and degree of punishment; it must be well understood, however, that *this determination [must be made] in the chambers of a court of justice* (and not in your private judgment)." Two requirements of retributive punishment, therefore, are that it is a sanction imposed by government and that it is in response to a crime.

Contrary to retributive justice, vengeance is a private act. An individual or individuals feel wronged by a party and respond to that wrong with injury inflicted *by themselves*. There is no recourse to law and the judicial system, just the response of individuals to an injury. Furthermore, this injury need not be real; it may be imagined and the injury involved may not even be a criminal offense. Persons may seek revenge for what *they think* is an injury or affront. The real or imagined injury which provides the motive for revenge need not be a criminal offense. For example, Nathanson (1987, 108) has noted that a criminal may seek revenge against the witnesses who testified against him. There is a further distinction between retributive punishment and revenge. Contrary to the criminal law which establishes that offenders must be seen as responsible for their actions before they may be punished, revenge may be sought for accidental injuries. We may seek revenge against the person who has physically injured us, or we may seek revenge against the eight-year-old child who vandalized our home. The extraction of vengeance does not require a real injury inflicted by a morally responsible agent.

Another important difference between retributive punishment and revenge or vengeance is that the former is limited by a principle of equality that the latter is not. Kant's principle of equality and the theme of the *lex talionis* is that offenders are to be punished *in proportion* to the harm they have inflicted on another. Minor injuries are responded to with minor punishments while offenders who inflict much more severe injury are, therefore, deserving of more punishment. Under a retributive principle the amount of punishment the state is justified in inflicting is limited by the amount of injury produced by the criminal act. There is no limiting principle to revenge, however. A minor injury may receive a severe or at least disproportionate response. Revenge knows no limit. I may respond by killing the one who has assaulted and terrified my child or elderly parents; I may assault and grievously injure someone who has hit my new car, whether or not they or the road conditions were to blame. As a private act there is no proportionality or equivalence limitation to revenge as exists for retributive punishment.

There is a final difference between retributive punishment and revenge or vengeance. Not only must punishment for the purpose of retribution be inflicted on a morally responsible party, it must be inflicted *only* on *the* morally responsible party. The state is justified in punishing the perpetrators of a criminal offense but not their family members or acquaintances. The only legitimate target of retributive punishment is the "guilty" party. Furthermore, notions of individual responsibility and culpability require that parties to the offense with diminished participation (such as an "aider and abetter") be punished less severely than the principals involved. Revenge is not so restricted. There is nothing in the idea of vengeance that requires that the person directly responsible for the original injury is the only legitimate target. Injuries against the victim can be retaliated by injuries against the offender or anyone connected to the offender, even if they took no direct part in the offense. In blood feuds, for example, a physical injury or dishonor to one family member may be responded to by agents of the victim by killing the offender, the offender's spouse, children, parents, or other relatives. The notion of "getting the wrong person" is not in the lexicon of a revenge-based punishment scheme. In sum, personal retaliation has no requirement for personal responsibility, has no limiting principle, and has no notion of an appropriate or "guilty" target.

Modern Retributivist Thought in Defense of the Death Penalty

Some version of retributive punishment, the *lex talionis* or the principle of equality, is frequently relied upon by those who would justify capital punishment today, since it so nicely comports with commonsense notions that criminals should be treated exactly as they have treated their victims. Two of the most vocal spokespersons for the morality of the death penalty in the academic community today are Ernest van den Haag and Walter Berns. In discussing the state's right to punish, van den Haag (1983, 30) adopts a Kantian position.[2] Criminals deserve to be punished because they have taken unfair advantage over those who have restrained themselves and obeyed the law. He states:

> The desire to see crime punished is felt by noncriminals because they see that the criminal has pursued his interests or gratified his desires by means they, the noncriminals, have restrained themselves from using for the sake of the law and in fear of its punishments . . . the offender, unlike the nonoffender, did not play by the legal rules and took advantage of those who did. He must be deprived of his illicit advantage if others are to continue to play by the rules. His advantage must be nullified in the minds of nonoffenders by the punishment the offender suffers.

The state is justified in punishing the offender at least in part because it is a morally required action—the unfair advantage taken by the criminal's noncompliance must be "nullified."[3]

Although the state has the moral right to punish because the offender, in taking an unfair advantage over the obedient, deserves it, we do not know yet from van den Haag *how much* punishment the offender deserves. Van den Haag seems to waiver in accepting the notion of strict equality between the injury produced by the crime and the injury deserved by the offender—the *lex talionis* or retributive principle of "an eye for an eye." On the one hand, he claims (van den Haag 1975, 193) that a strict equality between punishment and crime (that is, exactly duplicating the form of the victim's injury through punishment) cannot easily be achieved with some offenses:

> The *lex talionis*—an eye for an eye—is a simpler way of determining sanctions. It appeals aesthetically—to our sense of symmetry if not of justice—to make "the punishment fit the crime." But it is not feasible, if it were desirable, to do so literally. Punishments do not and cannot match in kind the crimes for which they are inflicted.

The *lex talionis* is not an effective general guide in determining the amount of deserved punishment, van den Haag concedes, because it cannot be literally applied—we cannot rape rapists, steal from robbers, or kill multiple murderers more than once. But he notes that there are instances when the injury inflicted on the offender can "match" the victim's injury, and in these instances the *lex talionis* should be imposed. The offense of murder is one of the crimes for which the injury can be duplicated in its punishment. Van den Haag's paragraph above concludes: "Punitive fines for some property crimes, or execution for murder, are among the few exceptions." Elsewhere he wrote that (1983, 33) "[t]he *lex talionis* cannot be literally applied . . . [s]till for some crimes we can do something of the kind . . . [t]hus we may fine those whose crimes are pecuniary and execute those who murder."

The *lex talionis* can be literally applied in the case of the one who murders one victim, van den Haag notes, since the execution of the one murderer is morally equivalent to the murder of the sole victim. He concludes from this that the murderer *should be* executed because death is the only appropriate moral response for those who have killed. It is the only appropriate response because it is the only penalty severe enough to match the severity of the offense. Murders are serious crimes because an innocent victim's life is gone and can never be replaced. However, according to van den Haag, the severity of an offense is not only a function of the harm done to the individual victim, it is also a function of what he called the "total gravity of the crime"—the total injury done to the social fabric (1985, 167). Murder is one of the most harmful crimes because it violates our sense of security in a peaceful community, and is therefore deserving of death. Under van den Haag's principle, therefore, most murderers would be executed, not the relatively small proportion that are today.

Van den Haag argues that the function of punishment is not merely to inflict equivalent harm on the offender, but to inflict *even more injury* than was originally produced. In one of his examples he notes that even if three days' confinement inflicts as much pain on a kidnapper as was suffered by the victim, justice would still demand that the kidnapper receive more punishment than three days' confinement (1985, 166). We would demand more punishment because the injury inflicted on the victim was undeserved. The offender, therefore, deserves punishment for inflicting an undeserved suffering on the victim. Van den Haag also insists (1985, 167) that more injury be inflicted on the offender than was inflicted on the victim because of his previously mentioned notion of the total gravity of the crime—the injury produced by a crime affects the entire community and not only the individual victim: "If my neighbor is burglarized or robbed he is harmed. But we all must take costly precautions, and we all feel and are threatened: crime harms society as it harms victims. Hence, punishment must, whenever possible, impose pain believed *to exceed* the pain suffered by the individual victim of crime" (emphasis added). To van den Haag, then, the limitation imposed by the principle of equality is the total social harm of the crime, not merely that experienced by the victim, and the harm produced by a murder can only be matched by the execution of the murderer.

In addition to his notion of desert, van den Haag offers two related arguments in support of the death penalty. He claims that the death penalty is the only morally appropriate sanction for murderers because he believes that in killing another the convicted murderer has forfeited his own right to life: "If the crime is great enough, [the criminal] may be deprived of his right to life. . . . The rights that we grant one another, on whatsoever basis, are forfeited if we commit crimes" (1983, 261). Van den Haag (1978, 64–65) also adopts the position that vengeance is an appropriate motive guiding punishment: "The motives for the death penalty may indeed include vengeance." This legitimate passion for revenge is, however, not to be inflicted by individuals without limitation, but is instead to be "regulated and directed by law." According to van den Haag (1978, 65), law and punishment (including the death penalty) gives expression to motives of private vengeance and is necessary in order to "solidif[y] social solidarity against lawbreakers." The justification for giving expression to motives of vengeance and revenge, then, is that in executing those who commit murder a society reaffirms and strengthens the value of life. When it fails to do so, it sends a message that life is cheap and insecure: "No matter what can be said for abolition of the death penalty, it will be perceived symbolically as a loss of nerve: social authority no longer is willing to pass an irrevocable judgment on anyone. Murder is no longer thought grave enough to take the murderer's life. . . . When murder no longer forfeits the murderer's life . . . respect for life itself is diminished, as the price for taking it is" (1975: 213). In an argument that seems paradoxical to those who oppose capital punishment, it is claimed that the execution of murderers is necessary to proclaim the sanctity of life.[4]

Walter Berns (1979) adopts a somewhat similar position. He begins by asserting the noncontroversial position that human societies are moral communities whose members are required to obey the laws. Similar to van den Haag's notion of the "total gravity of the injury," Berns (1979, 155) notes that those who fail to obey the law injure not only their victim but the entire community: "[t]he criminal . . . has injured not merely his immediate victim but the community as such. . . . [h]e has called into question the very possibility of that community by suggesting that men cannot be trusted freely to respect the property, the person, and the dignity of those with whom they are associated." The commission of an injury against the community produces a sense of outrage or anger among law-abiding community members which must be given expression. Berns's position is that the anger and indignation that we feel when someone is the victim of a crime is what makes us a moral community, and if this spirit of altruism is not to whither it must be vindicated. The expression and vindication of the moral indignation of the community at the offender is achieved through punishment. Capital punishment in particular is necessary, according to Berns (1979, 172–173), because it is the only way to satisfy that indignation and restore and reinforce the moral integrity of the community when a murder has been committed: "Capital punishment serves to remind us of the majesty of the moral order that is embodied in our law and of the terrible consequences of its breach. . . . The criminal law must be made awful, by which I mean, awe-inspiring, or commanding "profound respect or reverential fear." It must remind us of the moral order by which alone we can live as *human* beings, and in our day the only punishment that can do this is capital punishment."

Both van den Haag and Berns would argue, then, that murder is a horrible affront against the moral community which must be punished or else that morality is subverted. They would further suggest that the moral order is eroded when these horrible crimes are punished leniently, and that the only way to vindicate the moral community when a murder has been committed is by the death of the offender by judicial authorities. Both van den Haag and Berns, then, come perilously close to the position that retributive punishment is simply a form of communal revenge or vengeance. That connection is directly made by Oldenquist (1986, 73), who asserts that "[t]here is no doubt that retributive justice, the idea that a criminal deserves punishment and 'has it coming to him,' is the same as revenge. Retributive justice is the revenge a society visits on those who seriously harm it or its members." Oldenquist (1986, 76) does somewhat qualify his position by suggesting that retributive punishment is "sanitized revenge," which he contrasts with "simple revenge." Sanitized revenge is punishment that is assumed by judicial authorities and is limited by considerations of proportionality. Simple revenge, however, is the harm inflicted by victims (or their agents) which knows no limit and may be imposed on someone other than the one who inflicted the original harm. Oldenquist's definition of simple revenge is comparable to the meaning of vengeance given earlier here, and his definition of sanitized revenge is comparable to retributive justice. His point seems to be that retributive justice is simply a "cleaned-up" version of old-fashioned private vengeance, but that retribution should not on that basis be rejected as a motive for punishment. In his defense of capital punishment he notes (1986, 75) that the death penalty may be necessary in order to give expression to, and therefore strengthen, public morality: "The merit of execution (if there is any) is that without taking proportional retribution in grave and dreadful cases, a society compromises its honor, belittles itself, and undermines public confidence that the society takes itself and its values seriously."

There is a common belief that the execution of the murderer is the only morally just penalty for the crime. However, contrary to the other two arguments in support of the death penalty, the economic benefits and deterrence arguments, we cannot rely on empirical data to provide much insight into this issue. The argument for desert is a moral and philosophical position not easily addressed with empirical studies—how do we empirically determine whether or not convicted capital offenders deserve to be executed? How can we determine whether or not public morality would be strengthened if death (and only death) were the proscribed punishment for murderers? Opponents of the death penalty, on the other hand, have examined the moral implications of capital punishment. They offer compelling arguments why capital offenders do not deserve death, and even if they do deserve death, why principles of justice would suggest that we do not have to put them to death. We will now examine these counterarguments.

Life Imprisonment as Just Retribution for Murder

In his debate with Ernest van den Haag, John Conrad (1983, 60), a critic of capital punishment, responded to the claim that it is morally right to execute one who has deliberately taken the life of another by asserting that when the state deliberately executes a convicted capital offender, it "respond[s] to his wrong by doing the same wrong to him." Death penalty opponents argue that in deliberately, rationally, and with premeditation putting a convicted capital offender to death the state is simply committing an additional murder. Both acts, it is argued, involve the planned and coldly calculated killing of another human being. The equation of a state-sponsored execution with murder ("legal homicide") is related to the principle held by death penalty opponents that because we are better than they are, we should not kill killers.

Those who argue in favor of the death penalty would dispute the claim that in executing convicted capital offenders the state is committing an act which is morally equivalent to murder. We do not regard the killing of another as always morally wrong; for example, it is acceptable in times of war or for other reasons of self-defense. What we regard as morally offensive, they contend, is the killing of a person not in self-defense, or the deliberate killing of a truly *innocent* person, which the victim of a homicide is and the one executed for murder clearly is not. In taking the life of the murderer, then, the state is not repeating the same evil, nor is it clearly committing an immoral act. How, then, does one go about refuting the capital punishment proponent's claim that death is the only penalty that gives murderers what they deserve. Some critics of capital punishment have done so by articulating their own theory of retributive punishment which is at variance with Kant's and others' more literal version of the *lex talionis*.

Limitations of the Lex Talionis

A belief in retributive punishment does not logically compel a corollary belief in the death penalty. Death penalty opponents have been critical of capital punishment from a position of retribution. The essence of this argument is that a strict interpretation of the idea of *lex talionis,* "an eye for an eye," is inapplicable if it is taken to mean an exact proportionality between the offense and the punishment. These "abolitionist retributivists" would claim that there are clear and obvious limitations on the principle that criminals should be treated *exactly* as they have treated their victims, that the punishment should precisely duplicate the victim's suffering. These limitations call for a revision of the strictly literal notion of *lex talionis*.

One of the limitations of the *lex talionis* is that a strict principle of equality would mean that the death penalty is the appropriate punishment only for murder. Nonhomicide offenses such as rape, kidnapping, and armed robbery, which have been capital offenses in the past, would not be subject to the death penalty under the principle of equality. Furthermore, the principle of equality would require as just retribution the death penalty for *all murderers.* But there already are limitations and restrictions on the imposition of the death penalty for murder. We have learned in previous chapters that the death penalty may not be imposed on all who murder; it is reserved for those who commit murder in conjunction with an aggravating circumstance defined by law (a murder in conjunction with another felony, the killing of a police officer, etc.). In addition, not even all those who commit murder with an aggravating circumstance are sentenced to death. A constitutionally acceptable death penalty scheme requires the jury to hear and consider mitigating evidence which argues for a sentence of life, and juries are given the discretion to impose life sentences on even the most egregious murderer if they are swayed by such factors in mitigation. The principle of equality is tempered, then, with a liberal dose of mercy under existing capital sentencing statutes, and there is no reason to believe that these will be dramatically altered any time soon. Under existing law not all murderers are sentenced to death, just in those cases where the jury concludes that aggravating circumstances outweigh any claims for mercy. Nonetheless, the principle of equality is sacrificed.

A second limitation of the idea of strict *lex talionis* or equality is that it at times requires absurd, even uncivilized punishments. For example, as Nathanson

(1987, 74) has noted, the principle of equality would require that rapists be raped, torturers be tortured, and arsonists be burned if the crime resulted in the death of a victim. A strict, literal version of the "eye for an eye" standard would demand punishments that clearly are repugnant to contemporary moral standards, and would offer no suggestions on how to punish others, such as kidnappers (do they get kidnapped?), airplane hijackers (do they get hijacked?), or drunk drivers, to suggest only a few. Clearly, the strict *lex talionis* is in need of some revision if it is to serve as a general theory of punishment.

A third and related point is that the principle of equality cannot be met in instances of brutal murder. A strict "eye for an eye" retribution would require that brutal murderers be treated brutally, that they be tortured before their execution, bound and gagged or dismembered. It would require that we react cruelly and inhumanly in instances where the offender has so acted, and that we imitate the very acts of those that we so vehemently condemn. In addition, what do we do in instances of multiple murder, those offenders who have killed more than one person, maybe all in a brutal manner? These are the offenders referred to by public sentiment that suggests, "execution might be too good for them." A strict adherence to the *lex talionis* would require that we bring these multiple murderers to "within an inch of their life," then revive them for each victim killed, only to ultimately execute them for the last of the murder victims. But we cannot strictly reproduce the actions of these and other horrible offenders, nor would we want to in a civilized society, even though it may be their just desert. The *lex talionis* does not tell us why torturing even those who commit brutal murders would be morally repugnant and wrong. Clearly, principles other than "giving them exactly what they deserve" intervene in our efforts to punish such offenders.

A Revised Notion of Retribution and the Principle of Equality

In previous sections of this chapter we have referred to the notion of retributive punishment in its most literal form, the form requiring "an eye for an eye" (*lex talionis*), based on Kant's principle of equality. Nathanson (1987, 75–81) has referred to this form of retribution as "equality retributivism," since offenders are punished in equal and exact measure to their crimes. Death penalty opponents have been critical of this retributivist position, suggesting, among other things, that it fails to provide an adequate defense of particular kinds of punishment in general and specifically the death penalty. They would argue that a belief that one who has willfully injured another deserves punishment is not inexorably linked to a *particular punishment* that person deserves. More specifically, critics of capital punishment from a retributivist position have argued that to say that someone who has intentionally killed an innocent other deserves to be punished is not at all to say that *the only* punishment they deserve is death. Retributivism may demand that the murderer be punished severely but it would permit a range of punishments. This range may include capital punishment, but it would not require the death penalty for murderers.

The *lex talionis* and Kant's principle of equality are not, however, the only forms of retributivism. The abolitionist philosopher Jeffery Reiman (1985, 120) has suggested another form of retributive punishment which he calls "proportional retributivism." Reiman claims that proportional retribution offers a more defensible general rationale for punishment, one that does not require the death penalty for murder. Proportional retributivism is similar to equality retributivism in that those who commit crimes deserve to be punished because in committing a criminal act offenders have committed a moral wrong. Proportional retributivism differs, however, in that it does not require, as a principle of justice, that the offender be treated in the exact manner as the victim. Rather than an exact equality of injury between the victim and offender, proportional retributivism requires only that the worst crime in any society be punished with the worst penalty (Reiman 1985, 120). That worst punishment need not exactly reflect the nature or type of injury inflicted on the victim. In this proportional retributivism, the two ideas of retributive justice are still adhered to: (1) Offenders are perceived to be morally responsible agents who deserve punishment because of the harm they have produced and the unfair advantage they have taken; and (2) they are punished proportionate to the harm they have produced, that is, minor harms are punished with minor penalties and the most severe harms with the worst penalty.

Proportional retributivism, then, remains faithful to the premises of retributive punishment but abandons the requirement of the *lex talionis* and Kant's idea of the principle of equality by not demanding that the punishment precisely duplicate the criminal act. All that it requires is that the punishment be ordinally graded according to the seriousness of the offense. In terms of the upper limit of punishment that the state may inflict, Reiman (1985, 128–129) notes that proportional retributivism requires giving the offender only the most severe punishment that society currently would morally tolerate, what he calls the "closest morally acceptable approximation to the *lex talionis*":

> If we take the *lex talionis* as spelling out the offender's just deserts, and if other moral considerations require us to refrain from matching the injury caused by the offender while still allowing us to punish justly, then surely we impose just punishment if we impose the closest morally acceptable approximation to the *lex talionis*. Proportional retributivism, then, in requiring that the worst crime be punished by the society's worst punishment and so on, could be understood as translating the offender's just desert into its nearest equivalent in the society's table of morally acceptable punishments.

Reiman goes on to assert that this worst punishment must be severe enough so that it does not trivialize and therefore do an injustice to the victim's injury. Although he does not suggest in detail what equally serious alternative there is to death for those who murder, Reiman does offer the alternative of life in prison without the possibility of parole.

The critic of this argument would quickly respond at this point that the death penalty is the only appropriate punishment for those who deliberately take a life because no amount of prison time will be equivalent to the lost life of the victim. Reiman (1985, 130–131) concedes this point but suggests that the notion of proportional retributivism he offers would not require that the severity of the punishment *be identical* to the severity of the crime, only that the imposed penalty not be so lenient that it trivializes the offense. He points out that we already modify the severity of the penalty for other offenses; for example, we imprison rapists. But is ten years in prison truly the equivalent injury for one who has terrorized and raped another? Surely not, but ten years in prison is certainly a severe enough penalty that it does not do an injustice to the victim. Reiman would simply extend this argument to the case of murder. Life imprisonment without the possibility of parole is clearly not equivalent to the suffering of the murder victim, who may have contemplated for minutes or hours his/her own death and may, therefore, have been psychologically terrorized beyond any human attempt at equivalence. Reiman, however, would claim that life imprisonment is not such an insignificant penalty as to be completely out of proportion to murder.[5] Under his brand of proportional retributivism it would be just and fair not to execute convicted murderers so long as they received an extremely harsh sanction.[6]

The question may be raised at this point, why should we treat convicted murderers with less severity than they treated their victims? Do they not deserve to be "paid back" in full measure? There are two answers to this question. Reiman (1985, 131–132) suggests that we do not have the right to exact the full cost from the murderer in the form of the death penalty because of the fact that in the United States homicides are due in large measure to poverty, and "impoverishment is a remediable injustice from which others in America benefit." At least one reason why Reiman would not demand full punishment, then, is that murderers are themselves usually the victims of impoverished social circumstances, over which they do not—but we as a society do—have control. Until these conditions are remedied, he would argue, it is unjust to demand full retribution from the murderer. In addition, Reiman argues that in refusing to demand the full severity of punishment for murderers by not executing them, we are taking steps toward becoming a more civilized society. Refusing to put an offender to death has the effect of civilizing us, Reiman contends, because an execution involves the deliberate infliction of a physically and psychologically painful death. Such a refusal to put to death the most odious of our citizens, he claims, will also communicate to all in the society the sanctity of life.[7]

Nathanson (1987) provides a somewhat different answer to the question than Reiman, although he comes to the same general conclusion about the abolition of the death penalty. Somewhat skeptical of the notion of proportional retribution, he does agree with Reiman's position that the proportionality principle cannot be used by death penalty proponents to justify capital punishment or to *require* it as a punishment for murder. To Nathanson the proportionality principle requires not that murderers be executed but only that they should be punished by the most severe punishment on the society's scale of sanctions. This principle *does not,* however, state what that most severe punishment should be. It may tell us that armed robbers should be punished more severely than shoplifters and less severely than those who commit murder, but it does not provide any clue as to what specific punishment is deserved by a specific offense or what the upper and lower limits of punishment should be. The most severe offense, murder, should be punished with the most severe punishment, but the most severe punishment for a society need not be death.

To Nathanson, the problem of determining what punishment a criminal offender deserves is a subtle and complex issue. He argues (1987, 81–82) that we need to consider more than simply the result of a person's actions—did her action result in the death of an innocent person?—and take into account the "motives, intentions, and other features of a criminal's actions and character that are relevant to desert." The fact that a person has taken the life of an innocent other person is not enough in itself to conclude under Nathanson's scheme that death is a deserved punishment. Two additional pieces of information are required before a determination of moral blameworthiness can be made, the actor's motives and intentions. Those killings that are done intentionally deserve more condemnation and punishment than those done accidentally or negligently. In addition, actions pursued out of good motives are less blameworthy than those motivated by evil. The "mercy killer" who slays her suffering and terminally ill husband is less blameworthy, and therefore deserving of less punishment, than the one who does so for his insurance money.

A consideration of motives and intentions does not, however, completely exhaust Nathanson's view of moral desert. He also suggests (1987, 87–90) that we need to consider the amount of effort required to act in a morally appropriate manner. Persons brought up under unfortunate circumstances may not be as deserving of full moral blame as one reared in more fortunate conditions, because those circumstances make morally appropriate conduct much more difficult or nearly impossible. Nathanson notes that we use this effort dimension of moral desert frequently, as, for example, when we give more praise to one who has earned rather than inherited her wealth. Actions that are the result of overcoming great obstacles appear to us as more praiseworthy than those that occur effortlessly. Similarly, when persons face such obstacles to their moral conduct (such as poverty, drug addiction, and racism) that make it extremely difficult for them to act in an appropriate manner, Nathanson suggests that their acts may still be wrong, but they are not as blameworthy as they would have been had they not been subjected to adverse social conditions.

The role of effort and obstacles in Nathanson's notion of moral desert is similar to Reiman's suggestion that since murderers are frequently the victims of impoverished social circumstances, they should not be put to death, even if they deserve it. Where Nathanson and Reiman differ is in the determination of moral blame. Reiman claims that murderers deserve to die but that we should not exact the full amount of desert because of the fact that their actions were affected by their social conditions, conditions society both benefits from and could eliminate. Nathanson's (1987, 89) point is that we cannot clearly determine the blameworthiness of murderers nor therefore the exact amount of punishment they deserve until we completely understand the impact adverse social conditions have had on their behavior: "The idea here seems to be that we cannot legitimately blame someone unless we know that it was possible for that person to act otherwise than he did and that we could only know whether this was possible by being in the other person's shoes, that is, by seeing and feeling things from his perspective." To Nathanson, then, the determination of moral blameworthiness is a very complex process that cannot simply be captured by the results of a person's actions.

Nathanson's position regarding the effect of adverse social conditions on diminishing the moral culpability of offenders and the difficulty of precisely ascertaining the moral desert of persons was an integral element of Albert Camus's objection to the death penalty. In his remarkable essay, "Reflections on the Guillotine" (1974), Camus tells us that society bears some of the responsibility for the creation of its murderers. While this recognition does not exonerate offenders from all blameworthiness, it does make a clear determination of moral desert intractable.

> The state that sows alcohol cannot be surprised to reap crime. Instead of showing surprise, it simply goes on cutting off heads into which it has poured so much alcohol. . . . Does this amount to saying that every alcoholic must be declared irresponsible by a State that will beat its breast until the nation drinks nothing but fruit juice? Certainly not. No more than that the reasons based on heredity should cancel all culpability. *The real responsibility of an offender cannot be precisely measured* . . . there never exists any total responsibility or, consequently, any absolute punishment or reward. (pp. 208–210, emphasis added)

The point that Camus, and Nathanson many years after him, is making is that responsibility for murder is not anchored solely in the individual, that society bears some blame, and that the determination of culpability cannot be made with any degree of precision because there are so many factors to consider.

Now proponents of the death penalty will ask, don't we already have a mechanism where information about the intentions, motives, and "efforts" of those accused of capital crimes can be presented to those making moral judgments about the blameworthiness of murderers? They would argue that current guided discretion capital punishment schemes provide just such a mechanism. These statutes include enumerated aggravating circumstances which direct the jury's attention to the moral desert of the offender (how blameworthy she is), who during the penalty phase is entitled to present any and virtually all such mitigating information to the jury which would argue in favor of mercy. Such information would include, in addition to the defendant's intentions and motives, factors like previous drug addition, unemployment history, and emotional state at the time of the offense, which Nathanson includes in his notion of "effort" and "obstacles to appropriate moral conduct." The jury considers all of this information in making its assessment of the offender's moral culpability, and how much punishment she therefore deserves (life or death). Supporters of the death penalty might not disagree with Nathanson's notion of complex desert, they would merely claim that capital juries have such information available to them and are capable of making subtle conclusions as to how blameworthy particular capital defendants are.

Nathanson and other opponents of the death penalty would offer two responses to this. First, a full understanding of the moral desert of the offender may be impossible to attain because there are too many relevant factors and too much information required for an accurate assessment of moral blame. Nathanson notes that this conclusion might be adopted by those who believe that only God can make a reliable determination of a person's "real" blameworthiness because only an all-knowing Being could understand what actions a person could and could not take. There may be some truth to this. In our introduction to this chapter we learned that some proportion of death penalty opponents were against capital punishment because they believed that such punishment should be left to God.

This argument, that reliable moral judgments about moral blameworthiness and deserved punishment may be impossible because of too many relevant factors and too much required information, is a particularly ironic one. In his 1971 *McGautha* opinion for a majority of the Court, Justice Harlan cautioned that enumerated aggravating and mitigating circumstances for jurors to consider in determining whether or not a defendant should be sentenced to life or death cannot possibly hope to capture all of the important dimensions in making this awesome moral decision:

> To identify before the fact these characteristics of criminal homicides and their perpetrators which call for the death penalty, and to express these characteristics in language which can be fairly understood and applied by the sentencing authority, appear to be tasks which are beyond present human ability. [*McGautha v. California*, 402 U.S. 183 (1971) at p. 204]

Justice Harlan's warning is consistent with one of Nathanson's conclusions about the determination of moral desert: it is a complex judgment involving a large number of factors that might be impossible to have knowledge of and is probably not reducible to legal formulae such as the weighing of aggravating and mitigating circumstances.[8]

The second response that Nathanson and death penalty opponents would make to the claim that guided discretion capital statutes allow juries to make complex determinations of moral blameworthiness is that even if it is not impossible it is very difficult to reliably make such determinations in everyday discourse. Nathanson's objection here is that those making moral decisions in capital cases are under practical constraints and are thereby compelled to abandon the search for a precise determination of moral desert in favor of their own personal feelings and biases. These feelings would include racial discrimination and other arbitrary factors, such as their own idiosyncratic notion as to what a particular capital offender deserves. One of these "practical constraints" is the ambiguity of the law of capital punishment itself.

In his book *Capital Punishment: The Inevitability of Caprice and Mistake,* Charles Black (1981) makes the observation that the determination of who deserves to die is arbitrary under guided discretion statutes because important legal terms are vague and not easily comprehended by those making the life or death decision. What the law calls sentencing "standards" in the form of statutory aggravating and mitigating circumstances are not capable of precise meaning. What, for example, is a murder that is "outrageously or wantonly vile, horrible or inhuman in that it involved torture, depravity of mind or an aggravated battery to the victim"? And what does it mean for an offender to have "no significant history of prior criminal activity" or to be "under the influence of extreme mental or emotional disturbance" or that "the capacity of the defendant to appreciate the criminality of his conduct or to conform his conduct to the requirements of law was substantially impaired"? The first of these phrases is an aggravating circumstance under Georgia's post-*Furman* capital statute (see Table 2–1) while the latter three are statutory mitigating circumstances under the Florida law (see Table 2–2). Even if these terms could in particular cases be defined with some precision, there remains the problem of mentally *processing* those factors that argue for death and those that may argue for life. How, for example, does a jury *weigh* aggravating against mitigating circumstances—how much does each element weigh, do all aggravating and mitigating circumstances carry the same weight, is an aggravating circumstance of equal weight to a mitigating one?

Black is raising an important issue, that these terms or standards (and similar ones in other capital statutes) have no clear unambiguous meaning yet are supposed to guide the discretion of the jury as it makes its determination whether or not a particular defendant deserves to be put to death. Black's (1981, 29) contention is that these are illusory guides, what he calls "pseudo-standards":

[T]he official choices—by prosecutors, judges, juries, and governors—that divide those who are to die from those who are to live are on the whole not made, and cannot be made, under standards that are consistently meaningful and clear, but . . . they are often made, and in the foreseeable future will continue to be made, under no standards at all or under pseudo-standards without discoverable meaning.

The "standards" under post-*Furman* guided discretion capital statutes provide little or no guidance or help to the jury in determining the moral desert of convicted offenders, and Black concludes that jurors often resort to their own feelings and prejudices. Both he and Nathanson would conclude that even with such guided discretion statutes there is no basis for believing that we can reliably appraise the blameworthiness of murderers and assess the punishment they deserve.

What both Black and Nathanson are suggesting is that mistakes *can* be made in determining an offender's blameworthiness: she could be executed; when what she deserves, had a complete and accurate understanding of her intentions, motives, and "efforts" been possible, is a life sentence. In addition to punishing someone more severely than they deserve, there is another, more serious type of error that could be made: the execution of the innocent.

There can be little doubt that our adversary system of criminal justice, which includes substantial procedural protections for criminal defendants, is among the most advanced and civilized in the world today. Under our system, criminal suspects are afforded rights and protections that are intended to protect them against the excesses of state power. For the most part these protections work quite well. They are, however, institutions created and operated by humans with all their attendant limitations and frailties. Errors in judgments and decisions can be made at every step of the process, including the prosecutor's charging decision, the trial judge's ruling on the admissibility of crucial evidence, the jury's decision to convict and sentence, and the executive's power to pardon or commute. When one considers the number of decisions that are made, beginning with the commission of a capital crime and ending with the offender entering the death chamber, together with an appreciation of human fallibility, we can come to understand that however protective and effective our legal institutions are, inevitably mistakes will be made (Black 1981). In fact, if we assume that over the course of a number of years and a number of capital trials our legal system will make a mistake, then we have to face the prospect that *we will* unintentionally execute an innocent person.

Death penalty opponents would assert that the risk of executing an innocent person is a moral tragedy of the highest order, and a completely avoidable one if capital punishment were replaced with life imprisonment. But how likely is the execution of an innocent? Bedau and Radelet (1987) have investigated this issue. They reported that there have been some 350 instances in this century (1900–1982) of persons who were erroneously convicted of potentially capital crimes. Although some of these erroneous convictions occurred in non-death penalty states and some were quickly amended, many others occurred in death penalty states and went uncorrected for many years. Bedau and Radelet found that of the 350 persons who had been wrongly convicted of a capital crime, 139 were sentenced to death, and 23 were eventually executed. Given the difficulty of actually uncovering an instance of a wrongful conviction and execution, the authors take the position that the number of executed innocent persons is higher than twenty-three.

There is, in addition, no guarantee that the danger of executing an innocent person is eliminated under guided discretion statutes, even with extensive appellate review. There have been recent instances of innocent persons being convicted of capital crimes, and some came close to execution. Bentele (1985) describes the case of a Georgia man, Jerry Banks, who was convicted and sentenced to death in 1974 for the murder of two persons whose bodies he had found. Banks's conviction was reversed but he was retried and again sentenced to death. It was not until Banks had the services of new lawyers who uncovered crucial evidence and witnesses that the error of his previous conviction became known. He was successful in the appeal of his second conviction and death sentence, although the state dropped all charges against him in 1981.

There is also the case of Joseph Green Brown who was convicted and sentenced to death in Florida in 1974. Brown's conviction was based primarily on the testimony of his codefendant, Ronald Floyd, who had made a deal with the prosecutor in the case. The codefendant recanted his testimony eight months after Brown's trial, admitting that he had lied about Brown's participation in the murder and falsely told the jury that no agreement had been made between himself and the prosecutor. In addition, the prosecutor, Robert Bonanno, denied to the jury that any arrangement had been made with Floyd and knowingly gave the jury false testimony identifying a handgun of Brown's as the murder weapon. Brown, however, spent almost thirteen years on death row, and came within 15 hours of being electrocuted in Florida's electric chair before being granted a stay of execution. His conviction was not reversed by the Eleventh Circuit Court of Appeals until 1986 when it determined that the prosecutor in Brown's trial had lied to the jury about the agreement made with Floyd.[9] The state did not reprosecute the case. These are only two of the several known instances of innocent persons being erroneously convicted of capital crimes and sentenced to death under post-*Furman* statutes.[10] Although we will never know the precise number, that there have been instances of innocent persons being executed is not disputed. What is also indisputable is that there exists an alternative sanction for murder, life imprisonment, which would not entail the possibility of an innocent being put to death.

Don't Murderers Deserve Any Punishment?

Readers who are proponents of capital punishment must by now have reached a point of aggravation and exasperation. Having read that accurate and reliable assessments of moral desert are exceedingly complex if not impossible, even under procedurally reformed guided discretion capital statutes, and that the execution of those deserving less punishment and those deserving no punishment is possible, they must now want to loudly exclaim, "isn't it difficult to assess *any* blame, so that even if the death penalty were abolished some murderers could still be excessively punished if they received a life sentence when they really deserved only ten or fifteen years? And even when we decide to imprison murderers, aren't there going to be some unfortunate innocents who will be convicted and sent to prison? Is the logical conclusion of the abolitionist's argument that since an offender's blame cannot be determined accurately it should not be determined at all, and that since innocents might suffer no one should suffer any punishment for their misdeeds?" Of course not.

What abolitionists would claim is that the argument made by supporters of the death penalty—that murderers have to be executed because they "deserve it"—is not so straightforward. Abolitionists suggest that our ability to determine moral desert is not so fine-grained that we can determine with any degree of precision that Person A deserves to be executed while Person B, who is somewhat less blameworthy but we really do not know how much, deserves to have her life spared and be sentenced to life imprisonment. What we can determine, abolitionists would further assert, is that Person A and Person B have committed a serious offense, murder, and deserve to receive a severe punishment. This severe punishment will be at least as effective a deterrent as the death penalty, at least as cost efficient, will be morally deserved, and will not run the risk of an innocent person being put to death. This alternative punishment is life imprisonment. Moral blame, condemnation, and punishment would be assessed, but it would not *require* a *specific* form of punishment as the only just desert for murderers.

Those who would do away with the death penalty would also concede that even under a criminal justice system that excludes capital punishment, mistakes and errors will be made. Persons will be sentenced to life imprisonment who may only deserve ten or twenty years, and some innocent persons will be wrongly convicted and imprisoned. They would assert, however, that "death is different," punishing someone with an excess of years of undeserved imprisonment is not the moral equivalent of executing someone who does not deserve to die. They would also note that mistakes uncovered later cannot save the already-executed innocent person, but they may lead to the release and compensation of someone wrongly imprisoned. If mistakes are going to be made, abolitionists contend, let them be less-costly and morally consequential errors.

The proponent of the death penalty could finally assert a "rights" argument as van den Haag (1975) has, which claims that the state is justified in executing murderers because they have forfeited their own right to live. Bedau (1987, 9–63), however, has criticized this notion in what he calls the forfeiture theory of rights. His objection to the idea that murderers should be executed because they have by their action forfeited their right to life is that to say that an offender has forfeited *some* right due to his criminal action is not to say that he has forfeited a *specific* right, the right to life. That criminal offenders do indeed forfeit some rights is beyond dispute since they are punished by imprisonment (right of personal freedom and liberty). But Bedau (1987, 14) contends that there is nothing that *requires* a specific forfeiture such as death for the murderer: "while it would be necessary for the offender to forfeit some rights in order to be punished, it would not be necessary to forfeit the right to life." He further argues that even if it is accepted that the offender has forfeited his right to life it is not required that the state do so. The state may have the right to take the murderer's life, but that is only the right to do so, not the *duty* to take life away. The state may decline to execute someone even if it has the right to because as Bedau puts it, the state may have the right to take the murderer's life but if it does it may not be doing the right thing. The state does not do the right thing, he concludes, if it executes persons when a less-severe sanction is available which would achieve the state's purposes, and when it executes persons under a selection scheme that is inequitable. For Bedau, capital punishment fails both tests.

Nathanson also rejects the idea that murderers forfeit their right to life. Like Bedau his (1987, 139) position is that while murderers do relinquish some of their rights, they do not surrender all of them:

> Certainly, when people murder or commit other crimes, they do forfeit some of the rights that are possessed by the law-abiding. They lose a certain right to be left alone. It becomes permissible to bring them to trial and, if they are convicted, to impose an appropriate—even a dreadful—punishment on them. . . . Nonetheless, they do not forfeit all their rights.

One right which all criminal offenders retain, according to Nathanson, is the right to life. This right is never relinquished because all persons deserve "some level of decent treatment simply because they remain living, functioning human beings" (1987, 140). Similar to Reiman's belief that by refusing to take the life of a convicted murderer a society civilizes itself, Nathanson asserts that by rejecting the death penalty for any murderer we are thereby honoring our belief in the dignity of all human beings.

Summary and Conclusions

Many persons favor the death penalty because they believe that those who have deliberately taken the life of another person deserve to have their own life taken. This belief is an expression of a philosophy of punishment which holds that offenders should be punished for committing criminal offenses simply because it is deserved (even if there is no crime reduction or deterrent consequences), and they should be punished in proportion to the harm they have created by their criminal act.

This notion of deserved punishment is a central tenet of retributivism. The idea of deserved and proportional punishment is a very old one, extending back to the law of retaliation, or *lex talionis,* "an eye for an eye." It is most fully developed in Immanuel Kant's *The Metaphysical Elements of Justice.* Kant held that punishment of criminal offenders is deserved because in committing a crime they take an unfair advantage over other, law-abiding citizens. His principle of equality stipulates that the amount of punishment inflicted should equal the amount of harm produced by the criminal offense. Retributive punishment is not to be confused with simple revenge or vengeance. Unlike vengeance, punishment based on retributivism must be directed at the morally responsible agent, for a specific criminal offense, and by an official party, and is limited in its severity by the notion of proportionality.

Modern-day retributivists who support the death penalty, such as Ernest van den Haag and Walter Berns, echo Kant's theses. Van den Haag claims that those who intentionally kill another deserve to be executed because in killing another they have forfeited their own right to live. He also adheres to the notion that the total social injury produced by a murder is so great that the only commensurate punishment is that of death. Berns takes a similar view, noting that a murder destroys any sense people have of a safe community, and produces a feeling of outrage that must be given expression through official punishment.

Opponents of capital punishment would not dispute the fact that retributivism can be a legitimate justification for punishment or that notions of proportionality should provide a guide as to the amount of punishment to impose. They have, however, disagreed with the idea that the amount of punishment inflicted on an offender should be guided by a strict interpretation of the *lex talionis.* Their claim is that a literal interpretation of *lex talionis* would require punishments that would be either repugnant by contemporary moral standards (such as raping rapists or torturing those who have tortured) or impossible (such as a multiple execution of one who has killed more than one victim). The position of death penalty abolitionists who also claim to be retributivists is that there is only one moral requirement, that those who murder must receive one of the most severe punishments available in a society, which could include a long term of confinement.

Those who argue against the death penalty from a retributivist position have also been skeptical of our capacity to accurately divine the amount or type of punishment that is truly deserved by one who murders. Moral desert is such a complex issue, they note, that it is beyond the capacity of human reasoning. Given such limitations, and the possibility of making mistakes, which would include the execution of both the undeserving and the innocent, death penalty opponents would abandon executions in favor of an almost comparably severe penalty—life imprisonment.

Whatever the validity of the two competing positions, it is clear that the issue of what punishment murderers deserve is a difficult and contentious one. Unlike the economic benefits and deterrence arguments, there are no data that we can examine to help us through this thorny philosophical and moral quandary. Rather than coming to closure on the issue of deserved punishment for murderers, we have investigated the competing positions.

Notes

1. In the same Gallup poll, 61 percent of all respondents thought that the death penalty was a deterrent to murder.

2. It is difficult to classify van den Haag as a pure retributivist. Although he appears at times to adopt a retributive position regarding why criminals deserve to be punished and the amount of punishment they deserve, he claims (1983, 28) that retribution is not even a theory of punishment: "I cannot bring myself to regard retributivism as a theory of punishment, or anything. . . . [it] turns out to be no more than a feeling articulated through a metaphor presented as though a theory." Although he may disagree with his classification here as a retributivist, his position on the general justification of punishment (based partly on deterrence and partly on notions of desert) and on the death penalty are not inconsistent with retributivism.

3. What is clear from van den Haag's writings is that he also believes the state has the right to punish criminals, because, in doing so, it keeps others from violating the law (general deterrence), and may give the punished offender reason not to commit additional crimes (specific deterrence). Punishment is morally justified, then, because it produces a social utility—a reduction in crime.

4. This argument is held by philosophers like van den Haag and by the general public. It can also be found in the sentiments of at least one former Supreme Court justice:

> The instinct for retribution is part of the nature of man, and channeling that instinct in the administration of criminal justice serves an important purpose in promoting the stability of a society governed by law. When people begin to believe that organized society is unwilling or unable to impose upon criminal offenders the punishment they "deserve," then there are sown the seeds of anarchy—of self-help, vigilante justice and lynch law. [Justice Stewart in *Furman v. Georgia,* 408 U.S. 238 (1972) at p. 306]

5. Reiman (1985, 131) agrees that a prison term of eight to ten years after which a murderer is paroled would probably trivialize the injury produced by a deliberate killing. Reiman's argument is, however, vulnerable to the situation where an older person, say one who is fifty or sixty years old, commits murder. Because of their already advanced years their "life" sentence would only be approximately ten or twenty years in prison (given current life expectancy projections). There is no clear response to this, except to say that this would be the exceptional case, since the mean age for the average murderer is approximately thirty years.

6. This is also the position adopted by Hugo Bedau (1987, 61) in his recent book, *Death Is Different:*

> . . . murder, the gravest (or one of the gravest) of crimes, must be punished with the utmost permissible severity; and that society should spend considerable effort to arrest, try, convict, and sentence murderers. These principles, however, tell us nothing about *which* modes of punishment should be used. In particular, they are silent on the upper bound of permissible severity.

7. Advocates of the death penalty would, as we have seen, make the counterargument that in failing to execute those who deliberately take the life of an innocent person, we show a disregard for life: "Capital punishment for murder exerts a

moral influence by indicating that life is the most highly protected value" (Andenaes 1966, 967).

8. The conclusions that each drew from this were, however, quite different. Justice Harlan concluded that since the compilation of such information was beyond human ability the jury should be left free to make its awesome moral judgment without legal guidance. Nathanson's conclusion was that since moral blameworthiness cannot be reliably determined by mortals death penalty advocates cannot validly claim that death is the only morally appropriate sanction for murder, and would have it abolished.

9. *Los Angeles Times,* May 10, 1987, at p. 1, col. 1.

10. For additional recent examples of innocent persons being convicted and sentenced to death, see Bedau and Radelet (1987).

V
An Alternative to Capital Punishment

9

Future Trends and Prospects for the Abolition of the Death Penalty in the United States

Both the public and the judiciary seem to have a Janus-faced belief about the death penalty in the United States today. We have already seen that while most public opinion polls consistently suggest that more than three quarters of the public support capital punishment for murder, other polls indicate that this support would decline dramatically if there were an alternative, nonlethal punishment that promised to protect the public, such as life imprisonment without parole. This ambivalence is also shown by citizens who are closest to the death penalty, those serving on capital juries. Detailed research in one state has revealed that of those convicted capital defendants whose cases advance to a penalty trial, only about one half are ever sentenced to death (Baldus et al. 1990). The other side of this sentencing coin, however, is that about one half of convicted capital defendants *are* sentenced to death. Since 1980 nearly 300 new persons are added to death row across the United States each year. This would tend to suggest that the U.S. citizen's appetite for capital punishment (at least in the form of death *sentences*) may not have completely abated.

Our judicial system also shows mixed enthusiasm for capital punishment. Appeals courts continue to scrutinize capital cases with great care, vacating a high proportion of death sentences for either retrial or resentencing. As a result, many defendants sentenced to death by trial courts are eventually resentenced to life. For example, in 1980 192 offenders were sentenced to death. By 1987 only 10 of these 192 convicted offenders had been executed (5%), 9 (5%) died while incarcerated, 69 (36%) had their conviction and/or sentence vacated by an appeals court, 3 had their death sentence commuted, and 101 (53%) were still awaiting final disposition of their sentence. Even those whose death sentences are upheld are executed only after long delays. The average time between the imposition of a death sentence and the carrying out of that sentence is now approximately eight years.

Contrary to this is the judicial effort to restrict the opportunity of capital defendants to repeatedly appeal their case, thereby expediting executions. As we have seen, in *Barefoot v. Estelle,* the Supreme Court has already tried to hasten the processing of federal *habeas corpus* in capital cases through summary review procedures. We have also learned that it has tried to narrow the scope of federal *habeas corpus* for other capital defendants seeking relief, in *Teague v. Lane* and *Saffle v. Parks*.[1] Moreover, a committee of judges, appointed by Chief Justice Rehnquist, has recently proposed a modification of federal procedure which would limit convicted defendants to one round of appeals in federal court, and would establish a deadline of six months for inmates to file their motions. All of these efforts are devoted to reducing the time between conviction and execution.

In looking at the attitude of both U.S. citizens and their judiciary, therefore, we are drawn to the conclusion that there seems to be a love–hate relationship with the death penalty. There appears to be a surface enthusiasm for capital punishment, but a reluctance to see executions performed with any degree of regularity, and not without a growing body of legal restrictions. In this, the final, chapter we will examine the future of capital punishment in the United States. After making some conjectural observations on the pace of executions for the 1990s, we will suggest that U.S. citizens may have no real desire to retain capital punishment; instead, what we want is punishment for the serious offender and protection against dangerous offenders. We will also discuss the possibility that both can be secured with a noncapital alternative to the death penalty. We will then discuss the penalty of life imprisonment without parole as an alternative sanction to the death penalty. The chapter will close with a discussion of an abolitionist movement in the United States, a movement that if successful would place it within the company of the world's other democracies.

Is There an Impending Bloodbath in the United States?

We have learned in this book that capital punishment has been restored in most states, and that executions resumed in 1977. We have also discovered that there are now over 2,300 persons on death row awaiting their execution, with approximately 300 new inmates added each year. In addition, the federal government appears to be furthering its involvement in the death penalty business.[2] In October of 1989, Senator Strom Thurmond of South Carolina introduced a death penalty bill into the United States Senate which called for the death penalty for such federal crimes as treason, espionage, assassination or attempted assassination of the president, a murder committed in the course of a bank robbery, and first-degree murder. Crimes of first-degree murder that would fall under federal jurisdiction include murder on federal land, such as Indian reservations. The law proposed by Senator Thurmond also stiuplates that offenders committing crimes on federal lands would be subject to federal rather than state law. This could mean that those committing first-degree murder on an

Indian reservation could be sentenced to death even if the crime was committed in an abolitionist state.

Does this intensified support for capital punishment and a burgeoning death row population mean that we will soon be executing large numbers of persons? Will we soon be seeing executions taking place at a great rate, as in the 1930s when some 150 persons were executed each year? Will we soon be seeing a "bloodbath" across the United States?

It is very doubtful if executions will reach anywhere near their previous levels. From 1977 until the end of September 1990, there have been only 140 executions in the entire country, about 10 per year. Nor does it appear that this number will substantially increase any time in the foreseeable future. Although the number of executions increased from 1 in 1981 to 25 in 1987, there were only 11 executions in 1988, 16 in 1989, and only 20 by September of 1990. At least through the first half of the 1990s, it appears that the imposition of capital punishment in the United States will continue as it has in the immediate past. There will be a large number of offenders sentenced to death each year with but a handful of executions being performed. Many offenders will have their murder convictions and death sentences vacated by appeals courts, and the delay in executions, though perhaps reduced, will continue.

The reason for this situation will also be the same. There does not seem to be any great eagerness for the routine performance of executions. The political climate will remain ambivalent and cautious, as will the judiciary, which hears and rules on death penalty cases. The public does not seem to want the death penalty with any regularity. But if this is so, what do we want, and are there any policy alternatives to a system of capital punishment that sentences so many and executes so few?

The Illusion of Public Support for the Death Penalty

It is now time to return to an issue raised in Chapter 1, that although public opinion polls show support for the death penalty, this support does not run deep and strong. Public opinion polls from several states have shown that while from 70 to 80 percent of the public expresses "support" for the death penalty for murderers, fewer than one third continue to do so when it is compared with an alternative penalty, life without the possibility of parole with restitution (LWOP+R) (Bowers 1990). In a LWOP+R sentence, inmates spend the rest of their lives in prison without the possibility of parole, and with a requirement that they pay to the murder victim's survivors part of what they earn in their prison labors. When asked which penalty they would like to see imposed on convicted murderers, 67 percent of those polled in California said they would prefer LWOP+R, while only 26 percent preferred the death penalty; in Massachusetts 52 percent preferred LWOP + R to death (30%), and in New York 62 percent preferred LWOP+R to death (32%) (Bowers 1990). In Florida, a state which by 1990 had executed 24 inmates (the second highest number in the nation since executions were resumed in 1977) and currently has over 300 condemned inmates on death row, 70 percent preferred LWOP+R to the death penalty (24%) (Bowers 1990).

It should be noted here that in each of these states support for the death penalty expressed in general public opinion questions was quite high. The important point to remember, however, is that this "support" is not that strong in that it is substantially eroded when the public is provided with the alternative of LWOP+R. For example, in California 82 percent of those polled said that they approved of the death penalty for those who are convicted of murder. This declined 56 percentage points to 26 percent when these same Californians were provided with the alternative of LWOP+R (Bowers 1990). There was a 60 percentage point decline in support for the death penalty in Florida, from 84 to 24 percent, when compared with the alternative of LWOP+R, and 40 percent declines in New York and Massachusetts (Bowers 1990).

The expressed preference for LWOP+R may even increase with full public awareness and knowledge of this alternative. Bowers (1990) has presented some data to suggest that many persons are confused about LWOP, thinking that offenders serving such sentences may someday be released from their sentence back into the community. Although states that have implemented such schemes have differed with respect to what LWOP actually means (see Wright 1990), it can mean just that—that once sentenced to LWOP an inmate has no possibility of being released. It seems plausible to predict that support for LWOP as an alternative to the death penalty will be even greater when it is fully understood.

Politicians and members of the United States Supreme Court have traditionally taken general public opinion information to mean that the public is strongly in favor of the death penalty. We have just seen, however, that when more specific questions are asked, particularly those that provide other sentencing alternatives such as LWOP+R, this is simply not the case. While large numbers of U.S. citizens clearly express support for the death penalty in the abstract, this support does not at all mean that they *prefer* the death penalty. If this is so, then what do we want for those who have been convicted of murder?

Protecting the Public and Punishing Dangerous Offenders without the Death Penalty

An analysis of public opinion data seems clear; the public wants those who are convicted of murder to be punished severely, because they have committed a serious offense. They also desire to be protected from such offenders; they want some assurance that murderers will not be able to commit their offense again. Executing such persons is clearly one way to both punish them with severity and restrain them from committing another murder, but it clearly is not the *only* way to achieve these objectives. One other way to harshly punish offenders and prevent them from hurting other citizens is the penalty we have discussed in the previous section—life without the possibility of parole with restitution. In addition, when murderers are executed there are other desirable ends which may never be achieved, such as providing some form of compensation to the families of murder victims. LWOP+R affords a way for those convicted of murder to be punished severely, incapacitated from murdering someone else in the community, and to provide restitution for survivors of their tragic crime. We will discuss some of the advantages of this sanction.

Advantages of LWOP+R

LWOP+R Ensures Justice. Life imprisonment without the possibility of parole is indeed a severe punishment. In relation to our discussion in Chapter 8, there should be little doubt that LWOP+R does not trivialize or depreciate the significance of murder. Offenders serving LWOP terms are, of course, confined to maximum security prisons, have their basic freedoms restricted, are forced to live in a very controlled and regimented environment, and exist in great fear for their own safety because they are confined with other dangerous persons. Like other confined prisoners, those serving LWOP terms will be unable to have normal contact with family and other loved ones, and will be required to labor while confined. All of these pains of imprisonment will be imposed with no prospect of release. The requirements of justice, that those committing serious crimes receive severe punishments, will, then, be served by LWOP sentences. In being sentenced to prison for the rest of their life and required to make restitution, murderers would be punished severely, and their toils would not be for their benefit but to ease the suffering of the victim's family. There is an added advantage here in that by neither executing nor paroling convicted murderers, LWOP+R sends a symbolic message which demonstrates both society's abhorrence of murder and its fundamental respect for human life.

LWOP+R Enables Some Form of Restitution. One of the disadvantages of the death penalty is that the victim and those left behind by the murder are virtually forgotten. A criminal homicide is an act that does more than take away a loved one, it often creates financial hardship. Lives are shattered, and both immediate and long-term financial hardships must often be overcome in addition to the shock of the senseless murder. When convicted murderers are put to death the victim's survivors may receive some emotional gratification, but many misfortunes remain, burdens the offender's own death can scarcely relieve. One of the benefits of a LWOP+R sentence is that convicted murderers are required provide some of the money they earn while working in prison to the victim family, thus easing some of the financial loss. In this way the offender would repaying both society and the victim's family with both life and labor. T seems to be widespread support for the restitution requirement of sentence. Bowers (1990) reports evidence from public opinion polls in several states which show that while a life without parole sentence that does not involve restitution is not preferred over a death sentence, a majority do prefer it when restitution is added as part of the punishment.

LWOP+R Ensures Protection of the Public. Offenders who are sentenced to traditional life terms are normally eligible for parole when they have served a certain length of time. Although adequately prevented from killing a member of the public when incarcerated, such offenders may kill again if released. The traditional life term, then, offers some, but only temporary, protection to the public due to incapacitation. But we have already suggested the possibility of another kind of life sentence, a life sentence without the possibility of parole and therefore release. When convicted offenders are serving life imprisonment terms that preclude their release on parole, they are almost completely incapacitated from committing another violent offense in the community. Those serving LWOP+R terms would not be eligible for parole and could not, therefore, ever be returned to the community. Citizens would be adequately protected from such offenders. There are two possible ways LWOP+R offenders could commit another murder: if they were to escape, and if they were to kill an inmate or correctional worker while confined. Since offenders serving LWOP+R terms would be confined in maximum security prisons, the probability that they could escape is very remote. Although the possibility exists, escapes from such tightly controlled prisons have occurred very infrequently in the past. In addition, prisoners serving life terms have not traditionally been security risks to those who are confined or work with them (MacKenzie and Goodstein 1985). We have already reviewed a substantial body of literature suggesting that "lifers" re very unlikely to kill behind bars, and generally are model inmates.

It could be argued, however, that previous research concerning the tutional behavior of life inmates has not dealt with the issue of those serving ithout the possibility of parole. While murderers serving traditional life es may refrain from committing another homicide because they may bly be released on parole at some time, no such prospect is available to hose serving life without parole sentences. Although it may appear that without parole inmate may have "nothing to lose" by committing a hile imprisoned, such is decidedly not the case. As prison inmates, such would have normal prison privileges (watching television, taking or vocational courses, visits, telephone and mail privileges) which away. Those who work in correctional institutions have attested to f such losses of privileges in controlling the behavior of life term right 1990, 564–565). In addition, incapacitation works behind Disruptive inmates may be removed from the normal prison placed in isolation as punishment. In the long run, inmates without parole may be the best behaved because they may become institutionalized to the routines and limits of prison life. Experience with LWOP inmates in the Alabama penal system has shown that they commit about one half as many infractions as other inmates (Wright 1990, 565).

LWOP+R May Be Far Less Costly and More Certain Punishment. In Chapter 6 we learned how costly it was to maintain a criminal justice system that included the death penalty. When trying a death case, defense counsel uses every legal means at their disposal to prevent their client from being executed. Because of the finality and irrevocability of the death penalty, defense counsel is provided with a growing body of legal restrictions on the use of capital punishment, including extensive dual collateral review (appeals in both state and federal courts). We have also seen that because of this legal machinery and a public ambivalent about the death penalty, executions are rarely performed. The ideal of swift and certain punishment has simply broken down with respect to the death penalty in the United States. While hundreds continue to be sentenced to death only a handful are actually executed. Both the public and those working within the criminal justice system are disillusioned, and confidence in the law is undermined.

The alternative of LWOP+R promises to be both a less costly and more certain punishment. Defense counsel, free from the onus of having to defend their client's life, will be less likely to use every available legal maneuver at their disposal.[3] There would be fewer pretrial motions, and far less case preparation in general, since neither defense nor prosecution would be preparing for the bifurcated hearing of a capital case. In addition, the lengthy appeals process provided in capital cases because "death is different" would be eliminated. Courts, including the U.S. Supreme Court, have already determined the constitutionality of life without parole sentences (Wright 1990), and they have never determined that defendants facing the prospect of life without parole are required to have the "super due process" that is currently available to the defendant on trial for her life. A criminal justice system that included life without the possibility of parole with restitution as its most severe sanction would, then, be far less costly than one that included capital punishment.

It should also be noted that with a streamlining of the judiciary, a criminal justice system based on LWOP+R rather than the death penalty would be a far more certain one. Clearly the political climate of the country is such that LWOP sentences are preferred to death sentences. Prosecutors will be more inclined to seek them, and juries more inclined to impose them. We should expect to find far more consistency and evenhandedness than we have in state death sentencing schemes. Furthermore, without the interminable delays produced by an extensive appeals system, LWOP+R sentences would be imposed with a far greater degree of finality than death sentences, and the public's desire to see murderers punished would not be frustrated.

Critics of LWOP+R sentences may note here that a state's penal system may rapidly become overcrowded with those serving natural life terms. An over-crowded prison system would drastically reduce any cost savings. It is feared that existing prison space would soon "fill up" with those serving LWOP sentences, such that other, possibly dangerous, offenders would have to be released sooner than desired, or new institutions would have to be constructed. It could also be expected to easily erode the certainty of punishment, since prosecutors would seek fewer LWOP sentences as the prison system becomes overcrowded.

These fears may be misplaced, however. States that currently have LWOP provisions in their statutes for capital offenders have not been overburdened with them. In the Alabama and Kentucky prison systems, for example, murderers serving life without parole sentences comprise less than 2 percent of the entire prison population (Wright 1990, 562). These percentages are likely to increase as states sentence more of their offenders to LWOP, but the danger of overcrowding is minimal. Even if it is argued that LWOP inmates may eventually begin to compromise a larger proportion of a prison system's population, surely this group of serious offenders is exactly the kind that a state would like to incarcerate for a long time.

If a prison system becomes overcrowded, the answer does not necessarily lie in retaining capital punishment or building more prisons. It may mean that nonserious offenders will have to be given sentences that do not call for imprisonment. At the moment, the United States incarcerates more of its citizens than any nation in the world; 426 per 100,000 population compared to 268 in the Soviet Union, 97 in Great Britain, and 45 in Japan; costing the taxpayer some $16 billion a year (Black 1991). A good proportion of current inmates were incarcerated for nonviolent crimes that in the past were handled without recourse to incarceration. There is little doubt that the current prison population across the states could be substantially reduced if imprisonment were reserved for those committing the most violent offenses. Finally, even if the current rate of incarceration were to continue, millions of dollars would be saved through the abolition of the death penalty, which could finance new prison construction. Even if the frequency of LWOP sentences were to increase, then, it could still lead to considerable cost savings.

LWOP Would Ensure That the Innocent and Undeserving Are Not Executed.
In Chapter 8 we noted that one of the problems with any capital sentencing system is that human judgment is not infallible. Two kinds of errors could be made. One error would be in executing innocent persons. While the risk of this is minimal, we do know that it has happened in the past (Bedau and Radelet 1987), and when it occurs it is a moral failure of the highest order. The second and far more likely error occurs when offenders are sentenced to death who are guilty of a murder but may not be morally deserving of the death penalty. Although juries are provided with some guidance as to which convicted capital

offenders should be sentenced to death, such guidelines are too vague to provide much direction. The result is, as we have seen in Chapter 5, that many death sentences are imposed on some offenders while life sentences are inflicted on many more others who have committed comparable crimes. These death sentences can only be described as arbitrary, and therefore undeserved. Any capital sentencing system must, therefore, concern itself with the fact that some innocents and some not deserving of the death penalty will inevitably be executed.

If death sentences are abandoned in favor of life sentences without the possibility of parole, however, then these extreme errors will not be made. Neither the innocent nor undeserving would be put to death. Although other kinds of errors could be made—for example, innocent persons could still be convicted and those morally deserving of a lessor penalty could still be sentenced to LWOP—these mistakes would be far less costly. While nothing could be done for those innocent persons who are executed, those who were unjustly incarcerated could be released when the errors are discovered. Although the time offenders spent imprisoned could never be returned to them, they would, nonetheless, have their freedom, and could be compensated by the state.

Earlier in this chapter we learned that politicians and court justices may be misreading the public's appetite for capital punishment. While it is true that there is some general support for the death penalty, it cannot be said to be the preferred sanction or that it is in any way mandated by the public. What U.S. citizens want is that convicted murderers be punished severely, surely, and certainly. They also want to be protected from dangerous offenders, to see their tax dollars spent wisely, and that offenders somehow ease the suffering and loss to those victimized by their crimes. As many of us are now beginning to realize, the death penalty cannot meet all of these objectives. An alternative sanction, life without the possibility of parole with restitution, can, however, punish severely and with a greater sense of certainty, justice, and morality than capital punishment. With increasing public support for LWOP+R sentences, we may eventually see the abolition of the death penalty in the United States. We will now briefly examine the form and direction that this abolition movement could take, and how the elimination of capital punishment in the United States would place it alongside other democratic countries.

Abolition of the Death Penalty in the United States

From the Courts to the Statehouse

For death penalty opponents the case of *McCleskey v. Kemp,* which we discussed in Chapter 4, was hoped to be the beginning of the end for capital punishment in the United States. *McCleskey* brought before the U.S. Supreme

Court detailed and very sophisticated statistical information which suggested that even procedurally reformed, guided discretion statutes could not eliminate the historical legacy of racism from the administration of the death penalty. We now know that this research found that even after numerous legally relevant factors were taken into account, offenders who killed whites in Georgia were four times more likely to be sentenced to death than those who killed a black. Although the research study presented in *McCleskey* was acclaimed by the scientific community as the most rigorous and most careful study of criminal sentencing yet conducted, the Supreme Court dismissed the significance of its findings. The Court essentially concluded that condemned offenders must show that they were discriminated against by their own prosecutor or jury. However, just as smokers cannot definitively prove that their own lung cancer was produced by smoking, those claiming racial bias in their death sentence under the *McCleskey* standard cannot easily substantiate their case.

After *McCleskey* was decided it was thought that it marked the last chance for those seeking to have the death penalty abolished. But *McCleskey* was certainly not the last word for abolitionists. First of all, the case was a disagreement over the presence of racial discrimination, decided by a narrow 5–4 margin. It was also marked by very contentious opinions. Second, and more important, the Court's pronouncement in *McCleskey* was simply that the abolition of the death penalty would not come from the Supreme Court. The responsibility for ending capital punishment in the United States, Justice Powell suggested, would have to come from the people themselves, through their democratically elected bodies, state legislatures:

> McCleskey's arguments are best presented to the legislative bodies. It is not the responsibility—or even the right—of this Court to determine the appropriate punishment for particular crimes. It is the legislatures, the elected representatives of the people, that are "constituted to respond to the will and consequently the moral values of the people." Legislatures are also better qualified to weigh and "evaluate the results of statistical studies in terms of their own local conditions and with a flexibility of approach that is not available to the courts." [*McCleskey v. Kemp*, 107 S. Ct. 1756 (1987) at p. 1781 (citations omitted)]

The word given by *McCleskey* was that the courts will not be the salvation for those wishing to abolish the death penalty. It essentially rejected the notion of a judicial solution to the problem of racial discrimination in the imposition of the death penalty (and the abolition of capital punishment itself), and instead suggested an alternative arena for these issues to be addressed—state legislatures. The questions now are, how can those with a racial discrimination grievance be heard? and what specifically can be done to abolish this punishment? One step in this direction would be legislation that prohibits discriminatory or arbitrary death sentences.

The Racial Justice Act

Section 5 of the Fourteenth Amendment to the U.S. Constitution gives Congress the power to pass legislation to ensure that states actually comply with the due process and equal protection requirement. Out of this power came the proposed Racial Justice Act. Representative John Conyers introduced the House version of the Racial Justice Act on April 24, 1988. Senator Edward Kennedy of Massachusetts proposed a federal construction of the Act as an amendment to the Omnibus Drug Initiative Act of 1988. The House version of the Act would prohibit racial discrimination in the administration of capital punishment by either the state or federal government. Under this proposed bill, condemned prisoners would be given the opportunity to prove that their death sentence was influenced by race. Contrary to the requirement of *McCleskey,* however, the Racial Justice Act explicitly stipulates that statistical demonstrations of dispro-portionate racial impact, the kind of evidence presented by Warren McCleskey, could constitute a *prima facie* showing of racial discrimination. It specifically states that defendants would not have to demonstrate that they were the particular victim of intentional discrimination (see Berger et al. 1989). This proposed Act also declares that if a court makes a finding of racial discrimina-tion on the basis of such statistical evidence, the state will have the opportunity to rebut this evidence by demonstrating that the alleged racial disparity can be explained by legally relevant and racially neutral factors.

The Racial Justice Act would not spell the end of the death penalty, but its use would be severely restricted. If, for example, a petitioner demonstrated a statistically strong case of disparate racial impact of the death penalty within a state, the state could suggest that such racial disparity is only characteristic for those cases at the mid- or low levels of homicide aggravation. If it could then demonstrate that there is little or no racial disparity at the highest levels of aggravation, and that the defendant falls into that category, it would have successfully rebutted the claim of racial discrimination. The practical effect of the Racial Justice Act may be to limit capital punishment to only the most brutal and aggravated homicides.

At the time it was proposed, the Racial Justice Act had the support of the American Bar Association and diverse civil rights and civil liberties groups. Those who support this legislation could encourage its adoption and the consideration of similar legislation within individual states. The prospect for the success of these efforts appears promising. If politicians respond to anything, they do respond to the demands of their constituencies. In fact, members of state legislatures were probably responding to such a perceived demand when they drafted and enacted new death penalty schemes after *Furman.* We also can now appreciate the fact that politicians may be *misunderstanding* the political climate if they take at face value public opinion polls that indicate that eight out of ten support the death penalty for those convicted of murder. We have learned that such conventional public opinion questions hide the fact that the public may prefer a noncapital sanction, life without parole, to the death penalty. Proponents of the Racial Justice Act could emphasize that its provisions do not necessarily encourage the abolition of the death penalty, just one of its most obvious defects, that it has in the past and continues to be influenced by the race of the offender and victim.

Opponents of the death penalty need to ensure that politicians correctly understand the political climate relating to the death penalty—acceptability does not necessarily mean preference. Once politicians correctly read this climate, legislation comparable to the Racial Justice Act, or more explicit attempts to abolish the death penalty, may be successful. Other efforts may include attempts to get legislatures to adopt the alternative sanction of life without the possibility of parole. Although many states already have LWOP legislation, there is a need to better inform the public (and juries) about this alternative in order to increase the frequency of its use (see Wright 1990). If abolition is achieved, the United States will finally join a long list of democratic countries that have already made the move to eliminate or severely restrict the use of capital punishment.

International Trends in Abolishing the Death Penalty

In recent years, Amnesty International has led a movement directed toward the abolition of the death penalty in all retentionist countries. Amnesty International is a worldwide organization devoted to the protection of human rights. In conjunction with their work seeking the release of prisoners of conscience and fair trials for all political prisoners, Amnesty International has made the abolition of the death penalty a human rights issue. The practice of the death penalty is believed to be a fundamental human rights issue, because Amnesty International accedes to the United Nations Universal Declaration of Human Rights, adopted in 1948, which recognizes each individual's right to life (Amnesty International 1989). This right to life is held to be inalienable, and is grossly violated by the intentional taking of a life, whether by murder or state-sponsored execution.

Amnesty International has noted that there are thirty-five countries that have abolished the death penalty for all crimes, including such democratic contemporaries of the United States as Australia, Denmark, France, Germany, the Netherlands, Norway, and Sweden (1989, 259). There are another eighteen countries that have abolished the death penalty for all but exceptional crimes (crimes committed during wartime), including Canada, Israel, Switzerland, and the United Kingdom; and twenty-seven countries that have retained the death penalty for ordinary crimes but have not executed anyone for at least ten years, including Belgium, Greece, and Ireland (1989, 260–261). In sum, there are eighty countries that no longer use the death penalty as part of their criminal justice system. These forty *de jure* or *de facto* abolitionist countries comprise over 40 percent of the countries in the world. More important, most of the Western democracies are included in this group.

The United States is one of a minority of democratic countries that have retained the death penalty for ordinary criminal offenses. In using the death penalty for such ordinary crimes, the United States finds itself in the uncomfortable company of such repressive regimes as The People's Republic of China, Iran, Iraq, Korea, Libya, South Africa, and the Soviet Union. As Zimring and Hawkins (1986, 6–10) have noted, although there is no generally accepted penal practice in modern Western societies, it does correlate strongly among those nations that have retained the death penalty with a disregard for human rights.

Those who wish to abolish the death penalty in the United States could learn a great deal about how to go about it from those nations who have already done so. Historical analyses of other countries suggest that abolition of the death penalty has occurred in these countries even when expressed popular "support" for the death penalty was high. Zimring and Hawkins (1986, 12–15) have shown that successful abolition movements have not generally been in response to public demand for an end to the death penalty. In Great Britain, the death penalty was abolished even though a majority of the public favored retaining it. Zimring and Hawkins also note that public opinion often follows legislative effort. They reported that support for the death penalty in West Germany considerably diminished after abolition. If this is true, then abolition of the death penalty in the United States will not have to wait for public opinion to change. Abolitionist organizations can play an active role in convincing public officials that the death penalty is not needed, and is a punishment we can all live without.

Abolitionist Groups in the United States

We have just learned that in retaining the death penalty the United States places itself among some of the most brutal political regimes in the world. Although this in and of itself may not constitute grounds for abolishing capital punishment, as we have seen throughout this book, it is a compelling reason, and only one of several: Capital punishment is more costly than life imprisonment; it continues to be administered in an arbitrary and discriminatory manner; despite legal reforms it continues to be inflicted on the young, the mentally and emotionally handicapped, and the poor; it is a penalty that is subject to tragic moral errors which can be avoided; and it is a penalty that the public does not appear to demand or even prefer.

In addition to civil rights and civil liberties groups, such as Amnesty International, the anti–capital punishment movement in the United States is formed by a diverse coalition. Numerous religious groups have spoken out against the death penalty, such as the American Baptist Churches, the American Friends Service Committee, the Presbyterian Church of the United States, the

Union of American Hebrew Congregations, the Southern Christian Leadership Conference, the Unitarian Universalist Association, and the United Methodist Church.

In addition to religious groups, the medical profession has become actively involved in the death penalty, at least in forbidding its professions from directly participating. In 1980 the House of Delegates of the American Medical Association adopted a resolution stating that although one's opinion of capital punishment is a personal issue, physicians, as persons dedicated to the saving of life, could not ethically participate in a legally sponsored execution, as did the World Medical Association in 1981 (Amnesty International 1989, 78). The American Public Health Association, the American Psychiatric Association, and the American Nursing Association have also determined that members of their professions should not participate in an execution. There are as well diverse legal and professional groups that have joined the abolitionist movement. Although not yet successful, the abolitionist movement may gain strength in the United States; and the country will rid itself of an archaic and brutal penalty.

The End of the Death Penalty in the United States?

Will the death penalty come to an end in the United States? It already appears that the regular performance of executions is already over. In spite of a majority of states that have death penalty statutes, and over 2,300 persons awaiting death, there have been on average no more than ten executions per year since 1977. There is no indication that this number will dramatically increase in the years ahead. Rather than an abrupt end to the death penalty, by Supreme Court pronouncement, for example, it is more likely that capital punishment will simply wither away over the years.

The demise of capital punishment *will probably not* come about as the public becomes more aware of the problem and complexities of the death penalty business. They will be unmoved by scientific studies demonstrating that the death penalty is not better at reducing murder, that it is arbitrary and discriminatory, or that it is more costly than life imprisonment or sometimes inflicted on the innocent or undeserving. Some form of capital punishment may exist for a long time because of its symbolic importance. It is an institution society can use to express both its fear of crime and its revulsion of criminals (Zimring and Hawkins 1986). Having such symbolic or ritual importance, the death penalty may be impervious to directly rational or scientific argument. The best chance for eliminating the death penalty in the United States would be for abolitionist groups to stress the protection offered by alternative sanctions, and the strong moral reproach they carry, while attempting to restrict the kinds of offenses that would legitimate a death sentence. If states retain the death penalty in any form, perhaps it could be reserved by statute for only the very few that constitute the most heinous offenders (those that involve the brutal killing of multiple victims or by murderers repeating their crime). This will at least restrict the number of persons on death row, and further reduce the number of executions performed. It will also allow states to evaluate the prospect of not having the death penalty. After a time, when executions *de facto* cease to exist, perhaps full abolition will be successful.

Summary and Conclusions

The lesson to be learned from our recent history of capital punishment is that we as citizens must take on the moral duty of eliminating executions. We must not wait for the members of the Supreme Court to change in the hope of securing a more responsive audience, but must instead transform the climate of opinion that tolerates the existence of capital punishment.

There is evidence that clearly suggests that the public strongly prefers a penalty of life imprisonment without the possibility of parole with restitution to capital punishment. A sentence of LWOP+R offers many advantages over the death penalty. By keeping convicted murderers behind bars in maximum security prisons for the rest of their lives, it will ensure that they are severely punished for their crime. Although LWOP+R does not duplicate the harm done to the victim, it does meet the requirements of justice and deserved punishment by applying the harshest sanction short of execution. A LWOP+R sentence also promises to do more than the death penalty by requiring the offender to make financial restitution to the surviving family members of the victim. As such, it addresses some of the suffering and hardships left in the wake of the offender's crime. LWOP+R will also offer nearly as much protection to the public as the death penalty. Those serving true life sentences will not, short of escape, be able to murder another member of the public, and previous research has shown that "lifers" do not constitute a security risk to other inmates or prison employees.

We have also learned that LWOP+R sentences will be less costly and more certain than death sentences. A criminal justice system that includes LWOP will cost less than one with capital punishment, which, under current procedures, requires two separate trials and a lengthy appeals process. In addition, because of the careful scrutiny of capital cases by the judiciary, we have seen that while many death sentences are imposed, few are carried out, and those that are occur long after the crime and conviction. Without the long and successful appeals process normally attached to death sentences, a sentence of LWOP+R will be carried out more quickly and more certainly. Finally, LWOP+R promises greater protection for those who are innocent of their crimes or who do not deserve the ultimate penalty of death.

Many states already have LWOP provisions in their penal statutes. At least thirty states use some form of life without parole sentences for those convicted of murder (Wright 1990). Many persons, including those who would serve on capital juries, are, unfortunately, not always fully informed as to what a LWOP sentence really means. Although these states have not employed LWOP extensively, it is hoped that greater understanding and knowledge of this alternative will lead to its increased use.

If the United States does finally abandon the death penalty, it will join a number of democratic countries that have already abolished it in law or in practice, including most Western countries. The United States is today one of only a very few democratic countries that continue to retain the death penalty. Although there are about one hundred countries that have maintained the practice of capital punishment, these are among the most repressive political regimes in the world.

There are many groups in the United States today working toward the abolition of the death penalty. Among these include legal, religious, and medical organizations. Although they have had only limited success in the political climate of the 1980s, it is hoped that with time the citizens of the United States will realize that they do not need the death penalty, and will put an end to what is an unnecessarily cruel penalty.

Notes

1. See the discussion of these cases in Chapter 6.

2. There are currently thirteen federal statutes that contain some provision for the death penalty. In 1988, the Anti–Drug Abuse Act was passed which provided for the death penalty is some drug-related killings.

3. Even members of the U.S. Supreme Court have suggested that they give death penalty cases "special" consideration: "When the penalty is death, we, like state court judges, are tempted to strain the evidence and even, in close cases, the law in order to give a doubtfully condemned man another chance" [*Furman v. Georgia,* 408 U.S. 238 (1972) at p. 287, note 34 (Brenan, J. concurring); quoting *Stein v. New York,* 346 U.S. 156, 196 (1953)].

References

Amnesty International 1989. *When the State Kills.* New York: Amnesty International Publications.

Amsterdam, A. 1987. "In Favorem Mortis," *Human Rights* 14:889–890.

Andenaes, J. 1966. "General Preventive Effects of Punishment," *University of Pennsylvania Law Review* 114:949–983.

Arkin, S. D. 1980. "Discrimination and Arbitrariness in Capital Punishment: An Analysis of Post-*Furman* Murder Cases in Dade County, Florida, 1973–1976," *Stanford Law Review* 33:75–101.

Bailey, W.C. 1978a. "An Analysis of the Deterrent Effect of the Death Penalty in North Carolina," *North Carolina Central Law Journal* 10:29–49.

Bailey, W.C. 1978b. "Deterrence and the Death Penalty for Murder in Utah: A Time-Series Analysis," *Journal of Contemporary Law* 5:1–20.

Bailey, W.C. 1979a. "The Deterrent Effect of the Death Penalty for Murder in California," *Southern California Law Review* 52:743–764.

Bailey, W.C. 1979b. "Deterrence and the Death Penalty for Murder in Oregon," *Willamette Law Review* 16:67–85.

Bailey, W.C. 1979c. "The Deterrent Effect of the Death Penalty for Murder in Ohio: A Time-Series Analysis," *Cleveland State Law Review* 28:51–70.

Bailey, W.C. 1982. "Capital Punishment and Lethal Assaults against Police," *Criminology* 19:608–625.

Bailey, W.C. 1983. "Disaggregation in Deterrence and Death Penalty Research: The Case of Murder in Chicago," *Journal of Criminal Law and Criminology* 74:827–859.

Bailey, W.C. 1990. "Murder, Capital Punishment, and Television: Execution Publicity and Homicide Rates," *American Sociological Review* 55:628–633.

Bailey, W.C. and R.C. Peterson 1987. "Police Killings and Capital Punishment: The Post-*Furman* Period," *Criminology* 25:1–25.

Bailey, W.C. and R.D. Peterson 1989. "Murder and Capital Punishment: A Monthly Time-Series Analysis of Execution Publicity," *American Sociological Review* 54:722–743.

Baldus, D.C. and J.W.L. Cole 1975. "Statistical Evidence on the Deterrent Effect of Capital Punishment: A Comparison of the Work of Thorsten Sellin and Isaac Ehrlich on the Deterrent Effect of Capital Punishment," *Yale Law Journal* 85:170–186.

Baldus, D.C., C. Pulaski, and G. Woodworth 1983. "Comparative Review of Death

Sentences: An Empirical Study of the Georgia Experience," *Journal of Criminal Law and Criminology* 74:661–753.

Baldus, D.C., C. Pulaski, and G. Woodworth 1985. "Monitoring and Evaluating Contemporary Death Sentencing Systems: Lessons from Georgia," *University of California Davis Law Review* 18:1375–1407.

Baldus, D.C., G.G. Woodworth, and C.A. Pulaski 1990. *Equal Justice and the Death Penalty.* Boston: Northeastern University Press.

Balske, D.N. 1979. "New Strategies for the Defense of Capital Cases," Akron Law Review 13:331–361.

Barnett, A. 1978. "Crime and Capital Punishment: Some Recent Studies," *Journal of Criminal Justice* 6:291–303.

Barnett, A. 1981. "The Deterrent Effect of Capital Punishment: A Test of Some Recent Studies," *Operations Research* 29:346–370.

Baron, J. and A. Reiss 1985. "Same Time Next Year: Aggregate Analysis of the Mass Media and Violent Behavior," *American Sociological Review* 50:364–371.

Beccaria, C. [1764] 1963. *On Crimes and Punishments.* Indianapolis: Bobbs-Merrill.

Bedau, H.A. 1964. "Death Sentences in New Jersey 1907–1960," *Rutgers Law Review* 19:1–64.

Bedau, H.A. 1965. "Capital Punishment in Oregon 1903–1964," *Oregon Law Review* 45:1–39.

Bedau, H.A. 1982. *The Death Penalty in America* (3d ed.). New York: Oxford University Press.

Bedau, H.A. 1987. *Death Is Different.* Boston: Northeastern University Press.

Bedau, H.A. and M.L. Radelet 1987. "Miscarriages of Justice in Potentially Capital Cases," *Stanford Law Review* 40:21–179.

Belknap, M.R. 1987. *Federal Law and Southern Order.* Athens: University of Georgia Press.

Bendremer, F.J., G. Bramnick, J.C. Jones, and S.N. Lippman 1986. "*McCleskey v. Kemp:* Constitutional Tolerance for Racially Disparate Capital Sentencing," *University of Miami Law Review* 41:295–355.

Bentele, U. 1985. "The Death Penalty in Georgia: Still Arbitrary," *Washington University Law Quarterly* 62:573–646.

Berger, R. 1982. *Death Penalties: The Supreme Court's Obstacle Course.* Cambridge, Massachusetts: Harvard University Press.

Berger, V., N. Walthour, A. Dorn, D. Lindsey, P. Thompson, and G. von Helms 1989. "Too Much Justice?: A Legislative Response to McCleskey v. Kemp," *Harvard Civil Rights Civil Liberties Law Review* 24:437–528.

Berns, W. 1979. *For Capital Punishment.* New York: Basic Books.

Bienen, L.B., N.A. Weiner, D.W. Denno, P.D. Allison, and D.L. Mills 1988. "The Reimposition of Capital Punishment in New Jersey: The Role of Prosecutorial Discretion," *Rutgers Law Review* 41:27–372.

Black, C. 1981. *Capital Punishment: The Inevitability of Caprice and Mistake* (2d ed.). New York: Norton.

Black, C. 1991. "Paying the High Price of Being the World's No. 1 Jailer," *Boston Globe* (January 16):6–7.

Blume, J.H. and D.I. Bruck 1988. "Sentencing the Mentally Retarded to Death," *Arkansas Law Review* 41:725–764.

Bowers, W.J. 1983. "The Pervasiveness of Arbitrariness and Discrimination under Post-*Furman* Capital Statutes," *Journal of Criminal Law and Criminology* 74:1067–1100.

Bowers, ,W.J. 1984. *Legal Homicide.* Boston: Northeastern University Press.

Bowers, W.J. 1988. "The Effect of Executions Is Brutalization, Not Deterrence," in K.C. Haas and J.A. Inciardi, *Challenging Capital Punishment.* Beverly Hills, California: Sage Publications.

Bowers, W.J. 1990. "Massachusetts Voters Want an Alternative to the Death Penalty," (unpublished report). Department of Criminal Justice, Northeastern University, Boston, Massachusetts.

Bowers, W.J. and G.L. Pierce 1975. "The Illusion of Deterrence in Isaac Ehrlich's Research on Capital Punishment," *Yale Law Journal* 85:187–208.

Bowers, W.J. and G.L. Pierce 1980a. "Arbitrariness and Discrimination under Post-*Furman* Capital Statutes," *Crime and Delinquency* 26:563–575.

Bowers, W.J. and G.L. Pierce 1980b. "Deterrence or Brutalization: What Is the Effect of Executions?" *Crime and Delinquency* 26:453–484.

Brearley, H.C. 1932. *Homicide in the United States.* Chapel Hill: University of North Carolina Press.

Bureau of Justice Statistics 1988. *Capital Punishment 1987.* National Institute of Justice, Bureau of Justice Statistics. Washington, D.C.: U.S. Government Printing Office.

Bynam, A.E. 1988. "8th and 14th Amendments—The Death Penalty Survives," *The Journal of Criminal Law and Criminology* 78:1080–1118.

Camus, A. 1974. "Reflections on the Guillotine," in A. Camus, *Resistance, Rebellion, and Death.* New York: Vintage Books.

Capital Punishment—1982 1984. U.S. Department of Justice, Bureau of Justice Statistics. Washington, D.C.: U.S. Government Printing Office.

Capital Punishment—1987 1988. U.S. Department of Justice, Bureau of Justice Statistics. Washington, D.C.: U.S. Government Printing Office.

Cash, W.J. 1941. *The Mind of the South.* New York: Vintage Books.

Cavanagh, D.P. and M.A.R. Kleiman 1990. "A Cost-Benefit Analysis of Prison Cell Construction and Alternative Sanctions," Cambridge, Massachusetts: BOTEC Analysis Corporation.

Cloninger, D.O. 1977. "Death and the Death Penalty: A Cross-Sectional Analysis," *Journal of Behavioral Economics* 6:87–106.

Cohen, W. 1976. "Negro Voluntary Servitude in the South 1865–1940: A Preliminary Analysis," *Journal of Southern History* 42:31–60.

Colburn, D. 1990. "Lethal Injection," *Washington Post, Health: A Weekly Journal of Medicine, Science and Society* 6:12–14.

Conrad, J. 1983. *The Death Penalty: A Debate.* New York: Plenum Press.

Coyle, M., F. Strasser, and M. Lavelle 1990. "Fatal Defense," *The National Law Journal* 12:30–42.

Dann, R.H. 1935. "The Deterrent Effect of Capital Punishment," *Friends Social Service Series* 29:1–20.

Dix, G.E. 1979. "Appellate Review of the Decision to Impose Death," *Georgetown Law Journal* 68:97–161.

Donnelly, H.C. and G. Bala 1984. "1977 Releases: Five-Year Post-Release Follow-Up." Department of Correctional Services, Albany, New York.

Ehrlich, I. 1975. "The Deterrent Effect of Capital Punishment: A Question of Life and Death," *American Economic Review* 65:397–417.

Ehrlich, I. 1977. "Capital Punishment and Deterrence: Some Further Thoughts and Additional Evidence," *Journal of Political Economy* 85:741–788.

Ehrlich, I. and J.C. Gibbons 1977. "On the Measurement of the Deterrent Effect of Capital Punishment and the Theory of Deterrence," *Journal of Legal Studies* 6:35–50.

Ellis, I.W. and R.A. Luckasson 1985. "Mentally Retarded Criminal Defendants," *George Washington Law Review* 53:414–493.

Ellsworth, P.C. and L.D. Ross 1983. "Public Opinion and Capital Punishment: A Close Examination of the Views of Abolitionists and Retentionists," *Crime and Delinquency* 29:116–169.

Espy, M.W., Jr. 1980. "Capital Punishment and Deterrence: What the Statistics Cannot Show," *Crime and Delinquency* 26:537–544.

Espy, M.W. and J.O. Smykla 1987. *Executions in the United States, 1608–1987: The Espy File* [machine-readable data file]. John Smykla [producer], Tuscaloosa, Alabama, 1987; Inter-university Consortium for Political and Social Research [distributor], Ann Arbor, Michigan.

Fingerhut, L.A. and J.C. Kleinman 1990. "International and Interstate Comparisons of Homicide among Young Males," *Journal of the American Medical Association* 263:3292–3295.

Flanagan, T.J. and K. Maguire 1990. *Sourcebook of Criminal Justice Statistics 1989*. U.S. Department of Justice, Bureau of Justice Statistics. Washington, D.C.: U.S. Government Printing Office.

Flanigan, D.J. 1987. *The Criminal Law of Slavery and Freedom, 1800–1868*. New York: Garland Publications.

Forst, B.E. 1977. "The Case against Capital Punishment: A Cross-State Analysis of the 1960's," *Minnesota Law Review* 61:743–767.

Fox, J.A. and M.L. Radelet 1989. "Persistent Flaws in Econometric Studies of the Deterrent Effect of the Death Penalty," *Loyola of Los Angeles Law Review* 23:29–44.

Gallup, G. 1985. *Public Opinion, 1984*. Wilmington, Delaware: Scholarly Resources Press.

Gallup, G. 1986. *Public Opinion, 1985*. Wilmington, Delaware: Scholarly Resources Press.

Gallup, G. 1988. *Public Opinion, 1987*. Wilmington, Delaware: Scholarly Resources Press.

Garey, M. 1985. "The Cost of Taking a Life: Dollars and Sense of the Death Penalty," *University of California Davis Law Review* 18:1221–1270.

Garfinkel, H. 1949. "Research Not on Inter- and Intra-Racial Homicides," *Social Forces* 27:369–380.

Genovese, E.D. 1974. *Roll Jordan Roll: The World the Slaves Made*. New York: Vintage Books.

Giardini, G.I. and R.G. Farrow 1952. "The Paroling of Capital Offenders," *The Annals of the American Academy of Political and Social Science* 284:85–94.

Gibbs, J.P. 1975. *Crime, Punishment and Deterrence*. New York: Elsevier.

Godbold, J.C. 1987. " 'You Don't Have to Be a Bleeding Heart,' Representing Death

Row: A Dialog between Judge Abner J. Mikva and Judge John C. Godbold," *Human Rights* 14:22–25.

Goodpaster, G. 1983. "The Trial for Life: Effective Assistance of Counsel in Death Penalty Cases," *New York University Law Review* 58:299–362.

Goodpaster, G. 1986. "The Adversary System, Advocacy, and Effective Assistance of Counsel in Criminal Cases," *New York University Law Review of Law and Social Change* 14:59–92.

Gottlieb, G. 1961. "Testing the Death Penalty," *Southern California Law Review* 34:268–281.

Graves, W.F. 1956. "A Doctor Looks at Capital Punishment," *Medical Arts and Sciences* 10:137–141.

Greenberg, J. 1982. "Capital Punishment as a System," *Yale Law Journal* 91:908–936.

Gross, S.R. and R. Mauro 1984. "Patterns of Death: An Analysis of Racial Disparities in Capital Sentencing and Homicide Victimization." *Stanford Law Review* 37:27–153.

Gross, S.R. 1985. "Race and Death: The Judicial Evaluation of Evidence of Discrimination in Capital Sentencing," *University of California Davis Law Review* 18:1275–1326.

Gross, S.R. and R. Mauro 1989. *Death and Discrimination: Racial Disparities in Capital Sentencing*. Boston: Northeastern University Press.

Haney, C. 1984. "On the Selection of Capital Juries: The Biasing Effects of the Death-Qualification Process," *Law and Human Behavior* 8:121–132.

Hengstler, G. 1987. "Attorneys for the Damned," *American Bar Association Journal* (January):56–60.

Higginbotham, A.L., Jr. 1978. *In the Matter of Color: Race and the American Legal Process*. New York: Oxford University Press.

Johnson, E.H. 1957. "Selective Factors in Capital Punishment," *Social Forces* 36:165–169.

Johnson, G. 1941. "The Negro and Crime," *Annals of the American Academy of Political and Social Science* 217:93–104.

Johnson, R. 1981. *Condemned to Die: Life under Sentence of Death*. New York: Elsevier.

Judicial Council of California 1985. *1984 Annual Report 3*. Judicial Council of California, Sacramento, California.

Judson, C.J., J.J. Pandell, J.B. Owens, J.L. McIntosh, and D.L. Matschullat 1969. "A Study of the California Penalty Jury in First-Degree Murder Cases," *Stanford Law Review* 21:1297–1437.

Kansas Legislative Research Department 1987. *Costs of Implementing the Death Penalty*. House Bill 2062.

Kant, I. [1797] 1965. *The Metaphysical Elements of Justice*. Indianapolis: Bobbs-Merrill.

Kaplan, J. 1983. "The Problem of Capital Punishment," *University of Illinois Law Review* (No. 3):555–577.

Keedy, E.R. 1949. "The Early History of Murder and Manslaughter," *University of Pennsylvania Law Review* 97:759–777.

Kennedy, R.L. 1988. "*McCleskey v. Kemp*: Race, Capital Punishment, and the Supreme Court," *Harvard Law Review* 101:1388–1443.

King, D.R. 1978. "The Brutalization Effect: Execution Publicity and the Incidence of Homicide in South Carolina," *Social Forces* 57:683–687.

Kleck, G. 1979. "Capital Punishment, Gun Ownership and Homicide," *American Journal of Sociology* 84:882–910.

Kleck, G. 1981. "Racial Discrimination in Criminal Sentencing: A Critical Evaluation of the Evidence with Additional Evidence of the Death Penalty," *American Sociological Review* 46:783–805.

Klein, L.R., B.E. Forst, and V. Filatov 1978. "The Deterrent Effect of Capital Punishment: An Assessment of the Estimates," in A. Blumstein, J. Cohen, and D. Nagin, *Deterrence and Incapacitation: Estimating the Effects of Criminal Sanctions on Crime Rates*. Washington, D.C.: National Academy of Sciences.

Knorr, S.J. 1979. "Deterrence and the Death Penalty: A Temporal Cross-Sectional Approach," *Journal of Criminal Law and Criminology* 70:235–254.

Kobbervig, W., J. Invararity, and P. Lauderdale 1982. "Deterrence and the Death Penalty: A Comment on Phillips," *American Journal of Sociology* 88:161–164.

Koeninger, R.C. 1969. "Capital Punishment in Texas 1924–1968," *Crime and Delinquency* 15:132–141.

Layson, S.K. 1985. "Homicide and Deterrence: A Reexamination of the U.S. Time-Series Evidence," *Southern Economic Journal* 52:68–89.

Lempert, R.O. 1981. "Desert and Deterrence: An Assessment of the Moral Bases of the Case for Capital Punishment," *Michigan Law Review* 79:1177–1231.

Lempert, R.O. 1983. "The Effect of Executions on Homicides: A New Look in an Old Light," *Crime and Delinquency* 29:88–115.

Lewis, D.O., J.H. Pincus, M. Feldman, L. Jackson, and B. Bard 1986. "Psychiatric, Neurological and Psychoeducational Characteristics of 15 Death Row Inmates in the United States," *American Journal of Psychiatry* 143:838–845.

Lewis, D.O., J.H. Pincus, B. Bard, E. Richardson, L.S. Prichep, M. Feldman, and C. Yeager 1988. "Neuropsychiatric, Psychological, and Family Characteristics of Fourteen Juveniles Condemned to Death in the United States," *American Journal of Psychiatry* 145:584–589.

Lewis, P.W. 1979. "Killing the Killers: A Post-*Furman* Profile of Florida's Condemned," *Crime and Delinquency* 25:200–218.

MacKenzie, D. and L. Goodstein 1985. "Long-Term Incarceration Impacts and Characteristics of Long-Term Offenders," *Criminal Justice and Behavior* 12:395–412.

Mangum, C.S. 1940. *The Legal Status of the Negro*. Chapel Hill: University of North Carolina Press.

Marquart, J. and J.R. Sorensen 1988. "Institutional and Postrelease Behavior of *Furman*-Commuted Inmates in Texas," *Criminology* 26:677–693.

Marquart, J. and J.R. Sorensen 1989. "A National Study of the *Furman*-Commuted Inmates: Assessing the Threat to Society from Capital Offenders," *Loyola of Los Angeles Law Review* 23:5–28.

Marshall, T. 1986. "Remarks on the Death Penalty Made at the Judicial Conference of the Second Circuit," *Columbia Law Review* 86:1–8.

McFarland, S.G. 1983. "Is Capital Punishment a Short-Term Deterrent to Homicide? A Study of the Effect of Four Recent American Executions," *Journal of Criminal Law and Criminology* 74:1014–1031.

McGarrell, E.F. and T.J. Flanagan, eds. 1985. *Source Book of Criminal Justice*

Statistics—1984. U.S. Department of Justice, Bureau of Justice Statistics. Washington, D.C.: U.S. Government Printing Office.

Mello, M. 1988. "Facing Death Alone: The Post-Conviction Attorney Crisis on Death Row," *The American University Law Review* 37:513–607.

Mello, M. 1989. "Another Attorney for Life," in M.L. Radelet, *Facing the Death Penalty.* Philadelphia: Temple University Press.

Meltsner, M. 1973. *Cruel and Unusual: The Supreme Court and Capital Punishment.* New York: Random House.

Miller, A.S. and J.H. Bowman 1988. *Death by Installments: The Ordeal of Willie Francis.* Westport, Connecticut: Greenwood Press.

Myrdal, G. 1944. *An American Dilemma.* New York: Harper & Row.

NAACP Legal Defense and Education Fund 1990. *Death Row, U.S.A.* (September). New York: NAACP Legal Defense and Education Fund.

Nakell, B. 1978. "The Cost of the Death Penalty," *Criminal Law Bulletin* 14:69–80.

Nakell, B. and K.A. Hardy 1987. *The Arbitrariness of the Death Penalty.* Philadelphia: Temple University Press.

Nathanson, S. 1987. *An Eye for an Eye? The Morality of Punishing by Death.* Totowa, New Jersey: Rowman & Littlefield.

National Opinion Research Center, through Roper Public Opinion Research Center 1984.

New York State Defender's Association 1982. *Capital Losses: The Price of the Death Penalty for New York State.* Albany, New York: New York State Defenders Association.

Nietzel, M.T. and R.C. Dillehay 1982. "The Effects of Variations in *Voir Dire* Proceedings in Capital Murder Trials," *Law and Human Behavior* 8:1–13.

Note. 1972. "Capital Punishment in Virginia," *Virginia Law Review* 58:97–142.

Oberer, W.E. 1961. "Does Disqualification of Jurors for Scruples against Capital Punishment Constitute Denial of Fair Trial on Issue of Guilt?" *Texas Law Review* 39:545–567.

Oldenquist, A. 1986. "The Case for Revenge," *The Public Interest* 82:72–80.

Partington, D.C. 1965. "The Incidence of the Death Penalty for Rape in Virginia," *Washington and Lee Law Review* 22:43–75.

Passell, P. 1975. "The Deterrent Effect of Capital Punishment: A Statistical Test," *Stanford Law Review* 28:61–80.

Passell, P. and J.B. Taylor 1977. "The Deterrent Effect of Capital Punishment: Another View," *American Economic Review* 67:445–451.

Paternoster, R. 1983. "Race of Victim and Location of Crime: The Decision to Seek the Death Penalty in South Carolina," *Journal of Criminal Law and Criminology* 74:754–785.

Paternoster, R. 1984. "Prosecutorial Discretion in Requesting the Death Penalty: The Case of Victim-Based Discrimination," *Law and Society Review* 18:437–478.

Paternoster, R. and A.M. Kazyaka 1988. "The Administration of the Death Penalty in South Carolina: Experiences over the First Few Years," *South Carolina Law Review* 39:245–414.

Paternoster, R. and A.M. Kazyaka 1990. "An Examination of Comparatively Excessive Death Sentences in South Carolina 1979–1987," *New York University Review of Law and Social Change* 17:101–159.

Peck, J.K. 1975. "The Deterrent Effect of Capital Punishment: Ehrlich and His Critics," *Yale Law Journal* 85:359–367.

Peterson, R.D. and W.C. Bailey 1988. "Murder and Capital Punishment in the Evolving Context of the Post-*Furman* Era," *Social Forces* 66:774–807.

Phillips, D.P. 1980. "The Deterrent Effect of Capital Punishment: New Evidence on an Old Controversy," *American Journal of Sociology* 86:139–147.

Phillips, D.P. 1982a. "The Fluctuation of Homicide after Publicized Executions: Reply to Kobbervig, Inverarity, and Lauderdale," *American Journal of Sociology* 88:165–167.

Phillips, D.P. 1982b. "Deterrence and the Death Penalty: A Reply to Zeisel," *American Journal of Sociology* 88:170–172.

Powell, L. 1989. "Capital Punishment," *Harvard Law Review* 102:1035–1046.

Powers, E. 1966. *Crime and Punishment in Early Massachusetts 1620–1692: A Documentary History*. Boston: Beacon Press.

Pritchett, C.H. 1984. *Constitutional Civil Liberties*. Englewood Cliffs, New Jersey: Prentice-Hall.

Radelet, M.L. 1981. "Racial Characteristics and the Imposition of the Death Penalty," *American Sociological Review* 46:918–927.

Radelet, M.L. 1989. "Executions of Whites for Crimes against Blacks: Exceptions to the Rule?" *The Sociological Quarterly* 30:529–544.

Radelet, M.L. and G.L. Pierce 1985. "Race and Prosecutorial Discretion in Homicide Cases," *Law and Society Review* 19:587–521.

Radelet, M.L. and M. Vandiver 1983. "The Florida Supreme Court and Death Penalty Appeals," *Journal of Criminal Law and Criminology* 74:913–926.

Radin, M.J. 1980. "Capital Punishment and Respect for Persons: Super Due Process for Death," *Southern California Law Review* 53:1143–1185.

Radin, M.J. 1978. "Jurisprudence of Death: Evolving Standards for the Cruel and Unusual Punishments Clause," *University of Pennsylvania Law Review* 126:989–1064.

Radzinowicz, L. 1948. *A History of English Criminal Law, Vol. 1*. London: Stevens and Sons.

Reid, D. 1987. "Unknowing Punishment," *Student Lawyer* 15:18–23.

Reiman, J.H. 1985. "Justice, Civilization, and the Death Penalty: Answering van den Haag," *Philosophy and Public Affairs* 14:115–148.

Reynolds, H. 1981. *Cops and Dollars—The Economics of Criminal Law and Justice*. Springfield, Illinois: Charles C. Thomas.

Savitz, L. 1958. "A Study in Capital Punishment," *Journal of Criminal Law, Criminology and Police Science* 49:338–341.

Schmidt, B.C. 1982a. "Principle and Prejudice: The Supreme Court and Race in the Progressive Era. Part 1: The Heyday of Jim Crow," *Columbia Law Review* 82:444–524.

Schmidt, B.C. 1982b. "Principle and Prejudice: The Supreme Court and Race in the Progressive Era. Part 2: The *Peonage Cases*," *Columbia Law Review* 82:646–718.

Schneider, V. and J.O. Smykla 1991. "A Summary Analysis of Executions in the United States, 1608–1987: The Espy File," in R. Bohm, *The Death Penalty in America: Current Research*. Cincinnati, Ohio: Anderson Publishing.

Sellin, T. 1959. *The Death Penalty*. Philadelphia: American Law Institute.

Sellin, T. 1967. *Capital Punishment*. New York: Harper & Row.

Sellin, T. 1980. *The Penalty of Death*. Beverly Hills, California: Sage Publications.

Sellin, T. 1982. *The Death Penalty*. Beverly Hills, California: Sage Publications.

Southern Poverty Law Center 1981. *Motions for Capital Cases*. Birmingham, Alabama: Southern Poverty Law Center.

Spangenberg, R.L. and E.R. Walsh 1989. "Capital Punishment or Life Imprisonment? Some Cost Considerations," *Loyola of Los Angeles Law Review* 23:45–58.

Spitzer, S. 1975. "Toward a Marxian Theory of Deviance," *Social Problems* 22:638–651.

Stack, S. 1987. "Publicized Executions and Homicide, 1950–1980," *American Sociological Review* 52:532–540.

Stampp, K.M. 1956. *The Peculiar Institution*. New York: Vintage Books.

Stanton, J.M. 1969. "Murderers on Parole," *Crime and Delinquency* 15:149–155.

Stephen, J.F. 1864. "Capital Punishment," *Fraser's Magazine* 69:753–754.

Streib, V.L. 1987. *Death Penalty for Juveniles*. Bloomington: Indiana University Press.

Tabak, R. 1986. "The Death of Fairness: The Arbitrary and Capricious Imposition of the Death Penalty in the 1980s," *New York University Review of Law and Social Change* 14:797–848.

Uniform Crime Reports. 1988. Federal Bureau of Investigation. Washington, D.C.: U.S. Government Printing Office.

van den Haag, E. 1975. *Punishing Criminals: Concerning a Very Old and Painful Question*. New York: Basic Books.

van den Haag, E. 1978. "In Defense of the Death Penalty: A Legal-Practical-Moral Analysis," *Criminal Law Bulletin* 14:51–68.

van den Haag, E. 1985. "Refuting Reiman and Nathanson," *Philosophy and Public Affairs* 14:165–176.

van den Haag, E. and J.P. Conrad 1983. *The Death Penalty: A Debate*. New York: Plenum Press.

Vidmar, N. and P. Ellsworth 1974. "Public Opinion and the Death Penalty," *Stanford Law Review* 26:1245–1270.

Vito, G.F. and T.J. Keil 1988. "Capital Sentencing in Kentucky: An Analysis of the Factors Influencing Decision Making in the Post-*Gregg* Period," *Journal of Criminal Law and Criminology* 79:483–503.

Vito, G.F. and D.G. Wilson 1988. "Back from the Dead: Tracking the Progress of Kentucky's *Furman*-Commuted Death Row Population," *Justice Quarterly* 5:101–111.

Von Drehle, D. 1988. "Political Pressure Thwarts Clemency," *Miami Herald,* July 12, 1988, p. 1A, col. 1.

Vorenberg, J. 1981. "Decent Restraint on Prosecutorial Power," *Harvard Law Review* 94:1521–1573.

Weisberg, R. 1984. "Deregulating Death," in P.B. Kurland, G. Casper, and D.J. Hutchinson, *The Supreme Court Review 1983*. Chicago: University of Illinois Press.

White, W.S. 1984. *Life in the Balance: Procedural Safeguards in Capital Cases*. Ann Arbor: University of Michigan Press.

Wolf, E.D. 1964. "Analysis of Jury Sentencing in Capital Cases: New Jersey 1937–1961," *Rutgers Law Review* 19:56–64.

Wolfgang, M.E. 1958. *Patterns in Criminal Homicide*. Philadelphia: University of Pennsylvania Press.

Wolfgang, M.E. 1974. "The Criminologist in Court," *Journal of Criminal Law and Criminology* 65:244–247.

Wolfgang, M.E., A. Kelly, and H.C. Nolde 1962. "Comparison of the Executed and the Commuted among Admissions to Death Row," *Journal of Criminal Law, Criminology and Police Science* 53:301–311.

Wolfgang, M.E. and M. Riedel 1973. "Race, Judicial Discretion, and the Death Penalty," *The Annals* 407:119–133.

Wolfgang, M.E. and M. Riedel 1975. "Rape, Race, and the Death Penalty in Georgia," *American Journal of Orthopsychiatry* 45:658–668.

Wolfson, W.P. 1982. "The Deterrent Effect of the Death Penalty upon Prison Murder," in H.A. Bedau, *The Death Penalty in America* (3d ed.). New York: Oxford University Press.

World Almanac 1990. New York: Newspaper Association.

Wright, J.H. 1990. "Life-without-Parole: An Alternative to Death or Not Much of a Life at All?," *Vanderbilt Law Review* 43:529–568.

Yunker, J. 1976. "Is the Death Penalty a Deterrent to Homicide? Some Time-Series Evidence," *Journal of Behavioral Economics* 5:1–32.

Zedlewski, E.W. 1987. "Research in Brief: Making Confinement Decisions." Washington, D.C.: National Institute of Justice.

Zeisel, H. 1976. "The Deterrent Effects of the Death Penalty: Facts v. Faith," in P.E. Kurland, *The Supreme Court Review*. Chicago: University of Chicago Press.

Zeisel, H. 1981. "Race Bias in the Administration of the Death Penalty: The Florida Experience," *Harvard Law Review* 95:456–468.

Zeisel, H. 1982. "A Comment on 'The Deterrent Effect of Capital Punishment' by Phillips," *American Journal of Sociology* 88:166–169.

Zimring, F.E., J. Eigen, and S. O'Malley 1976. "Punishing Homicide in Philadelphia: Perspectives on the Death Penalty," *University of Chicago Law Review* 43:227–252.

Zimring, F.E. and G. Hawkins 1973. *Deterrence*. Chicago: University of Chicago Press.

Zimring, F.E. and G. Hawkins 1986. *Capital Punishment and the American Agenda*. New York: Cambridge University Press.

Index